Hungry for Peace

Hungry for Peace

*International Security,
Humanitarian Assistance,
and Social Change in North Korea*

Hazel Smith

UNITED STATES INSTITUTE OF PEACE PRESS
Washington, D.C.

United States Institute of Peace
1200 17th Street NW, Suite 200
Washington, DC 20036-3011

First published 2005

Printed in the United States of America

The paper used in this publication meets the minimum requirements of American National Standards for Information Science—Permanence of Paper for Printed Library Materials, ANSI Z39.48-1984.

Library of Congress Control Number: 2005936704

To Mihail with love

Contents

Foreword

NORTH KOREA IS TYPICALLY PORTRAYED in American media as at best bewilderingly unpredictable and at worst as a brutish hell-on-earth. Either way, the regime in Pyongyang is seen as profoundly unsuitable as a diplomatic partner, given that diplomacy demands of its participants a degree of both transparency and reliability, if not a degree of commonality of interests and values. Explicitly or otherwise, this line of reasoning is frequently used to justify a policy of treating North Korea as a boxer would treat an unknown opponent: keeping him at arm's length, eyeing him warily, waiting for his inevitable attempt to land a painful punch. Ironically, given that so many voices in the West proclaim North Korea to be paranoically fearful of the outside world, this pugilistic stance mirrors Pyongyang's own edgy, snarling attitude when dealing with other countries.

It is time, argues Hazel Smith in this challenging volume, that the West changed its approach. Not only is it unproductive, contends Smith, who has spent more time in North Korea than all but a handful of Westerners, it is ultimately self-defeating. If North Korea was ever an unknown quantity, it is no longer; if the narrowest of military-political calculations once circumscribed and poisoned its national outlook, now a broader range of national interests, including the welfare of its people, dictate a less confrontational outlook.

What prompted this apparent change in North Korea's approach to the outside world was a tragedy of dreadful proportions. The famine that ravaged North Korea in the 1990s obliged the obsessively self-reliant regime to work with the international humanitarian community and to allow aid agency personnel—including Smith herself, who was seconded into the agencies—to live and work in the country. Interaction with UN relief agencies and with various NGOs from South Korea, Europe, North America, and other parts of the West gradually led North Korea to accept some international norms and spurred the social changes that followed the regime's decision to permit the growth of markets. As North Korea gained experience working with members of the international community, it learned, too, that its security as a nation depended not just on the strength of its armed forces but also on the health of its people. This shift, says the author, has been gradual, and there is still a very long way to go before North Korea finds it natural and easy to cooperate with foreign partners. But the change, however driven by dire events, presents the West—not least the United States—with what may be an important opportunity to encourage Pyongyang to exchange the boxing ring for the negotiating table. At a time when policy for dealing with North Korea seems paralyzed by indecision, Smith's analysis presents a perspective that may offer a new approach to dealing with this beleaguered regime.

Given the more than half century of seemingly zero-sum relations between North Korea and the rest of the world, Hazel Smith's arguments certainly challenge conventional wisdom. They are also compelling in several respects, notably in demolishing the notion that North Korea is altogether inscrutable and unchanging. They are a counterpoint to far more common images of the Kim Jong Il regime and thus deserve to be heard by policymakers and analysts from Washington to Seoul and from Tokyo to Brussels, as well as in universities and think tanks in both the East and the West. That is not to say, of course, that Hazel Smith's views will be accepted. The subject of North Korea excites strong feelings, and policy advocates on all sides have firm opinions that will not easily be modified, let alone transformed. Even so, the United States Institute of Peace, whose congressionally mandated mission is to promote and disseminate thoughtful research into the ways in which international conflict can be peacefully prevented, managed, and resolved, is pleased to have supported Professor Smith's work. The Institute does not endorse or reject the arguments in *Hungry for Peace,* but it does support the idea of injecting new, constructive perspectives into debates on topics of great import for national and international security. (This same commitment to spurring serious debate lay behind the Institute's publication of Andrew Natsios's book, *The Great North Korean Famine,* which, though it addresses much the same subject as *Hungry for Peace,* offers a very different assessment of the regime in Pyongyang and of the best way to deal with it.)

In addition to bringing challenging ideas into the intellectual marketplace, the Institute is dedicated to disseminating useful knowledge. And even those readers who may remain unpersuaded by Hazel Smith's thesis will surely appreciate the contribution she makes to our knowledge of North Korea in general and of its response to the great famine of the 1990s in particular. The author not only draws on her very considerable first-hand experience of the international relief efforts but also complements it with material culled from a wide variety of sources, including documents and data generated by relief agencies working within North Korea. *Hungry for Peace* provides a rare, perhaps unique close-up account of the dreadful spread and terrible impact of the famine, of the relief community's heroic efforts to battle it, and of the eye-opening interactions between aid workers and North Korean officials and ordinary citizens.

Offering, as it does, much needed information as well as a fresh perspective on international relations with North Korea, *Hungry for Peace* will appeal to a wide range of audiences: policymakers from numerous countries, humanitarian workers from a yet more numerous array of NGOs and intergovernmental agencies, area specialists, international relations theorists, students of the region and of relief operations, and anyone interested in evolving definitions of "security" and of the unfolding story of North Korea, its nuclear weapons program, and its government, economy, and society.

Hungry for Peace joins a growing library of titles published by the United States Institute of Peace that focus on the diverse countries of East Asia— but that have implications and lessons that stretch far beyond that part of the world. These titles include two other volumes on the peculiar problems and outlook of North Korea: Andrew Natsios's *The Great North Korean Famine,* which I have mentioned above; and Scott Snyder's exploration of

North Korea's distinctive approach to international interaction, *Negotiating on the Edge.* Snyder's work is part of a larger Institute endeavor that examines cross-cultural negotiation, a project that has generated studies of half a dozen important nations, among them two neighbors of North Korea, *Case Studies in Japanese Negotiating Behavior* by Michael Blaker, Paul Giarra, and Ezra Vogel, and my *Chinese Negotiating Behavior.* These book-length studies are complemented by shorter pieces that likewise analyze how best to encourage peace and stability within the Asian region. Just within the past two years, for instance, the Institute has published chapters by David Steinberg on human rights in the Republic of Korea and by Merle Goldman on human rights in China, both of which appear in *Implementing U.S. Human Rights Policy,* edited by Debra Liang-Fenton; assessments by William Drennan of recent U.S. policy toward North Korea and by Robert Ross of the U.S. approach toward the Taiwan Straits dispute, which are to be found in *The United States and Coercive Diplomacy,* edited by Robert Art and Patrick Cronin; and special reports such as *The Mindanao Peace Talks: Another Opportunity to Resolve the Moro Conflict in the Philippines, A Comprehensive Resolution of the Korean War,* and *U.S.-China Cooperation on the Problem of Failing States and Transnational Threats.*

Individually, many of these studies are designed, like *Hungry for Peace,* to appeal to a diverse audience. Collectively, they reflect the great breadth of the Institute's interests and its commitment to bringing challenging ideas, fresh perspectives, and new knowledge to as wide an audience as possible. Bold, illuminating, and instructive, *Hungry for Peace* embodies this commitment perfectly.

Richard H. Solomon
President
UNITED STATES INSTITUTE OF PEACE

Acknowledgments

ANY PEOPLE HAD A HAND in the making of this book—consciously and unconsciously—the genesis of which occurred during my first visit to the DPRK, back in 1990. I was then researching and writing on the Nicaraguan revolution and the international system—and was interested in the whole phenomenon of what happens when "non–status quo" states collide with status quo patterns of international relations. So first I want to thank Fred Halliday, without whose exemplary teaching I would never have started on a research career, and whose example reinforced my view that solid, high-quality scholarly research can and should be done on even the most non–status quo of states. Second, I wish to thank Keith Bennett, who facilitated my first visits to the DPRK, in 1990, 1991, and 1994.

This book would never have been written if I had not had the good fortune to be selected to spend a year as a Jennings Randolph Senior Fellow in Washington, D.C., at the United States Institute of Peace in 2001–2. Joe Klaits, Elizabeth Drakulich, and John Crist made me welcome and provided a research home of which most writers can only dream. Jacob Bercovitch, a fellow "fellow," shared in the general writing anxieties and was a hugely supportive colleague and friend. Clara Cole was a wonderful research assistant in every way—intellectually, organizationally, ethically, and humanly. I feel fortunate to have worked with her at this early stage of what I'm sure will be a prestigious future career.

This book would also not have been written without continued, consistent, and generous support from the University of Warwick, which permitted me to take large chunks of time away from the university. I thank all those who demonstrated confidence that I would eventually produce this book, particularly Professor Stuart Palmer, who, as deputy vice chancellor, authorized my research leave.

Some of the ideas developed in this book started life in earlier forms. The theoretical framework of chapter 1 builds on an article titled "Mad, Bad, Sad or Rational Actor? Why the 'Securitization' Paradigm Makes for Poor Policy Analysis of North Korea," which appeared in *International Affairs* (vol. 76, no. 3 [July 2000]: 593–617). Other concerns and ideas developed through the interactive and cumulative process of research and writing, as illustrated in articles and papers mentioned in the bibliography. I am grateful to all those who have offered comment on these ideas along the years.

I would like to thank those in Pyongyang, Washington, DC, New York, Tokyo, Beijing, Seoul, London, and elsewhere who have been kind enough both to share their views on the DPRK over the years and to listen to my ideas. I have been privileged to get to know some very remarkable and very decent human beings as a by-product of my work on the DPRK, among them Fred Carrière and Ambassador Donald Gregg at the Korea Society, New York, whose sterling efforts to help the United States understand both Koreas have never been more necessary; Brad Babson, Sig Harrison, Svante Kilander, Karin Lee, John Merrill, Yi-Sook Merrill, Kathi Moon, Oh Jae-Sik, Jong Park, and Jon Watts. Tom McCarthy, a good friend and one of the few sane voices in the Washington debate on the DPRK for a very long time, is very badly missed after his premature death on May 8, 2003.

The research for most of this book comes out of my experiences working with and for various humanitarian organizations in the DPRK in 1998, 1999, and 2000–2001, in the United Nations World Food Program (WFP), UNICEF, UNDP, and Caritas. In my view, the individuals who have worked in the DPRK for these organizations are the unsung heroes of the North Korea story. These are the individuals who have chosen to live and work, sometimes accompanied by their families and sometimes separated from them, in an isolated, psychologically difficult, and sometimes physically tough environment for periods of up to four years, sometimes more.

These individuals work consistently, patiently, and professionally to provide food, medical assistance, agricultural support, and clean water, and to resuscitate the education system so as to help orphaned children, babies, infants, schoolchildren, pregnant and nursing women, the elderly, the disabled, the unemployed, poor farmers, and the poor in general. Since the first humanitarian officials became resident in 1996, they have also, in a quiet and unheralded way, and as a result of sustained involvement in the DPRK, done more toward the "opening up" of the DPRK to contemporary international norms than most of the high-profile political interventions from abroad. The quiet process of confidence building and the institution of channels of communication with the outside world for the North Korean population have been undertaken by large numbers of people who have never sought publicity for themselves and are largely unknown to the public at large. They are in the DPRK simply doing their job.

This book, inasmuch as it captures any of the contribution made by these individuals—not some amorphous "humanitarian community" but real, live, complicated human beings—is meant as a tribute to them. They include Fathia Abdalla, Yvette Adda, Mohammed Adil, Pedro Amolat, Michel Anglade, Alpha Bah, Laurence Bardon, Jennifer Bitonde, Kuhmud Bomick, Douglas Broderick, David Bulman, Nina Busch, Leona Cayzer, Maria del Carmen Leal, Hom B. Chhetri, Roberto Christen, David Cole, Jean Cole, Rick Corsino, Doug Coutts, Denise Crilly, Rosa Maria Delgadillo, Annette Denny, Evaline DiangA, Eric Donelli, Rudi Fankhauser, Marta Fontana, Soraya Franco, Kim Fredriksson, Anna Gevorgyan, Edisher Giorgadze, Umberto Greco, Fe Guevara, Kauko Hakkinen, Thi Van Hoang, Zhen-Zhen Huang, Per Gunnar Jenssen, Sven-Erik Johansson, Kirsten Jorgensen, Mirjana Kavelj, Al Kehler, Ingrid Kolb-Hindarmanto, Patricia Kormoss, Oliver Lacey-Hall, Tomas Liew, Xuerong Liu, Karin Manente, Georgio Maragliano, Joe Martinico, Mike McDonagh, Brendan McDonald, Elaine McDonald, Albert Mettler, David Morton, Hanne Mueller, Hans-Joerg Mueller, Ueli Mueller, Hans Peter Müller, Aline Mutagorama, Nasiba Ghulam Nabi, Vu Viet Nga, Joseph O'Brien, John O'Dea, Iyabo Olusanmi, Omawale Omawale, Baton Osmani, Jane

Pearce, Prahbu Prabhakaran, Diane Prioux Debaudimomt, Aurelie Rajaonsin, Narayan Rajbanshi, Helmut Rauch, Andrea Recchia, Susan Riddle, Emma Roberts, Owen Saer, Hasana Shakya, Xin Shen, Kyi Shinn, Rebecca Sirrell, Eigil Sorensen, Runar Sorensen, Dierk Stegen, Temmy Tanubrata, Ahmed Tayeh, Nguyen Van Tien, Sungval Tunsiri, Pedro Vila, Andreas von Ramdohr, Zhigang Weng, Sonali Wickrema, and Ahmed Zakaria. A special mention goes to Kathi Zellweger, who cannot be praised enough for her sheer tenacity, goodwill, efficiency, and solid analysis—in other words, her personal and professional contribution to the DPRK. I would be remiss if I did not emphasize that these are only some of the individuals with whom I have worked; I cannot name them all as there have simply been too many, but I apologize to those I have not mentioned.

This list does not include the many dedicated North Koreans with whom I have worked in the humanitarian agencies over the years; they will forgive me, I know, for not mentioning them by name. They know, as much as I do, that it would not necessarily do much for their career prospects to be picked out and named in a book principally designed for a non-DPRK readership. This list does not include, for the same reasons, and also because there are too many to name, all the North Koreans I have worked with in the counties, farms, hospitals, orphanages, schools, and food-for-work sites throughout the country. These officials are as unsung as the international officials with whom they work—and much worse off in human security terms. Their incomes remain either nonexistent or so pitifully small that many continue to have difficulties even providing enough food for themselves and their families.

I also want to give credit to the humanitarian organizations themselves, which continue to respond to the needs of individuals who suffer from hunger and deprivation in many parts of the world, not just in the DPRK. When I started this research I subscribed to the conventional cynicism about the motives of humanitarian workers and the effects of humanitarian activity. Some of that cynicism remains, as no human being's motives are ever entirely "pure" and humanitarian activity manifestly does not and cannot respond fully to all humanitarian needs. It is now, however, tempered by my own understanding and experience of the often no-win situations in which workers and humanitarian organizations are placed. Sometimes it seems as if they are expected to solve all the political and humanitarian problems of every country, especially countries where even the best efforts of the world's politicians have failed. In the end, humanitarian organizations can achieve only the limited objectives set out in their mandates—to relieve humanitarian need. They do this in each country in which they work to a better or worse degree, depending on circumstances often completely out of their control.

Of all the humanitarian organizations, I wish to mention the United Nations World Food Program in particular. It may not have as high a public profile as other UN organizations but, in my view, its focused mission allows it to work effectively, efficiently, professionally, and humanely —and it does so in the most difficult and often the most dangerous circumstances anywhere in the world. It gets things done—food to hungry people—when others are often still contemplating what to do next in what can seem completely intractable circumstances.

Thanks to Kathi, Joe, Denise, Ingrid, Susan, Marta, and Umberto for their continued friendship. As always, nothing would have been completed without the continued tolerance, affection, and unconditional support of my family. And a final acknowledgment to Mihail Petkovski, whom I met in Mount Myohyang, where it all started.

Humanitarian/Development Organizations Based in North Korea, 2003

Legend

1. PYONGYANG
UN: FAO, UNDP, UNICEF, WFP, WFP-FALU, WHO, UNFPA, OCHA

Donors: AidCo (Food Security Unit), Humanitarian Aid Office (ECHO), Italian Development Cooperation, (ITDCO), Swiss Agency for Development Cooperation (SDC)

IOs: International Federation of Red Cross and Red Crescent Societies (IFRC), International Committee of Red Cross (ICRC)

NGOs: Resident: Adventist Development and Relief Agency (ADRA), Campus fur Christus, Cooperazione e Sviluppo (CESVI), Concern Worldwide, Deutsche Welthungerhilfe (GAA), Handicap International (HI), Premiere Urgence, PMU Interlife, Triangle GH Non-Resident: (via FALU): Caritas, World Vision, ACT, CFGB

2. NORTH HAMGYONG
ADRA, FALU, UNICEF, WFP, WHO, UNDP

3. RYANGGANG
FALU, SDC, UNDP, UNICEF, WFP, WHO

4. CHAGANG
FALU, FAO, IFRC, SDC, UNICEF, UNDP, WFP, WHO

5. NORTH PYONGAN
Campus fur Christus, DWHH, FALU, FAO, ICRC, IFRC, UNDP, UNFPA, UNICEF, WFP, WHO

6. SOUTH PYONGAN
ADRA, Concern, EC, DGDev, FAO, ICRC, IFRC, PMU, Premiere Urgence, SDC, Triangle, UNICEF, UNDP, WFP, WFP-FALU, WHO

7. NAMPO
FALU, UNDP, UNICEF, WFP, WHO

8. NORTH HWANGHAE
ADRA, Campus fur Christus, FAO, IFRC, SDC, UNDP, UNICEF, WFP, WHO

9. SOUTH HWANGHAE
ADRA, Campus fur Christus, CESVI, DWHH, AidCo, FALU, FAO, UNDP, UNFPA, UNICEF, WFP, WHO

10. KAESONG
ADRA, FALU, FAO, IFRC, UNDP, UNICEF, WFP, WHO

11. KANGWON
CESVI, FALU, FAO, ITDCO, UNDP, UNICEF, WFP, WHO

12. SOUTH HAMGYONG
Campus fur Christus, FALU, FAO, ITDCO, UNDP, UNICEF, WFP, WHO

Source: UNOCHA, Resident International Organizations, 2003 Provincial Programme Map.

Hungry for Peace

Introduction
Reframing the Debate

WAR IS STILL A POSSIBILITY on the Korean peninsula. No peace treaty was ever signed following the armistice that ended the Korean War in 1953.[1] More importantly, Korea is still divided into two mutually antagonistic camps: the Democratic People's Republic of Korea (DPRK, or North Korea) and the Republic of Korea (ROK, or South Korea).[2] Conflict between North and South still has the potential to spill over into large-scale killing and destruction. In that event, the United States would be directly involved because of its defense commitments to South Korea. China, Japan, and even Russia might also intervene, directly or indirectly. In other words, the unresolved Korean conflict is inherently an international security problem. Its resolution would help bring stability, not just to Koreans on both sides of the border, but to East Asia as a whole. Bringing peace to the peninsula would eradicate a continuing threat to international peace and security.

This book argues that understanding the possibilities for reducing international insecurity and promoting a stable peace inherently requires understanding the reconstituted national security priorities of the DPRK. After the creation of the state in the 1940s, a conception of national security as territorial integrity underpinned the DPRK's national security doctrine. After the economic crisis of the 1990s, the DPRK government included human security priorities, in terms of providing for the basic food needs of the population, along with the more conventional policies of national defense, in a reoriented national security policy. The dominant goal of regime survival was the primary reason for both the former and the latter approach to national security.

The human security concerns shaping the DPRK's new international orientations were to secure freedom from want, mainly in terms of providing enough food to feed the population. These new priorities were consciously developed in the wake of the state's inability to feed the population in the 1990s—a policy failure that resulted in nearly a million dead of starvation and malnutrition-related diseases. More problematic for the DPRK government was any recognition of the necessity of incorporating the other half of the human security equation—freedom from fear—in a reconstituted system of national priorities. On the contrary, fear of violence from a foreign military invasion was used to justify the maintenance of a political system in which political and civil freedoms remained restricted. Some signs of the possibility of change could be glimpsed by the early years of the twenty-first century, however, when the DPRK government demonstrated some willingness to engage seriously with external actors even on these most sensitive of policy issues. The human rights dialogue with the European Union and Switzerland provided the most visible demonstration of this new thinking.

This book investigates three related themes. The first is the dramatic socioeconomic change that has taken place in North Korea since the early 1990s. The second is how freedom-from-want concerns reshaped DPRK national security policy. The third is how the international humanitarian community addressed changing North Korean security dilemmas and found a way of working with the DPRK government.

Helping external actors to learn from the experiences of the humanitarian community in responding to human security needs in the area of freedom from want and in the realm of freedom from fear provides a core objective of the book.

The overall purpose of the book is to contribute to improved understanding of the DPRK so as to find feasible alternatives to war as a method of conflict resolution on the peninsula. The alternative proposed assumes that the conditions for radically improved human security for the North Korean population must be first articulated and evaluated before good policy can be developed and implemented. Sustainable improvements to the human security of North Korea's population will contribute to the creation of a stable peace. They are also, most importantly, an ethical end in themselves.

The Theoretical and Analytical Framework

The framework for consideration of what I call the human/national/international security nexus in the DPRK is provided by a reconsideration of international relations theories as they have been applied to the study of the DPRK. Conventional ways of understanding (theories) of the DPRK and international security argue both for the DPRK's unpredictability and for its evil intent in international relations. The development of weapons of mass destruction is viewed as an example of evil intent that, combined with the country's purported unpredictability, makes for a grave threat to international peace and stability. Underpinning this approach is the assumption and assertion that little is or can be known about the DPRK and that, therefore, worst-case options must always be assumed.

The Arguments

In this book I first argue that the DPRK is both knowable and predictable. Second, I argue that conventional state-centric notions of international relations can contribute to a partial explanation of DPRK foreign policy, but paradigmatic blinkers need to be abandoned to allow researchers and analysts to make full use of the knowledge about the DPRK that has become available since the mid-1990s. Third, I argue that orthodox theories always fail to understand fully interstate relations and activities, including (but not confined to) those of the most inscrutable states, such as the DPRK. The reason is that they fail to comprehend that, in the end, states are a conglomeration of human beings, organized in social groups, across as well as within territorial boundaries, who propel the state into action in international (and domestic) affairs. States pursue different policies and objectives as a result of volitional acts (including decisions and nondecisions) taken by human beings—sometimes as individuals and sometimes acting within groups, most importantly within governments. States' actions and reactions also result from the unintended consequences of social group activity.

Knowledge of the DPRK substantially increased as an unintended by-product of humanitarian activity in the country from the mid-1990s on. This accretion of knowledge in itself can contribute to peace and security on the Korean peninsula without any radical reorientation of theories of international security. This is because increased knowledge can lead to more predictability, reduce the possibility of dangerous miscalculations, and lessen threat perceptions. Better knowledge of the DPRK can, for instance, contribute in the short run to an attenuation of North-South Korea conflict and therefore a diminution in the immediate risk of violent conflict—helping in the creation of "passive peace" on the peninsula.

I argue, however, that because classical international relations theories cannot extend beyond the confines of the "state as black box" approach, we also need to understand the status of human security needs in the DPRK, to evaluate when these are satisfied and when they are not. In this way we can more fully understand the conditions that would allow for a consolidated or sustainable peace and stability on the Korean peninsula. A passive peace will be inherently unstable if human security needs are not met in the DPRK. In the end, an "active" or stable peace will come to the Korean peninsula only if the human security needs of the DPRK's population are more or less met in a sustainable, credible, and long-term manner.[3]

I further argue that an unanticipated effect of humanitarian community operations was to contribute substantially to the potential for active peace on the peninsula. In some ways these operations provided a motor and model for peacebuilding initiatives. I do not argue that an overt objective of humanitarian intervention was to bring peace or that humanitarian community activities could achieve peace on their own. This outcome can only be attained through cooperation between South and North Korea, the growth of interdependent societies, and the implementation of a regional peace and security agreement. I do, however, argue that for an active or stable peace to be attained, all actors need to better understand processes as much as outcomes of negotiations and peacebuilding. Thus they need to carefully choose appropriate means as well as desirable ends in building an effective security strategy for the Korean peninsula. The processes of confidence-building and negotiated compromise, alongside the judicious use of economic instruments, are part of the panoply of instruments available to diplomats. The experience of humanitarian diplomacy in the DPRK provides lessons for state diplomats in the modalities of achieving objectives in the DPRK.

The book argues that international policymakers need to recognize the DPRK government's shifting priorities in its efforts to provide for human security for its population. By channeling policies so as to assist the population but also to encourage change in a way that does not militarily threaten the DPRK government, international policymakers could support peaceful political, social, and economic change on the Korean peninsula. International policymakers should continue to assist the DPRK government in its efforts to provide for human security in terms of freedom from want. In practical terms this means continued humanitarian support to relieve the chronic food and health crisis facing most of the country's population and economic cooperation for agricultural and industrial redevelopment and restructuring.

International policymakers should also work with the government to encourage the implementation of policies and the building of institutions that can provide the framework for the population to enjoy freedom from fear—an equally important component of the notion of human security. In practical terms this means supporting the transfer of economic assistance only in the context of institution building, including the building of the rule of law, an independent judiciary, an accountable policing and penal system—all based on predictability and transparency in the justice sphere of civil administration.[4]

Another significant contribution that international policymakers can make is to negotiate and conclude a peace agreement on the Korean peninsula. This would cut the ground from under the feet of those conservative elements in the DPRK who continue to advocate the internal suppression of personal liberties on the grounds that war is still a possibility.

Positive change in governmental policy can and should be encouraged through what I call "intelligent intervention" by those outside powers that have the potential for diplomatic and economic engagement with the DPRK. Misdirected external policies are not neutral but dangerous. They will reinforce domestic policies that cannot relieve the misery of a hungry, poor, and deprived population and increase regional and international instability.

The Politics of Data

Questions of assumptions, methodology, and data in the study of the DPRK have never been of merely technical or academic interest. Disputes as to reliability, quality, and accuracy of information have, for instance, formed the basis for U.S. congressional resolutions condemning the DPRK for its lack of transparency. Such disputes were also part of the rationale for the cutoff of Japanese food aid to the North Korean population in 2001. The DPRK, in turn, often viewed demands for more data as akin to requests to allow foreign spies unimpeded access.

A Knowledge Vacuum

One of the key inhibitors to normalizing the relationship between the DPRK and the rest of the world was the absence of credible information about the country. The DPRK's overweening obsession with national security meant that all socioeconomic data were viewed as potentially helpful to the enemy and therefore not made public. The DPRK's isolation meant that very little credible sociological, anthropological, or cultural analysis of the society has ever been completed or disseminated outside the country. The lack of information on this country prior to the 1990s can hardly be overstated, and its consequences have been severe and detrimental to building peace. Those with genuine fears of potential DPRK aggression were forced to use worst-case scenarios as a substitute for empirical analysis.

Others viewed the possibility of a DPRK-initiated attack as slight, particularly from the late 1980s. Nevertheless, their ability to "talk up" the threat from the DPRK was made all the more easier because of that country's unwillingness to reveal the most insignificant and mundane (to the outside world) pieces of information. Its society, because it was largely unknown except through the understandably biased testimonies of defectors, was presumed evil, demonic—literally *indescribable*. The consequences for foreign national security analyses were grave. If a society was so outlandish, outside the pale, and bizarre, then the predictable reaction would be the one most prevalent in what I describe in this book as the "securitization" literature. The society must be destroyed or, at best, absorbed by its southern neighbor.

The DPRK had active interchanges with China, Russia, Eastern Europe, and members of the nonaligned movement during the Cold War and had much more contact with foreigners than is generally understood or reported.[5] Reporting from these sources, however, tended to be uncritical. In some cases foreign interlocutors were themselves from closed or Communist societies where the free flow of information was not possible or encouraged. In other cases the links were superficial, and visitors were not inclined or able to investigate DPRK society independently. During the Cold War period, however, UN agencies such as UNDP and UNICEF started to report basic social information.[6] The latter conducted an important nutrition survey in the southeastern province of Kangwon in 1988.[7]

The Impetus for Opening . . . and the Limitations

From the mid-1990s, as a consequence of the nuclear crisis of 1993–94 and the humanitarian crisis of the 1990s, the government faced pressures toward transparency from a number of different external sources. It was pushed into intensive negotiations with adversaries, not just on the food and humanitarian crisis, but also on nuclear issues, economic reconstruction, and a whole host of political and security issues, including armaments and proliferation. In engaging with the DPRK, various foreign actors gained relatively large amounts of information about the country, particularly in their discrete sectors of expertise. The DPRK was initially deeply uncomfortable with the data-gathering aspects of foreign activity and seemed unable to distinguish between legitimate data collection and espionage. By the beginning of the twenty-first century, however, these knowledge-collection exercises began to be accepted with a little more equanimity, particularly those that were clearly necessary for effective planning of humanitarian and economic programs and activities.

From the mid-1990s on, in a development that accelerated after the breakthrough June 2000 Pyongyang Summit of North and South Korean leaders, the DPRK hosted literally thousands of foreign visitors. These included foreign businesspeople, particularly from South Korea. They also included hundreds of foreign technical experts, including U.S. military personnel working to recover the remains of those reported missing in action during the Korean War (1950–53). Compared to those who visited the DPRK for short delegation-type visits and tended to be shown only the sights, these visitors were engaged in serious interactions with North Koreans and often made repeat visits. Some—not only South Koreans but also foreigners—spoke Korean fluently. They were thus in a relatively good position to develop useful analyses of the sectors of the economy or the society with which they were engaged. Unfortunately, the nature of the business conducted by many of these visitors precluded wide dissemination of their analysis, given that pressure from both sides limited disclosure of findings and activities.

Diplomats, even in these days of "open diplomacy," prize confidentiality and discretion and were therefore less able than the international humanitarian agencies to publicize their myriad interactions with DPRK officials. Most resident foreign diplomats also had little exposure to life outside Pyongyang—or sometimes, to life outside the diplomatic compound in Pyongyang. International business, to preserve its competitive edge, also tended not to disseminate its research on the DPRK.[8] The Korean Peninsula Energy Development Organization (KEDO), predominantly consisting of South Koreans and Americans, was active in the DPRK from 1994 until the breakdown in 2002–3 of the agreement that had established its operational framework. Throughout, KEDO stuck to its energy briefs, not wishing to complicate an already sensitive activity with extensive publicity.[9]

The U.S. military, which since 1997 has sent teams that included Korean speakers to search for the remains of soldiers missing in action in the Korean War, provided summaries of its activities but did not use its experiences to provide expanded public analysis of the country.[10] Like businesses, militaries in any country are not structurally open organizations. The U.S. Department of Defense was also sensitive to the potential for domestic political fallout over its payments to the Korean People's Army in return for assistance. It was anxious to maintain a low profile and avoid political controversy, so as not to jeopardize the operation.

Facilitating Knowledge: The Crucial Role of the Humanitarian Community

From the mid-1990s on, the growing role played by the humanitarian community in responding to government requests to help provide relief for famine victims brought an increasingly useful, systematic process of data collection and dissemination.[11] More by accident than design, external humanitarian intervention helped outsiders gain an understanding of the country, increasing knowledge of the DPRK's society, economy, and governmental behavior. Most of the humanitarian agencies demanded transparency and accountability and, because of their unique and necessitous relationship with the DPRK government, were able to achieve results in the production of data on the DPRK that had not previously been possible. If the DPRK had not complied, at least to some extent, with the demands of the international agencies, the population would have again faced starvation, with unimaginable political consequences for the government.

Publicity, visibility, and transparency are imperatives of humanitarian agency operations, as agencies must report back to donors and convince the public in donor countries to continue to support and finance humanitarian assistance. An intrinsic aspect of the mission and mandate of the humanitarian communities in the DPRK, therefore, was to obtain information about humanitarian needs and to disseminate that information to the wider world. Another objective of collecting and disseminating good information was to demonstrate the necessity of giving scarce resources to the DPRK in the face of many other equally compelling human tragedies competing for donor attention and assistance throughout the world. The pressures to justify humanitarian assistance to the DPRK were particularly intense, given the initial lack of reliable knowledge about social and economic conditions and the reluctance of the DPRK government to allow independent monitoring of food aid distribution.

In the case of the DPRK, the implications of implementing standard operating procedures for humanitarian organizations were revolutionary. Collecting and disseminating information—a routine operation anywhere else in the world—had potentially enormous consequences for the wider politics of the Korean peninsula. The immense distrust between the DPRK and major donors was such that every action or omission on either side could inadvertently become a potential trigger for serious political conflict. At the same time, information obtained for legitimate humanitarian purposes also contributed to the "normalization" of the DPRK. It provided a better understanding of the country and thus helped to bring an element of predictability into its relations with major humanitarian donors—countries that were also the DPRK's major political adversaries.

The international humanitarian community did, of course, encounter difficulties with reliability, verifiability, accuracy, and access to information.[12] But even with these problems, the information made available was uniquely usable both for humanitarian activity and as a contribution to peacebuilding. Data from humanitarian community sources helped to elucidate social change in the DPRK by allowing an evaluation of who got what and where and how this had changed, particularly since the 1990s. This was so because the scale of the crisis resulted in a nationwide humanitarian operation, by April 2002 covering 85 percent of the population and 163 out of 211 counties.[13] The information gathered by the humanitarian community on basic human needs, particularly in relation to food, health, and agriculture, although incomplete, was nevertheless comprehensive in that it was virtually nationwide in coverage. By 2001, comparisons could be drawn among different parts of the country, and by 2003, eight years after the establishment of the humanitarian presence, data were available over a fairly long period—allowing for temporal as well as spatial comparative assessment of socioeconomic diversity and change.

Some agencies, and certainly some donors, were aware that the unintended consequence of humanitarian activity was to provide a transmission belt for information sharing and dialogue between the DPRK government and donor governments. Indeed, an argument raged within the humanitarian community as to whether it was ethically acceptable for humanitarian assistance to have any connection with politics or peacebuilding.[14] This debate was largely resolved by the 2000s. Pragmatically, it was accepted that, while the job of humanitarians was to respond to humanitarian crisis, particularly to food insecurity and hunger, they were also responding, whether intentionally or not, to a different type of hunger—the population's hunger for peace.

The Consequences of Analytical Failure

Analysts were slow to catch up with the scope and scale of the socioeconomic change that followed the breakdown in the state's capacity to feed the population in the 1990s. They were caught up in paradigmatic assumptions that were long past their sell-by date. The DPRK continued to be seen as an unchanging society and state, despite mounting evidence that the DPRK socioeconomy had undergone irrevocable transformation.

An analytical error that bedeviled study of the DPRK polity was to equate the category of social change with the category of policy change. Social change is different from policy change. It is a simple question of logic and observation to note that governmental policies can help to facilitate social change, negatively or positively, but there is clearly no automatic correlation between the two categories. As often as not, policy is a response to social change. It is a way to manage change. In the case of the DPRK, because there were no dramatic policy changes in the past decade, analysts sometimes assumed an absence of socioeconomic change. This assumption provided a false picture of DPRK society and, inevitably, where this analysis was used as a foundation for policy, led to poor policy outputs.

One of the reasons international security policymakers poorly understood social change in the DPRK was that they were not able or willing to separate analytically socioeconomic change from policy or political change, or to disaggregate state and society in the DPRK. Continuing to treat the DPRK as a monolithic entity or as an impenetrable "black box," international policy analysts could not differentiate between discrete sources of security threats for DPRK policymakers. Many of these were related to the human (in)security conditions of the population. These analytical failures meant that, at critical junctures, the international security community failed to appreciate opportunities both to develop nuanced interventions in support of desired changes and to discourage negative developments. The broader objective of obtaining a durable peace on the peninsula thus suffered.

The Analytical Alternative

The DPRK should be analyzed exactly as social scientists would analyze any other state—democratic or authoritarian, theocratic or secular. As with all states, the DPRK was not and is not a monolithic actor. Like all governments, the DPRK government was propelled and motivated by a mix of domestic and international imperatives that changed over time. Understanding the relationship between the diversity and complexity of the society and the socioeconomic change that followed the economic and food crisis of the 1990s helps to explain why some policy options were chosen by government and other actors, and other policies were not.

Methodology

The methods used in this book include research in libraries, in archives, on the Internet, and in the field, as well as interviews and observation. My work in the field introduced an element of participant observation to the process. I was fortunate enough to be able to work in the DPRK for extended periods of time with the major agencies: UNICEF from April to May 1998; UNICEF and the United Nations World Food Program (WFP) from October to December 1999; the WFP from August 2000 to July 2001 (during which period I was transferred to the UNDP for a few weeks); and the Caritas program in September 2001, as an evaluator. I have also directed and implemented a training project with DPRK Ministry of Foreign Trade officials since 1999. I left the country in 2001 but returned regularly on shorter visits in the context of that project. All of the extended periods of research could have generated a book in themselves about doing research in the DPRK, but here I want to illustrate how international agencies conduct investigations in the DPRK by reviewing two projects I undertook in-country.

Field Research on Gender in the DPRK

One investigation I undertook for the WFP was to review, for internal use, the gendered aspects of WFP programs and activities. This task involved several interviews with North Korean staff in the WFP, particularly with one woman who was extremely knowledgeable and helpful about culture and customs regarding food habits and pregnancy. The second part of the research involved field visits to rural and urban districts in the vicinity of Hamhung, Wonsan, and Kaesong. Days were spent interviewing nursery, primary school, secondary school, and orphanage staff, pregnant and nursing women in their homes, women and men working on large food-for-work sites, county engineers who supervised the projects, and county and provincial officials in each area. Most of the interviews were conducted with a North Korean WFP staff member and colleague also acting as translator.

Officials were much more forthcoming than the women interviewed in their homes. That was not surprising, given that home visits involved me, a male interpreter, and the local county and provincial officials interviewing often very shy women who had either just given birth or were about to.

The term "gender" was a new concept to the DPRK. However, in practice the chief engineers had routinely taken into account the different gendered or social roles of men and women in planning projects. Officials had often given some thought to how work tasks might have a disproportionately negative impact on women's health and nutritional status. One particularly memorable discussion took place on the edge of a large embankment reclamation site employing 5,000 male and 5,000 female workers, on a very cold December afternoon (minus twenty degrees centigrade). Seven or eight elderly Korean male engineers and I discussed the sanitary needs of menstruating women working on the site. Without prompting by an outside observer, these engineers had provided for makeshift toilet and washing facilities for women (and men) through local contributions of material and labor. They had reasoned that the UN, through the aegis of the WFP, would not provide financial support for these particular "non-food" items.

Restructuring the Information Base

While working for the WFP in 2000–2001, my main task was to evaluate and restructure the information, monitoring, evaluation, and reporting systems. This mammoth task involved reviewing every piece of information available to the WFP and trying to better systematize future collection, organization, and dissemination. The whole country team was mobilized over one year to carry out this task. Dozens of meetings were held throughout the entire process, involving North Korean and international staff, to work out what could and ought to be done (not always the same). Restructuring involved a range of discrete areas, from considering what the information would be used for (program management and donor reporting) to computer database development, revision of the sixteen monitoring checklists used throughout the country, and training of staff in interviewing, reporting, agriculture, and nutrition.

Technically the process was straightforward, involving first of all deciding on the unit of analysis. The county was chosen, as the province would have been too large a canvas for programming purposes, and it was politically and logistically unfeasible to consider the household as a fruitful source of data for comparative analysis. Part of the exercise involved agreeing on a common romanization for the county names, as different spellings were being used both within the DPRK government and among the various international agencies. In some cases the agencies were using the South Korean names for the counties, as opposed to the sometimes quite different names prevailing in the DPRK. This ostensibly simple choice of unit of analysis then involved a massive follow-up exercise of standardization, undertaken with the active participation of the North Korean counterpart in the management of humanitarian operations, the Flood Damage Rehabilitation Commission (FDRC).

Second, a structured pilot evaluation in three different counties in three different parts of the country with three separate WFP teams, including local and national staff, was undertaken. The WFP teams were allocated one county each in three different provinces. They were given a set of questions to be used as a base both for archival research in the profuse but, at the time, nonsystematized Pyongyang WFP records and for discussion with North Korean officials at the county level. Interview techniques were discussed prior to the field trips so as to develop a common, nonthreatening approach that could not be interpreted as "spying" or information collection for its own sake rather than for program-related objectives. International and national officers were chosen for the pilot exercise based partly on their longevity in the field and partly on the trust they had developed with the county officials, with whom they already had working relationships. The results of this survey demonstrated what kinds of quantitative and qualitative data were available or could reasonably be collected on a regular basis (in the DPRK, the aim is to visit counties at least once every two months).

In the end the restructured system allowed for spatial and temporal comparison of detailed demographic, infrastructural, agricultural, nutrition, and beneficiary data. The general concern about reliability of quantitative information was balanced by a systematic use of qualitative data in the system. Reporting developed the use of comparative analysis—thus figures did not need to be completely accurate as long as they were consistently compiled from the same source. Throughout, a WFP computer programmer developed a county database into which quantitative and qualitative data could be entered, collated, and compared over time and space. This was to make regular reporting systematic and consistent.

The process of standardization revealed new areas in need of systematization, particularly in the initial stages. Potato production figures, for instance, had been calculated sometimes in gross metric tons and sometimes in what agronomists called the "cereal equivalent." The cereal equivalent describes how many calories or how much nutritional value is obtained from a given quantity of potatoes compared with a given quantity of cereals—with corn and milled rice considered "cereals." The potato-to-corn cereal equivalent in terms of tonnage harvested is 4 (potatoes) to 1 (corn). Analysis that treats production/tonnage figures and nutrition/cereal equivalent figures as one and the same is simply meaningless. Likewise, the term "malnutrition" was often used loosely by Korean and international staff alike. Some recorded severe malnutrition, while others identified situations as falling into the much larger category of chronic malnutrition. The process of systematization was aimed at eradicating all these sources of inaccurate reporting. The system also allowed for cross-referencing with information gained from other multilateral agency and NGO monitoring.

Knowledge . . . Not Anecdotes

The point of this rather detailed exegesis is to demonstrate the very serious and continuous evaluation by the WFP and all the other agencies of the basis for their knowledge claims. This means that when information from the agencies enters the public arena, it is not a product of anecdotal wisdom, or a weeklong delegation visit that assesses the conditions of the entire country from the safety and isolation of the country's main hotel, the Koryo, or the Kobangsan Guest House (where U.S. short-term visitors tend to be housed). It is instead the product of serious and professional assessment.

Data and Sources

I have tried to substantiate knowledge claims throughout the book with references to sources that can be checked. For this reason I have, in the main, eschewed anonymous sources and nonpublic documentation as references.

Confidential information derived from the WFP system or any other source does not provide the foundation for anything written in this book. In some parts of the book, I have relied on my local knowledge of the DPRK. However, I have attempted throughout to build the core argument on sources replicable or accessible to a researcher.

Primary source material includes government documents, mainly from the DPRK, the ROK, and the United States. Extensive use is made of data from multilateral and bilateral humanitarian agencies and NGOs, mainly from Europe, South Korea, the United States, and Japan. I have made direct and indirect use of interviews in and outside the DPRK. I have also used material from interviews, talks, and conferences outside the country —mainly in the United States, China, Japan, and the United Kingdom. Over the past decade and a half I have interviewed North Koreans in English and through interpreters throughout the DPRK and outside the country. I have also drawn on interviews and discussions with many people concerned with the DPRK, including Americans, Japanese, South Koreans, Chinese, Europeans, Australians, and Canadians. I have spoken with those working in different sectors, particularly humanitarian assistance officials, the military, diplomats, intelligence agency officials, agronomists, health personnel, journalists, academics, and policy analysts.

Also useful have been a number of excellent websites that bring together primary source material in English, including translations of the South and North Korean media. These are referenced in the bibliography.

The secondary material is less useful, as much of it is still bounded by Cold War frameworks in the assumptions on which it is founded and the questions it sets for itself. The literature on external actors' relations with the DPRK, particularly the United States, is relatively profuse, compared to the scant analysis of DPRK domestic social and economic structures and processes. Useful secondary literature can be found in the references.

The core data for this book, however, come either directly or indirectly from work carried out by the humanitarian agencies in the DPRK. Before the humanitarian community began systematically collecting and disseminating information, it was virtually impossible to evaluate social change in the DPRK—much less to separate analytically socioeconomic change from DPRK governmental policy and further investigate how one affects the other. This was not the case by the early 2000s. The enormous amount of data thus recorded provides the base for the preliminary assessment of key socioeconomic variables and the response from government and outside agencies that form the substantive core of this book. These data also provide the foundation for an evaluation of the differential impact of socioeconomic change on different sectors of society.

Assumptions and Terminology

The Kim Il Sung era and the post–Kim Il Sung era should not be regarded as different from each other because of the titular ruler. Ample evidence indicates that Kim Jong Il was the effective ruler of the DPRK for at least ten years before his father's death. I have used the periodization, however, to distinguish roughly the period of absolute crisis, under the rule of Kim Jong Il, from the previous era under the presidency of Kim Il Sung, who died in 1994. This periodization is legitimate, given that Kim Il Sung's policies framed the pre-crisis era and Kim Jong Il's policies must shape the era of crisis.

In this book the term "regime" is used in a conceptually specific manner. It is not necessarily used in a pejorative manner—for instance, to describe a government we do not like. It is used more in the way the term is used in the international relations literature. Regime, therefore, is more "a set of governing arrangements" or "a set of principles, norms, rules and decisions-making procedures."[15] Ethical judgments are made in this book, but these are founded on substantiated argument rather than conceptual implication.

The Structure of the Book

I have chosen to write this book around a more or less chronological narrative, with the main exception of the theoretical and analytical framework provided by the next chapter. The chronological narrative is occasionally superseded for the sake of narrative and thematic coherence. For instance, in the short evaluation of land rezoning in chapter 3, I have continued the discussion to take account of how the policy developed into the new century, although the chapter focuses on the transitional period of 1994 to 1998. The chronological framework is of course only a narrative and analytical device designed to indicate important events in the particular time frame under consideration. Real life never fits so neatly into analytical time periods, and that caveat applies also to this book. I have argued, for instance, that government policy could be characterized as being in a state of paralysis during the mid-1990s. I would not wish to imply, however, that elements of proactivity were not present in this period or that trends toward continuing stasis were not very evident well after the mid-1990s. I am here using the chronological device merely to identify what I consider to be dominant characteristics of the period.

The substantive chapters deal with the conceptual and theoretical framework for understanding the DPRK; the heritage of the Kim Il Sung period and the human and economic disaster of famine; the transitional period when socioeconomic change took place in the DPRK but the government remained in policy paralysis; the response of the international humanitarian community to hunger and poverty and the process of interaction with the government; the government's more proactive domestic policies from the late 1990s on; the analogous government proactivity abroad; and the response of the DPRK's main external interlocutors and adversaries. The final chapter provides a summary of the arguments. It also posits policy recommendations based on the reconceptualization of Korean security dilemmas argued for in this book.

1

Preventing War and Forging Peace

ONVENTIONAL APPROACHES TO INTERNATIONAL SECURITY are incapable of analyzing change in the DPRK polity and politics, including foreign policy behavior. This is because explanations of the DPRK are so far embedded in the international security discourse of which they are a product that they are incapable of seeing, let alone analyzing, the change in DPRK society that has occurred since the mid-1990s. International security analysis has become part of the international security problem. In this sense, theory and explanation have become "securitized."

This chapter argues for two alternative, although not mutually exclusive, ways of thinking about international security and the DPRK. The first is an adaptation of classical international relations theory. The second develops a "human security" analysis of peace and security on the Korean peninsula. These two approaches offer theoretical alternatives that are empirically well founded, analytically coherent, and policy relevant.

The Inadequacy of International Relations Theory

International security questions tend to be treated in the international relations literature in an abstract manner, divorcing discussions of war and peace from the very bloody and messy realities of real-life violent conflict. In these abstract models of international relations, the state is reified.

Whether through balance-of-power theories, deterrence theories, or theories of alliances, institutions, regimes, or the construction of international norms, "states" are studied almost as if they were autonomous of the people who live in them.[1] Indeed, within these theoretical frameworks, the inhabitants of states are simply eradicated as an analytical variable in the discussion of how and why war occurs and is prevented.[2]

Within this perspective, states are sometimes understood as being constrained by other states—but the assumption is that state behavior can be understood separately from the people who live in it. The exception is sometimes made in the attempt to understand how governments or sometimes bureaucracies or, in days gone by, "great men" shape the behavior of states.[3] In the end, though, within this dominant theoretical prism, states per se can be understood as rational, self-interested, optimizing actors. Their behavior can, ultimately, be predicted. The rationality (of states) assumption permeates the academic study of international relations, from the dominant "realist" perspective through to and including its rivals for disciplinary sovereignty—the liberals, institutionalists, and social constructivists.[4]

This approach has always relied on some pretty heroic assumptions—in much the same way as have the theories of self-regarding economic man from which these international theories are derived. For this reason alone, the theories that are generated from within this worldview should be used with extreme caution. More significantly for the study of the two Koreas, when one of the states concerned seems to act not at all like other states, this dominant perspective encourages an interpretation that assumes—because that state is unpredictable within the context of prevailing paradigms—it must be "abnormal," "rogue," and ultimately a "threat" to other states and to international security.[5]

Radical state-centric views argue that in explaining international relations and managing foreign policy, because the international system has no central state to maintain order (it is "anarchic"), states must always be prepared for self-defense. They must preemptively arm themselves so as to be ready for any eventuality. In the end only superior military force can preserve the security of states. States must be ever prepared to respond to perceived threats to stability with military force. Thus it does not take too much imagination to jump from identifying the DPRK as a "rogue state" to concluding that the most appropriate way to deal with such a threat is through the application of military force.

Poor Theory + DPRK Opacity + Worst-Case Analysis = Bad Policy

Conventional approaches to the DPRK and its international relations receive extra force because, the argument goes, so little information is available about the country. Given the absence of reliable empirical data, all there are to guide analysts are conventional international relations models of interstate behavior. This has never been a completely persuasive argument for the field of foreign relations, given that it was possible, even prior to the end of the Cold War, to obtain data from the DPRK's international partners about policies, activities, and outcomes.[6] Other sources, inevitably more partial, but still providing a part of the jigsaw puzzle of information about DPRK international behavior, came from the pronouncements of the DPRK itself, as well as the investigations of interested adversaries.[7] Certainly, with the plethora of contacts the DPRK has had with the outside world since the mid-1990s, this argument has lost the plausibility it may have once had.

This is not to say that DPRK governmental decision making is not about as opaque as it is possible to be in this contemporary world of transparency norms and relatively free flows of information. It is difficult to ascertain what the DPRK government might be thinking or what its objectives might be with any degree of certainty. This, of course, contributes to international anxieties—to a sense of unpredictability that heightens security dilemmas, makes for arms racing, and causes conservative politicians and militarists in Western countries to consider seriously pre-emptive strikes on the DPRK.[8]

It also means that Western policymakers too often import worst-case analysis of DPRK intentions and capabilities into the political arena as established fact. The capacity to produce fertilizer and pharmaceuticals, for instance, is transposed as the technical capacity to make biological weapons. The conclusions are, strictly speaking, truthful—if the DPRK can manufacture pharmaceuticals, it can probably manufacture biochemical weapons. The combination of the DPRK's own culture of secrecy and the activities of ideologically driven Western politicians who are predetermined to find in the DPRK the epitome of barbarism—heightened by the fear of the unknown and the possibly known—easily and reasonably sharpens international anxieties.

For these reasons, therefore, conventional approaches have "securitized" discourse on the DPRK and international security.[9] By "securitization," I mean that the scholarly literature has become partisan, contributing to the escalation of conflict rather than to analysis of it. I take issue with the conventional approaches but accept that they assume the status of "common sense" in the scholarly, policy, and media coverage of the DPRK.[10] This also means that scholarship representing a different position, however well supported intellectually, is sometimes deemed questionable simply because it does not fit the sociological consensus of the research community.[11] On a less academic but more practical level, the securitization paradigm provides a very bad guide for policymakers, based as it is on extraordinarily flawed premises.

The Securitization Perspective: What It Is and What It Does

The securitization paradigm accepts the classical security assumptions that military power and military instruments are ultimately the only significant factor of analysis in respect to Korea, but the paradigm goes further than this by sublimating all other issues, including DPRK economic, cultural, and humanitarian policies, within a military-based analysis. In addition, its inherent normative assumption is that the domestic and foreign politics of North Korea provide the root cause of all tension on the Korean peninsula.

The securitization perspective portrays North Korean politics as mad in the sense of being irrational and unknowable and bad in the sense of the motivation and impetus for policy being ascribed to normatively unacceptable characteristics of the state and its leadership. That these two aspects of the paradigm are sometimes contradictory—if the state is mad, can it really be understood as bad, in the sense of being consciously directed by evil intent whose instigators could take responsibility for their action?—is not a problem for the paradigm, given that these assumptions are made prior to analysis. Thomas Kuhn, the eminent philosopher of science, taught us that assumptions underpinning a tradition of scientific inquiry—what he calls a paradigm—do not have to be "rational."[12] As long as these assumptions prove fruitful in solving research puzzles, at least within Kuhnian theory, they will continue to shape the direction of research. Nor must these paradigmatic assumptions always give rise to precisely the same conclusion. Kuhn informs us that paradigms shape research questions, acting as a filtering device to weed out assumptions that do not fit paradigmatic frameworks. They may thus narrow the theoretical agenda, but they also permit differing research outcomes *within the confines of the paradigm's fundamental assumptions*. Thus, within the securitization paradigm, we can find different strands—what I will call the "bad" or "mad" approaches; within each, one can find "hard" and "soft" variants.

The "Bad" Thesis

The "bad" thesis assumes that the DPRK pursues alien objectives that are anathema to the rest of the civilized international system. The assumption that the North Korean state and its leadership are fundamentally outside the pale of the global community underpins the terminology sometimes used to describe North Korea as a "rogue state."[13] From this perspective, the DPRK is motivated by malevolence and belligerence, and its leadership's foreign and domestic policies can be ascribed to malice aforethought. Internationally, North Korea is ready to make war upon its southern neighbor, perhaps even to attack the United States itself, and in pursuit of these offensive aims is constantly engaged in a furtive arms buildup.

This perspective underlies much of the U.S. foreign policy community approach. One typical example is of a 1998 document whose style conveys an extreme picture.[14] Hostility is "unremitting," diplomats "demand," and actions are "all too clear." North Korea is likened to the ultimate of U.S. bogeymen, Saddam Hussein. That particular paper was premised on claims that the North Koreans were developing a clandestine nuclear site —claims that subsequent U.S. inspectors found to be without foundation.[15] The North Korean state is presented as immoral, as resources were "diverted" to the military instead of to a population that was suffering from severe food shortages; the fact that the humanitarian community found no evidence of diversion of food to the military was not acknowledged.[16]

The DPRK certainly maintains an overweening military capacity. Whether it sees this capacity as defensive and whether it sees its exports as a source of hard currency to purchase necessary inputs into its economy (as do most arms-producing Western states, like Britain) remain matters for interpretation.[17] Russian analysts working with U.S. colleagues pointed out that, while DPRK arms production and development were undesirable because they increased tension due to possible "disproportionate counter-measures by the United States and Japan," international law nevertheless permitted the DPRK to develop missiles for defensive purposes and to use space for peaceful purposes.[18] This was quite unlike the case of Saddam Hussein's Iraq, which, as a defeated power in war, was subject to UN resolutions prohibiting and controlling arms development. Nevertheless, the impressive conviction of those writing from this perspective brooks no caveats and no acknowledgment of the existence of alternative interpretations of DPRK policy.

In the "bad thesis," much is also made of the North Korean armed forces' offensive posture, with "60–65 percent of those forces . . . close to the border, in a high state of readiness, well primed for an attack on the South."[19] To equate the former with the latter point of the previous sentence, however, is rather disingenuous. As others pointed out, "Pyongyang is only 120 kilometers from [the border with South Korea]. Thus it might be more accurate to say that 65 percent of North Korea's troops are deployed in front of their capital."[20] As the same author remarked, "it would be far more surprising if the DPRK deployed its troops in the north, away from where potential conflict could occur."[21]

North Korea is, within the "bad" perspective, a "garrison state" and "the most militarized society on earth," with its population ready, willing, and able to wage total war against its peace-loving neighbors.[22] Evidence for this perspective includes the one million people in the DPRK's armed forces, the expenditure of more than 30 percent of the country's budget on defense, and the incorporation of up to 30 percent of its population of 22 million in the armed forces or in local militias.[23] This picture, however, leaves out what might be relevant data for any policymaker interested in assessing, say, the comparative military strengths of South and North Korea.

If, for instance, we refer to the International Institute of Strategic Studies' (IISS) annual survey of the military strength of the world's states, we find that in 2000 the DPRK spent an estimated $2.1 billion on its armed forces, compared to an estimated South Korean military expenditure of $14.4 billion.[24] IISS data for 2001/2002 inform us that the North had 300,000 more personnel on active service than the South but about the same number of reserves (4.7 million for the North and 4.5 million for the South).[25] This means that the DPRK army, with its very low level of per capita spending compared to South Korea's, must be operationally weak in terms of hardware and software support.

The comparative advantage of the DPRK lies in its 300,000 extra personnel in uniform; but this again is somewhat qualified by the much larger South Korean population that would be called on in time of war—47 million, compared to 24 million in the North.[26] Economically, the DPRK's estimated GNP in 2000 was just $15 billion, compared to $457 billion for South Korea.[27] These figures hardly suggest that North Korea is an overwhelming military threat to the South. Indeed, former South Korean president Kim Dae Jung argued that South Korean–U.S. combined forces were enough to prevent any offensive from North Korea.[28]

The perceived threat from DPRK forces derives not only from the financial support allocated to the military but from the alleged efficiency and sheer volume of North Korean forces. Here the securitization paradigm both underestimates and overestimates North Korean military capacity. It grasps one aspect of DPRK defense capacities—the readiness for war of the entire population. All the social organizations (women's, children's, and work units) regularly train their members to be prepared should war break out. The million or so adults who form the core of the permanent army remain in the armed forces for a maximum of five to eight years before they go on to be part-time members of the militias.[29] The turnover ensures that most adults receive some military training. The North Korean military structure functions in effect as a giant "Home Guard" where the entire population (not just 30 percent of it) can be mobilized if necessary. In this sense the much-cited figure of a million-strong army vastly underestimates the North Korean military forces.

On the other hand, capacity is overestimated because of inadequate accounting of military and civilian activities in the DPRK economy. Neither the militias nor the armed forces are separate from the "economic" structure, in that "military" activities include the construction of "civilian" infrastructure and a contribution to national requirements such as transplanting and harvesting food. The 30 percent of GDP cited for military expenditure in conventional accounts ignores the contribution of the military to the "civilian" economy. That the military also takes part in nonmilitary activity is recognized in some of the securitization literature, although there is little evidence of such information feeding back into the discussion of the total sums attributed to military expenditure.[30]

In its domestic affairs, the DPRK is perceived as a human rights violator of magnitude. A prime example is an unsourced U.S. government document published in 1999, stating that the DPRK "state leadership perceives most international norms of human rights, especially individual rights, as illegitimate, alien social concepts subversive to the goals of the State and party."[31] Individuals are routinely "disappeared," tortured, or subjected to arbitrary arrest, detention, or forced resettlement. The report tells us that no fair trials were permitted and there were no rights to privacy, with individuals constantly subject to surveillance at home and in the community. According to the same sources, there was no freedom of speech, assembly, association, worship, or movement.[32] Unrest is such that "an unsubstantiated Reuters report stated that following a March [1998] coup attempt against Kim Jong Il, authorities arrested several thousand members of the military."[33]

It is difficult to substantiate some of these claims, although, again, the activity of the humanitarian community helped deliver some solid information on some of these issues. For instance, we know that household surveillance exists for preventive health purposes and might also be used for political surveillance. We know also that there is some freedom of worship for Christians, but we do not know how much.[34] What we are beginning to find out, however, suggests a more complex picture than that portrayed by the "bad" thesis. Unquestionably, the Protestant and the Catholic churches built in Pyongyang in the late 1980s are seen by authorities as showplaces to indicate that religious tolerance is part of DPRK society. At the same time, visiting priests have repeatedly confirmed that elderly congregations attending services appeared to be genuine believers.

Data made available from humanitarian community reports were also able to direct analysts toward more specific questions. Why, for instance, has there been a rise in the number of children in the orphanages since the food crisis began?[35] Is it that there are simply more orphans due to increased mortality? Is it a sign that familial and community support structures are breaking down? Or is there more dissidence and have these children somehow been separated from their parents for more sinister reasons?[36] We simply do not know the answer, although outside analysts are increasingly able to start responding to these questions in an informed manner. In 2001, for instance, the United Nations Organization for the Coordination of Humanitarian Affairs (UNOCHA) undertook to document all the UN, bilateral, and NGO activity in the orphanages since the start of the humanitarian activity in the DPRK. This activity generated a cross-referenced picture of numbers of children, locations of institutions, and qualitative information about the conditions of institutions and the state of the children.[37]

The "bad" paradigm is, furthermore, founded on a logical contradiction. Citizens suffer such extreme deprivation at the hands of their government, yet the assumption is that these same citizens would be able and willing to fight, with some chance of success, a total war in a sustained manner involving every member of the population. This contradiction can, however, be absorbed by the "bad" paradigm. Citizens have been so effectively brainwashed by the propaganda of the regime (goes the argument) that they have lost their capacity for independent thought. Rather than using war as an opportunity for liberation from an authoritarian leader (as, for example, happened in Serbia after the Kosovo war), the North Korean people would be more likely to act as an undifferentiated mass in support of the leadership.

The Hard Version

The hard version of the "bad" thesis argues that the North Korean state is irredeemable. Writing on nuclear issues in the context of reunification, but from within a framework intended as a generalization about the nature of the DPRK, Nicholas Eberstadt states, "The North Korean regime *is* the North Korean nuclear problem and unless its intentions change, which is unlikely, that problem will continue as long as the regime is in place."[38] "Western governments" should "unflinchingly" assess whether they can change the North Korean state.[39] The inference is clear. Only eradication of the regime will do. The methods are not made explicit, but given North Korea's unwillingness to be bulldozed into a quick unification,

the hastening of reunification implies coercion, which, in the circumstances of the Korean peninsula, would very likely mean war. If such a
policy were implemented, South Koreans and U.S. citizens (though not
U.S. policy analysts, of course) would have to "unflinchingly" step forward to fight and die (again) in Korea.[40]

The "Softies"

The soft version of this thesis accepts the assumptions of the bad perspective. North Korea "extorts" aid from the United States; it engages in "blackmail efforts" and in "provocative behavior."[41] The DPRK "undoubtedly"
would like to "rule the entire Korean Peninsula," even though "it knows
that . . . goal unachievable and foolish to pursue."[42] The soft approach
does not view the DPRK as possessing overwhelming military capabilities
or as totally intractable. The "softies" do not believe the DPRK possesses
"a plausible invasion capability against South Korea."[43] Nor do they rule out
the possibility of negotiation with North Korea. However, because they
remain convinced that the DPRK is an inherently untrustworthy partner,
they find it difficult to see how a deal could generate the confidence
building and trust necessary for its success.

The "Mad" Thesis

The "mad" thesis is essentially a subfield of the "bad" thesis, relying as it
does on a notion of evil intent as one of its fundamental assumptions. The
difference between the "bad" and the "mad" theses is that the former pre-
sumes the DPRK to be a rational instrumental actor, the latter an irrational
actor, unknowable, unpredictable, and dangerous because of the presumed
underlying ill intent of its leadership. Another difference is that, while the
"mad" thesis implies something primeval and atavistic, with policy arising from a sort of primitive, chaotic, and fundamentally unknowable
polity and society, the "bad" thesis assumes strategic intentionality on the
part of DPRK authorities.

North Korean politics is viewed as "mad" in the sense of tending, often
inexplicably, toward noncompliance with international norms and irra-
tionality in its apparent refusal to follow optimal preference-maximizing
behavior.[44] North Korea is therefore unpredictable in its domestic and

foreign policy behavior. For these reasons, the thesis goes, negotiating with North Korea will always be fraught with danger. DPRK negotiators cannot be trusted to behave in the way that conventional diplomacy requires; nor can they be trusted to honor agreements.

The Hard Version

The extreme, or "hard," version of the madness thesis argues that terrible, inexplicable things that would be outside the pale of normal human existence go on inside North Korea—such as cannibalism. Claims of cannibalism should be taken very seriously—but those who have made these allegations did not assume the responsibility of systematically investigating them. A classic example of these unsubstantiated claims presented as fact appeared in the *Economist's* July 1999 survey on Korea, with its front cover given entirely over to a demonic-looking portrait of Kim Jong Il.[45] The commentary inside the magazine rounded off its analysis of North Korea by stating: "And there is madness. A family talking to a journalist for the first time since escaping to the mountains in China say they left because they had run out of hope. The mother, in her 50s, had visited a neighbor, who had been due to give birth. There was no sign of the baby. The woman had something boiling in a pot on the stove. She said it was a rabbit. It wasn't."[46]

The "Softies"

The "soft" version of the mad thesis asserts that North Korea is unknowable and therefore uninterpretable because, it is alleged, there is no reliable information about the country. Marcus Noland, for instance, in what became a benchmark article on the DPRK, stated baldly that "there is an acute lack of information [about North Korea]" and that "virtually all economic and social data are regarded as state secrets."[47] Robert Scalapino pointed to the DPRK as a "mystery" but argued at the same time that it "would be a serious mistake to assume that . . . we know nothing about the DPRK."[48] The eighteen-page report "North and South Korea" in the *Understanding Global Issues* series stated that in any discussions of North Korea, "lack of hard information is a constant problem" (before going on to present a perfectly adequate account of North Korean politics and economy, along with source references in the document itself!).[49]

This is not to say, of course, that the DPRK is an open polity and that it is not a struggle to obtain accurate and usable information from and about the country. However, the "soft" perspective denies *in principle* that it is possible to gain reasonable knowledge of North Korea. More recently, this perspective has not acknowledged the success of the aid community in making inroads into DPRK impenetrability.

Perhaps the least subtle accounts in this genre were those that argued that the DPRK was such an expert in deception that critical evaluation of DPRK politics was almost impossible. This assumption is largely based on the contention that, even when the DPRK went so far as to plan a war against South Korea in 1950, absolutely no evidence could be found of a premeditated invasion of the South in captured Central Committee files when the U.S.-led UN forces took Pyongyang.[50] That this lack of evidence might warrant a different interpretation from the standard account was not considered. Instead, the absence of evidence demonstrates the "regime's devotion to strategic secrecy," even to the extent of hiding its intention from its own senior officials.[51] Even, therefore, "the formal evidentiary record of officially revealed DPRK pronouncements and actions . . . must be treated as problematic." This is a "preternaturally secretive" state. (The irony that the lack of reliable evidence did not prevent the author from drawing some very strong conclusions indeed about DPRK policy seemed lost.) The DPRK, goes the argument, has retained a commitment to strategic deception throughout its existence as a state, right up until the present day.

Then there is the "damned if you do and damned if you don't" mode of analysis. This approach views North Korean compliance with an agreement as a sure sign of intended noncompliance. It is beautifully exemplified by one analyst, who, writing on the 1994 U.S.-DPRK agreement on nuclear energy, stated in 1998 that "although it has carefully fulfilled its obligations initially, North Korea will at some point make trouble over the implementation of the Agreed Framework."[52]

Securitizing North Korea

With few creditable exceptions, Cold War assumptions, despite being contradictory and often unsubstantiated, remain embedded in the post–Cold

War literature about the DPRK.[53] That many of the strong claims of the securitization paradigm remain unsupported by evidence does not imply a weakness from this perspective. If a government is so far beyond the norms of international society, it stands to reason that such a government will do everything in its power to prevent an independent assessment of the facts. Lack of corroboration, in a manner Orwell would have appreciated, thus became corroboration of those things needing to be corroborated.

Securitization as a Faulty Road Map to Stability and Peace

The securitization approach no doubt captures elements of North Korean politics. DPRK policymakers can be unpredictable—as the "mad" thesis implies—but they can also be very predictable indeed, as the "bad" thesis asserts. The state has engaged in practices that would not be acceptable in liberal polities and should not be acceptable anywhere, most starkly in its suppression of dissidence.[54] Yet this perspective does not tell the whole story about the DPRK. Worse, it distorts the complexities of North Korean politics and policies. This means, among other things, that the perspective is not much use as a guide for policymakers seeking to build better strategies to help bring stability and peace to the Korean peninsula.

There are five major problems with the securitization approach—none of them mutually exclusive. The first is that many of the strongest claims are not supported by evidence. The second is that the perspective cannot assimilate change. The third is that the fundamental assumptions are so stark that they brook no qualification. The fourth is that the perspective actively ignores data that contradict the approach. The fifth is that when data that do not fit the approach cannot be ignored, they are distorted to meet the requirements of the perspective—in other words, they are *securitized.*

Where Is the Evidence?

The first of these problems is perhaps the easiest to deal with. Given increased access to the DPRK, one could expect to see more research backed up by the conventional rules of scholarly inquiry in the future. This is already happening with some of the work that is being carried out on economic options for North Korea's future.[55] Of course, the provision of more data does not necessarily lead to a change in perspective if the researcher is so committed to its basic assumptions that they become unquestionable.

One article about possible outcomes in North Korea came to the conclusion that if "famine materializes, its roots will be in political decisions made in Pyongyang, not material resource constraints."[56] For a serious economic analysis this conclusion is interesting. The vast body of economic analysis from international organizations working within the country—analysis which is pretty uncontroversial for adversary (but donor) countries such as the United States and the Republic of Korea—holds that famine was the product of both domestic inability or unwillingness to change policy, at least on the macrolevel, and a serious lack of material inputs.[57]

The (also uncontroversial) consensus was that with major material inputs, such as fertilizer, agricultural production could be massively reinvigorated. This consensus was borne out in concrete terms in 2001 when, largely thanks to the inputs of South Korean fertilizer, cereal harvests increased forty percent over the previous year's, after a change in agricultural policies—for instance, introducing more double-cropping initiatives.[58]

A Society That Never Changes?

The second problem—the assumption that the DPRK has an unchanging as well as belligerent persona in world and domestic affairs that cannot be altered unless the regime is eradicated—cripples analytical clarity and purpose.[59] Diplomacy or negotiation with DPRK policymakers becomes fruitless, as the interests of the DPRK and the international community can never coincide. Furthermore, the DPRK's inherent aggression means that it will always be an intransigent partner in negotiations.

By definition, if the securitization perspective cannot assimilate change as an explanatory variable, it cannot help inform negotiators of how, when, and why DPRK foreign policy behavior is changing.[60] The only choices available for policymakers using this approach are *paralysis* (nothing can be done with the DPRK) and *confrontation* (nothing should be done with the DPRK, as diplomacy constitutes appeasement, and therefore the military option is all that is left on the table).[61]

What Happened to Qualified Analysis?

Third, a problem for those interested in developing successful policy on the DPRK is that the DPRK is viewed as such a singularly bad or mad entity that only the starkest descriptors are appropriate. It is difficult for analysis informed by these extreme descriptions to be qualified—because then the approach loses its foundation, thus threatening the verisimilitude of the entire perspective.

Ignoring Data That Don't "Fit"

Fourth, and directly linked to the third analytical problem, given the rigidity of the assumptions, data that do not fit the framework tend not to be examined. In practical terms this can mean that the detailed data collected by the humanitarian community, which may allow for a more nuanced picture of the DPRK, are implicitly judged "out of court"— inadmissible as evidence.

Distorting the Data

The fifth and final problem is that data that might contradict the securitization worldview and that do manage to be acknowledged are incorporated selectively into analysis so as to confirm the prior assumptions. An example is taken from the opening paragraphs of an otherwise useful economic analysis that manages to use an anecdote about DPRK soldiers pulling bananas out of their rucksacks to impress upon readers the sinister nature of DPRK society.[62] These soldiers could have been taking an unauthorized snack break, but the interpretation is of "a surreptitious trade in bananas."[63] Data were *securitized* to fit the message of a normatively unacceptable and bizarre system and society that was the DPRK.

Securitization Theory— Making for a More Dangerous World

Combined, these problems make for dangerous decision making. Decision makers operating in the thrall of the "mad" or the "bad" approach—and often these are combined—have few options other than to make war or to remain isolated from contact with the DPRK. Both these options lead to unacceptable political, humanitarian, and strategic consequences. This perspective also leads to a failure of the diplomatic imagination. If, for instance, former U.S. president Jimmy Carter had thought nothing could be done with the DPRK in 1994, he would not have made the visit that helped break the nuclear deadlock on the peninsula and prevent war.[64]

Using Mainstream Theory More Rigorously

I do not argue that classical security threats, for instance, in terms of proliferation of weapons of mass destruction, should not receive the serious attention they obviously deserve. These, by their nature, are the ultimate threat to human security. Instead I argue that classical security studies have underutilized resources capable of understanding and therefore dealing with very real security tensions on the Korean peninsula and that can help analysts differentiate negative from positive stimulus as far as potential security threats are concerned. The securitization perspective cannot do this because it interprets *all* DPRK actions (even those in contradiction with each other) as constituting a challenge to international security.

A Historicized and Contextualized Rational Actor

In contrast, a useful and standard theoretical contribution, but one that has not been utilized in the analysis of the DPRK, is Graham Allison's "rational-actor model" of international politics.[65] Devised partly to analyze the Cuban missile crisis, it posits an interpretive model that suggests that states (including revolutionary states) can be understood as being led by unitary governments engaged in more or less purposive acts in international politics.[66] Governments, in this model, pursue goals and objectives through choosing alternative policy and behavior, to which are attached potential "utility," or consequences. Rational choice in this scenario consists therefore in selecting alternatives that maximize utility, that is, those that achieve the government's goals and minimize unpleasant consequences.

Allison's model can be used to interpret DPRK behavior through a *historicized and contextualized rational-actor framework.* This approach would assume that the DPRK is hugely conditioned by its late-twentieth-century experience of war and threats of war and, equally important, its sense of self-directed Korean nationalism. It also assumes a DPRK knowable in principle, even if it acknowledges the real difficulties of researching the country.

Some analysts have never abandoned the exigencies of scientific rigor by using the excuse that "nothing can be known" about the DPRK, and their research continues to be informed by tough empirical reasoning. Bruce Cumings, who has spent many years studying Korea, is the exemplar in this field.[67] Neither has the security studies field completely given itself up to the securitization approach—with a credible body of literature allowing for a research agenda that treats the DPRK as a rational or knowable actor. For instance, in what has become the standard account of U.S.-DPRK negotiations during the 1994 nuclear crisis, former *New York Times* editorial board member Leon Sigal shows how Cold War presumptions of North Korean politics brought the United States literally to the brink of war.[68] Conflict was only prevented at the last minute by former president Jimmy Carter's "track-two" diplomacy in Pyongyang. Carter's shuttle diplomacy was itself partially underpinned by personal intervention from U.S. scholar Selig Harrison, who has persistently worked from the perspective that the DPRK is a knowable entity.[69]

A historicized and contextualized rational-actor model could also incorporate discussion of economic instruments as means of achieving security goals. Another direction of research might reassess, empirically, the predictability of DPRK foreign policy behavior—building on those aspects of Sigal's work in which he has demonstrated the consistent failure of U.S. intelligence and foreign policy communities to read what he argues is a predictable (and rational in Allison's sense) negotiation strategy.[70] A model that assumes rationality might help provide interesting answers to the question, for instance, of how the North Koreans achieved what could be considered a diplomatic success in securing a formal agreement through which its major adversaries—the United States, South Korea, and Japan—financed the development of its nuclear power program.[71]

More practically, policymakers need accurate information that can assist in the pursuit of successful negotiating outcomes. An analysis of the DPRK that attempts the difficult task of sifting through the evidence to assess and separate out negative and positive signals from Pyongyang will make for more effective and less costly policies than one that ignores the difference.

The securitization paradigm assumes that conflict with the DPRK can be resolved only through coercion, because the DPRK is both intransigent and belligerent at all times and inherently unable to negotiate good-faith settlements. Assuming rationality may, however, allow for the possibility of achieving compromise and trade-offs through a process of diplomacy that specifically seeks to resolve conflict through peaceful means.[72]

Making the DPRK More Explicable

Orthodox international relations theory can thus be used to help explain the DPRK in a more sophisticated manner than before through the development of a model of the DPRK as a historicized and contextualized rational actor. The theory assumes a rational actor in the sense that the policy objectives and goals of the DPRK can be understood through a conventional means/ends costs/benefits calculus.

A soft version of the thesis might minimally argue that using the increased knowledge of the DPRK available since the mid-1990s in the context of a rational-actor intellectual framework allows for some predictability to DPRK domestic and international behavior. If predictability is increased, threat perceptions may be reduced (or not, depending on the results of the empirical evaluation).

A hard version of the thesis might want to assert that the DPRK should be understood as a "rational actor" like all other states that operate within the international system. This would mean that partner and adversary states could engage the DPRK with a reasonable amount of certainty that agreements would be kept, international law upheld, and war used only as a last resort. These assumptions would also have to be explored through empirical research. Their advantage is not that they always describe the "reality"—most states do not always keep their agreements, for instance. The advantage is that they provide an analytical framework against which the empirical data can be tested—historically, in different time periods, and geographically, in terms of the DPRK's relationships to different states, ranging, for example, from the United States to China.

Whether soft or hard versions are adopted, if this more nuanced approach is used, DPRK policy can become more explicable. Decision making can then be based on more rigorous analytical criteria than the theological assumptions too often underpinning the "bad" or "mad" theses.

Rational Policy Options

Rational-actor approaches have underpinned some of the most successful policy choices of those who must work out how to attain stability and peace on the peninsula. Former South Korean president Kim Dae Jung's engagement policy, which resulted in a proliferation of North-South political, economic, social, and cultural contacts, was underpinned by the idea that it was possible to negotiate with the DPRK—the same as with any other international actor. The Clinton administration, as evinced in the October 2000 visit to Pyongyang by then secretary of state Madeleine Albright, also moved in this direction. In the closing days of that administration, U.S. policymakers developed an approach to the DPRK that was informed by the view that cooperation with North Korea both was possible and would serve the U.S. national interest—helping to achieve stability in East Asia in a way that coercion could not.

A Better Option—for Peace and Security

I argue, however, that an active or stable peace on the peninsula that is durable and can be taken for granted will come about only when Koreans in the DPRK (and the ROK) attain a level of human security that ensures freedom from want and freedom from fear.[73] Furthermore, I argue that this can be done only if these freedoms are embedded in institutions and practices that can safeguard those freedoms. I do not argue that human security can be attained without long-term reconstruction of the Korean economy and polity. How that is achieved will be the product of political negotiations between the various actors. I do, however, argue that the conditions for human security needs can be identified and that the response to meeting these needs can be tracked. I also argue that understanding whether or to what extent North Korean and international policymakers are able or willing to respond to these needs helps explain the possibilities for stability, security, and long-term peace on the peninsula.

Human Security

The concept of human security emerges from the 1994 Human Development Report, which argued,

> The battle of peace has to be fought on two fronts. The first is the security front where victory spells freedom from fear. The second is the economic and social front where victory means freedom from want. Only victory on both fronts can assure the world of an enduring peace. No provisions that can be

written into the [UN] Charter will enable the Security Council to make the world secure from war if men and women have no security in their homes and their jobs.[74]

Different analysts conceptualize human security needs differently. My approach is to include both freedom from want and freedom from fear as twin fundamentals of human security.[75] Freedom-from-want basics are, at minimum, the right to food, shelter, a reasonable standard of health, and equitable access to a good standard of education. Freedom from want includes the right to live in an environment where there is freedom from fear of economic and natural disaster affecting life and livelihood. Freedom from fear includes the right to live a life absent of arbitrary violence or political and religious repression. Human security includes access to positive freedoms, including the right to a cultural identity, to make personal choices, and to take part in decision making at the individual and the collective level.

Assessing Human Security

Human security is never gained to the same degree by the entire population of any country, even democratic countries. It is a truism, for instance, that in the United States a presidential candidate must have access to wealth and status to have any chance of winning an election. Formal legalistic freedoms, in other words, are often qualified by informal unfreedoms—most often related to wealth differentials and lack of access to status networks. This does not mean to say that human security needs should be considered as normatively neutral analytical categories that should then be used to measure that which can be attained in practice—to a greater or lesser degree in different societies. There are limits to what can be considered an acceptably unequal endowment of human security within societies. What should constitute these limits remains a question of judgment. This, in turn, does not mean that there are not intellectually rigorous ways to assess what may or may not be acceptable levels of inequality within societies. The criteria used to assess human security in a given society need therefore to be made explicit and to be publicly justified.

The criteria for assessing "acceptable" limits of inequality can be elicited from diverse sources. These include, at one end of the scale, the ethical liberal philosophy of "fairness" most famously developed by John

Rawls, which, crudely speaking, stresses equality of process and is less concerned about inequalities in outcome. At the other end are historical materialist approaches, drawn from the works of Karl Marx, that (again crudely speaking) are less concerned with achieving the level playing field of fairness of process and much more exercised by inequality of outcome.[76]

The first, or "process," approach lends itself to an emphasis on the individual, who, as long as he or she has the same ability as others to make choices, must take personal responsibility for outcomes that end in insecurity. The second, or "outcome," approach lends itself to an emphasis on the ethical priority of the community, whose responsibility it is to collectively provide for relative equality of outcomes.

My approach is that both process and outcome should be understood when assessing whether human security standards are met. Political fairness in opportunities for the individual should be balanced by a view that in some circumstances the good of the community needs to be weighed against the good of the individual. This would be so, for example, if the choice in human security was between providing the opportunity for a few to benefit from having access to arable land and food while others starved and enforcing a level of redistribution of food so that individuals without access to arable land could be saved from hunger and starvation.

In other words, I argue that the individual should be considered as providing the definite focus of ethical life, although I also recognize that no individual grows up separate from society. The opposite is true. The individual becomes individuated through participation in society. All sorts of communities—whether these be the family, kinship network, local community, wider society, ethnicity, or state—may be extremely highly valued by the individual, to the extent that if these communities are threatened, the individual's personal security is directly challenged.

Threats to an individual's security should be understood through a prism that encapsulates both personal and community insecurity. Understanding the ethical value of community as well as the value given to more directly personal threats such as hunger is crucial to understanding whether human beings in a given society feel secure or not, or to what extent.

Human security is not made up of many absolutes. Some aspects of human security are clearly not negotiable, such as the right to enough food to eat to survive. Some human security rights, however, can be qualified and need to be understood in the context of the particular society. The right to sufficient food to lead a decent quality of life is, for instance, very negotiable. In times of food stress, for example, a community may decide to forgo sufficient food for some to lead a decent quality of life so that all can survive at a basic level. This suggests that human beings are prepared to accept a degree of human insecurity if they are convinced that some greater good is being worked for—the nation, for instance—but only also if the society is convinced that things will improve for succeeding generations. Societies also find it difficult to tolerate too much visible inegalitarian distribution of human security benefits and too much millennialism, where the payoff disappears behind an ever-receding horizon.

Who or What Provides Security?

For the past four or five hundred years, the actor that has ultimately provided or guaranteed human security has been the state. Classically, the core functions of the state were not, however, to provide a broad range of human security guarantees but were instead only to provide for a narrow range of freedom-from-fear human security rights. The core function of the state was, and arguably remains, to provide an ordered society and to prevent military aggression against its inhabitants. The state provided freedom from fear in that protection was provided against external aggressors and internal disorder. Policing and military functions remain at the heart of the modern state. Classical state functions also contributed to human insecurity in some cases, however, as security apparatuses were (and are) used to quell dissent and to suppress opposition to state rulers.

With the rise of liberal democracy as a worldwide (although not universal) form of government and the theoretical valuing of every individual (not just the individual as owner of property as in Lockean democracy) as the ethical core of society and as an end in himself (and later herself), the emphasis on what the state should and should not do changed. States are expected to perform welfare functions and to be the guarantors of a broad range of human security provisions. Not all states perform these functions very well and most not very well at all. The UNDP reported that as of 1997 1.3 billion people lived on less than a dollar a day—a rule-of-thumb benchmark of poverty.[77] A 2002 United Nations Conference on Trade and Development (UNCTAD) report shows that these poorest of the poor are also becoming worse off.[78] The number of people trying to survive on less than a dollar a day in thirty African states and Haiti increased from 125 million between 1965 and 1969 to 278 million between 1995 and 1999.

Irrespective of the empirical reality, the expectation that states should provide for basic human security needs constitutes a worldwide norm and is applied to all states, whether democracies or not. States are expected to provide the ultimate backstop to secure freedom from want as well as freedom from fear for their populations.

Assessing Human Insecurity in the DPRK

Given the absence of an uncontested and unambiguous analytical framework, it is not an easy methodological task to operationalize human security categories. It is not, in other words, possible to provide an analytical category, divorced from society and history, space and time, that could provide a means of defining what constitutes a secure human being. Instead the operationalization of human security is, within the context of the caveats developed above, a matter of ethical and intellectual judgment.

Since the mid-1990s the central, overweening human security question for almost all the population of the DPRK was of chronic food shortages. The analytical focus in the sphere of freedom from want in this book is therefore a focus on food (in)security. The freedom-from-fear focus is personal safety, political freedom, rule of law, and national security. Not all individuals suffered to the same degree, and so central also to the analysis of this book is an attempt to understand the different experiences of different groups in DPRK society—as shaped by gender, age, geographical location, occupation, and social class.

Policies for Peace and Human Security

The securitization perspective is inadequate as an analytical framework to help understand the DPRK. The empirical work produced by and through the presence of the humanitarian community in the DPRK calls into question the rigor and rationality of the fundamental assumption of the DPRK as an unchanging state and society, impervious to change. Policymakers were, however, one step ahead of the analysts in revolutionizing thinking about the DPRK. This was shown most clearly in the South Korean government's bold adoption of the "sunshine," or engagement, policy—designed to deal with the DPRK as a rational actor, motivated by decipherable interests and context.

The securitization perspective provided a poor guide for policymakers because it fails to grasp the complexity of DPRK polity and politics and the socioeconomic transformation that began in the 1990s. The alternative approach seeks to explore the context and motivation for changes in DPRK government policy. A revised understanding helps foreign policymakers develop policies that can intercede to promote beneficial change and discourage and prevent negative developments. Alternative approaches do not have to be normatively committed to either the continuation or the demise of the North Korean regime. They should, however, be committed to supporting moves toward peace, stability, and freedom from hunger for the people of North Korea.

The Human Security Trade-off
Constitution and Collapse

U
P UNTIL THE EARLY 1990S, the North Korean population more or less accepted a trade-off in human security. Most people gained material benefits as large national achievements were made in the areas of food, health, education, and work.[1] Advances in freedoms from want compensated somewhat for the absence of individual political freedoms.[2] The population more or less accepted the human security trade-off for two reasons. The first was that gains were visible to all, while costs, on the whole, became clear only when individuals found themselves in direct conflict with the state. The second was that the regime rigorously pursued a socialization, organization, and management practice that provided incentives for those who cooperated with the system and disincentives for those who did not.

The Kim Il Sung regime built and managed the social consensus that legitimized the principle of human security trade-off. Economic growth provided the context for a sophisticated social management strategy, backed up by enormous political-socialization efforts as well as judicious use of the instruments of coercion. The socioeconomic growth strategy, while securing achievements for three decades, contained intrinsic weaknesses. Understanding the built-in fragility of the system helps explain both the economic crisis of the 1990s and the tragedy of famine in the mid-1990s.

The Socioeconomic Management Strategy of the Kim Il Sung Regime

Kim Il Sung used the rewards of economic growth as leverage in a system of social management whose aim was to preempt opposition by building social consensus. Potential divisions in the society, which could have jeopardized regime stability, arose from socioeconomic differences between country and town, provinces and the capital, civilians and the military, and the poor and the better off. The Kim Il Sung regime carefully balanced competing claims for economic and political rewards and accommodated the interests of key social groups.

Complementary to the social management strategy was the building of an elaborate apparatus that attempted nothing less than the complete socialization of the population through culture, media, and education. For those who expressed doubts or otherwise broke the law, alternative means of social control included community surveillance, the use of physical repression, and the legal system.

The "consensual" approach to the human security trade-off was never uncontested. Purges eradicated potential opposition leaders in the late 1950s and again in the late 1960s.[3] From the 1960s until the death of President Kim Il Sung in 1994, however, there was no uprising against the government or expression of unrest such as to threaten domestic stability. The management strategy paid off.

The Foundations of Consensus

One reason that the authoritarianism of the Kim Il Sungist system was relatively easily assimilated into North Korean society was that North Koreans had little experience of political liberalism and none of democracy.[4] Thus they had only a minimal comparative base from which to assess the merits of liberal democracy versus Communist society.[5]

Up until the early twentieth century Korea was still mainly an agricultural society without adequate railways, road networks, bridges, or communications facilities—preconditions for the development of substantial nationwide commerce.[6] Korea's incipient commercial and industrial development took place under the aegis of a repressive Japanese occupation, which lasted from 1910 until liberation in 1945. Under these conditions it was almost impossible for Koreans to become anything other than subordinates within the modernization of Korea.[7]

In other circumstances, the introduction of capitalism in Korea might have seen the development of an indigenous middle class and concomitant political liberties. In the context of the Japanese occupation, most Koreans were excluded from economic and political benefits. The Japanese colonial and military authorities suppressed national identity and personal freedoms as potentially providing a vehicle for the expression and mobilization of Korean nationalism.[8] Incipient liberal notions and practices that had been imported into Korea from Japan and elsewhere continued to coexist with much older and still prevalent ideas of hierarchy and the importance of community.[9]

In comparison to the Japanese colonial system, the Kim Il Sung regime allowed much more opportunity for a wide range of individuals from previously marginalized social classes to participate in decision making through the party and local government. The system of "democratic centralism" demanded unquestioning loyalty to higher authorities yet at the same time admitted input into decision making on nonstrategic issues at the lower levels. A certain amount of local initiative was permitted within the confines of overall policy direction provided by the Korean Workers' Party (KWP). The political system also encouraged decentralization because of the assumption that, should war break out, local areas would have to operate relatively autonomously, providing for their own defense and survival.

The system stabilized around the autocratic and personalistic leadership of the president, Kim Il Sung, who nevertheless achieved political legitimacy through his acknowledged leadership of nation building in the new state. These activities included a significant role in the anti-Japanese liberation struggle and leading what was pitched as a victory over U.S. and UN forces in the Korean War.[10] Kim Il Sung was also credited with presiding over the building of an industrialized economy, including a reasonably well-developed welfare and educational infrastructure. The establishment of an independent nation after decades of subordination to Japan (and before that, to China) also aroused pride in the population.[11] The system was further legitimized through the state's efforts to associate the new regime with the rescue and revival of a specifically Korean cultural and historic identity.

Managing Consensus

Kim Il Sung promoted social policies that accentuated commonalities of interest and responded to potential social cleavages so as to forestall grievances against the regime, especially from potentially powerful groups such as farmers, industrial workers, regional interests, and the military. Farmers were given land (collectively), industrial workers were given relatively high wages (based on a collective work-points system), representatives of the remote though populous northeastern regions were disproportionately represented in the party, and the military was given access to privileges and status within the state and society.

The president supported and implemented policies that promoted the interests of women, a previously legally second-class group within the society.[12] He promoted campaigns against "bureaucratization"—ostensibly attempting to encourage innovative answers to local problems but, as a result, leaving the bureaucracy inefficient and ineffective. The leadership considered a functioning, systematic civil service operating with any level of impartiality a threat to its political dominance, and so such a development was actively discouraged.

Incorporating the Farmers

Support from farmers was pivotal for the North Korean development strategy, which aimed for food self-sufficiency to lessen its reliance on outside powers and to build grain reserves in case of war. In 1946, in the immediate aftermath of liberation from the Japanese, the government began a massive land reform project. This ended with the collectivization of agriculture and the effective eradication of individual farming as a social or economic force in 1958.[13] The state granted free of charge 1 million hectares of land—that is, just less than half of North Korea's arable land—to 725,000 poor and landless families, possibly 3 million people.[14] The highly skewed pattern of land ownership under Japanese colonialism meant that there were relatively few Korean landlords, and thus only a relatively small group, some 44,000, who had their land expropriated.[15] Many of these landlords were either absentee or chose to move south. Land reform was therefore both popular and relatively conflict free.

By 1964, 3,800 cooperative farms had been set up on the basis of established demographic and kinship patterns. Many farms were amalgamated so that each *ri*, or village, would consist of one cooperative farm, varying in size depending on the size of the village.[16] The strategy was to collectivize around existing social structures and settlements. Farming management practices solidified the social bonds consolidated and institutionalized through collectivization even further, as work teams and subwork teams were built on existing small settlements within the *ri* and family groupings.[17]

Cooperative farms stayed more or less constant in number, continuing to provide the country's basic staple food. About 500 state farms were also established, but these concentrated on nonbasic grain production of items such as seeds, fruit, vegetables, and livestock.[18] Unlike cooperative farmers, who received their food and income directly from their own production, state farmers were salaried workers and received food and income through state distribution channels.

Cooperative farmers, who provided the country's staple food supplies, remained rewarded through incentive structures geared toward the collective at the level of either the farm, the work team, or the subwork team. Individual families were, however, permitted to own small family plots or "kitchen gardens," and there was some evidence that productivity on family plots was significantly higher than on collective agricultural land.[19] In the cooperative sector rewards were therefore much more tightly linked to effort than in the state sector, whether at the farm or household level.

Kim Il Sung's management of collectivization helped consolidate support from a large rural social group that benefited from the transfer of land but whose motivation for production and loyalty to the community was based much more upon very old social ties than on ideological commitment to Communism or its North Korean variant, the *Juche* idea. Unlike workers on the state farms, cooperative farmers maintained some independence from the party and the state machinery.[20] Social solidarity in the rural areas therefore was founded less on party ideology than on the basis of very old community ties.

By 1996 just over 5 million cooperative farmers and their families—about 22 percent of the population—provided about 90 percent of all agricultural production and nearly all staple food production.[21] These farming families benefited from redistribution of land. Many also associated collectivization—"cooperativization," as it is always called in the DPRK—with the provision of social benefits such as health services, education, and electricity. Few of these benefits had been available to this sector of the population prior to the establishment of the Kim Il Sung regime.[22]

Privileging Industrial Workers

Much of the country's heavy industrial and mining sector was located in the northeast, in the provinces of North and South Hamgyong, based around the largest cities in the country after Pyongyang, including Chongjin, Kimchaek, Hamhung, and Tanchon. These cities, as well as mining counties such as Musan on the DPRK-China border, still have some of the highest population densities in the country but little arable land to support food self-sufficiency, particularly in North Hamgyong.[23] A priority for the Kim Il Sungist management strategy was to ensure that industrial workers maintained high productivity levels and a commitment to the regime.

Unless they had the good fortune to have relations living and working on productive farms out of town who could send food, northeastern industrial workers had no direct access to agricultural production and had to purchase food as well as other goods. Many lived in large blocks of highrise apartments and so did not have their own household plots of land, and most of these apartment blocks did not have surrounding green space where food could be grown.[24] Before the crisis of the 1990s, the government compensated heavy industrial workers for lack of access to land by awarding them higher points and higher income through the national workpoints system.[25] More work points guaranteed access to highly subsidized food and basic goods, and relatively high income meant that nonrationed goods could also be bought when they were available.

It is doubtful whether the aspirations of this group of well-organized, educated, often skilled, and highly politicized workers could have been wholly met, especially from the 1980s on, when the monotonously regular calls to ever-increasing effort for national shock brigade–type activities were no longer accompanied by increased material rewards. Reports of labor unrest in Chongjin in 1981 and in Ryanggang (another northern province) and Wonsan (South Hamgyong) in 1983 indicate that this group did not believe its needs were being met by the Kim Il Sung regime.[26]

Nevertheless, in the context of the developing economy, northeastern industrial workers probably took some pride in the scale of the achievements in industrial output. While never well-off in the sense of being able to live a life of ease and guaranteed freedom from want, they could also take some comfort in their privileged status within the DPRK social and political firmament and their priority access to economic rewards within the DPRK socioeconomy.

Satisfying Regional Interests

The Kim Il Sung regime paid some attention to incorporating "anti-regionalist" sloganeering in calls for party and national unity, but in practice it privileged the industrial northeast in party positions. In 1980, for instance, at least 114 of the 523 Central Committee members of the Korean Workers' Party were identified as coming from North Hamgyong.[27] This was a disproportionately high 21 percent, given that North Hamgyong province contained only 10 percent of the total population. The priority given to the northeast had less to do with giving credit to the location of the anti-Japanese struggle, as has been suggested by one analyst, and was much more a result of prosaic political necessity. The northeastern region was home to an organized working class that could potentially oppose the Pyongyang-based elite.[28] The objective was to maintain the loyalty of this organizationally developed sector of the population.

Controlling the Military

Building a powerful army was at the center of Kim Il Sung's national policies—a policy more or less supported by the population. The army developed popular legitimacy as a necessary, useful, and integratory national institution. The reasons for the army's high social status had little to do with the official propaganda, which included the often-repeated statements that the Korean People's Army (KPA) was the descendant of the anti-Japanese struggle.

More concrete reasons underpinned popular support for the army. First, the North Korean people had lived through a brutal Japanese occupation, followed by a vicious war that by 1953 had left between 1 and 2 million North Koreans dead and another 2 million wounded, out of a total population of around 10 million.[29] Since the war had ended without a peace treaty—only with an armistice—it was relatively straightforward for the regime to mobilize popular support for a national security strategy that reinforced the national capacity for self-defense.

Second, Kim Il Sung institutionalized civilian-military relations to reinforce practical integration between military and civilian sectors but to divorce the military from political power. Relatively short periods of service in the armed forces meant a constant turnover in military personnel, which discouraged the evolution of an institutionally distinct military cadre separate from the population at large.[30] The government insisted on preparing the entire adult population for civil defense through regular training and defense exercises. This meant that the broader population was brought into regular contact with the military for a joint purpose—self-defense—whose necessity seemed self-evident to most.

Another integratory policy was to mobilize the military in the busy agricultural seasons. Soldiers helped with the labor-intensive chores of transplanting and harvesting. They were visibly employed in providing support for projects that would benefit the majority of the population—for instance, in construction, irrigation, and road-building projects.

The military enjoyed genuine social support. Families were proud and relieved when sons and daughters joined the army, both for the status it conferred on the families and for the secure career and improved life opportunities it provided their children. Young people were rewarded, for instance, with preferential access to education after the completion of their stint in the military. The population at large therefore viewed many of their own personal interests as being linked to the perpetuation of a strong military.

Though the military was an important social force, it was not a major political actor. The army, as in the former Soviet Union, remained subordinate to civilian decision makers. Nor was the military, as it is in some authoritarian countries, a day-to-day oppressor and a force to be avoided or one that instilled fear in the population. Instead the military was positioned to help deliver freedoms from want, most visibly in food production. It was also legitimized by its freedom-from-fear role as the guarantor of national security.

Providing a Safety Net

The state provided a functioning welfare safety net for those who were not members of key socioeconomic groups. All the population who worked and those who had a legitimate reason not to work (children, the sick, the elderly, etc.) were guaranteed a minimum food ration and access to basic household goods at highly subsidized prices.[31] The entire population was entitled to basic goods, including health care, education, shelter, and a job. The state provided a welfare safety net—at least for those who did not run afoul of the state. Food and other goods were not made available to able-bodied adults who did not work—who were considered outside the pale. This was made clear in a 1987 DPRK publication, which noted that "in our country . . . there are no loafers and all people faithfully work to the best of their ability."[32]

There were many genuine advances in social provision. A free system of universal education that offered child care for children aged three months or older and a vast network of tertiary colleges were established. Adult literacy climbed to almost 100 percent, and adults were encouraged to maintain lifelong learning, with study and training facilities established in workplaces throughout the country.[33] Health-care facilities and services were made universal and free. Women's rights were implemented in practical ways. For instance, maternity-leave provisions were generous and did not remain a paper exercise but were implemented throughout the society.[34] The DPRK was never a socialist paradise, as some of its more self-serving propaganda proclaimed, but it did succeed in delivering substantial social goods for the population.

Socializing and Organizing the Population

The socialization process proclaimed the virtues of President Kim Il Sung and decried the political systems of Western societies. The regime succeeded in that the system was naturalized to the extent that the society in which North Koreans lived appeared normal, even commonsensical, making it less necessary to use the security apparatus to prop up the regime.[35] It is highly unlikely, however, that the regime ever completely convinced North Koreans that they were living in the "perfect" society trumpeted by its propaganda.

The government pursued the ideology of what it called *Juche*—independence or self-reliance. The core of *Juche* was the idea that material help from other countries was welcome but only within the confines of a definite policy of self-determined decision making in domestic and foreign affairs.[36] Appeals to Communism as a unifying or nation-building mythology provided only a secondary and ultimately dispensable ideological framework for the DPRK government. The ideological cement of North Korean society was founded on a Korean nationalist project. The particular version of Korean nationalism systematically propagated by the government was integrated around the nation-building activities of the Kim Il Sung family.[37] Culture, education, and social organization continually reinforced nation-building images constructed around the exploits, both real and imagined, of Kim Il Sung; his mother, father, and great-grandfather; and his son.[38]

Another feature of the socialization project was the continued priority given to the community over the individual. An individual's welfare and life opportunities could be advanced only through membership in a group. Individual effort and individual initiative were encouraged only if they supported group efforts. Even as collective needs for welfare and cultural identity were addressed, individual needs for freedom and personal self-expression were suppressed.

Culture as Socialization

Under Japanese occupation, many Korean children could not expect even to finish primary school. Under Kim Il Sung, education was greatly expanded: all children could receive primary and secondary education, and most would have the chance to enter some form of adult or college education program. This expansion, however, came at a price.[39] From the time the child entered nursery at three months old to the time she or he left high school, the child attended daily classes that taught the history of the Kim family as the history of the modern nation. Songs were sung every day in praise of the "Great Leader," poems and novels were read, plays performed, and artwork created with this one central theme.

Daily press and TV broadcasts reiterated the beneficent works of the Kim family, for which the population was educated to show gratitude and adoration verging on the religious. The movie industry consolidated these images. Few other images were allowed as subject matter for any of the arts, apart from Korean scenery or scenes from ancient folkloric Korean art. The only public art—for instance, sculptures in provincial towns—also consisted of either sayings or representations of Kim Il Sung.[40]

The immense nationwide effort to build cultural legitimacy for the regime was accompanied by a parallel effort to exclude from people's consciousness any day-to-day knowledge of alternative interpretations of the world.[41] Those who went to university to study foreign languages or diplomacy had access to foreign literature and images, but the average citizen living in a farm in rural South Hamgyong or the small mining towns of South Pyongan would have little clue how the rest of the world functioned.[42]

The Organizational Framework

The political organizational framework was provided by the Korean Workers' Party, a mass party whose membership between 1967 and 1991 was estimated at 15 percent of the population. (Given a population of about 22 million in 1991, party membership then must have totaled about 3.3 million people.)[43] If this figure is at all accurate, some 30 percent of all adults were party members. Given the highly gendered roles of men and women in the DPRK, in which women give priority to the private sphere over the public sphere, it would be reasonable to suppose that 50 percent of all adult men were party members. These very high levels of party membership made the party ubiquitous as a form of social control and surveillance. However, they also allowed for the possibilities of input into party decision making by very large numbers of people.

The myriad of community organizations—the children's and youth organizations, the workplace- and neighborhood-based collectivities—also had very high levels of membership.[44] The most important of these was the League of Socialist Working Youth of Korea.[45] The membership of the Youth League was 3.8 million in the mid-1990s.[46] It effectively incorporated all children of secondary-school age and college students into a party/state organization that directed free-time activities into collective contributions to the nation. These ranged from participating in mass gymnastics to helping keep neighborhoods clean to participating in civil defense activities.

All North Koreans were involved in collective organizations to a greater or lesser extent. These functioned simultaneously as a means of participation and as agents of social surveillance. In short, they acted as agents of socialization into the Kim Il Sungist ideological framework.

Methods of Social Control

Social control relied on persuasive and coercive mechanisms but not primarily on the use of physical force. Combined with state policies that took for granted the right of the community and the state to intervene in personal and family lives was a legal system that subordinated the interests and rights of the individual to those of the state or the party. North Koreans and their families were never free from minor and sometimes major state interference in their everyday affairs. Physical repression was a last resort, although the potential for brutal treatment should an individual fall foul of the law was well understood.

Many individuals accommodated themselves to the political system in which they lived. Political dissent was effectively outlawed through the constitutional decree that state policies were always subordinated to the policies of the Korean Workers' Party.[47] It was, therefore, a criminal offense to be disloyal to the party. Dissenters suffered repression and punishment. National security threats were used to legitimize a complete intolerance of dissent.

Community Surveillance

Social control mechanisms included the systematization of community oversight of community activities.[48] Social or community surveillance over the individual's day-to-day activities was possible partly because social and cultural norms gave a degree of legitimacy to ideas that subordinated individual interests to that of the community.[49] Community surveillance mechanisms were also recognized as contributing to the prevention of personal crimes; murders or rapes were rare. The government justification for community surveillance schemes was to prevent enemies and spies infiltrating the society to obtain information pertaining to national security.

The role of the leader of the local neighborhood organization was not of

> intimidating . . . but his task consists of creating a climate in which citizens cannot behave in a way that differs from the commonly accepted. Everything and everybody is in the public eye . . . everything which is generally adopted is decent but if it doesn't agree with the established rules and traditions, it is not. Neighbors [for example] can be accused of buying goods that are too expensive or modern.[50]

Accountability Mechanisms

The sociopolitical community structures that exerted social and political controls were considered legitimate, if oppressive. Their legitimacy derived partly from the fact that community organizations provided for some limited accountability by officials to the community.

By definition, neighborhood leaders lived in the same area as the constituencies they oversaw. In addition, party chairpersons, county administrators, farm and enterprise managers, and their families tended to live and work in the same locations for very long periods of time, because the political structure did not permit wide latitude in personal mobility for employment purposes. The major exception was when a youth joined the military or was recognized as suitable for advanced training or education at provincial capitals or in Pyongyang. A measure of accountability was therefore built into local political structures simply by virtue of the nonmobility of local cadres.

The pressures on leaders and managers to deliver were intense, given their day-to-day contact over very long periods of time with the people they managed and directed. These direct links to feedback and criticism were particularly accentuated in rural areas and in the smaller towns. The norms of the system, if not always the practice, demanded public-policy responses to public grievances. The ruling philosophy of "anti-bureaucratization" also allowed a limited space to voice criticism of the system.

The Legal System as an Instrument of Party Discipline

The DPRK criminal and civil legal system did not separate the party from the state, and the notion of an independent (of the party) judiciary did not exist. Legal norms in the DPRK supported an opposite notion of what constituted good governance—the conflation of party and state interests. It is therefore a tautology to argue that the DPRK's evidentiary procedures would have not been acceptable in any liberal democratic polity. The DPRK legal system reflected its political system of democratic centralism and institutionalized that system within its domestic legal framework.[51] As a corollary of this system of legal norms, the security apparatus was institutionally unconstrained by rules of law that separated the interests of the party from the interests of the state.

The legal system incorporated party representatives into the judicial process and allowed wide catchall provisions that could be used to find any defendant guilty if she or he breached party statutes, customs, or practices. The structure of the legal system therefore allowed for possible arbitrary imposition of the rule of law. This could in theory have been mitigated by local community involvement in criminal and civil procedures that could have brought some level of transparency and accountability to proceedings. In practice, given the powerful pressures on citizens not to disagree with official representatives, it is unlikely that dissenters could expect impartial treatment through the judicial process.

Physical Repression

Individual brutality and arbitrary violence by security forces was not a visible feature of day-to-day life in the DPRK. Punitive measures were, however, consistently taken to suppress political criticism. There is sufficient evidence of harsh treatment of dissidents.[52] Those showing any inclination toward opposition to the regime were punished. As late as 1999, a DPRK official representation to a United Nations Human Rights Committee noted, "The state does not tolerate the expression of ideas that severely infringe upon the honor and dignity of others or state security and public order."[53]

There was a very well-founded fear of the consequences of falling outside the boundaries of what was "permissible." One standard punishment was to send offenders—sometimes accompanied by their families—to remote areas of the countryside for "reform through labor" programs. Offenders worked on farms and in mines until their sentences were completed. Living conditions in remote and disadvantaged rural and mining areas are tough and brutal enough for local inhabitants. With the added physical repression from prison guards, these "reform through labor" camps must be very barbaric places. There is virtually no verifiable information on these "reform" camps, so it is difficult to assess the numbers of individuals and families who underwent this punishment and for how long their sentences might have lasted. There is enough evidence, however, to indicate that conditions for societal outcasts were harsh, if variable, and subject to arbitrary interpretation by local prison officials.[54]

The Contradictory Economy: Growth and Fragility

The population of North Korea had benefited from rising standards of living from the creation of the DPRK in 1948 and its consolidation after the 1950–53 Korean War until the late 1970s, possibly even the mid-1980s.[55] The average life span increased from around 28 years in 1944 to a reported 74.5 years in 1994, and infant mortality rates decreased from 204 per thousand live births in 1944 to 14.1 in 1993.[56] There was probably always regional variation in these figures. Those living in remote provinces with inhospitable conditions and without arable land were likely worse off than those living in the more productive farmland and the major conurbations. Nevertheless, the figures do indicate quite remarkable increases in living standards for very many people. As counterintuitive as it might be today, when the Republic of Korea is the twelfth most important economy in the world, until around the mid-1970s living standards in the North were higher than those in the South and, in aggregate economic terms, the DPRK was the wealthier nation.[57]

Faltering Growth

Growth faltered in the late 1970s, although basic living standards were maintained by the continuing willingness of the Soviet Union and China to provide concessionary imports of fuel, spare parts, and technology.[58] Toward the end of the 1980s, however, even before the collapse of the Soviet Union, the DPRK began to lose its preferential trading agreements with the former Communist bloc. In 1991, even China, the DPRK's major ally in the Communist world, insisted that beginning in 1993 the DPRK must pay for goods in hard currency.[59] One problem for the DPRK was the absence of domestic oil production. Even though the DPRK was successful in building an economy that minimized oil dependence, it still required oil for crucial sectors, including for military and agricultural purposes.[60] The DPRK was not a subsistence agricultural economy but instead an industrialized, urbanized society. When Russia and China were no longer prepared to provide cheap or free oil, and with the DPRK unable to afford international market prices, oil imports dried up, contributing to steady economic decline in which agricultural and industrial production diminished.[61]

DPRK economic activity entered into precipitous decline in the 1990s, as illustrated by South Korean figures of North Korean economic activity from 1989 to 1995. Taking 1989 as the baseline indicator at 100, gross national product declined to 96 in 1990, 93 in 1991, 88 in 1992, 84 in 1993, 83 in 1994, and 79 in 1995.[62] Foreign trade volumes halved between 1990 and 1991. Imports dropped from $1,852 million in 1990 to $945 million in 1991.[63] Exports for the same period declined from $2,888 million to $1,644 million.[64] Export values stabilized at around $1 billion from 1992 to 1994, with import values around $1.5 billion during the same period.[65]

The low level of economic activity was one problem for the DPRK. A continued trade deficit was another. In addition, key economic sectors of agriculture and industry showed signs of structural disintegration, while the military sector continued to absorb a disproportionate share of domestic resources.

The Agricultural Sector

The DPRK's agricultural sector aimed at food self-sufficiency for the country and for each cooperative farm. The rationale for this policy was to lessen overall food dependence on outsiders (in exactly the same way that European countries pursued food self-sufficiency after World War II). The government feared it could face war at any time. If enemies attacked the cities, it wanted to provide functioning food-producing bases in rural areas to which civilians could be evacuated. Food self-sufficiency was difficult to achieve given that, among other things, only 15 to 20 percent of the land was suitable for arable purposes.[66] The DPRK's topography—mountainous and more than 60 percent forested—provides major constraints on agricultural production. Of the approximately 2.3 million hectares of arable land, only 1 million hectares is suitable for staple-food production.[67] Available arable land is subject to the constraints of very short growing seasons due to extreme winter weather. Northern provinces of the DPRK face up to nine months of frost every year, and southern provinces experience around five months of winter.[68]

Land availability constraints meant that agricultural production depended on high energy inputs of electricity, fertilizer, chemicals, and pesticides. Gravity-fed irrigation is not a feasible option for many parts of the country. Thus the agricultural southern provinces, which are the most suitable for main-crop rice production but which face heavy rains every summer during the rice-growing season, are almost entirely dependent on electrical irrigation to prevent flooding. Electricity-fed irrigation was also necessary to distribute water for the early spring crop when spring rains failed, as they often did. Agricultural production was therefore dependent on domestic industrial production of electricity, fertilizer, and chemicals.

Despite the natural obstacles to agricultural production, the DPRK achieved sufficient grain production to meet the basic needs of its population beginning in at least 1973, with harvests in the late 1980s achieving record levels.[69] Reductions in agricultural output started in 1990, as the DPRK lost its ability to obtain sufficient imported inputs to produce enough fertilizer, chemicals, and electricity to satisfy agricultural needs.[70] The agricultural sector suffered from antiquated or obsolescent machinery, lack of agro-industrial products, broken-down irrigation facilities, and shortages of transport and fuel.

Deficiencies in the agricultural sector were not due primarily to lack of knowledge by farmers. Agriculture was not as insulated from modern practices and techniques as other sectors of the economy. The DPRK had participated in international agricultural research institutions, producing world-class seed varieties.[71] When the international community developed policies of promoting double-cropping in the late 1990s, for instance, visiting agronomists found that farmers were fully cognizant of both the advantages and drawbacks of these policies. Double-cropping, which introduces an additional but minor crop in the spring, carries the risk of importing additional pests. With pesticides in short supply, it can prove a hazardous strategy for poor farmers. Additionally, with the vagaries of weather, waiting to harvest the early spring crop can mean a delay in planting the main crop, which could mean risking lowering main-crop output.[72]

Debate continues as to whether the social organization of agricultural production provided disincentives to increases in productivity. The DPRK agricultural policy dilemma remained how to feed the increasing urban and nonfarming population. To achieve this aim it veered between encouraging decentralized responsibility and attempting to impose the most detailed planning on every aspect of the farming process. The continuing constraint for the whole agricultural process across the entire history of the DPRK was insufficient inputs—including of land, labor, capital, and technology.[73]

Industry

DPRK development strategy was founded on the premise that the rapid construction of a modern industrial sector would provide the foundation for the establishment of a modern multisectoral economy. At the center of the DPRK national emblem is a power station, symbolizing the significance of heavy industry as a priority developmental sector for the state.[74]

State policy was to develop a comprehensive domestic industrial capacity, providing capital goods for the agricultural, manufacturing, and military sectors—thus minimizing foreign dependency.[75] The machine-building sector provided the pivot for industrial strategy and was supposed to provide necessary heavy equipment and a catalytic center of technological innovation for the entire economy. Fertilizers and pesticides were produced and priority given to the development of a chemical industry, which provided the foundation for domestic production of medicines and agricultural products. Similarly to agriculture, DPRK industrial production demonstrated strong growth up to the early 1980s. Industrial output increased substantially in the important sectors of electricity generation, coal, minerals, metallurgical products, fertilizer, machine tools, ship-building, chemicals, and building materials.[76]

The government ostensibly also promoted light industry, or consumer-goods industries. Provinces and counties were given the responsibility of setting up "local factories" that were supposed to generate inputs from local resources after the needs of heavy industry and agriculture had been met. In practice this sector was relegated to a lesser priority. The continual calls in President Kim Il Sung's New Year's messages for development of the light industrial sector betray a recognition of lack of success in meeting the demand for consumer goods. These messages also hint at some realization of limits to the population's continued acceptance of the lack of availability of basic goods.

The industrial sector displayed structural weaknesses similar to those of agriculture in three areas—energy dependence, limited markets, and over-reliance on improvised, short-term—and hence unsustainable—

solutions to long-term problems. First, the use of energy in factories was disproportionately large, wasteful, and inefficient. Second, DPRK heavy industry was geared toward the domestic market and markets of other Socialist countries. When the latter disappeared at the end of the Cold War, few alternative markets were available.

Third, the government adopted a "make do and mend" approach to industry, responding to resource constraints by encouraging workers to make their own tools if they could not obtain them elsewhere.[77] Government policy promoted innovation through the creative recycling of every piece of household and commercial "waste."[78] The practice of "technical improvisation in every area" was encouraged. The results ranged from the widespread use of vehicles powered by charcoal-burning stoves to the expectation that doctors would make their own operating tools and medical equipment in the backyards of hospitals. Continuing resource shortages embedded the improvisation approach, demonstrating a continued ingenuity by the workforce. The downside was that industrial output was invariably of poor quality and, often, obsolescent only a short time after production.

Industrial organization suffered from bottlenecks typical of planned economies, with industrial capacity often underutilized and insufficient attention paid to the efficient use of inputs.[79] Systems of outputs based on quantitative targets encouraged a concentration on volumes or quantity of output as opposed to focusing on marketability or quality of output. Some countervailing tendencies in the system encouraging efficiency did exist, however. Skilled workers were rewarded with relatively high incomes and work points that could be exchanged for food rations. On the other hand, the nationwide system of quarterly targets encouraged workers to idle for a couple of months before rushing to complete the planned quotas at the end of every three-month period. Workers developed social solidarity, learning to cover for each other and slowing down when necessary to help ease heavy physical exertion. Financially, there were no economic or material incentives to do otherwise.

Energy

The population of the DPRK benefited from visible and important improvements in power supply up until the late 1980s. A unified energy grid was created by 1958, and most areas of the country probably had at least intermittent access to electricity for domestic and industrial purposes by the 1960s.[80] Rural households benefited as well as urban dwellers, as electricity was made available for domestic usage as well as for agricultural and commercial sectors.[81] The major consumer of energy, however, was the heavy industrial sector. The DPRK relied mainly on coal and hydro-power for electricity generation for agricultural, manufacturing, commercial, and domestic uses and for railway transportation.

Oil was not a major component of DPRK electricity generation, although it was used to fuel two of the country's power stations and was necessary as a vital component of agricultural products and as fuel for vehicles. The energy sector was highly dependent on Soviet technology and equipment and was cost-inefficient. Energy production and distribution, as with all national economic planning, was mechanically organized through centralized planning that concentrated on achieving high output at the expense of quality controls and efficient management of resources.

The Military Sector

By its nature the military sector in any society is difficult to penetrate. In the DPRK, with its obsession with secrecy, the costs and contribution of the DPRK military to the wider society are even more difficult to assess than in other countries. According to the International Institute for Strategic Studies, the $2.1 billion spent in 2000 on defense came out of a gross national product for the same year of $15 billion—14 percent of GNP.[82] The costs of defense were, however, inflated due to the inclusion of what, in other socioeconomies, would be "civilian" activities. Defense spending in the DPRK includes a relatively high percentage of civilian costs, such as housing, communications, food production, health care, education, and road building.

The costs and benefits of the military to the DPRK economy are impossible to quantify, but qualitative assessment indicates positives and negatives for the economy. A decrease in the numbers in the armed forces would have increased the number of workers with some skills that could have contributed to the civilian economy. On the other hand, this could have happened only if capital investment was available to pay for jobs. A contrary result might have been the creation of a large group of hungry, demobilized soldiers, not necessarily a positive development. In addition, given that the DPRK suffered from perennial labor shortages, the economy as a whole benefited from having an easily mobilized supply of disciplined labor that could supplement the civilian labor force as required, particularly in agriculture and construction. The military also generated earnings through its own production and export industries, such as the bottling and export of mineral water. Ballistic missile technology and weapons also provided hard currency, although how much is unknown.

Planting the Seeds of Insecurity

The development model contained inherent institutional flaws that provided limits to growth irrespective of the loss of Soviet bloc support. These flaws could be summarized as the replacement of systematic organization with intermittent mobilization capacity, the substitution of ideological exhortation for economic rewards as a means of providing incentives, and reliance on a "make do and mend" mentality as a substitute for a modern conception of systematic maintenance.

Government policies of mass mobilization and the active discouraging of "bureaucratic" organization came with hidden costs to the long-term health of the economy. The government's capacity to mobilize large numbers of the population to attain defined goals, such as the building of a road or assistance with seasonal agricultural labor shortages, was remarkable. The archetypal mobilization method was to launch shock brigade–type activities, called Chollima campaigns after the Korean winged horse of legend, which was said to be able to cover 1,000 *ri* (a Korean unit of distance) in a day. These campaigns emphasized the production of large outputs over short periods of time. Mobilization tactics as a substitute for organizational efficiency were wasteful, as other activities were neglected and quality of output was a secondary target.

Management techniques relied on exhortation, as opposed to a systematic organization of production and economic incentives. They inevitably could not guarantee continued quality and reliability of output.

The mentality of "make do and mend" became institutionalized in each sector. Improvisation replaced the concept of regular maintenance. Makeshift solutions were neither efficient nor sustainable. Lack of regular maintenance and the inability to maintain consistent standards in production and agriculture because of lack of resources and bottlenecks meant that deterioration in production capacity set in almost as soon as a project was completed.

The Failure of the Old Policies

After 1989, with the collapse of ideologically compatible international part-ners, the economy was no longer sustainable and entered into steep decline. The government initially responded with an intensification of policies that had succeeded in previous decades. It relied mainly on increasing physical labor to try to wring every ounce of productivity out of human individuals already working hard and long hours. The government exhorted the pop-ulation to ever-more-exhausting physical efforts to make up for the limited access to technology, spare parts, and necessary inputs such as fuel and fer-tilizer.[83] Students, youth, and the military were engaged in construction projects over and above their "normal" activities.[84] The government also resorted to austerity measures—from 1990 on most visibly in the calls to limit food consumption in the "eat two meals a day" campaign.[85]

These policies were unsuccessful in helping to stem increasing eco-nomic deterioration and social deprivation. The methods of the past that had produced short- to medium-term gains might have continued pro-ducing further small economic benefits if the Soviet Union and the Eastern bloc had remained and continued to supply oil, technology, and exper-tise. Without external support in the form of capital and technology, these old methods and policies were wholly unable to respond to the food shortages that turned into the famine of the mid-1990s.

The Onset of Famine

Economic decline provided the context for the inability of the country to feed its people from the mid-1990s on, but the proximate cause was the natural disasters of the mid-1990s, most especially the floods of July 1995, which independent observers described as being "of biblical pro-portions."[86] The chronic deterioration in the economic environment, which already threatened human security as food production diminished and health and welfare services deteriorated, was transformed into an acute crisis when severe hailstorms in 1994 and "devastating" floods in

1995–96 savaged the country, destroying arable land, social and economic infrastructure, harvests, and grain reserves.[87] A tidal wave in 1997 caused further damage to this stricken economy.

The 1995 floods had catastrophic consequences. The United Nations Department of Humanitarian Affairs reported that

> between 30 July and 18 August 1995, torrential rains caused devastating floods in the Democratic People's Republic of Korea (DPRK). In one area, in Pyongsan county in North Hwanghae province 877 mm or nearly a metre of rain was recorded to have fallen in just seven hours, an intensity of precipitation, unheard of in this area . . . water flow in the engorged Amnock [*sic*] River, which runs along the Korea/China border, was estimated at 4.8 billion tons over a 72 hour period. Flooding of this magnitude had not been recorded in at least 70 years.[88]

Major fuel sources were lost. Emergency responses were hampered by destruction of the country's coal supplies, which caused, among other things, deterioration in electricity supplies. This in turn prevented electricity-driven railways from being used to transport relief goods.[89]

. The most immediate and pressing problem was the destruction of large parts of the crop and of grain reserves. The United Nations reported "major devastation for the agricultural sector" and quoted DPRK figures of 359,936 hectares of damaged arable land.[90] According to a U.S. State Department official, the floods of 1994 and 1995 destroyed possibly as much as 3 million tonnes' worth of emergency grain reserves, as much of it was stored underground.[91] The United Nations reported a total of 1.5 million tonnes of grain lost.[92] Another U.S. source, the respected Centers for Disease Control and Prevention, stated that 1.2 million tonnes, that is, 12 percent of grain production, was lost to the 1995 floods.[93] Whatever the exact figures, the result was that food became a scarce commodity. Since the DPRK lacked an export capacity and foreign reserves with which to buy food from abroad, its people faced starvation.

The Tragedy

In 1995–96 some 186 people were reported dead as a direct result of flooding, with over half a million persons displaced from their homes.[94] This meant that during 1995–96 at least 2.5 percent of the population was homeless and on the move, at a time when the country's own food resources could not meet the necessary calorific requirements for human survival. The crisis was most evidently grave in its effect on human security for those who faced actual starvation. It also affected those who could find just about enough food to survive but who suffered from malnutrition-related disease and incapacity through lack of sufficient food and adequate nourishment because they had little access to protein, minerals, and vitamins.

Multiple threats came from the sheer absence of food, the devastation done to water and sanitation systems and energy supplies, and the lack of basic medicines, medical equipment, and supplies (including soap and cleaning materials). Hundreds of thousands of people were reduced to eating grass and tree bark, which staved off acute hunger pains but which were useless for survival.[95] Worse, eating such "alternative" foods caused both acute and chronic damage to digestive systems.

Severe and Widespread Malnutrition

The first assessment visit by UN humanitarian agencies, which took place between August 29 and September 9, 1995, involved WHO, FAO, UNICEF, and WFP representatives and was supported by UNDP officials.[96] UNICEF and the WFP made field visits to Chagang province, in the north of the country, and North Hwanghae province in the south in November 1995.[97] It was not possible to quantify the levels of malnutrition until 1998, when the first joint international-government nutritional survey took place, and initial evaluations of the crisis relied on qualitative assessments from humanitarian professionals. These first humanitarian workers tended to have many years of experience working in difficult countries where quantitative assessment of need was not possible, usually because the society was in the middle of war. Consequently, they were able to apply their training, experience, and ability to make comparative analyses to assess humanitarian need in the DPRK. Their reports indicated widespread malnutrition, with the worst cases concentrated in the children's centers or baby homes, which provided residential care for children aged zero to four years (the same age as nursery school children) without parental support.[98]

The DPRK government established the children's centers, developed what the international humanitarian community called "orphanages" for five- to six-year-olds (the same age as kindergarten children), and expanded boarding schools for seven- to seventeen-year-olds (the same age as primary and secondary school children) without family support as a direct response to the food and economic crisis. Prior to the crisis, adoption had been a common social practice, but now families could no longer afford to feed extra children.[99] Not all children living in baby homes, orphanages, and boarding schools were orphans. A number of these children had living parents who, for sometimes unspecified reasons, could not care for and feed them.

Most of the international agencies concentrated their efforts on assessing the needs of children and women, judged to be always the most vulnerable in humanitarian crises. Initial reports identified widespread severe malnutrition, called "wasting" by professional nutritionists, which is indicated by a low weight for height. Severe wasting cannot be treated except by medical intervention and without appropriate nutritional rehabilitation often leads to death. This is because the immune system becomes damaged and the person becomes very vulnerable to disease. The digestive system is also damaged, so specially prepared food must be obtained—the severely malnourished person will not be able to digest and absorb normal food. With children, particularly those under two and babies who cannot communicate and cannot understand why they might have to eat odd-tasting but "nutritious" foods, the threat to life is magnified. Wasting is different from "stunting" or chronic malnutrition, which is evidenced by low height for age and which was visible throughout the country and reported on by all the humanitarian agencies.[100]

Runar Soerensen, a trained nurse and experienced humanitarian assistance official, was posted to the DPRK in January 1996. Soerensen was UNICEF's first resident international officer and one of the first representatives of the humanitarian agencies to take up residence in the DPRK. He described the condition of children as

> bad from the time I [arrived]. . . . It was a little difficult to get a grip on the situation. But we detected that up to 70, 80% of the children in the nurseries and kindergartens had disappeared from these institutions and since nurseries and kindergartens are representing the backbone . . . of the education and formation of children in Korea, something must have been extremely wrong and . . . at the beginning of April 1997, the government asked us to

visit certain areas. We visited Huichon . . . and saw extremely malnourished children.

When I say malnourished children, in medical terms, we say that they have either suffered from marasmus, or kwashiorkor, and that would mean, when they have marasmus, they have a total lack of fat, protein and carbohydrates in what they are eating, and they become as thin as skeletons. When we talk about kwashiorkor, that will mean they are lacking protein in their food, and they become swollen and they look very bad, they look unhealthy, extremely swollen, both in face, body and extremities.[101]

In the DPRK, because nearly all adult women under the retirement age of 55 participated in the workforce, nearly all children attended one of the nurseries, kindergartens, or primary and secondary schools that provided nationwide care and educational facilities for children from age three months upward. Nurseries and kindergartens have kitchen and dining facilities, unlike primary and secondary schools, and one of the early major signs of lack of food available to the state was the reduction in attendance at nurseries and kindergartens. Children were being kept at home, where families were trying to find some way to feed them. Reports from some of the first international observers, particularly from the UNICEF investigations, indicated that on average a "normal" attendance at these institutions was around 95 percent but dropped to 20 to 35 percent when food ran out.[102]

Sanitation and Energy Breakdown

The threats to human life from lack of food were compounded by severe damage to water, sanitation, and energy distribution systems. The country lost up to an estimated 85 percent of its hydroelectric capacity in the floods, along with coal supplies, coal mines, and coal transport facilities, sharply reducing the ability of the country to generate electricity.[103] Flooded sewage systems overflowed into drinking water systems in Pyongyang and other cities, and lack of electricity made pumping systems for water and sewage networks malfunction, with sewage and waste flowing into potable water supplies. Only those in rural areas and elsewhere who relied on basic dug latrines could avoid drinking water from polluted sources.[104] This meant that, paradoxically, those with the most developed water and sanitation systems—the 70 percent of the population with access to piped water systems—were most endangered from the threat of water-borne disease.[105] At the beginning of the DPRK's hot and humid rainy season in July 1996, cholera outbreaks were reported in the west and the north of the country and said to have caused the deaths of "malnourished soldiers and civilians."[106]

UN officials reported a complex set of problems in the energy sector, pointing out that the power shortage problem of 1995–97

> was not due to a shortage of oil as only two of two dozen power stations were dependent on heavy fuel oil for power generation . . . and these two were supplied by KEDO [the Korean Peninsula Energy Development Organization]. . . . About 70% of power generated in the DPRK came from hydropower sources, and the serious winter-spring droughts of 1996 and 1997 (and a breakdown on one of the Yalu River's large hydro turbines) created major shortages throughout the country at that time, severely cutting back railway transportation (which was almost entirely dependent on electric power), which in turn resulted in coal supply shortages to the coal-fueled power stations which supplied the remaining 20% of power in the country.[107]

Health System in Crisis

Health services were unable to cope. Health service providers had difficulties in responding to disease and sickness due to lack of inputs as well as lack of up-to-date training and knowledge about care and health techniques and procedures. Medical personnel had had good contacts with the Socialist countries, including Cuba, which had an advanced medical and health-care system, but had little experience of treating severe malnutrition. There was little evidence that malnutrition had been a prevailing medical and social problem since the 1950s. The most recent experience of food shortages had been between 1969 and 1974, which the government had been able to respond to by importing grain.[108] A 1988 UNICEF survey of children in Kangwon province (in the southeast of the country) had noted that children's nutritional status, except in the case of six- to eighteen-month-olds, compared favorably with World Health Organization standards.[109] While the survey results could not be extrapolated to the entire country, they do indicate a very great difference with the Kangwon of ten years later, when children were dying of starvation.[110]

The treatment of malnutrition demanded specialist inputs such as high-energy milk (HEM), which was not available in the country. Acute respiratory illnesses and diarrheal diseases, which UNICEF and the DPRK Ministry of Public Health (MoPH) identified as being the primary causes of death in children, required medicines and supplies that were also not widely available.[111] The health system had trained doctors and medical personnel and provided clinics and hospitals nationwide, but without basic medical inputs—including everything from soap, oral rehydration solution, and antibiotics to anesthetic supplies—trained personnel could not function. Health-care facilities remained unheated in the viciously cold winters. According to a 1997 UNICEF delegation, hospitals were clean, but wards

> were devoid of even the most rudimentary supplies and equipment; sphyg-momanometers, thermometers, scales, kidney dishes, spatulas and IV giving sets etc. The mission saw numerous patients being treated with home made beer bottle IV sets, clearly unsterile. There was an absence of ORS [oral rehy-dration solution] and even the most basic drugs such as analgesics, and antibiotics.[112]

Another symptom of the health-care crisis was the changing pattern of drug use. The World Health Organization (WHO) reported that, whereas prior to 1995 some 80 percent of the population was likely to be treated by "modern" medicine and 20 percent by "Koryo," or traditional medicine, by 1998 that ratio had reversed.[113] Disease increased, with those illnesses directly linked to poverty and poor sanitation emerging on a large scale. Tuberculosis was a major concern. The Ministry of Public Health reported 57 cases of tuberculosis in 1996, but by 1997 the World Health Organization was reporting 10,000 cases per year, estimating that half of these sick people were dying due to lack of drugs and functioning tuberculosis surveillance, prevention, and control programs.[114]

National immunization campaigns, which DPRK authorities reported had been successful in reaching 95 percent of children under five until 1994, were disrupted after the 1995 floods due to a breakdown in the cold chain that is necessary to keep vaccine effective, and difficulties in transport—partly due to lack of fuel.[115] Immunization campaigns were resumed with the help of UNICEF and the WHO after 1995. Nevertheless, the Ministry of Public Health reported seven confirmed cases of polio in 1995, six in 1996, and three during January–March 1997.[116]

The Scale and Scope of the Famine

The acute phase of the crisis lasted from 1994 to at least 1998 and resulted in many deaths from starvation and malnutrition-related disease. Huge swathes of the population became desperate for food, including in the established food-producing areas in the south of the country. In 1996 people in the agricultural producing areas, the so-called better-off parts of the country, were so hungry that they ate the maize cobs before the crop was fully developed. In places this reduced expected production of an already diminished grain harvest by 50 percent.[117] Farming families would have been fully aware of the implications of their actions in eating the early maize but, facing starvation, were forced into adopting what in normal times would have been a socially unacceptable coping strategy.

The entire nation was adversely affected; severe malnutrition was recorded in Pyongyang as well as in the more remote regions. Figures, however, were notoriously difficult to come by. The DPRK at first offered only the barest of information to outsiders; many also doubted the DPRK's capacity to carry out accurate statistical analysis.[118] Nevertheless, some estimates of the number of deaths were later made.

Famine Deaths

The total number of "excess deaths" from famine will probably never be fully determined, although various figures have been promulgated. Independent analysts and observers placed the figure at between 800,000 and 1.5 million, with the most rigorous research indicating a figure of about two-thirds of a million people dead through starvation or disease and sickness caused by lack of food.[119] Others cited figures ranging from an estimated 220,000 (calculated from government-supplied base figures) to 3 million (claimed by ideological opponents of the DPRK government).[120] It is impossible to know how many people died due to the economic and food crisis, for a number of reasons. There has been no census of the population since 1993 and no independent national survey of mortality rates since the crisis started. Numbers extrapolated from surveys based on one province, usually the northern mountainous province of North Hamgyong, did not factor in the varying impact of the food crisis on different provinces. Some provinces, like Ryanggang, for instance, also situated on the northern border, became receivers of population as land was developed for extensive potato production in the late 1990s and resettlement of families from other provinces took place.

The debate about numbers sometimes misses the point. There is no contesting that a substantial humanitarian crisis occurred in which many, many people died. Even the lower estimates would mark a major tragedy in a country of 21 to 22 million people. For every family, the death of every single person from food shortage was a human and humanitarian disaster.

From Inbuilt Fragility to Outright Disaster

The DPRK socioeconomy achieved enormous aggregate advances for large sections of the population between the late 1950s and 1989. The agricultural, industrial, and energy sectors grew, and surplus was invested in national projects, with benefits distributed toward the population at large. The economic system was, however, increasingly anachronous as well as inefficient. It could not compete in an export-led, quality-conscious international economy and could not, ultimately, generate sustainable growth. With the end of the Cold War, the economic strategy of growth and redistribution to offer balanced benefits to most social groups was no longer possible, at least in its former incarnation.

Agriculture, industry, and the energy sectors folded into an interrelated crisis. The government was no longer able to obtain or produce the necessary fertilizer, pesticides, and electricity necessary to support the highly input-intensive agricultural sector. Soil was already facing exhaustion after years of efforts to increase food production out of a small amount of agricultural land, much of it not optimal for arable purposes.[121] Factories ground to a halt as fuel supplies dried up, and a countrywide lack of energy supplies adversely affected all sectors of the economy, including agricultural and industrial production, health and education sectors, and, in turn, consumption.[122] Factories no longer had energy or spare parts, and as most were modeled on Soviet bloc technology, machinery was obsolescent. If they produced anything, it was uncompetitive goods that could not be sold on reconfigured world markets, where international trade transactions were dictated by the logic of liberal capitalist norms and priorities. The drastic reduction in energy supplies provided the transmission belt for the crisis to spread through every economy sector and affect every social group in the country.

As Ian Davies, former UN director of industrial development for China and the DPRK, commented:

> Power shortages reduced coal output, and breakdowns caused by flooding of coalmines and a shortage of spare parts in coalmines (both coalmining machinery and pumping equipment) and power stations also created chaos. Most of these spare part problems were the result of difficulties in obtaining critical spare parts from former Soviet suppliers, the difficulties being exacerbated by the problems of identifying former suppliers, and the collapse of the bilateral trade agreement, currency clearance systems and barter systems that prevailed for forty years until 1992.[123]

The Collapse of the Human Security Trade-off

Kim Il Sung had promised and delivered to the vast majority of the population improvements in food security, health, education and social service provision, and employment. He had been astute enough to develop and manage a social system that provided a human security trade-off that maintained social stability and national cohesion, allowing for a more or less united people and thus providing an enhanced capacity for national security.

By the 1980s, government policy had stabilized around the human security trade-off—a management strategy that delivered economic benefits to wide sectors of the population and ensured that key social groups benefited economically and politically, with a welfare safety net provided so that those who could not work could survive. At the same time the government limited political freedom and built a structure of social control located within a nationalist and personalistic, dynastic ideology. The system was tough and always brutal against dissenters but achieved a degree of legitimacy through the provision of benefits and the effective management of social tensions—both of which provided an imperfect but stable sense of human security for most of the population. The system had always, however, depended on the availability of increased economic resources to meet the increasing expectations of the population and as compensation for the absence of political freedoms in the country.

By the 1990s, the human security trade-off so carefully developed and managed in the Kim Il Sung era was visibly enfeebled, disintegrating totally in the disaster of the mid-1990s. The human tragedy of the famine manifestly could not be dealt with through old methods and policies. The people, as well as the government, would have to find new ways of living and working—if only to guarantee simple survival.

3

Human Insecurity
and Socioeconomic
Reconstitution

FROM 1994 ON, THE REGIME COULD NO LONGER DELIVER its side of the bargain in the human security trade-off, which had delivered material and political rewards to key social sectors in return for acceptance, more or less, of restrictions on individual political freedom. Kim Jong Il did not display his father's strategic and political adroitness in the management of the socioeconomy, responding with only minor alterations to economic policies that had already demonstrably failed to prevent chronic economic crisis.

In lieu of effective government direction of the economy, the social consensus that had underpinned the Kim Il Sungist period disintegrated in the mid-1990s. The state could not continue to provide a functioning safety net for formerly less well-off groups or the newly economically disenfranchised. The unanticipated consequence of a population left to fend for itself and to find its own coping solutions was irreversible socioeconomic reconstitution around a new, marketized form of socioeconomy. "Marketization by default" was implemented throughout the country as the product of the accumulation of millions of individual acts of economic survival —sanctioned and supported by local party officials and only reluctantly accepted by the central state and party apparatus.

A Government in Shock

From the mid- to late 1990s, the government's economic policy adjustment was tentative and vacillating. Initial responses to the crisis were still dominated by the one economic instrument at the direct disposal of government. This was the intensification of human labor so that annual production targets were obtained "at any cost by arousing workers to greatly increased activity."[1] Official policy promoted the "arduous march" and the "forced march"—efforts supposed to rebuild the nation through collective labor motivated by ideological exhortation.[2]

Only minor policy changes were introduced, mainly in the agricultural sector—reflecting a government that was reluctant to adopt wholesale change yet increasingly aware that the old policies would not suffice. Government legislation indicated only a grudging and belated recognition of the vast socioeconomic changes that were taking place as a result of the state's inability to maintain its previous system of rewards—and punishments. In every case, government pronouncements of policy change demonstrated an enormous lag factor in decision making. Like Canute trying to push back the waves, it was surrounded by socioeconomic change that it did not at first wish to acknowledge and over whose pace and direction it had only tenuous control. The adoption of the government's only significant policy change in this period, the "Army First" policy, should be understood as a means to maintain regime survival in the face of potential opposition from those newly disenfranchised within the emerging marketized economy.

Policy Change in Agriculture

The government attempted to redirect policy in the farming sector in 1996 when it sanctioned small-scale agricultural markets, changed incentive schemes, and implemented improved land management schemes by introducing double-cropping.[3] New incentive systems allowed subwork teams, usually consisting of families and relatives, to function as economic units in which, theoretically, members could benefit from increased productivity.[4] Families were allowed to sell surplus produce, including basic grains, in the newly sanctioned private markets, and farm managers were also allowed more autonomy.[5]

Changes in farming principles were, however, tentative, limited, and cautious. They left in place the overall formal command structure in which agricultural planning and food production were subject to direction from the Pyongyang-based party leadership. These minor changes in agricultural policy did not produce major increases in agricultural production. They did, however, legitimize a changed mindset, which recognized that production would increase only if market incentives were established.

The "Army First" Policy

Kim Jong Il did not take the title of president when his father died; instead he led the country as supreme commander of the Korean People's Army.[6] The DPRK had no formal presidential office except that Kim Il Sung was deemed "eternal president" after his death, with this title ratified in the 1998 constitution. Kim Jong Il continued as unchallenged leader of the DPRK through his role as chairman of the National Defense Commission; as such his interests were synonymous with the interests of the military.

The "Army First" policy gave the military a central role in domestic politics as well as in national defense—decisively moving away from the position held by Kim Il Sung that had subordinated the army to the civilian leadership. Kim Jong Il thus provided himself with insurance against his inability to secure compliance from key social sectors—particularly in the troubled period after the start of the food crisis. The policy was not merely a reaction to the acute crisis of 1995, however, as it had been set in motion immediately after the death of Kim Il Sung in July 1994. Deteriorating regime legitimacy and loss of physical resources to reward formerly privileged geographical and economic groups, however, made a policy choice a policy necessity.

Kim Jong Il's pursuit of the "Army First" policy was perhaps the clearest indication that he did not feel as secure in terms of popular political legitimacy as did his father.[7] That Kim Jong Il could not command acquiescence to his policies was visibly evidenced in 1997 with the defection to Seoul of former senior ideologue and government official Hwang Jang Yop. This incident indicated opposition to the government at very senior levels indeed.[8]

The Consensus Disintegrates

Very few were protected from the effects of the acute crisis of the mid-1990s, although each individual experienced the breakdown of food, health, water, sewage, power, transport, and education differently and to a different extent.[9] Only the very well-off, mainly Kim's family and his immediate cohorts, could wholly protect themselves from the fear of death through starvation or malnutrition-related disease. Some were lucky enough to have access to coping mechanisms such as arable land undamaged by floods, rivers for fishing, or goods from licit or illicit border trade with China. In the main, because of aggregate national food shortages, all social groups faced threats to what had been relative security in terms of freedom from want, including those who had been protected and privileged under Kim Il Sung's "consensual" regime maintenance policies. Farmers, industrial workers, and even the armed forces were no longer exempt from the effects of the country's chronic food shortages. Individuals and families had to learn how to fend for themselves, as the state could no longer protect and provide for its population.

The Poorest . . . and the Best Off

For the poorest living in the most remote areas, the breakdown in state support may not have been entirely new, especially in the brutal winters, when many mountain roads become impassable. The difference between "crisis" and "normal" times would be in the availability of individual coping mechanisms. If poor individuals could engage in petty trade or receive food and income subsidies from relatives, or if they had been fortunate enough to store some food, they would have been protected for a while. If not, they would have certainly suffered grievously and probably not survived the worst of the shortages.

The very wealthiest would simply continue to buy food from abroad (using hard currency stored in foreign bank accounts) and to go overseas for medical treatment. They would not, however, be exempt totally from the crisis. Electricity shortages, for instance, meant that street lights, even in Pyongyang, were dark more often than not. Furthermore, the water and sanitation systems were so compromised that even Pyongyang ministry buildings did not have functioning sanitation systems or running water.

Farming for the Community and Family— No Longer for the State

The approximately 5 million cooperative farming families were no longer guaranteed either food availability or physical survival after the crisis of the 1990s. During the acute phase of the disaster, after the hailstorms and floods of 1994 and 1995, agricultural production and the state's capacity to guarantee inputs for farming such as fertilizer, pesticides, irrigation, and machinery were destroyed. Social infrastructure that had hitherto been provided from profits made from excess harvests—such as nurseries, schools, clinics, and cultural inputs—could no longer be funded.[10] The poorer cooperative farmers, who in any case had not always been able to find their entire year's food supply from their own agricultural production, could no longer be given state support for food supplies or for other basic goods such as soap or medicines.

Farming families had never been beneficiaries of the public distribution system, which had been designed to distribute farming surplus to non-farming families.[11] Even if they had been entitled, the Public Distribution System had little food to distribute in the years of crisis as food shortage affected the entire country. Between the failed harvest of 1995 and the next main harvest of October 1996, farming families were allowed 100 kilograms a year per person—about half an individual's minimum physical survival requirements.[12] Farmers made homeless by the 1995 floods in North Pyongan, North Hwanghae, and Chagang were early recipients of food aid.[13] Relief stocks came from bilateral as well as multilateral sources—including generous donations from Japan—but these were not enough to stem hunger.[14] Rural families resorted to eating tree bark. Farmers living in northern border areas engaged in legal and illegal border trade with neighboring China and Russia. Farming families, like the majority of the population, had to either find ways to fill the food gap or face sickness and death.

The state's inability to deliver inputs to farmers was accompanied by a de facto recognition that individuals and their families were more likely to produce more, even in difficult times, if they were permitted to reap rewards directly from their own efforts. Farmers' individual plot holdings were increased, and they were also permitted to sell their produce in the farmers' markets, where urban dwellers came to sell or barter manufactured goods for food.[15] Although it was still illegal to buy and sell basic grain, that is, rice and maize, on markets, private grain sales became tolerated. The government made halfhearted attempts to control prices and times of opening, but by summer 1997, effective market prices were operating for all commodities, and markets were ubiquitous throughout the country, functioning daily and sometimes in the evening.[16] At first the government considered them a temporary expedient and either denied their existence or only admitted to their marginal contribution to the distribution system.

Farmers began systematically to underdeclare agricultural yields from family plots and aggregate farm production, leaving less to be allocated to the state for redistribution to national priority groups like the army and the poorest and more to sell on the markets. Some cooperative farms entered into direct swapping arrangements with urban enterprises, exchanging part of their crop for use of trucks or other unobtainable but necessary farming inputs. Poor farming families continued to farm the most marginal land, often illegally cutting down forest land and planting on rocky, unsuitable mountain slopes. This caused soil erosion and ensured future flooding after heavy rains.[17]

These new, semilegal, always non-state-controlled socioeconomic practices were tolerated and sometimes encouraged by authorities at the county and provincial level.[18] Local authorities were told in the mid-1990s that they would have to take responsibility for feeding local populations and had had to respond in a pragmatic manner given the simple impossibility of utilizing old ways of working. Markets were useful for local officials, as they provided an extra instrument through which local populations might possibly obtain food.

Even as it permitted some freedoms in the farming sector, the state also attempted to maintain control where it could. The government invested in state farms in which employees were directly employed. There it could attempt to exert stronger labor discipline than it could over cooperative farms. Major new investments were, for instance, channeled into state farm potato production in Daehondang, Ryanggang province. Investments were also made in farms that were settled by demobilized and serving military personnel and their families, in an effort to ensure that the military would have guaranteed access to food.[19]

The military carried out "land rezoning" in the breadbasket provinces, ostensibly to create larger fields that would be easier to farm efficiently and economically.[20] Land rezoning also fulfilled the objective of physically eradicating old rural boundaries to make it difficult for former landlords to claim title post-unification.[21] There were negative agricultural effects of rezoning. Immediately problematic for food-insecure rural populations was the elimination of the possibilities of growing narrow lines of soya bean or other crops between formerly smaller fields. These tiny areas of intercropping had provided a valuable source of food for subwork teams or cooperative farm families who had been permitted to use the production for their own purposes—either for family consumption or to sell on markets. Rezoning also disturbed the topsoil, causing additional difficulties for agricultural production.

Farmers became used to a certain degree of freedom in production and distribution, although there were also countervailing tendencies. The central state authorities still attempted to maintain control over sectors of agricultural production—mainly to provide a steady food supply to the military and "key" workers but also to ensure a minimum safety net for the vulnerable.

The New Underprivileged—
Industrial Workers and Urban Residents

Factory closures escalated from the mid-1990s as a result of lack of necessary inputs, lack of credit, and the government's inability to attract external support. By 1998 even the showpiece Chollima steel complex and the Taean heavy machine factory—long trumpeted as organizational models for the rest of the country—displayed no sign of economic activity.[22] By the late 1990s the government had accepted that some factories would never reopen, stripping many for scrap metal.[23] Workers in former industrial heartlands, the land-poor, population-dense provinces of North and South Hamgyong, were some of the worst off in the country. Surveys consistently reported high death tolls from famine in these provinces.[24] Huge concentrations of former industrial workers lived in the northeast of the country, in the factory cities of Chongjin, Kimchaek, and Hamhung. They were neighbors to unemployed miners living in the northern border counties.

The DPRK had previously provided all non-cooperative-farm families basic food requirements through the Public Distribution System (PDS). Postcrisis, the government attempted to maintain some food distribution to avoid starvation for the worst off, including land-poor industrial and urban workers, but it could not maintain a continuous supply of even basic rations. Each year beginning in 1995, from January to March—when harvests ran out—the PDS reduced basic allocations. From April to October, when the next harvest came in, the PDS was sometimes closed down altogether.[25] The PDS would reopen in particular counties if or when that area benefited from a second harvest as a result of a double-cropping capacity or when a vegetable or other harvest became available.

During the worst food shortages, the PDS acted as a vehicle to deliver "alternative food." Alternative foods were made in local food-processing factories by county administrations. They consisted of a base of about 30 percent maize or corn residues combined with maize husks, edible bulbs, grasses, and seaweeds—made up as a food bar or a kind of noodle.[26] Such barely digestible, non-nutritious foods were designed as a desperate substitute for real food and as a way of staving off hunger pangs by filling stomachs. Frequently this was the only "food" available to urban unemployed and underemployed workers and their families. International aid did not target adults, except for pregnant and nursing women, so unless these adults could find some coping strategy they were at risk of certain malnutrition and possible starvation when the harvest ran out in the spring and summer lean season. Given the lack of food at home and lack of access to aid, it is no wonder that adults from northeastern industrial areas increasingly chose to try their luck in China.

Formerly privileged heavy industrial workers and other urban workers were supplied only with the barest minimum of food and sometimes no food at all. Urban residents, particularly those from the big cities with little access to arable land, had few options when the state could no longer provide food or other basic necessities. The World Food Program reported that they had "reduced or no income."[27] Urban residents also did not have the same regular access to farmers' markets as their rural compatriots—because of lack of transport, money to buy goods, and lack of assets to swap.

Coping responses varied. Former industrial workers resorted to selling or bartering assets such as family jewelry, furniture, and household possessions for food. Some families regularly walked miles to nearby mountains to try to secure food and fuel. The unemployed, destitute urban workers and the poor farmers of the agriculturally deprived northern region engaged in licit and illicit trade with China.[28] Lumber, labor, and assets were swapped for food and some cash. Some families relocated to other provinces.

Some Koreans migrated to China and some became refugees, fleeing to bordering Yanji, the capital of the Korean autonomous region of Yanbian in the Chinese province of Jilin. There North Koreans without valid papers or a good command of the Chinese language could be assimilated with less fear of being arrested than in neighboring provinces and regions.[29] Many had family connections and some were helped by sympathetic local Chinese Koreans. Those who visited China legally had to leave their families behind as an inducement for them to return. Those who attempted to move to China without authorization risked penalties both in China and, if repatriated, back in the DPRK. Some migrants stayed for long periods, while most moved across the border to obtain food and income before returning home to families, heading back to China when food and other supplies again ran out. In 1998, one study found, "[North Korean] migrations into China [could] be characterized typically as short-term movements by a single member of a household whose other members remained in North Korea."[30]

Some industrial and urban workers stayed at work. The government attempted to maintain power supplies, basic irrigation capacity, and some industrial capacity. Workers in functioning mines, plants, and factories in key sector industries were rewarded with food where it was available and also paid in the local currency, the *won*, although this could buy nothing of value from the mid-1990s on. Basic supplies of food for workers operating in key industries were not munificent; workers were expected to respond to government calls for reconstruction efforts primarily out of a sense of national pride.[31]

Workers creatively used the system to try to minimize the most debilitating effects of the extra physical work they were supposed to undertake. Workers drew on their experience of meeting quantitative output targets only in the last few weeks of the three-month planning period so as to reduce communal work norms to manageable proportions. Remuneration was still geared toward the group, so individuals were not penalized for slow or inefficient working, provided the group norms supported frequent rest breaks and made allowances for the different capacities of individuals. Households were also permitted to alternate different members for work activities. The focus on the collective as the unit of economic activity continued to give some protection against burnout through sheer physical exhaustion, even as the government continued to respond to the crisis by calling for the intensification of human labor.

In the DPRK of the mid- and late 1990s, only a few workers could hope to become food secure, and such a status was often obtained semi-legally. A small proportion of urban workers with access to foreign business, governments, aid organizations, and visitors had the opportunity to become relatively well-off, if they could leverage access to hard currency and food out of these connections.[32]

The Provinces—and the Capital

Each of the DPRK's nine provinces and three "cities under central authority"—Pyongyang, Kaesong, and Nampo (also categorized as provinces for administrative purposes)—fared differently in the breakdown of economic and food security. Overall, Pyongyang coped best and North Hamgyong worst, but this did not mean that all in Pyongyang were secure from want or that all in North Hamgyong were vulnerable. Whether the population managed to survive or not depended mostly on the capacities and reactions of county-level authorities. Differences could be explained by the differential coping solutions available to the county authorities, the relative flexibility of local authorities, the availability of assistance from central state authorities, and to what extent the county had access to foreign assistance.

The border areas of mountainous Chagang and southern Kangwon provinces remained off-limits to humanitarian organizations, but counties in those provinces that were accessible displayed signs of widespread poverty, including malnutrition in children. Parts of Ryanggang, in contrast, also a northern border province, remained overall slightly better off than its neighbors. Containing only 3 percent of the country's population, the province benefited from dense forestry that could be cut and sold—legally and illegally—to neighboring China. Its low population density also attracted both organized and spontaneous in-migration from other provinces, given the opportunities for land cultivation.

The picture of human insecurity was differentiated *within* provinces. Poor coal mining counties in South Pyongan, for instance, existed side by side with counties that continued to produce enough food, at least for subsistence. Nampo, the country's major port, provided a hub for employment and access to food for port workers, but at the same time, in the mid-1990s, it displayed high levels of severe malnutrition in young children in the city's children's institutions.[33] (This changed in the early 2000s, when children in Nampo and Pyongyang were recorded as best off in the country in terms of nutritional status. They had benefited from the relatively high levels of economic activity in Nampo in the later period of modest economic recovery.)[34]

Provincial authorities reacted to human insecurities by attempting to maintain a minimum food distribution to the most needy of their populations. They were also flexible in permitting the wide variety of decentralized coping mechanisms that included the toleration of markets and the growth of unregulated petty trade. Provincial authorities in North Hamgyong and other industrial areas faced some of the toughest, most intractable food security problems. All international agencies recognized that families living in the dense conurbations of North and South Hamgyong, including formerly well-off industrial workers and their families, were particularly severely affected by food shortages and were "the most vulnerable" people in the country.[35]

The coping strategy of legal or illegal migration to bordering China and Russia was not an option, however, for the entire province of North Hamgyong, which had a population of more than 2 million.[36] The desperation caused by food shortages and lack of alternative means of provision led to one of the few reported outbreaks of protest against the government, when riots broke out in October 1999 in the mining county of Onsong, North Hamgyong.[37] These riots were violently suppressed by the DPRK's core military "elite squads," not by local militias—perhaps indicating a rift between North Hamgyong party leaders and their counterparts in Pyongyang.

The Military—Not All Benefited

The armed forces were given priority for food distribution, but this did not mean that all members of the armed forces received generous rations.[38] The army was told to find ways to grow its own food and to develop industries so that it could purchase food and other necessities from the markets and from abroad. There were no indications that the ranks of the army were given excessively large rations, but unlike the general population they were more or less assured of a basic food supply all year round. These were basic rations, however, and ordinary soldiers of the million-strong army often remained hungry, as did their families, who did not receive preferential treatment simply because a son or daughter was serving in the armed forces.[39]

All families were connected in some way to the military. If youth were not on active service, they would serve in the reserves. More comprehensively, all members of the family would occasionally be mobilized for civil defense duties. Given the overall aggregate food and basic goods shortages, it was not possible to exempt the military from economic decline or to privilege all members of the armed forces. The interests of the military, therefore, were very practically intertwined with the interests of the population as a whole.

Giving Up on the Safety Net— the Growth of Endemic Poverty

DPRK society was reconstructed in the aftermath of the acute crisis of the mid-1990s with only a minimal food, health, and economic safety net. The worst off included those who either had no employment or, although earning work points that in former times would have guaranteed them food, such as light industrial workers, were not a priority group for allocation of the little food available. To maintain entitlement to food should any become available in the Public Distribution System, unemployed male and female factory workers still had to show up at the workplace. They were allocated unproductive "make-work" jobs, which had the additional effect of keeping them busy—off the streets and with little time on their hands to think about allocating blame for their problems. At the same time, many workplaces adopted a de facto policy of ignoring worker absences as individuals went scavenging for food and for means of survival.

Women (especially pregnant women), children (especially under two years old), the elderly, the disabled, and the sick suffered real deprivation —extreme enough to lead to what must have been high death rates for all these vulnerable population groups.[40] All received insufficient and inadequately nutritious food and, unless lucky enough to live in parts of Pyongyang or to have some access to China, had very little hope of obtaining medicines. Doctors were often well trained and caring but could do little with the infinitesimal inputs available. Hospitals and clinics lacked regular supplies of the most basic equipment, including soap, cleaning materials, and electricity. They became places where cross-infections could proliferate.

Women—Multiply Disadvantaged

Women suffered particular hardship. The strongly gendered structure of North Korean society deemed it natural for women to carry the physical responsibility for obtaining and preparing food and securing water and fuel for the family, including the extended family.[41] In the time of food crisis, this gendered role remained unchanged, and it was in the main women's responsibility to try to find food for the family. The demands of domestic responsibilities meant huge increases in physical activity, while women's calorie intake diminished, often to well below what was needed for healthy human growth and development.[42] Women went without food so that their families could eat whatever food was available. Women also ate the most dangerous of the "wild foods," sometimes dying from eating poisonous vegetation or suffering crippling digestive illnesses as a result of eating indigestible foodlike material.[43]

At the same time women in the DPRK, according to the UNDP, had the highest participation in the workforce of any country in the world, at 89 percent.[44] Women had to continue finding some way to carry out their formal work role, as otherwise they would not have been eligible for whatever food or income could still be obtained within the formal system of state distribution. Yet workplace directors tolerated high absenteeism by women from work, without in the main cutting back on their workpoints entitlement. This was partly because women were concentrated in the lowest-paid service sectors, such as health and education. County authorities prioritized food distribution to those deemed to be contributing to the resuscitation of the national economy, so in practice women did not often benefit from the limited food distribution. This policy was maintained even though, as the nutritional status for the majority worsened, illnesses increased and more children required institutional care, so that workers in the care professions were in demand as never before. Women, therefore, were unlikely to receive anything but the barest minimum of food allocation through state distribution.

In "normal" times combining the domestic role with participation in the labor force might have caused added irritation and fatigue. In the aftermath of chronic food shortages in the mid-1990s, carrying out the food- (and fuel-) collection role became literally a question of life and death, and women with their primary responsibility for domestic functions carried the real brunt of the absence of state support.

Except for the lucky minority who had access to the prestigious Pyongyang Maternity Hospital, pregnant and nursing women faced particularly severe difficulties in staying healthy. Maternal mortality rates increased, and although accurate figures are not available, UNICEF reported in 1996 a maternal mortality rate of 41 per thousand.[45] It was in any case impossible for women who lacked vitamins and minerals, most importantly iron, to avoid common complications of pregnancy, including anemia, hemorrhage, and premature births.[46] Birth rates went down as death rates went up—partly due to the physical inability of women to carry healthy babies but probably also because women were deciding not to have babies when they could no longer assure children of enough food to eat.[47]

Children—Starving Toddlers and the Rest Chronically Malnourished

Children, especially those under two, were recognized by both the government and the international community as highly likely to be suffering from the extreme and pervasive poverty of the mid-1990s on. Unlike in some poor countries, where children enter the workforce at a very early age as a way to earn income, children in the DPRK do not work, apart from helping out at harvest times. They are thus entirely dependent upon state or community provision of food and other goods.[48] When the state could no longer guarantee food for the entire population and when the county had no food locally, children became heavily reliant on international food aid. From the start of chronic aggregate food deficits in the mid-1990s, children in food-deficit localities faced hunger every year. Children aged twelve and under, apart from a small minority, have faced food deprivation throughout their entire lives. A decade of undernutrition means that children's immune systems are fragile and thus children are ever more susceptible to diseases such as tuberculosis, which has assumed epidemic proportions since the 1990s.

The World Health Organization reported DPRK government figures of death rates of 93 children per thousand in 2001.[49] Even though these figures are unlikely to be accurate, they vividly indicated the worsening of health conditions for children—especially when compared to the government's figures for 1993 of an under-five mortality rate of 55 per thousand.[50]

Babies and toddlers had the worst rates of severe malnutrition, and death rates were probably very high in this group. UNICEF cited what must have been very understated infant mortality rates at 23 per thousand live births—although accurate infant mortality rates do not exist.[51] The reasons for this extreme state of human insecurity at the level of simple survival are very well documented. Undernourished mothers found it difficult to maintain exclusive breast-feeding, and no suitable alternative was available. Infant formula was not produced locally, and only a miniscule amount was imported.[52]

Nor was there any regular supply of weaning or semisolid food, which a baby needs before its digestive system is fully developed and can absorb solid foods. Women in North (and South) Korea make rice porridge for weaning food, and before the crisis even non-rice-producing communities would try to ensure that pregnant and nursing women obtained rice for this purpose. During the crisis many, possibly most, families did not have access to rice and literally had no food that the child could digest. Neither was milk readily available. Much of international food aid assistance was corn, indigestible to very young children. With these chronic shortages of basic food, babies and toddlers continued to face the most extreme hunger and probably had the highest death rate of any age group in the population.

The Elderly and the Disabled—Major Threats to Survival

There is little data on the welfare of the elderly, but it is likely that elderly people would have given up their food for children and grandchildren during the worst of the crisis. It is certain that they could not have survived moderate illnesses or cold during the severe winters, as they lacked medicines and heating. There is similarly little data on the disabled, except for information reporting nine provincial institutions for deaf and mute children and three schools for the blind.[53] One international aid agency, Handicap International, helped in the supply and manufacture of prosthetics and had access to a beneficiary group of about 2,000 amputees.[54] How children or adults with other disabilities fared in the context of the crisis is simply not known, however. Given their difficulty in coping in "normal" times and most families' precarious ability to sustain themselves, it would be difficult to envisage that individuals with moderate to severe disabilities could physically survive.

The Sick—the Absence of Hope

Chronic and acute illnesses increased in prevalence, partly because of an absence of food, partly because hygiene and sanitation systems disintegrated, and partly because there were too few medical and health inputs. Chronic digestive failure associated with the eating of nonfood substances to fill the stomach was one result of the food crisis of the mid-1990s. Tuberculosis, malaria, and acute respiratory and diarrheal illnesses increased dramatically. In 1999, for instance, an estimated 40,000 new cases of tuberculosis a year were being reported—up from zero reported cases in 1976.[55] Also in 1999, an estimated 100,000 malaria cases were reported in six of the country's twelve provinces.[56] Sick adults who could not work were triply vulnerable. They were unable to work in either the formal or informal sector and obtain food; they were not beneficiaries of international food aid; and they had to rely on what the county could provide when food supplies were short or nonexistent.

The Consequences of Central Government Paralysis

The inability or unwillingness of the central state and government to respond to crisis further delegitimized the regime. State socialization capacities were diminished at the same time that individuals and local authorities started to adopt non-state-directed private initiatives for simple survival. The cumulative effect of these uncoordinated and spontaneous activities was to unwittingly facilitate socioeconomic restructuring and the establishment of the foundations of a marketized economy.

Loss of Legitimacy

The Kim Jong Il regime continued to pump out propaganda expressing the centrality of the Kim family to nation building through TV, newspapers, posters, and performance arts. This campaign continued even though practical issues such as the lack of electricity and lack of paper placed some restrictions on dissemination, particularly between 1994 and 1998. Given the nationwide visibility of lack of state efficacy in delivering basic goods, it is doubtful whether campaigns portraying Kim Jong Il as synonymous with the state did much more than cause the population to associate continuing hardships with their leader.

The state-controlled media acknowledged the "difficulties" of the 1990s and responded by exhorting the population to ever-increasing physical effort to increase production and to defend the country.[57] No amount of ideological or nationalist sloganeering, however, could bring about enthusiastic participation in the hard physical work that was necessary to compensate for lack of technology and transport and that left the majority in poverty while bringing visible benefits to only a small minority.

Children suffering from malnutrition were unable to attend nurseries, kindergartens, and schools on a regular basis. In winter, if schools could manage to open without adequate heating, electricity, and materials, children were often too cold and hungry to learn effectively.[58] Women, who accounted for 100 percent of nursery teachers and the vast majority of kindergarten and primary school teachers, spent their time looking for food and fuel. This curtailed the time available for teaching and child care in the children's institutions, which were often closed or operated with large classes or on a shift system.[59] In many parts of the country, understaffed, unheated nurseries, kindergartens, and schools, lacking fundamentals such as electricity, paper, and pencils, were unable to do little more than carry out basic care, including assisting in feeding children if and when international food aid became available. Educational institutions were left with little capacity to keep inculcating the Kim Il Sung family state-building mythology.

From Public Distribution to Private Markets

The Public Distribution System as a guarantor of a basic ration for all nonfarming families disintegrated from 1995 on as scant food or goods were available for distribution.[60] The organizational capacity to distribute food, however, remained more or less intact, and the government continued to use the system to provide a distribution mechanism for international food assistance and, in some provinces at some times of the year, a basic ration for specific sectors of the population. As food flows through the system were insufficient to make necessary a permanent distribution infrastructure, however, the public distribution centers fell into disuse. Some were converted for alternative use, such as schools.[61]

The reconstituted PDS distributed international food aid and channeled food to key workers such as miners and those who were working in occupations designated as crucial for economic reconstruction. The PDS became a distribution system of last resort rather than, as it had been, a primary source of cheap food organized so that all the population could have access to guaranteed food supplies.[62] The PDS also changed from a distribution mechanism organized around principles of equity to one based on selection and targeting. At the same time that the PDS became both less equitable and less of a reliable source of food, the semilegal but increasingly ubiquitous markets provided an alternative supply, distribution, and price-setting mechanism—of food and other goods.[63]

Markets were also organized around principles of selection, but unlike with the PDS principles of equity and transparency (through the work-points system, which was public knowledge), markets were instead based on the principle of purchasing power, or lack thereof. Many were multiply disadvantaged by the new market-based system of distribution.[64] Unemployed industrial workers, for instance, were unlikely to receive food from the new PDS, which directed any food that became available to those in work, and the unemployed, by definition, had no income with which to purchase food in markets.[65] Neither were these workers likely to have access to land on which they could grow food.

Local Parties as the Motor of Socioeconomic Change

The county and provincial party and state authorities had much more reason to be tolerant of the semilegal ways of getting by that the population had been forced to adopt than the Pyongyang-based party center. Although far from being a democratic state, the DPRK maintained some measures of accountability within its party and state structures. Party and government officials throughout the country were faced on a daily basis with a population that was suffering hunger with no alternatives other than nonlegal routes for survival. The party also retained some measures of accountability because of its sheer size. Only very senior party officials remained immune from the food crisis. Most officials and members were in the same position as the population as a whole in that they were forced to circumvent the law in order to find food and the means of survival.[66] There were few food-surplus counties, and no geographical area unaffected by the food and energy crisis of the mid-1990s. Thus no section of the party could, in practice, insist on adherence to old doctrines. Doing so would have meant denying survival mechanisms to its own members as well as most of the population.

Markets, illegal migration, and illegal clearing of forests and mountain land for food and fuel became tolerated by local authorities as sometimes the only coping mechanisms available for survival for the people who lived under their jurisdictions.[67] The authorities in the northern counties of the DPRK colluded in the illegal semimigrations of North Korean people across the Chinese border. County and local party officials could not guarantee food to the local population, and migration was a way in which the people for whom they were responsible could help themselves. Local government officials permitted and supported large-scale population movements from province to province, as families moved to find food and fuel that the state could no longer provide. Some of this population movement was organized by central government and some was spontaneous—locally sanctioned to deal with acute food shortages, particularly in the "lean season" when already inadequate harvests had run out.

The party hierarchy in the provinces and the counties did not necessarily approve of the socioeconomic change taking place around them from the mid-1990s on. Even the most ardent supporter of the Kim Il Sung regime, however, had little option but to participate in the new semilegal market economy—not to do so might mean literally not to survive.

Marketization by Default

The central government was much more ambivalent than local governments about the moves to marketization that had taken place as the unintended effect of lack of state capacity. Official public pronouncements stressed the baleful effects of "imperialist" ideology that the government argued was being imported along with the foreign aid that prevented out-right starvation.[68] The government periodically recognized the socio-economic change it was powerless to stop, but it declared such change "temporary"—due to economic difficulties that, once overcome, would allow for reversion to the old economic and political system of planning and state control.[69] In other words, the government vacillated in response to these new methods of economic operation—sometimes attempting to offer support for the new quasi-private economy and sometimes attempt-ing to rein in such change.

Although limited policy change was approved in the agricultural sec-tor, it was not the central government that initiated the major socio-economic change of the mid-1990s. Instead households, farms, local com-munities, counties, and provinces implemented coping strategies as best they could, using options that varied according to their differentiated ability to barter, swap, sell, or buy for themselves. The severity of the crisis forced socioeconomic change as the population adopted self-help methods to find ways to survive physically. The state could no longer systematically redistribute food from the few counties that were still capable of produc-ing agricultural surplus or provide inputs so that food production could again meet the survival needs of the population. Private markets replaced public distribution systems as the main source of food and goods.

Social change came to the DPRK as the unintended effect of individual attempts to survive the crisis. In practice the problem-solving methods adopted by local officials and communities were based around market-based provision of food and other basic goods. Local officials facilitated marketization, as the alternative would have been starvation for neighbors and the communities they represented. Government became an economic bystander as people began to fend for themselves—in the process institu-tionalizing private farmers' markets as a major source of food and goods.

The Human Security Trade-off (Partially) Reversed

In a very limited sense, there was a reverse in the human security trade-off generated during the Kim Il Sungist period. Economically, incipient marketization that developed as a response to state failure was cause and consequence of increased economic inequalities and widespread poverty.

Politically, effective control over the entire population became much less uniform than that prior to the crisis of the mid-1990s.

The "forced march" effectively legitimated the self-help activities of local communities, which were encouraged to "solve the problems of food, clothing and housing by themselves without looking to the state for help."[70] Unorganized in-country migration reflected de facto increases in personal freedoms, as individuals crossed most county and provincial boundaries without prior authorization while looking for food or fuel. Much more freedom was given to individuals to fend for themselves as a response to the state's inability to provide the population with basic goods for survival.

These increased personal freedoms, particularly of mobility, resulted from the breakdown and loosening of security controls in the wake of the crisis. These were highly visible freedoms, with individuals traveling throughout the country looking for fuel, food, the possibilities of barter trade, or the opportunities for casual work. A heightened condition of human insecurity in terms of lack of guaranteed access to food, shelter, health, education, and work had not led to a complete intensification of physical and political repression. Instead the effects on individuals in terms of their potential "freedom from fear" were contradictory. Crime, including prostitution, became more prevalent. Paradoxically, these developments signaled new constraints on the state's ability to control deviant behavior.

The negative side of increased personal mobility and the decrease in the security capacity of the state was the increase in lawlessness—as farms and communities faced threats of theft of crops and other goods.[71] Migrants, refugees, and defectors reported a breakdown in public order, evidenced by a rise in murder rates, as police and security forces could no longer curb the actions of individuals searching for food and income.[72] Neither was the state security apparatus immune from the crisis; security personnel supplemented their income and obtained food by accepting bribes to ameliorate punishments. Corruption became an entrenched part of the prison and security system.[73]

Even in this early period the state showed signs of accepting a loosening of economic controls, despite its intermittent attempts to take back control over grain prices. No such signs of flexibility appeared in the political sphere. The government made recurrent attempts to reinstitute central security controls and to reconsolidate restrictions on personal freedoms.[74] On the other hand, the visible presence of the security apparatus remained minimal, and men and women in military uniform seldom carried guns. Nevertheless, the state remained insistent on overt loyalty to Kim Jong Il, continuing to punish dissenters severely. A vivid example was the 1996 shooting of a defector who had sought refuge in the Russian embassy in Pyongyang.[75]

Human Insecurity and Social Reconstitution

In the aftermath of the crisis of the mid-1990s, the already-disabled state could no longer provide its half of the grand bargain of the human security (wants)/human insecurity (fear) trade-off. Many social groups lost former privileges and became less well-off, and others suffered absolutely. Cooperative farmers, industrial workers, and urban dwellers were often made desperate by the crisis, particularly when they had become unemployed or underemployed, with only a few able to reposition themselves to take advantage of economic recovery. Women, children, the elderly, the disabled, and the sick faced overwhelming deprivation and continued to die prematurely and in unacceptably large numbers.

The visible inability of the state to deliver basic goods, combined with the decline of the effectiveness of the state's socialization capabilities, the economic and political disenfranchisement of key social groups, the spread of poverty, and the growth of visible corruption, was accompanied by only one major domestic policy decision—to reinforce the security capability of the state through the implementation of the "Army First" policy. Otherwise, domestic policy paralysis was the hallmark of initial reactions to the acute crisis of the mid-1990s. Under the Kim Il Sung regime, government had led the process of socioeconomic change in the DPRK, but the new government of Kim Jong Il was unable to do so. Government policy was forced into a predominantly reactive position, following events rather than leading them.

A by-product of the economic and food crisis was damage to the state's ability to implement the socialization processes that had made the overt use of the security apparatus to control dissent relatively unnecessary.

Propaganda efforts continued, but few resources were available to support the educational and cultural activities that socialized the population into Kim Il Sungism. The state's lack of capacity to deliver human security in terms of regular access to food and basic supplies was evident, reinforcing the bankruptcy of any notion of the DPRK as paradise, socialist or otherwise. The regime lost legitimacy except for that derived from its durability, familiarity, and ties to the nation-building activities of the Kim Il Sung period.

4

Humanitarian Assistance
and Human Security

THE BANKRUPTCY OF GOVERNMENT IDEAS to deal with the food and economic crisis was most visible in the 1994–95 decision to ask "enemy nations," such as the United States, Japan, and South Korea, for international assistance to feed the population.[1] The government's ostensibly most radical policy change—to ask for help from the West— was a sign of desperation. With it the government demonstrated not only that it could no longer feed its people or guarantee their physical survival but also that it recognized it had exhausted all options available within the prevailing domestic and foreign policy framework. The decision to ask for help was, for a long time, immensely controversial within the government and party. It was initially made tolerable to those political currents opposing any form of exposure of North Korean weaknesses to the West only on the grounds that aid would be restricted to "inputs" and any perceived interference into domestic affairs challenged.

Diverse humanitarian agencies operating with different mandates responded to appeals for humanitarian assistance, although food aid remained at the core of the international effort. Millions of tons of food were channeled through the UN World Food Program. As a consequence the WFP became both the major provider of humanitarian assistance and the chief negotiator with the government on behalf of the entire humanitarian community. Humanitarian agency operations provided a practical response to the immediate need of safeguarding basic human security interests—that of physical survival through avoidance of starvation.

Humanitarian agencies' interaction with the government was often conflictual. All agencies expressed a number of dissatisfactions in their working relationships with the DPRK authorities. Issues of principle concerning access to beneficiary populations constituted the core of conflict, although the process of negotiation and dialogue between the agencies and the government over time brought improvements in access as well as a more positive attitude by the DPRK government to working with the agencies.

The slow process of continued negotiations contributed to an increase in mutual knowledge, trust, and predictability. The confidence-building processes generated provided a potential enabling context for broader political negotiations with the major donors of humanitarian assistance, which were also the DPRK's major adversaries. The intensive process of agency interaction proved relatively successful, but ultimately, it also demonstrated the limits of humanitarian diplomacy as a catalyst for policy change and increased human security for the population of the DPRK.

Humanitarian Strategies

From 1997 on, the humanitarian community institutionalized operations. It developed a common strategy that, first, continued to respond to emergency needs—intended to directly save lives—and, second, attempted to provide a bridge into more long-term reforms to support sustainable economic recovery.[2] By 1998 residential UN agencies, bilaterals, and NGOs had more or less adopted a collective and coordinated approach and were coordinating appeals for the DPRK through the annual common humanitarian appeal mechanism coordinated by the United Nations. The three key sectors of assistance were food aid, health support, and food security, the latter category mainly involving assistance with the reclamation of flooded agricultural land and other agricultural activities.

The strategy did not change much over time. It was first formalized in the 1998 UN country team articulation of a "three-track" approach. This was to provide humanitarian assistance, to support the UNDP-sponsored Agricultural Rehabilitation and Environmental Protection (AREP) plan, and to stress "capacity-building" as an essential component of humanitarian operations.[3] The first and second parts of the strategy were, to a greater or lesser degree, supported by the DPRK government, donors, and all the humanitarian agencies and were therefore uncontentious. The third part of the strategy raised questions of economic and political change, which both donors and the DPRK government found controversial. The government wanted change but at its own pace, and not necessarily in the same direction as that desired by donors.

The first part of the strategy, providing humanitarian assistance, was implemented through provision of food aid, medical assistance, and short-term projects intended to bring some immediate agricultural recovery, such as the rebuilding of embankments destroyed by flooding and the clearing of silt from streams and rivers. The target beneficiaries were women and children. Given the abundance of evidence that the vast majority of the population continued to face starvation on an annual basis, this first part of the strategy remained uncontroversial. As late as 2002, the UN remained concerned that starvation was still a possibility in the DPRK, arguing in its appeal documents that "only generous food-aid contributions can prevent a major famine."[4]

The second part of the strategy—the implementation of the AREP plan—was envisaged as a bridge between relief and rehabilitation work. Although developed by the UNDP in coordination with the government, the agricultural recovery program was always meant to act as an umbrella program for individual projects that could be undertaken by many different agencies, including NGOs and bilateral and multilateral organizations.[5] The UNDP was also able to use the regular joint government/agency mechanisms of dialogue developed through the policy-planning elements of the AREP plan to provide a framework for discussions of long-term agricultural and economic reform.

Humanitarian officials, however, had to use a good deal of tact and diplomacy in addressing the subject of reform. Throughout the 1990s even the word "reform" itself was distrusted by the North Koreans, as they equated it with attempts to dismantle their political and social system. Thus, for instance, the UNDP document for the 1998 joint government/UNDP Geneva workshop on agricultural recovery made judicious use of quotes from the late president Kim Il Sung to explain why peasants' markets

could be an appropriate instrument for the provision of goods not supplied by the state.[6]

The third part of the humanitarian strategy built on the understanding common to all the agencies that the continuing life-threatening emergency of chronic food insecurity, in the sense of the country being unable
to feed its citizens without international aid, would end only when the
DPRK was able to revive its export industries and that to do this, it would
need to attract Western development assistance.[7] As relations intensified
between the humanitarian organizations and the government and as the
DPRK became more incorporated into conventional international relations,
some of these more sensitive political and economic issues became easier
to discuss. The June 2001 paper produced by the in-country Humanitarian Development Working Group, consisting of UN agencies, donors,
bilateral organizations, and NGOs, which was overtly critical of DPRK
government policies—referring to the negative effects of DPRK arms sales,
international bad debts, and lack of government openness—illustrated
how robust the government/agency dialogue had become.[8]

The policy ramifications of humanitarian agency ideas for long-term
recovery could only be hinted at, however, for fear of causing a backlash
against individuals and agencies seen as "interfering" in government policy
on issues that were understood, by both agencies and government, as "sensitive." As the relationship between humanitarian actors and government
evolved, a common means of resolving the sensitivity dilemma was to make
specific the analysis of the country's multifaceted economic and political
problems but to refrain from offering far-reaching recommendations for
policy reform.[9]

UN agency managers, with their comparative international experience,
also understood that however the country changed, it was not going to be
without costs, and that this was also well understood by the government.
The 1998 UN strategy document explained,

> The local reluctance to change stems from history, mistrust and the fear to
> loose [sic] face. We should not expect the leaders of this country to contem-
> plate any type of "reform" or further major opening if they are unaware of,
> particularly, social implications. These fears are not unfounded; they range
> from the loss of social values, welfare and cohesiveness to the introduction of
> crime and HIV/AIDS. In addition, there are no good examples of sudden

change bringing prosperity anywhere! Listening and understanding is needed on both sides.[10]

The agencies adopted a policy of confidence building and familiarization, increasingly proposing and implementing approaches designed to expose government officials and institutions to alternative policies, particularly in other Asian countries, like China, India, and Vietnam. The euphemisms adopted for this approach were many and various, including "capacity building," "study tours," "familiarization," and "training." The objective was both to increase technical skills and to show DPRK officials that they had little to fear from increased transparency and much to gain. An implicit hope was that increased confidence in the benefits of transparency might spill over into broader political and economic domains.

Underlying the Strategy: The Issues of Principle

The key principles underlying international humanitarian operations included an adherence to norms of transparency, accountability, and efficiency. These latter principles also underlay the operations of liberal market economies and were antithetical to the principles underlying the DPRK economy—of a national security-centered, closed polity. Thus humanitarian agencies and the government were both aware that giving way on operational requirements for the DPRK often meant a breach in the standard methods of operation of the society itself.[11] Negotiations on operational issues were, therefore, always heavily loaded for both the government and the agencies. Concessions agreed on specific projects, such as increased access to information or facilities, were viewed by the government as concessions of principle, not just agreements over enhancing technical capability.

The government could not entirely ignore the norms underpinning humanitarian operations. It could not risk alienation of the major agencies and possible withdrawal of food aid, which would have resulted in widespread starvation. This does not mean that the process of negotiation between the humanitarian agencies and the government was ever easy or harmonious, but it does mean that both sides were involved in very serious negotiations from the beginning of the humanitarian operation. The DPRK government was forced into a steep learning curve, not just about humanitarian operations but about the principles underlying them.

The World Food Program as the
Crucial Humanitarian Actor

The food aid organization of the United Nations, the World Food Program, became the key actor in responding to direct threats to human security, as the large volumes of assistance requested and obtained remained overwhelmingly in the sector of direct food aid. Donors regularly fulfilled appeals for food, while other sectors were constantly underfunded—even though the humanitarian community recognized that food assistance alone could not address the interrelated causes of malnutrition in the DPRK. From 1999 to 2001, the next-largest multilateral agency, UNICEF, received just $12 million in contributions through the CAP appeal.[12] The decline in support for UNICEF meant that its programs became less significant than some of the NGOs. The relatively well-funded International Federation of the Red Cross and the World Health Organization (WHO) became as important, if not more important, than UNICEF in the health sector.

The relative numbers of resident international staff illustrated the overwhelming dominance of the WFP in humanitarian work in the DPRK. The WFP in 2001 had authorization for 56 international staff, while UNICEF, with the next-largest number of international staff, had just 10.[13] The preponderance of the WFP in terms of the size of the operation, its contacts with key donors, and its lead role in humanitarian community negotiations with DPRK authorities gave it a significant role in introducing DPRK officials to the standard operating procedures of multilateral organizations and the donors. These procedures, based on norms of transparency, accountability, and efficiency, were antithetical to the DPRK's historic modes of organization. Thus every step in agency/WFP/DPRK cooperation involved long processes of negotiation in order to explain and persuade the government of the necessity and rationale of agency methods of operation.

The World Food Program's central role in the relationship with the DPRK government was formalized in 1998, when the first UN humanitarian coordinator role was allocated to the WFP representative, Douglas Casson Coutts.[14] The job of the humanitarian coordinator is to coordinate all humanitarian agencies in-country—UN agencies, bilaterals, and nongovernmental organizations.[15] David Morton, an extremely experienced senior humanitarian official, assumed the humanitarian coordinator role for the WFP in late 1998. He incorporated four roles in his person—WFP representative, UNDP country director, UN resident representative, and UN humanitarian coordinator. In 2004, after four years' service in-country widely recognized as superlative by UN agencies, bilaterals, NGOs, and donors alike, Morton moved on to WFP Rome headquarters as director of logistics for the global WFP operation. He was replaced by Masood Hyder, whose two decades of field experience with the WFP included negotiating humanitarian access in the enormously difficult wartime environment of Sudan.

Enemies or Friends—the Key Donors

Generous food assistance came from a wide variety of donors, but the large volumes of basic grains that significantly helped avert starvation in the DPRK came from nations that had large grain surpluses as well as the most difficult and often antagonistic political relations with the DPRK. A wide range of motivations underpinned aid, within and across these governments. Some political groups had genuine humanitarian motivations, while others gave food aid to help avert wholesale collapse of the DPRK and consequent instability in Northeast Asia. South Koreans were also horrified by the pictures of fellow Koreans, especially children, dying and suffering from severe malnutrition. This propelled the South Korean government to ease restrictions on contacts with the DPRK from as early as the mid-1990s so aid could be sent north.

Food aid recorded by the UN system for the DPRK in 1995–96 included a very large bilateral donation from Japan, which had always had mutually hostile political relations with the DPRK and with which diplomatic relations did not exist. Japan donated about $60 million in this period. In comparison, DPRK ally Syria gave $8 million in food assistance, and Switzerland, a longtime diplomatic partner of the DPRK, provided $2.5 million in aid.[16] The UN Office for the Coordination of Humanitarian Affairs (UNOCHA) attempted systematically to record total assistance for the year 1998, although it recorded only reported donations and therefore under-recorded total assistance. Nevertheless, it reported that in 1998 the United States provided just over 50 percent of total assistance to the DPRK, worth about $173 million. The EU, China, and the Republic of Korea provided the next-largest sums of assistance, at 15 percent, 8 percent, and 8 percent respectively.[17]

For 1999, the major donor was the United States, with a massive 85 percent of total assistance, a cash value of $161 million.[18] Neither Japan nor South Korea was recorded as a donor in this calendar year. For the year 2000 some 77 percent of all recorded humanitarian assistance to the DPRK —worth $135 million—came from three countries: the Republic of Korea (41 percent of the total), Japan (20 percent), and the United States (17 percent).[19] The analogous figure for 2001 was 78 percent, with a value of about $265 million.[20] Japan provided 46 percent of total assistance, the United States some 40 percent, and the Republic of Korea some 7 percent.[21] In 2002, Japan declined to give further assistance, and the United States and the Republic of Korea remained by far the largest donors.

A New Dynamic in DPRK Politics and Society

The various humanitarian agencies active in the DPRK had diverse mandates and methods of operation, even if their main assistance remained food aid. Initial responses came in the form of individual and largely fragmented donations of food and health assistance from UN agencies, bilateral governmental agencies, and NGOs. These ad hoc responses became institutionalized after 1997, in such a way as to eventually have a significant impact on DPRK society. Westerners became resident in the DPRK as the agencies for whom they worked established a long-term presence. Many of these foreigners had very different views on what constituted a "good society" than did their hosts. Those most free to express these alternative views were NGO staff.

Prior to 1995, the DPRK had only a very limited experience of international humanitarian or development agencies. The UNDP, the oldest of the resident agencies, had established an office in Pyongyang in 1980, but it had a tiny staff complement, and activities were more or less limited to formal dialogue with government officials in Pyongyang.[22] The only other significant experience that the DPRK had of humanitarian agencies was contact with the Red Cross movement, but these relationships had operated at very senior levels, mainly when political contacts had needed to be made between North and South Korea.[23]

The DPRK had hosted delegations from Western NGOs such as the American Friends Service Committee. Nevertheless, these nongovernmental contacts had had only a superficial effect on DPRK society. Visiting Westerners, including scholars from universities and cultural delegations from abroad, were able to catch only glimpses of DPRK society. Moreover, few DPRK citizens other than senior party officials had had anything other than the most cursory contact with these visitors. In contrast, the humanitarian NGOs with which the DPRK came into contact after 1995 were enormously diverse in terms of their country of origin, methods of operation, and mandate, as well as in terms of their expectations of the DPRK government.

The residential nature of humanitarian operations brought large numbers of inquisitive foreigners to the DPRK. Among them were a wide variety of NGO staff whose experience of humanitarian operations, Asia, or living in poor countries ranged from extensive to nonexistent. This brought a brand-new dynamic into DPRK society. The DPRK, which had never before had serious interaction with humanitarian agencies, did not understand initially that humanitarian agencies operated on the foundation of common norms with which it would also have to engage. The government also had no idea at first about how to work with genuinely independent nongovernmental organizations.

The Multilateral and Bilateral Agencies

The UN response to the emergency can be traced to the 1995 visit of a UN Disaster Assessment and Coordination (UNDAC) team, consisting of representatives of the WFP, WHO, UNICEF, and the Food and Agriculture Organization (FAO), which visited the country to evaluate flood damage.[24] As a consequence UN missions were expanded and became residential in the DPRK.[25] Between 1995 and 1997, what had started as a negligible in-country international community presence was transformed into a relatively substantial residential operation, including governmental, multilateral, and nongovernmental agencies.

The UNDP remained in-country, but as its mission was primarily in the development sector as opposed to humanitarian operations, its scope was limited—except in the agricultural sector, in which relief and rehabilitation work were conjoined. The WFP established an office in Pyongyang in

November 1995. UNICEF, an important provider of health-related hu-
manitarian assistance throughout the world, opened an office in January
1996; the WHO did so in late 1997.[26] By 2000 the UN Family Planning
Association also had in-country international representation, while the
FAO employed a national officer.[27] Regular visiting missions from smaller
UN agencies, including those with developmental mandates as opposed
to directly humanitarian spheres of interest, such as the World Tourism
Organization, became a feature of the later UN landscape in the DPRK.

In July 1997, the Swiss Disaster Relief Unit (SDR) opened an office in
Pyongyang, followed in August by the European Commission, which employed six international staff members—four from the Commission's Food
Security Unit and two from the Humanitarian Aid department of the
European Community (ECHO).[28] The Italian Development Cooperation Office of the Italian Ministry of Foreign Affairs had a resident presence in Pyongyang from 2001 on.[29] In 2004 the Swiss Agency for Development and Cooperation (under which the old SDR is now subsumed)
and the European Commission retained a major presence in the DPRK.[30]

Nongovernmental Organizations Come to the DPRK

The International Federation of the Red Cross, Caritas, Children's Aid
Direct, and Médecins Sans Frontières (MSF) were among the first NGOs
to offer assistance to the DPRK.[31] Some nongovernmental organizations
became resident, but many more did not. European NGOs were mainly
residential. (It was a condition of NGO funding by the European Community's Humanitarian Office that the agency be resident.) U.S. NGOs
were mainly nonresidential (with the exception of in-country health and
food aid monitors during parts of 1998, 1999, and 2000). South Korean
and Japanese NGOs were nonresidential. The Canadian NGOs operated
as nonresidents. A huge number of nonresidential NGOs from all over the
world, including Hong Kong, South Korea, Japan, the United States, and
Canada, maintained a steady stream of humanitarian and later development assistance to the DPRK.[32]

The Residential NGOs

The residential NGOs became an established presence after 1997, when
the International Federation of the Red Cross (IFRC) set up an office in

Pyongyang along with seven much smaller nongovernmental agencies.[33] These seven were Children's Aid Direct (CAD), Concern Worldwide, Cooperazione e Sviluppo (CESVI), Deutsche Welthungerhilfe—known in English as German Agro Action (GAA), Médecins du Monde (MDM), Médecins Sans Frontières (MSF), and Campus fur Christus (Switzerland).[34] In 1998 Action contre la Faim (ACF or Action against Hunger), Help Age International, Oxfam, and Cap Anamur also became resident.[35]

The NGO community fluctuated in number. Between 1995 and 2002, six left and five more arrived. Médecins Sans Frontières (1998), Médecins du Monde (1998), Oxfam (1999), Action against Hunger (2000), Help Age International (2000), and Children's Aid Direct (2002) were the six that left the DPRK.[36] Additions to the resident NGO community were Adventist Development and Relief Agency (ADRA) (Switzerland, 1999) and PMU Interlife (Sweden, 1999); in 2000, Triangle from France; and in 2001 Handicap International, also a French NGO.[37] In 2001 Hungarian Baptist Aid established what it calls "semi-residential" status.[38] In 2002 the French agency Premiere Urgence joined the NGO residential community, followed in 2003 by Save the Children–UK and an Italian Christian NGO, Associazione con i Fatebenefratelli per i Malati Lontani (AFMAL).[39]

The Nonresidential NGOs

Of the nonresidential NGOs, four distinct although not mutually exclusive groups could be discerned by 1997. The first group coordinated their activities through the NGO-funded Food Aid Liaison Unit of the WFP.[40] The second consisted of NGOs from the United States that operated through the Private Voluntary Organization Consortium.[41] A third group worked via sister NGOs, some of which were resident in the DPRK and some of which were not. A fourth group operated bilaterally, directly with the DPRK government, and included South Korean, Japanese, and United States–based NGOs. The first two groups of NGOs (with overlapping membership) operated through a semiresidential presence in the DPRK.

The first consisted of a number of faith-based agencies, which established a coordinating mechanism for logistics, monitoring, and evaluation in 1997 in what they called the Food Aid Liaison Unit (FALU).[42] Operating with one international staff and two national staff tasked with monitoring, evaluation, and reporting, FALU was physically based in the WFP office and benefited from the huge WFP logistics capacity. FALU provided a value-for-money residential base for substantial aid inputs from Caritas, Canadian Foodgrains Bank (CFGB), ACT/Church World Service, World Vision International (WVI), ADRA, Food for the Hungry, and Mercy Corps. As of 2004, FALU remained an important source of assistance, although by 2002, its constituent membership had shrunk, leaving Caritas, CFGB, ACT, and WVI as member organizations.[43]

The second group was also united in a formal, if loose, association. The Private Voluntary Organization Consortium (PVOC) was established in 1997. It consisted of ADRA, Amigos Internacionales, CARE, Catholic Relief Services, the Carter Center, Church World Service, the Korean-American Sharing Movement, the Latter Day Saints Charities, Mercy Corps International, and World Vision.[44] PVOC monitors were based in the DPRK in 1997 for three months with the WFP, in 1998 for six months with UNICEF, and, from late 1998 to 2000, intermittently with the WFP.[45] Three Korean speakers were employed in a team whose numbers changed but consisted of around eight people.[46] The PVOC team left the country when its potato-seed project and food-for-work activities, which its member NGOs had supported, ended in 2000.[47]

The third group consisted of those NGOs that worked through international counterparts, including American NGOs such as the American Red Cross, which supported the International Federation of the Red Cross, and South Korean NGOs such as Caritas-Coreana, which worked through Caritas–Hong Kong.[48] Prior to the thawing of relations between North and South Korea in 2000, South Korean NGOs took advantage of the "partnership" route to avosid direct control over their operations in the DPRK by the South Korean government.[49] South Korean NGOs also channeled their early assistance through their international links or U.S. affiliates because of their anxiety that direct involvement might bring them into conflict with the South Korean National Security Law, which prohibited and punished support for the DPRK. The South Korean Association of Evangelism in Korea, for instance, donated rice through the Eugene Bell Foundation U.S., and the South Korean organization Health Care Workers to Aid North Korean Flood Victims channeled assistance through

UNICEF.[50] World Vision Korea, which sent substantial amounts of assistance to the DPRK, worked through World Vision International. This was a special case, however, since World Vision was founded in South Korea, and its primary mission, despite its worldwide focus, was to alleviate need in Korea.[51]

The fourth group was of NGOs that worked largely bilaterally with the DPRK government, including United States, Japanese, and Korean agencies. Predominant among the U.S. NGOs were AmeriCares, the American Friends Service Committee, and Mercy Corps (in addition to its work within the PVOC).[52] Since there were no diplomatic relations between the DPRK and Japan, and informal relations were minimal, Japanese NGOs tended to work closely with the General Association of Korean Residents in Japan, a long-established organization with close ties to the DPRK government.[53] These NGOs included the Association to Send Eggs and Bananas to the Children of the DPRK, Caritas-Japan, the Relief Campaign Committee for Children, and the National Christian Council in Japan.[54] As restrictions eased on the activities of South Korean NGOs, many openly began to operate directly with the DPRK government. By 2000 the most important sources of South Korean NGO assistance to the DPRK included the Korean Sharing Movement, Iussaran Association, World Vision, Join Together Society, the Eugene Bell Foundation, the Korean People's Welfare Foundation, and Caritas-Coreana.[55] By June 2001 at least eighteen South Korean NGOs were donating humanitarian assistance to the DPRK.[56]

Safeguarding Human Security

The first international agencies to respond to DPRK appeals for assistance were those with an already-established relationship with the DPRK —the WFP, UNICEF, and UNDP—along with the International Federation of the Red Cross (IFRC) and the Catholic NGO Caritas–Hong Kong.[57] UNDP was known to the DPRK authorities because of its presence in Pyongyang since 1980. UNICEF had been carrying out work with the DPRK since 1985, and the FAO and the WFP had first signed a "Basic Agreement" with the DPRK in 1986. Of the NGOs, Caritas–Hong Kong first started meeting with DPRK officials in 1993.

The WFP delivered just over 18,000 metric tons of rice, to a value of about $4.5 million, excluding freight and monitoring costs, between November 1995 and May 1996.[58] UNICEF's initial response in 1995–96 was to provide around $2 million worth of supplementary food for young children, measles immunization, oral rehydration salts, and multivitamin tablets.[59] The IFRC appealed for 26 million Swiss francs in September 1995, March 1996, and November 1996 and donated a variety of food aid, including 22 metric tons of cereals, along with nonfood items such as winter clothing.[60] Caritas mobilized $5.5 million in its first year of assistance, 1995–96, allocating $4.5 million to food aid, about $0.5 million to agriculture, and the rest to various social sectors, including education.[61]

Less visible and less recorded—because of the fear of home government restrictions—was the delivery of aid from Japanese and South Korean NGOs, which also began in 1994–95. World Vision Korea, for instance, began an emergency relief program in the DPRK in 1994, and Korea Food for the Hungry International sent medical equipment and clothes in 1994 and 1995.[62]

The Scope and Scale of the Aid Effort

From mid-1996 on, appeals for assistance were integrated through the United Nations' coordinating mechanism of the consolidated inter-agency appeal process. This worldwide mechanism for coordinating responses to humanitarian disasters produced nine appeals for the DPRK, up to and including the appeal for 2004. The first two UN appeals incorporated only UN agencies, but later appeals included all other residential and some nonresidential humanitarian activity. The volumes of assistance requested increased exponentially from 1996 until 2001. Only in the seventh appeal, for 2002, did the amount of the appeal decrease. This reduced appeal reflected both an improvement in the previous year's harvest (in 2001) and an acknowledgment of "donor fatigue" in fund-raising for the DPRK.

The first UN Consolidated Inter-Agency Appeal was for $43.6 million and ran from July 1, 1996, to March 30, 1997.[63] Food assistance, support for the recovery of arable land, and health assistance were requested.[64] By the close of the appeal some $34 million had been raised.[65] The second consolidated appeal was for $126,226,177 for the period from April 1, 1997, to March 31, 1998. In July 1997, the total requirement for the second appeal was increased to $184 million.[66] Some $158 million was raised—an over-80 percent response rate.[67] Some 80 percent of the total appeal was for food aid, and here donors overfulfilled the target, providing 119 percent of the food assistance requested.[68]

The third appeal, which was the first to incorporate resident NGO with UN agency requests for funding, ran from January 1, 1998, through December 31, 1998. It was for $415,648,979, of which $345,801,900 (or 90 percent) was for food assistance.[69] Although only about 57 percent of the appeal was funded, the entire cereal component of the appeal was received, and 99.6 percent of the food tonnage originally requested as lower-value commodities replaced commodities of a higher monetary value.[70] Food and health needs remained reasonably well covered by donors in the 1998 appeal. Agriculture fared less well: the FAO received just over 80 percent of the $3 million requested, and the UNDP received none of the more than $5 million it had sought.[71]

The fourth appeal, in 1999, was for $376,112,894, although of that sum $101,358,000 worth of food was already in the pipeline at the time of the appeal, leaving $274,754,894 to be raised.[72] Of the latter sum, about 89 percent, or approximately $243 million, was for food assistance and the promotion of food security.[73] In contrast to the huge sums requested for food assistance, only small amounts were allocated to other sectors—with $28 million given over to the health appeals.[74] Again, just over 50 percent was funded—the WFP received over 100 percent of its appeal, while the UNDP again received zero percent of its requested funds, UNICEF just under 25 percent of the $20 million requested, and the WHO just over half a million of the $7 million requested.[75] UNICEF and the WHO were the major agencies involved in health assistance, and underfunding meant that urgent health programs could not be carried out.

The initial fifth appeal, for the year 2000, was for $331,706,092, with about 92 percent, or approximately $241 million, for food assistance.[76] The appeal was reduced during 2000 to $197,466,381, after the WFP recalculated the dollar value of food aid required—with $106,250,000 destined for the WFP.[77] Again, although overall the appeal was only funded to just over 50 percent of the target, food aid through the WFP was fully funded. The UNDP/FAO received just 6 percent of the $53 million requested, and the UNDP and UNFPA received zero percent of their individual appeals, while the key health agencies of UNICEF and the WHO received just 11 percent (of $18 million) and 17 percent (of $8 million), respectively.[78]

The sixth appeal, for 2001, was for $383,984,914—with all but about $60 million destined for WFP food aid.[79] Even though relatively small sums were requested for health, water, sanitation, and support for agricultural recovery, these sectors continued to attract very limited support from donors. Indeed, the agencies warned that the basic humanitarian program was jeopardized due to the agencies' inability to deliver an integrated response to the humanitarian crisis.[80] By October 2001, for instance, UNICEF had been pledged just 30 percent of the $10.5 million it required, and the WHO received 16 percent of approximately $8 million requested.[81]

In 2002, for the first time, the UN consolidated appeal for the DPRK was for a reduced amount compared to the previous year's request: $258,136,111 was the target.[82] The vast majority of the appeal was again destined to support food aid, with $213,605,401 targeted for the World Food Program.[83] Support for agricultural recovery, health, water, and sanitation support and education were to be funded from the balance of about $45 million, subject to donor support.[84]

The eighth and ninth appeals, for 2003 and 2004, respectively, stabilized at about $222 million; the 2003 appeal was funded at about 56 percent of its target.[85] The vast majority of the appeal continued to consist of requests for food aid to be channeled through the World Food Program—some $197 million for 2003 and $190 million in the 2004 appeal.[86]

The NGO Contribution

NGO assistance to the DPRK was much smaller in dollar and volume terms than aid from the multilateral and bilateral agencies. The value of these residential operations was more in the ability of small NGOs to operate in "niche" sectors other than food—water/sanitation, agricultural recovery, and health—and in a more in-depth manner than was possible for the larger operations.[87] NGO interaction with DPRK authorities also provided an intangible asset to humanitarian operation, as NGOs continually reinforced expectations of improved transparency and accountability.

It is not easy to quantify the precise amount of NGO assistance from various sources, as there is no central record of NGO activity in the DPRK. From 1998 on, the UN Office for the Coordination of Humanitarian Assistance (UNOCHA) collected and published details of all assistance to the DPRK in the annual consolidated inter-agency appeal document, including that *not* donated via the UN consolidated appeal process. These records, however, were entirely dependent on reports made to UNOCHA, and inevitably some aid will have been unaccounted for.

The International Federation of the Red Cross and the Caritas agencies provided the most significant volumes of NGO assistance. Of the resident NGOs, by far the largest contributor to the DPRK was the International Federation of the Red Cross, which spent some $90 million between 1995 and 2002.[88] The IFRC's main activity remained in the health sector, but it also supplied food aid and, in 2002, was the lead agency in disaster-preparedness planning for the humanitarian community.

Of the nonresident NGOs, Caritas–Hong Kong made a significant contribution. It acted as liaison agency on behalf of the worldwide Caritas network and, between 1995 and March 2001, supplied some $27 million worth of assistance.[89] Caritas–Hong Kong also coordinated contributions from the Canadian Foodgrains Bank and the U.S. faith-based NGO the Mennonite Central Committee (MCC). If CFGB and MCC contributions are included, the Caritas effort amounted to some $42 million worth of assistance.[90] Caritas worked mainly in the food, agricultural recovery, and health sectors, while CFGB and the MCC mainly provided food.[91]

There is no aggregate data on the volumes of assistance provided by the dozen or so European resident NGOs, but their programs were relatively small. Between 1996 and 2000, a total of 49 million euros (about $35 million) was spent on programs by seven NGOs—CESVI, Concern, Children's Aid Direct, Action contre la Faim, German Agro Action, Médecins Sans Frontières, and Triangle—as well as the IFRC.[92] None of the other resident NGOs' programs involved very large expenditures: the 2002 appeal for seven resident NGOs amounted collectively to about $7 million, out of a total of $258 million.[93]

South Korean NGOs provided the bulk of nonresidential NGO assistance. That from Japan, the United States, and other countries remained tiny, if symbolic of a broad international coalition to provide humanitarian relief to the DPRK.[94] The South Korean government estimated that South Korean NGOs transferred about $130 million worth of assistance to the DPRK between 1995 and 2001, compared to a U.S. NGO expenditure of probably less than $10 million in the same period and a Japanese NGO expenditure of even less.[95] Assistance provided by these NGOs was important for its intrinsic value: to feed hungry people and help in agricultural recovery. Another important contribution was to open non-governmental channels with South Korea and Japan, countries with which the DPRK had had little interaction for nearly half a century.

Assessing the Effectiveness of Humanitarian Agencies

The alleviation of human insecurity through saving lives was and is the primary aim of humanitarian agencies. The secondary aim was to help create the conditions for sustainable human development—aiming to produce an exit strategy that would ensure human security in terms of freedom from want without a continued dependence on humanitarian assistance. Humanitarian agencies shared an analysis that the latter objective was not likely to be achieved without domestic economic and political change. They differed on how to promote such change.

The vast majority did not demand radical policy change from the DPRK government. Either their mandates precluded their direct advocacy of this position, or they did not expect that such direct advocacy would achieve the desired results. Instead, most agencies chose to engage in long-term confidence building while at the same time, in their technical negotiations with the government, insisting that in-country humanitarian operations were underpinned by the basic organizational principles that underpinned their activities worldwide.

How Do We Know Who Benefited?

In any humanitarian emergency, it is difficult to assess whether international assistance made the crucial difference to survival. Personal survival is always the result of a combination of individual coping mechanisms, which may or may not include access to international aid. In the DPRK, assessing the impact of international assistance was especially difficult, because the government restricted unmonitored evaluations by agencies. The government's frame of reference was that the country was constantly vulnerable to military attack and that therefore the provision of any socio-economic information had the effect of supplying data to its enemies, who could then better assess its vulnerabilities.

Nevertheless, the government did regularly provide social statistics to the agencies. This data was systematically used by the agencies from 2001 on, after the WFP reorganized and restructured its information, monitoring, reporting, and evaluation systems. A comprehensive information collection and dissemination capacity was created in 2000–2001 to try to make better use of the various information available to the WFP.[96]

Agencies never gave up on the battle to secure reliable quantitative information. Indeed, they managed to negotiate the implementation of three nutrition surveys, in 1998, 2002, and 2004. These, along with the 1998 UNICEF Multiple Indicator Cluster Survey (MICS), provided valuable quantitative data on vulnerability.[97] Nutrition assessments were considered an essential tool for the agencies but were not welcomed by the government, again because of its reluctance to share information with foreigners. Smaller institutional or geographically specific nutrition surveys were also implemented by NGOs.[98] The twice-yearly FAO/WFP food and crop assessment reports also supplied "hard" analysis based on a mix of satellite imagery, government data, and reports from field visits.[99] NGOs, because they concentrated on just a few institutions in a small number of counties, were able to complement WFP breadth of analysis with NGO depth of activity and involvement.[100]

Another constraint on monitoring capacities was the sheer scale of the operation. By 2000 the food aid program was the largest in the WFP's history and the largest in the world in that year.[101] In 2001 the World Food Program delivered 1 million tons of food aid, feeding at the height of the lean season some 8.5 million people, the largest operation in its history.[102] This 1 million tons of food aid was distributed in 50-kilo bags. In this operation not every bag of rice could be counted, nor could every child receiving aid be visited.

The difficulties in obtaining good quantitative data meant that the humanitarian agencies also relied on qualitative data. Assessments combined quantitative and qualitative analysis to give some indication of whether

assistance was meeting the needs of hungry people.[103] Qualitative data
was provided from the thousands of visits from experienced professional
humanitarian workers, who systematically and regularly documented
needs, vulnerabilities, and the impact of international assistance. In 1999,
the largest of the agencies, the World Food Program, increased its monitoring activities to some 400 to 500 visits per month. All counties, except
the minority that were off-limits to humanitarian workers, were visited
regularly.[104]

All NGOs carried out prior assessment and postevaluation of projects.
Although these were often tiny compared to the major UN projects, all
agency fieldwork activities and observations were regularly shared through
in-country coordination. Interagency meetings were held weekly, and
intersectoral meetings were held biweekly or monthly.[105] NGO, bilateral,
and multilateral agency workers were thus able to build a comparative
picture of need and to cross-check experiences where they overlapped in
the field. The system did not always work perfectly, but the point is that
an operable and operational coordination system was institutionalized by
1998 and grew to provide an efficient method of sharing and disseminating information.

A small minority of counties, mostly sparsely populated and in remote
areas, remained excluded from humanitarian assessment and therefore
humanitarian programming.[106] The DPRK government stated this was
for "security reasons." In practice, these counties were situated mainly on
the northern or southern borders and were home to military garrisons and
munitions factories. There were some exceptions to the rule of "no access
—no aid." Nationwide immunization programs supported by UNICEF
and the WHO, for instance, were also carried out in nonaccessible counties. Some of these counties gradually became accessible for humanitarian work, although as of June 2002 there were still 43 counties out of
203, accounting for about 18 percent of the population, not accessible
to humanitarian agencies.[107] It was impossible to obtain information on
who might be hungry and how the poorest were managing to cope in
these areas.[108]

It was not possible to conduct surveys of households; the county provided the lowest available level of useful analysis. Neither was it possible
to monitor the impact of assistance on individuals, other than to make an

assessment from an individual visit. This was partly because of the size of the operation and partly because repeat visits to the same individual beneficiaries were rarely permitted.[109] Nor was it possible for the agencies to assess whether all of the beneficiaries were being fed through international assistance. If a child was sick and could not attend kindergarten or school, for instance, it always remained unclear whether that child received international food assistance, since all international food aid targeted for children was channeled through the children's institutions and not directly to families.

Agencies were, however, able to measure humanitarian "inputs" and "outputs." The amount of food as "input," for instance, could be derived from various fairly reliable international sources of data on trade, aid, and agricultural production as well as government figures. Outputs could also be measured pretty reasonably and accurately—for example, the number of people fed in aggregate terms, the number of trees planted in reforestation schemes, the number of individuals sent on study trips abroad. Measuring "outcome" or "impact"—to what extent aid had made a difference—was more difficult, given the lack of direct access to beneficiaries of assistance.

In summary, aggregate and county-level analyses of food shortages and vulnerability analysis of different sectors of the population became possible through the increasingly systematic and well-researched documentation provided by the humanitarian community itself, notably the FAO/WFP crop and food assessment reports and the three nutrition surveys. Humanitarian agencies had available to them increasingly sophisticated if imperfect data through which they could evaluate overall needs and vulnerability, that is, which groups of the population were more vulnerable and for what reasons. The weakest aspect of the information base was the absence of direct data from individual households so as to evaluate more efficiently the impact of assistance.

Saving Lives

There is no way to assess how many lives were saved through international aid, including food aid. Proxy indicators as to the effectiveness of food aid include changes in rates of malnutrition, incidence and prevalence of low birth weight, usually counted as 2.5 kilograms or less, and qualitative assessments.[110] In the DPRK quantitative and qualitative evidence on change in rates of malnutrition provided the baseline evidence for making judgments as to whether or not international assistance saved lives.

The incidence of severe malnutrition observed throughout the country from the time humanitarian agencies first arrived in 1995 was quantified in 1998 after the WFP, UNICEF, and the European Union carried out an extensive nutrition survey in collaboration with the government.[111] About 16 percent of children under seven demonstrated severe malnutrition, which meant that between 400,000 and 500,000 young children were at imminent risk of death.[112] Some 62 percent of children aged under seven suffered from chronic malnutrition—a staggering 1.7 million children whose nutrition was so inadequate that they could not achieve normal height for their age.[113]

The agencies, again in conjunction with the government, carried out another national nutrition survey in late 2002. The results of the 2002 survey confirmed the hundreds of reports from government officials, nurseries, schools, and hospitals that, from 1998 on, the rate of severe malnutrition in children had visibly declined and chronic malnutrition had somewhat decreased.[114] This nutrition assessment, published in 2003, allowed for comparisons between nutritional levels in 1998 and in 2002.[115] Chronic and severe malnutrition still existed, but the nutritional levels of children aged under seven were now on a par with those in Cambodia and Indonesia. The only source of food for the vast majority of these children was international aid and domestic grain production. Thus this food must have been reaching the targeted beneficiaries of children under seven.

Regular reporting from humanitarian officials confirmed the improvement in nutritional status, but they also showed that the worst cases of child malnutrition were in the "orphanages" in each of the twelve provinces. Not all children in these institutions were orphans. Increasingly, the poorest families with parents and relatives unable to cope placed hungry and sick children in these institutions, knowing they were guaranteed 24-hour access to food and both international and state support.

Humanitarian agencies were sure they had saved lives. What they did not know but never stopped trying to find out was whether they were saving all the lives they ought to be. They knew they were reaching the most vulnerable in aggregate terms—women, children, the sick, the elderly—

but they could not tell if they were meeting the needs of all these most vulnerable people. In October 2001 David Morton, the UN humanitarian coordinator, argued that "we know that there is a very serious crisis that affects millions of people. We have no doubt that our aid has saved many, many lives."[116]

Relief to Recovery

The exit strategy for the DPRK, as in any emergency food operation, was that indigenous economic recovery needed to take place so that the country could meet its own food needs through a combination of increased agricultural production and food imports. The international community's most substantial contribution in this respect took place in the agricultural sector and was led by the UNDP, which worked in coordination with the government and donors using the 1998 Agricultural Recovery and Environmental Protection (AREP) plan. The AREP plan was unrealistic in its ambitions, declaring that the country could become self-sufficient in food by 2001. Nevertheless, it was successful as an effective and surprisingly transparent mechanism for government–international community collaboration.[117] The AREP model also provided a pattern for future cooperation when the government and UNDP agreed in 2001 that the coordinating mechanisms used for agriculture should be adapted and used to frame future collaboration in the energy and transport sectors.[118]

The AREP process supported agricultural policy changes that included increased emphasis on double-cropping, a massive campaign to introduce potato as a staple crop, reorganization of farm-working practices, and, more discreetly, the eventual acceptance of farmers' markets as legitimate arenas for price-setting and distribution.[119] Policy changes combined with inputs from international assistance programs resulted in sharp increases in grain harvests in 2001, despite few signs of a resuscitation of the wider economy.[120] Grain harvests continued to improve—although not to the extent that the chronic food shortage could be solved by the government through domestic production as of 2004.[121]

With agencies, donors, and government working jointly through the monitoring and evaluation aspects of the AREP plan, the agricultural sector of the DPRK economy became very open to international scrutiny. The UNDP was careful to fulfill its mandate to report to donors and to the wider international community on its activities in the DPRK. In addition, foreign agronomists, including those from South Korea, made frequent visits to farms, the Academy of Agricultural Sciences, and the Ministry of Agriculture and were able to make direct professional assessments of changes to crops, yields, and social infrastructures. As the operation wore on, many of these professional and technical assessments could be compared over time, as agronomists and agencies made regular repeat visits to the same farms, counties, and officials. The UNDP operated only as an umbrella organization, coordinating and monitoring overall progress, which meant that regular visits from international officials were not confined to UNDP representatives but included technically qualified personnel from agencies ranging from small NGOs (CESVI and Concern Worldwide, for example) to large multilaterals, most importantly the International Fund for Agricultural Development (IFAD).[122]

International organizations developed much more trust-based relationships with DPRK counterparts and the government in agricultural recovery work than in the area of food assistance. The reasons were partly that the relatively small scale of the program made monitoring an easier task, partly that technical experts from overseas and from the DPRK were able to work closely together on the basis of a common professional knowledge base, and partly that the effective consultative process concerning the creation and implementation of the AREP plan ensured joint ownership of the program.[123] In comparison with specifically targeted agricultural assistance, food aid is inherently fungible. Food assistance does not have to be clandestinely diverted to nonbeneficiaries, as the simple existence of international food aid facilitates the allocation of domestic food production to governmental priority groups, such as the military.

The relative success in promoting transparency and accountability in agriculture did not mean that the agencies remained without concerns. In late 2001 the residential agencies were still calling on the government to provide more extensive social and economic data to allow better planning for rehabilitation and development in the future.[124]

Agricultural recovery was not as well supported by the international donor community as food aid. Donors were ambivalent about the merits of pursuing a recovery program that might assist in the strengthening of a government and system of which they disapproved. At the same time, donors recognized that agricultural aid was an appropriate form of development assistance for the DPRK because of its obvious contribution to the restoration of national food security. Despite these tensions, the agricultural sector effectively formed a "bridge" into development assistance for the DPRK, especially after the June 2000 North-South summit, when the South gave more support for fertilizer aid and South Korean NGOs, particularly the International Corn Federation and World Vision, took a prominent role in financially supporting agricultural recovery.[125]

Building Capacity

Early efforts at agency involvement with capacity building were resisted by the DPRK government. It argued that only inputs were necessary to resuscitate agriculture and the economy. DPRK policymakers were aware of the implicit, sometimes explicit, aims of the humanitarian community and the major donors to encourage a more open society in the DPRK and wary of "training" elements of humanitarian programs that might contribute to that end. Initially, official pronouncements commented that aid was like "sugar with poison"—needed and wanted but containing the germs of debilitation, perhaps destruction, of the DPRK model of society.[126] By the late 1990s, however, the DPRK authorities were persuaded of the benefits of retraining. By 1999–2000 the agencies were incorporating capacity-building projects throughout their programs at the request of the government as well as at their own instigation.[127]

The WFP sent DPRK officials to India and Cambodia in 2001 to familiarize them with other food aid operations. UNICEF attempted to deal with what it called the "knowledge gap" through training and, for example, sent DPRK statisticians to Australia and DPRK officials to Thailand to research HIV/AIDS in 2001.[128] Campus fur Christus sent Koreans to Switzerland to receive training in goat farming.[129] The Swiss Agency for Development and Cooperation (SDC) developed a systematic program of training where they sent officials abroad, including to Switzerland and China. In 2002 the SDC, in coordination with the UNDP, also supported a comprehensive capacity-building project designed to help DPRK officials learn about development assistance and resource mobilization.[130]

The DPRK government developed a proactive policy to learning from the resident international organizations. It placed government officials

within the agencies—often for periods of two or three years, and sometimes more. DPRK officials effectively received on-the-job training in
international policies, procedures, and methods of operation, developing skills and experience useful for those later in contact with the outside world.

Government attacks on the motivations behind assistance did not continue past 1998. Although suspicions remained, by 2000–2001 the DPRK
government was actively seeking training opportunities from multilateral,
bilateral, and nongovernmental agencies. Evidently, it was persuaded that
ideas and skills from the capitalist West had something to offer the DPRK.
The humanitarian agencies, as the only regular source of intensive contact
with the outside world, were clearly the source of this new openness in government policy. They were committed to the often frustrating practice of
patient negotiating, aiming at long-term paybacks as well as short-term
achievements. This strategy proved successful, at least in the context of the
limited goals of introducing alternative ways of working into the DPRK.

Negotiating and Implementing
Humanitarian Norms and Principles

As the in-country presence of international agencies lengthened, agencies
that had more or less agreed on the nature of the emergency in the DPRK
and the necessity for food and other assistance disagreed on how to deal
with the DPRK government on the issue of humanitarian norms. A minority argued that there was no humanitarian space whatsoever in the DPRK
and that agencies should not continue operations.[131] Another minority
stated that the DPRK was being held to standards higher than those
expected of governments in other humanitarian contexts. The majority,
however, argued that the implementation of humanitarian norms in the
DPRK was not satisfactory but that it had improved since the start of the
operations, and negotiations were appropriate and effective as a mechanism to achieve objectives. By 2004 this majority voice remained the prevailing and uncontested approach. The withdrawal approach was rejected
by the vast majority of humanitarian agencies. Instead the 2001 consensus statement from resident multilateral, bilateral, and nongovernmental
organizations continued to provide a common platform for negotiating
with the DPRK government.[132]

The most extreme reaction was that of four agencies that withdrew from the DPRK between 1998 and 2000, citing unacceptable restrictions on monitoring and evaluation activities. These were Médecins sans Frontières, Médecins du Monde, Action contre la Faim, and Oxfam. Oxfam returned in 2002, although this time as a nonresidential partner with the DPRK.[133] MSF, MDM, and Action contre la Faim voiced concerns that they were not reaching the most vulnerable children and that the difficulties and constraints they faced prevented adequate assessment, monitoring, and evaluation activities.[134] Oxfam left because it was concerned about constraints on adequate monitoring and assessment, not of beneficiaries, but of the water facilities it was testing. MDM had also experienced funding difficulties, as did Help Age International, another agency that also withdrew from the DPRK, although without publicly stating its reasons.[135] Children's Aid Direct also terminated its operations worldwide in 2002, including in the DPRK, after it could no longer attract funds for its programs. Of the nonresident NGOs only two U.S.-based NGOs decided to cease operations in the DPRK, citing operational constraints, including the inability to conduct adequate assessment, monitoring, and evaluation activities. These were CARE and Catholic Relief Services (CRS).[136]

The second view, also in the minority, was more sympathetic to DPRK efforts to support international humanitarian agencies. The major Canadian humanitarian agency involved in the DPRK, the Canadian Foodgrains Bank (CFGB), which had supplied assistance since 1996, argued that monitoring worked relatively well in the DPRK and found that the quality of monitoring "would exceed the average monitoring of CFGB program[s]."[137] Explicitly cautious about making comparisons to other operations, the CFGB nevertheless commented that "the provision of humanitarian assistance is [a] messy business which requires the weighing of options between 'less than ideal' approaches . . . in comparison with some other contexts, the concerns in the DPRK do not come close to the diversions and human rights violations of other contexts."[138] This view was implicitly corroborated in a U.S. government publication, generally critical of the DPRK, which nevertheless reported that U.S. NGOs monitoring activities on-site exceeded those in other countries.[139]

By far the vast majority of resident NGOs, all the bilateral multilateral agencies, plus the dozens of nonresident NGOs working in the DPRK took the view that humanitarian assistance benefited hungry and needy people in the DPRK, that it did reach targeted groups, particularly women and children, and that it did save lives. The agencies, however, were not satisfied that they ever achieved the optimal conditions for assessment, monitoring, and evaluation and engaged in consistent, patient negotiation to try to improve these conditions.

Agencies negotiated jointly and singly on operational issues but cooperated when negotiating on broad "humanitarian principles" with the government, working through the good offices of the UN humanitarian coordinator, whose function it was to coordinate UN, bilateral, and NGO in-country humanitarian operations. Individual and joint negotiations with the DPRK government focused on access—to information, facilities, geographical regions, and beneficiary groups. Access to beneficiary groups was for diverse purposes—assessing needs and vulnerability, monitoring distribution of assistance, and evaluating the impact or outcome of providing international assistance. Humanitarian agencies also tried to negotiate to improve conditions for international officers operating in the field outside Pyongyang. In late 1998, after Médecins Sans Frontières made its well-publicized exit from the country, resident agencies collaborated to produce a set of humanitarian principles, developed initially partly with the involvement of DPRK officials and later used as a foundation for collective negotiations with the DPRK government.

Humanitarian Principles

The November 1998 set of humanitarian principles was reaffirmed in April 1999 and again in March 2001, on the last occasion after the withdrawal of Action contre la Faim from the country. The agencies also issued three "consensus statements" in November 1998, December 1999 (after Oxfam's withdrawal), and March 2001.[140] The humanitarian principles were monitored through a series of "benchmarks" developed by the in-country humanitarian-development working group consisting of all the resident humanitarian agencies. Progress on the benchmarks was regularly recorded in reports on the implementation of the Common Humanitarian Assistance Plan, which was coordinated by UNOCHA.

Seven of the nine humanitarian principles were intended to directly address the needs of beneficiaries or potential beneficiaries. They were the insistence on knowledge being available so as to assess needs; an assurance that aid reaches those who most need it; access for assessment, monitoring, and evaluation; distribution of assistance only to where access is granted to humanitarian agencies; protection of the humanitarian interests of the population; support to local capacity building; and beneficiary participation in program planning and implementation.[141] The two remaining principles were concerned with improving conditions for international humanitarian workers—calling for adequate capacity in terms of international staff and a commitment to address the health and safety needs of humanitarian workers in the field.[142]

The consensus statements stressed progress that had been made as well as the value of staying involved with the DPRK. While explicitly calling for improved humanitarian working conditions, the statement reiterated the bottom line, which was that lives were being saved in the DPRK through the humanitarian presence. The 2001 statement argued:

> We are convinced that our engagement, maintenance of an in-country presence and an adherence to the Humanitarian Principles have been positive factors in improving the situation for the people of DPR Korea and that this approach continues to be the best way to proceed. In particular the humanitarian and rehabilitation programmes implemented in the country during the last five years have, without doubt, achieved positive results for people in much of the country.[143]

Some Successes . . . but a Long Way to Go

Negotiations with the government continued to be difficult, and progress was not discernable in all areas. Access to information relating to specific agency operations increased through the years of the emergency, and the quality of data improved, although suspicions remained as to the veracity and reliability of quantitative data. This was partly because it was never clear how information had been collected and partly because of doubts about the government's continuing capacity to collect reliable data on a nationwide basis. As the extent of the operations deepened and broadened, however, and the government became more relaxed about the motivations of agencies, much more opportunity became available for cross-checking and comparison between agencies. Access to the population also increased. By June 2002, 163 out of 206 counties were accessible, compared to 159 counties out of 211 in May 1997 (the total number of counties diminished with administrative reorganization in 2002).[144]

The negotiations around the implementation of the first two nutrition surveys—which took place in 1998 and 2002—symbolized the various perspectives on the role of aid and agencies as well as the change in attitude over the four years dividing the two sets of negotiations.[145] The DPRK government had to be persuaded of the rationale for what it considered intrusive investigations of its society, and the international agencies demanded random surveys as a litmus test of the DPRK government's commitment to transparency and accountability. The 1998 negotiations provided a crash course in international humanitarian agency operating procedures for the DPRK government. Real, if small, gains were made in the direction of mutual trust and increased openness.[146]

The 1998 nutrition survey produced an internationally credible survey, but the government was deeply angered when the international agencies unilaterally released the results in November 1998. Negotiations for the next survey took four years; for the international community the survey became a totem of the DPRK government's commitment to honesty and openness in its dealings with the West. The 2002 negotiations, although still arduous, were informed by a government side that had increased its understanding of the value and necessity of providing accurate information and transparency of operations—if only because this was what was required by donor governments. The government also had learned that it could not operate unilaterally. In 2001 it had attempted to do so, presenting a survey of its own that had included ludicrous statements, such as that the country had 100 percent access to safe water. The agencies had chosen to studiously ignore the 2001 government survey, which would have had the effect, if publicized, of bringing the government into further disrepute with key donors.

Negotiations also resulted in some increased beneficiary input. The WFP, for instance, held a number of participatory provincial workshops on nutrition and food-for-work procedures involving local medical personnel, care workers, and officials. The Swiss Agency for Development Cooperation increasingly demanded and achieved greater input by what it terms its "stakeholders"—farmers and counterparts from the Ministry of Agriculture.[147] Increased acceptance of capacity building or training as a necessary component of programs was particularly significant. Initial attempts to persuade the DPRK government of the value of training had been repeatedly rejected, as the government had previously insisted that only "inputs" (food, money, and equipment) were required to reinvigorate the economy.

Some improvements took place in the working conditions of humanitarian workers living in Pyongyang. They moved out of hotels and into apartments, earned driver's licenses, and were permitted to drive freely around Pyongyang and down to the west coast port of Nampo.[148] Restrictions remained on the field workers based in the remote areas outside Pyongyang, who were not permitted outside hotels unaccompanied and who were left virtually in solitary confinement after daily visits were completed, remaining isolated for up to three weeks at a time. Conditions were somewhat mitigated after the WFP established telephone and e-mail access for its field workers, but radio communication among staff in the field remained prohibited "on national security grounds." The five WFP suboffices throughout the country acted in effect as resources for the wider international community, being based in provincial hotels in which aid workers from other agencies were also accommodated.

The agencies never argued that they were wholly able to fulfill the most important of the humanitarian principles: the protection of the humanitarian interests of the population. This would have required control of factors outside the purview of humanitarian agency control, including donor capacity and willingness to aid the DPRK and DPRK governmental willingness to radically change its system of government and society. Instead, the majority of agencies chose to work within the parameters given and to attempt to "push the envelope" to try to overcome constraints and negotiate to improve humanitarian operating conditions.

Trickle-Down Diplomacy

The unprecedented call for international assistance from the DPRK government meant that it came into contact with major donors of international humanitarian assistance—including the United States, Japan, and South Korea—as a dependent but, importantly, interactive partner, even if this partnership was often one step removed, via mediation of the multilateral and nongovernmental humanitarian agencies. The constant negotiations that took place between the DPRK and officers of major international humanitarian agencies had to take into account the interests and concerns of adversaries, because these were also the major donors of humanitarian assistance to the DPRK.

Contact with donors came about through visiting donor delegations. The UNDP-AREP process provided the most systematic mechanism of engagement between the DPRK government, the agencies, and donors, as the AREP plan had included as an essential element an enormous process of preparation and consultation between the DPRK, UNDP, and donor governments. This started with a joint briefing by government and international officers of donor countries and international organizations represented in Pyongyang in March 1998.[149] This briefing was followed up by joint government-UNDP visits to twelve Asian and European capitals, New York, and Washington to consult on the document, prior to another presentation to an EU mission visiting Pyongyang in May 1998. All this "sensitization" effort was undertaken before the official meeting to discuss the plan, held in Geneva in late May 1998.

The AREP negotiation gave DPRK ministers and representatives of donor nations the opportunity for direct and frank dialogue. The 2002 Geneva meeting heard the director of USAID say that the United States "cannot support the AREP proposal" as it "was prohibited by law for the provision of development assistance to the DPRK" before discussing the shortcomings of the plan in some detail.[150] At the same meeting the vice minister of foreign affairs of the DPRK reported on how difficult it was for the DPRK to become a beneficiary nation, commenting that "in the past, the DPRK was a donor country, and it had had to learn how to receive assistance."[151] Here the DPRK representative was referring to its former agricultural aid to some of the poorer countries in Africa.

The AREP negotiations were never regarded as merely technical by any of the actors concerned, as agricultural and food security policy was for all sides simply one aspect of the socioeconomy of the DPRK. Donors saw the AREP talks as an opportunity to discuss what they considered were necessary reforms in the direction of a market economy in the DPRK. For the South Koreans, the AREP process was seen as a contribution to

South-North cooperation, whose aim was to support North Korea in its efforts for agricultural recovery and economic development, arguing that "the AREP 2000–2002 win [*sic*] provide the necessary impetus for North Korea to use the progress made so far as stepping stones towards a much brighter future."[152]

The AREP process permitted direct talks between donors and the DPRK and provided one channel in which formal and informal discussion could take place between partners whose political relations were highly conflictual. It was not the only channel of dialogue, as the United States, the Republic of Korea, and Japan had also worked with the DPRK government since 1994 within the Korea Peninsula Energy Development Organization (KEDO).[153] The difference is that, unlike with KEDO, its negotiations and output were public and participatory, propelling DPRK representatives and diplomatic partners into a transparent and visible conflict resolution framework.

Humanitarian Assistance and Human Security

Humanitarian agencies operated on two human security fronts. They responded to human insecurity by helping to provide the most basic freedom from want—the right to food and basic medical care. International humanitarian actors responded to desperate human insecurity in the DPRK, and their activities saved lives and assisted in modest economic recovery. Humanitarian agencies also, as a direct consequence of attempting to fulfill their mandates, introduced liberal norms to the DPRK government. To the extent that these ideas were made less threatening and more acceptable to the government, the humanitarian agencies also contributed to a potential increase in human security for the population. The first contribution was the direct effect of humanitarian activity. The second was a product of the unintended effect of agency activities. This latter contribution to human security should not be overstated, but neither should it be ignored.

By consistently aiming for more openness so that they could better do their job, the agencies were able to demonstrate the value of operating methods that were not subordinated to a war/national security mentality whose consequence was, among other things, to rationalize the lack of political freedom for the population. The culture of secrecy generated as a direct product of the national security mentality meant that humanitarian norms, based on transparency, accountability, and efficiency, were antithetical to the country's standard operating procedures. The agencies, through their insistence on the application of humanitarian norms in their operations and negotiations in the DPRK, were able to demonstrate to the government that a decline in secrecy in the society did not necessarily lead to invasion or increased vulnerability.

The agencies were also able to demonstrate that conflict could be settled through negotiation. Not all conflicts were resolved to all parties' satisfaction, but many were resolved to the extent that conflict could be ameliorated. A "win-some, lose-some" conflict resolution framework was created, built around norms that had direct relevance for the wider economic and political debates surrounding the transformation of DPRK society.

The humanitarian agencies opened up formal and informal channels for the familiarization of DPRK officials with the West. The agencies contributed to confidence building between the DPRK government and, indirectly, the West, as their own activities demonstrated that strong disagreements of principle between the DPRK and the West could be negotiated. The agencies thus helped to create a new political climate in which the possibility of resolving conflict between the DPRK and the West through negotiation, not war, could be conceived. The small though important contribution of the agencies to conflict prevention was both to make the DPRK a more knowable and therefore a more predictable entity to the outside world and, at the same time, to make the outside world more understandable and therefore less threatening to the DPRK authorities.

There were, however, inherent limitations of humanitarian activity as a means of achieving durable human security. Humanitarian actors could help provide food and support economic reorientation, but they were not peacemakers per se. An improved climate of understanding between the DPRK and the West came about as the unintended effect of humanitarian activity in the DPRK. It remained up to the DPRK government and its international adversaries and partners as to whether they would take advantage of the process of confidence building begun by the humanitarian agencies—and choose negotiation to settle conflict and bring a durable human security to the people of the DPRK.

5

The New Human Security Patchwork

I N THE EARLY TWENTY-FIRST CENTURY, socioeconomic change in the DPRK continued to be an unintended consequence of millions of citizens making day-to-day decisions to optimize personal and family survival. The central government did, however, become more actively engaged than in the previous decade, reasserting a proactive leadership in economic policy. By 2004 the government had publicly embraced the incorporation of market principles as providing the new dynamic of economic redevelopment. The internal debate on how far and how much reform had been resolved to the extent that even the naysayers accepted that there was no turning back in adopting economic marketization. DPRK policymakers were, however, much more willing to facilitate economic reform than to promote domestic political change.

Recovery and reconstitution of the economy took place along market lines. Given the classical definition of a market economy—where price is determined by the relationship of supply to demand, not by government —market forces predominated in the DPRK by the early twenty-first century. Underpinning the new marketized economy were new dynamics of economic exchange—driven no longer by state planning, allocation, and distribution but instead by the logic of hard-currency transactions. The DPRK did not, however, become a politically liberalized economy. Individuals remained subject to political control and lacked civil liberties. The

DPRK did not, in other words, become a *free* market economy. Instead, what took place was a process of *marketization without liberalization*.[1]

The reconstituted and marketized socioeconomy achieved stability, albeit at very low levels of economic activity. Socioeconomic reconstitution was founded on fragile human security conditions. Survival for the majority remained precarious and unsustainable without continued international humanitarian assistance, particularly in food. Marketization without liberalization brought new social cleavages as well as new threats to regime survival.

Marketization without Liberalization

By the late 1990s the government more or less accepted that the society had moved toward a system where individuals and communities took primary responsibility for their economic lives. The government understood that the economy could no longer be based on direct state-based provision. The government did not try to reimpose the old mechanisms of economic control, but it did attempt to channel the new dynamics of economic marketization toward government goals of regime survival and economic redevelopment. In this context the government promoted new principles of economic rationality in economic planning as well as new economic sectors that it thought might have export earning potential, most importantly in information technology.

From 1998 on, economic units that generated a surplus—including provinces, counties, farms, and enterprises—were permitted to engage more directly in market transactions. They could sell products, purchase inputs and basic goods, and redistribute goods to their constituents. Economic units used these new-found freedoms, selling surplus locally or developing export capacities by selling local produce abroad (for instance, potato starch to China). Economic transactions increasingly took place via markets, which became much more visible after 2000. Markets became institutionalized as the primary system of supply, allocation, and distribution of basic goods.

Markets spilled over into the corners and streets of small towns and villages throughout the country. Petty traders, usually women, could be seen peddling low-value commodities such as cigarettes, unconcerned about

being observed by passing foreigners or officials.[2] These street-corner ped-
dlers were very different from the licensed stallholders seen on streets in
small and large towns beginning about 1998. The latter were spruced-up
women in white catering hats with clean stalls offering usually hygieni-
cally prepared snacks. The former were poor, dirty, tired women offering
goods for sale in the same way as petty street traders in any poor country
in the world.[3]

The government encouraged a shift into information-technology industries, working with foreign companies to develop expertise and to earn hard
currency from joint productions of animated cartoons and computer programs.[4] Government strategy, made explicit in the New Year's Day edito-
rials of the party newspapers, identified the development of information
technology as a foundation for future prosperity as well as a necessary component of modernization efforts.[5] The strategy was supported by a plan of
action in which "large numbers of personnel proficient in advanced tech-
nologies will be trained."[6]

Promoting the information-technology sector as a strategic priority for
economic development had a significance beyond its potential to increase
export earnings. The nature of the information-technology sector implied a
potential opening to information, data, and ideas from other cultures. Skills
development that included facility with the Internet and e-mail was likely
to ensue. Large numbers of technocrats would become acquainted with
technology that by definition—*information* technology—would grant unprecedented levels of communication with and knowledge about the outside
world. Increased government emphasis on training in computer-related
applications for wide swathes of the workforce meant that access to information from outside the country was, potentially, much more accessible than it had ever been—and not just to selected personnel.

Legislating and Legitimating Economic Reform

The government legalized moves away from state to private provision,
gradually recognizing socioeconomic changes that had been tolerated out
of necessity since 1995 but which by 2001 had become the norm. The
first legislative amendments to reflect the socioeconomic transformation
were enacted in 1998. Changes to the constitution extended the right of
economic entities other than state-led enterprises to own and dispose of

property. They also legalized the small-scale acquisition of private property.[7] These changes were a lag factor in socioeconomic organization, not a lead factor as they have sometimes been understood.[8] By the early years of the twenty-first century, the government had publicly accepted that a return to previous economic practices was impossible. In June 2000, for instance, at a meeting attended by U.S., South Korean, and other governmental representatives, as well as senior officials of UN agencies, Vice-Minister of Foreign Affairs Choe Su-Hon reported that the DPRK was "underlining economic efficiency and profitability. . . . Production entities whose economic efficiency is not justified will have to be closed down."[9]

The repeated references in official documents to profitability as a major principle of economic planning from 2002 on reflected a resolution to the internal debate about the speed and scope of marketization.[10] A consensus that economic reconstruction would take place along capitalist lines had been forged. One indication of this consensus was the government's pursuit of training opportunities for its foreign trade and foreign banking personnel in the West, with the overt goal of introducing the country's foreign trade bureaucracies to liberal trade norms, principles, and rules. The public espousal of market principles prefaced the July 2002 government announcements that freed prices (to a certain extent), increased wages, and recognized and legalized the market system, in terms of markets determining price.[11] The system of free rent and utilities was abolished; only education and health care remained free of charge. The state would continue to provide a basic grain ration at subsidized prices, but it was not expected that this would be the only or even the primary source of food for households.

In addition, the government declared Sinuiju, the busy border town with China, a free-trade zone.[12] Sinuiju was permitted autonomy in its local affairs and was to be managed by a controversial figure, the Dutch-Chinese entrepreneur Yang Bin, one of China's richest businessmen.[13] The Sinuiju free-trade zone proposal eventually disintegrated due to Chinese opposition, but the principle of collaboration with capitalist business within the DPRK was maintained. From 2003 on, the Kaesong industrial development zone as a joint activity between the DPRK government, the South Korean government, and South Korean business was the major example of this new approach to working with Western business.

The 2002 government legislation legitimated and institutionalized markets in two senses. First, markets were accepted as the physical location for economic transfers. Second, the 2002 legislation indicated an acceptance of marketization as a new system of socioeconomic relations. In the first sense local markets had effectively replaced the Public Distribution System as the primary source of goods by 2002. In the second sense, the 2002 "reforms" legalized the de facto system of price setting that had occurred since 1996, as price became increasingly determined by the relationship between supply and demand—unlike the old system of government price setting.[14] As of 2004, it was not clear what proportion of a household's goods remained supplied by the state, the province, the county, or the market. It is fair to say, however, that farmers' markets, where local household production was "sold or bought at free market rates," became the norm as a means of distribution of goods and supplies for the entire country.[15]

Socialism as a Relic of the Past

The 2002 legislative changes sent a strong signal to the outside world and to the population that the socialist planned economy was a relic of the past. The government legalized economic practices that had hitherto only been tolerated as "temporary" measures. The sections of the party that had hoped the new economic trends could be reversed had lost out in intraparty debates. The government attempted to reassert control over the economy, but in a different form than in the Kim Il Sung era. Government control could now be understood as a dirigiste, policy-setting approach rather than the all-encompassing intervention in production, distribution, and consumption characteristic of the pre-1990s command economy. It was also a geographically contingent control in that the government could no longer enforce its writ nationwide. Government policies were less assured of success, mainly because the state could no longer provide economic and social rewards to the population or to local cadres in return for compliance with state edicts.

How Markets Worked in Practice

The DPRK's marketization without liberalization took place in the context of the slight economic recovery of the early years of the new century.

New market mechanisms became integrated with fragments of the old system, such that two overlapping market systems evolved by that time. In analytical terms these could be distinguished by their differing participants, means of exchange, relationships of inequality, and significance for economic institution building. The first, the food market economy, was constituted around the buying and selling of food. The second, the hard-currency economy, was constituted around the buying and selling of hard currency. In the food economy, distribution remained regulated to a certain extent, and money was sometimes not used at all, as swapping and bartering remained an important economic mechanism. In contrast, the semilegal hard-currency, or "dollarized," economy, while used by only a minority of the population, institutionalized hard-currency dynamics, making them the motor of economic redevelopment in the DPRK.

A Precarious Recovery

The economic free fall bottomed out in 2000 but stabilized at a very low level of economic activity. Exports rose to $515 million in that year, a year-on rise of 8 percent, and imports amounted to $1.4 billion, a rise of 46.5 percent over the previous year.[16] The government estimated average per capita national income for 1998 at 982 *won*—just $446 at the 2001 official exchange rate of 2.2:1, but a mere $37 at the July 2001 Pyongyang black market rate of 26:1.[17] Nevertheless, the figures indicated that the government—without significant assistance from the multilateral financial institutions or from foreign investors—had started to implement a strategy that allowed for some reconciliation with the new politico-economic trading conditions of the post–Cold War period.

The leveling-off in economic decline took place in the absence of trading partners prepared either to offer substantial concessional trade in fuel, food, or any other commodity or to import goods that were more expensive or of a lesser standard than could be obtained elsewhere. In other words, the DPRK achieved some limited success without substantial economic or political support, as it had had during the Cold War from the Soviet Union and China. This was some indication that the DPRK government was learning to operate within a harshly competitive global free-trade system.

The New Dual Economy

The food market involved the entire population (all have to eat to survive), and the state retained some control over pricing. The absolute necessity to obtain food to ward off starvation motivated this market. The means of exchange were only a secondary factor in the food market, and these means were various. People bartered goods and food. They obtained food to barter from direct agricultural production, sometimes from state distribution (swapping corn, for instance, or potatoes for vegetables or milk). Food was sometimes obtained directly through the Public Distribution System or via international assistance. In this case no means of exchange would be necessary—although in some cases labor was required, for instance, in humanitarian agency–sponsored food-for-work projects.

Sometimes food was obtained through theft. During the preharvest months locally appointed youth guarded harvests in makeshift wooden watchtowers, prepared to ward off hungry marauders attempting to steal the crop for food.[18] Similarly, those living in first- and sometimes second-floor apartments in all the small towns throughout the country used wire meshing to enclose balconies—partly to keep livestock reared on balconies in, but also to keep thieves out.[19]

Some direct food purchase could take place. Individuals used the local currency, the *won,* where they could or, if they were fortunate enough to have access both to hard currency and to shops that had food to sell, they used hard currency to buy food. Outside the major cities there were few food shops, with markets the first and most common supplier of food. From the early 2000s, market traders were also happy to accept hard currency on a fairly open basis. The local currency was used, but it was virtually worthless and used only as a currency of last resort, because it could not carry out the functions that a currency performs in a market economy—for savings (a store of value), as a means of exchange, or as a unit of accounting. It was not worth saving in *won* because there were so few domestically produced goods and hard currency was needed to purchase any imported good—even the basics such as shoes, bicycles, tools, soap, meat, material for clothes, and any imported food. Rampaging inflation meant that savings in *won* could easily become literally not worth the paper on which the currency was printed. The *won* was also hardly used as a means of exchange, as it had no stable value—food was a more reliable currency in most of the country. It was also rarely used as a unit of account, given its valueless nature.

By the 2000s, most nonfood goods and some foods could normally be supplied only through hard-currency transactions. On national holidays, such as President Kim Il Sung's birthday on April 15, some attempt was usually made to hand out extra goods like school uniforms. These were exceptional efforts, however, and reflected an absence of readily available goods in the Public Distribution System at other times of the year. Goods of any value, in use and money terms, could be bought only by those with access to hard currency.

The significance of the hard-currency market was not that the majority of the population had direct access to hard currency. They did not. Its significance was that its causal dynamics replaced those of planning and egalitarianism as mechanisms and principles of economic organization. By the beginning of the 2000s, an individual's access to hard currency provided the only reliable guarantee of human security. Individuals no longer expected that they could rely on the state as a guarantor of basic human security in terms of freedom from want. The 2002 economic reforms explicitly accepted these new principles of socioeconomic organization.

In the era of the planned economy, the problem for individuals and communities had been, "If hard currency can be obtained, how can it legally be spent?" In the new era, the greater problem was how to acquire hard currency so that it could be spent—openly if not totally legally.

Dollarization

"Dollarization"—the widespread use of hard currencies in the DPRK economy, including the dollar—irreversibly changed DPRK society. The government sought to restrict the use of the U.S. dollar with its 2003 declaration that the euro would be the only hard currency of "legal" tender. Nevertheless, since 1998 the U.S. dollar, along with other hard currencies, had unofficially replaced the *won* as the currency unit used for exchange, as a store of value, and for accounting purposes.[20] Even transactions between government agencies were carried out in dollars.[21] The government itself made use of the U.S. dollar in all serious international exchange calculations. Korean nationals, as well as foreigners, needed U.S. dollars (later euros) and other hard currencies to buy items of any value in local shops and markets. Foreigners living in, working in, and visiting the country used dollars in all domestic transactions until 2003, when they were instructed to use the euro, but in practice dollars continued to circulate, along with other hard currency. The *won* operated in extremis, as a subsidiary currency for those who did not have access to hard currency, including U.S. dollars, euros, Japanese yen, and Chinese RMB.

Hard-currency use came about partly due to the lack of a developed and reliable banking and credit system. Dollars entered the country through foreign businesses and aid organizations—some of which chose not to operate through the banking system and instead, partially or fully, operated on a cash-dollar basis. South Korean organizations were particularly involved in transactions involving large cash-dollar flows. The South Korean government-backed Hyundai tourism project in Mount Kumgang, for instance, had paid slightly less than $400 million to DPRK officials by August 2001.[22] All these payments were made in cash.[23] Such methods allowed, among other things, clear opportunities for corruption.

The government countenanced the dollarization of the economy, which took place in an extraordinarily short amount of time. In 1998, it was not possible to give dollars away, for instance, as a tip for good service in restaurants, hotels, etc. This was because the security services would have questioned any Korean, other than those in the higher echelons, who was spending foreign currency. From 2000 on, in contrast, it was possible for poor working persons to use dollars—if they could obtain them—throughout the nation. This did not imply that the security forces would never show interest in those individuals spending dollars. The dollarization of the economy, while comprehensive and tolerated as an economic necessity, was not "legalized" in the sense of the government having officially replaced the *won* with the dollar. However, there were disincentives to the prosecution of those engaged in the dollar economy. The most salient was that those with the most access to dollars and other hard currency were also likely to be those most privileged or influential in the society, including those in the security apparatus.

Dollarization accompanied an increased openness of the society. Hard currency had to be obtained from foreigners or North Koreans who had contact with foreigners. Thus as individuals gained access to increasingly necessary dollars and other hard currencies, they also had increased access to knowledge and information about the outside world. Some of this knowledge was through personal contacts at ports, in hotels, and at tourist facilities. Other interactions were more systematic. Local staff employed in international humanitarian organizations, for instance, had continuous and open access to Internet sources of news about their own country as well as to news about other countries.

Human Security and Socioeconomic Reconstitution

The process of marketization and dollarization was intimately bound up with ancillary processes of fragmentation and immiseration. Socio-economic inequalities increased, and these inequalities could be stark. At their worst, they meant the difference between survival and death. While some benefited, the vast majority of the population lived in poverty, facing malnutrition, disease, and hardship every day.[24] The social safety net was so damaged that health- and social-care facilities were inoperable in many areas due to lack of inputs of basic equipment (including soap, for instance) and medicines. A minority, who had access to income and contacts from abroad, perhaps from relations in Japan, had relative health and food security.

Freedoms from fear were more unequally and paradoxically distributed. Those out of reach of the deteriorating security apparatus, particularly away from major cities, had increasing freedom of movement and personal choice. Some of the economically better off would still face the possibility of arbitrary interpretation of the law. (This was particularly true in the capital, where the political and security apparatus had remained intact and in some cases been rejuvenated because of access to resources in the limited recovery of the early years of the new century.) All would still be unable to express political disagreement with the government.

In the new era of marketization, social fragmentation did not occur between some large, easily identifiable preexisting groups and others. It did not emerge between Pyongyang and the rest of the country, the party and the rest of the population, the army and civilians, or the few who worked for profitable enterprises and the majority who worked for unproductive factories or public services that could no longer pay wages. Instead social differentiation developed between groups of individuals who had access to hard currency and food and those who did not. New social cleavages were created around new axes of privilege, as some obtained access to benefits and others were excluded. Social groups were reconstituted—not, as previously, in relationship to their access to the state, but in terms of their access to the market.

Fragmentation

Individuals with access to hard currency and benefiting from dollarization were concentrated in specific geographic regions—in the capital and port and border towns—and had contact with foreigners either directly or indirectly through their work. They included senior personnel in both the party and the state apparatus, but they also included ordinary workers such as port personnel and employees of restaurants catering to foreigners. Four discernible groups formed the small minority with relative human security in terms of freedom from want. Only one group had real freedom from political repression—a crucial aspect of freedom from fear—and this was the Kim Jong Il family.

The first and best off of the four groups consisted of the small elite surrounding the Kim Jong Il family. They had access to riches and assets rivaling those of some of the world's wealthiest people, much of their wealth located in foreign bank accounts. They had food, medicines, and the best of health care flown in from abroad. This was a tiny group but by far the wealthiest. This elite did not engage in conspicuous consumption but lived in isolated and guarded villas, hiding its wealth and lifestyle from the North Korean people.

The second group was that of the North Korean nouveau riche. It consisted of midlevel or senior members of the party, government, and businesses who came into regular contact with foreigners through trade, diplomatic, and aid connections. They either were paid in hard currency, as were the North Korean officials who worked for international organizations, or received informal cash handovers designed to "facilitate" the work of the foreign organization in the DPRK. This group was small compared to the total population but was visibly growing. It was much more visible than the Kim Jong Il elite, because it did engage in ostentatious consumption—buying wide-screen televisions, video and DVD players, and, in some cases, automobiles. This was a new social group that grew out of the reconstitution of the DPRK economy and was mainly Pyongyang based.

The third group also obtained hard currency from foreigners but was from lower social strata. It consisted of service workers in foreigners' homes, restaurant and hotel workers, and dockyard workers. Hard currency was used to buy food and other basic goods. The significance of this group was that its existence was made possible only as the economy became dollarized. As the dollar or hard currency in general began to be taken for granted as the source of value in the new DPRK socioeconomy, it became "normal" for poorer people to use hard currency without fear of retribution from the security apparatus. This was a very new aspect of DPRK social relations, reflecting new freedoms and the possibilities of increased personal choice and decision making for large numbers of people.

The fourth group consisted of those who had relative human security in terms of food availability but not much else. These were mainly farmers and their families who were fortunate enough to live on productive cooperative farms. Productive cooperative farms were those that could produce enough grain to feed the entire farm community the whole year round. Officially, farmers in 2001–2 received 210 kilograms of cereal per person—more than enough to cover aggregate basic food needs.[25] However, many families on these farms still suffered from inadequate access to a well-balanced diet, including the minerals and vitamins necessary for healthy development, such as calcium and iron. In addition, even in the most productive cooperative farms, there was little possibility of earning hard currency with which to buy medicines for the farm clinic, spare parts for farm machinery, and fuel for farm equipment, among other things. If a farmer was particularly fortunate, the farm might generate some surplus, some of which could be sold or bartered in the farmers' markets.

Human security in terms of freedom from want did not exist in a stable manner for cooperative farm families. Human insecurity was even more pronounced for those farming unproductive lands. Some rural families had access to "firefields"—generally pieces of cleared forestland, often on precipitous slopes that could provide food for two or three agricultural seasons—but these were inherently unsustainable enterprises.

Pyongyang and the Provinces

The slight economic recovery of the early 2000s was most visible in Pyongyang and in some parts of the food-producing provinces. Pyongyang as a whole—although not all its inhabitants to the same degree—benefited from the influx of foreigners and the spending power they brought with them. As grain production increased marginally in 2001, so did food security for those in the more productive parts of the provinces of North Hwanghae, South Hwanghae, North Pyongan, and South Pyongan. North Hamgyong remained devastated with little industrial or agricultural activity, except in the port areas of Chongjin and the free-trade zone of Rajin-Sonbong. South Hamgyong, with its large industrial cities, also remained acutely food insecure.

The ostentatious consumption of the Pyongyang nouveau riche provided a stark contrast to the Stone Age lifestyles of formerly economically privileged and politically powerful industrial workers in North and South Hamgyong in the northeast of the country. This latter group was reduced to near starvation and scavenging for food and edible roots after wholesale factory closures in the 1990s.[26] Urban adults were not normally eligible for international humanitarian assistance, including food, and unlike their rural counterparts, they did not have access to agricultural production. These factors explain the November 2000 observations by the FAO and the WFP that the "indications are that the urban population have between 20 and 25 percent less cereal available per caput compared to individuals in rural areas."[27]

This was why poverty was visible in the cities, side by side with the observable privilege of the minority with access to dollars. John Powell, senior official in the United Nations World Food Program, reported that as late as 2002, "urban residents were worst affected by food shortages as they had no access to farmers' markets where rural residents buy, sell and barter agricultural products."[28] Some, of course, would have had indirect access via relatives in the country or occasional visits to rural areas, but this access would have been irregular and not available to most. In the new postcrisis DPRK, urban workers, including formerly privileged industrial workers, formed the new underclass.

Immiseration

Immiseration was prevalent throughout the country. It could be found in Pyongyang as much as in the mountainous remote regions in the north and east. It was entirely a product of a household's inability to grow or purchase food and to obtain basic goods such as medicine and fuel. Lack of household capacity to produce or buy food and goods was compounded by government inability, since the mid-1990s breakdown of the Public Distribution System, to regularly and systematically channel food, clothes, and other basic goods to the nonfarming population.

Rural families were generally better able to survive than urban families because they had access to land and could grow food. This was particularly so for the breadbasket provinces in the south and less so for the northern mountainous counties in North Hamgyong and Chagang. In the north of the country, the growing season is short, agricultural land is marginal, and agricultural production, even at the best of times, is insufficient to feed local populations.

One indication of the continuing fragility of human security throughout the country was that in 2003, the World Food Program still judged that it needed to provide basic rations for all children under seventeen and all pregnant and nursing women, if they were not to be at severe risk. In health terms, although reporting of the incidence of disease was not systematic, the widespread lack of basic drugs and medical equipment meant that diseases such as tuberculosis and hepatitis and the high prevalence of diarrheal and acute respiratory illness were likely contributing to increases in mortality rates.[29] By the early years of the new century, the international humanitarian community was providing enough food to allow for the survival of most of the population. It could not, however, meet the national need for medical and health-care inputs or rehabilitate the dilapidated and unsafe water and sewage systems that brought disease to the majority.[30]

Limits to Growth

The economic reforms of 2002 highlighted not only the government's efforts to provide the conditions for increased productivity but also how many constraints still remained on economic expansion. Agricultural and industrial production remained hampered by the residue of controls from the era of the planned economy and the lack of confidence in the currency. The lack of functioning infrastructure; the absence of a domestic legal framework to regulate the newly marketized economy; and remaining overintrusive state controls on land, labor, and production inhibited growth. Economic activity remained at a low level, and some state-organized redistribution of production, particularly food and fuel, remained necessary in order to sustain survival for the majority. These factors militated against the new instruments of economic liberalism acting as a mechanism for substantial economic growth. In turn, however flexible the government became, there was a limit to what it could achieve by its own efforts. Foreign investment, as the government well appreciated, was the sine qua non of economic recovery.[31]

In the farming sector, even though grain harvests improved beginning in 2001, a chronic food deficit remained. The country required an additional 1 million tonnes of cereal to give its population a minimum caloric intake.[32] Structural disincentives to increases in output continued to obstruct agricultural expansion, for although government prices for grain to farmers increased, farms that managed to produce food surplus to the requirements of its own farmers were still supposed to relinquish much of that production for sale to the state (at prices determined in *won*) for national redistribution. Farms could earn much more from selling their grain production on the private markets than to the government. Farmers also gained much more flexibility in economic and personal choice if they channeled food through markets instead of through bureaucratic and often corrupt governmental procedures. Undeclared surpluses could be given to relatives or swapped and sold for necessary goods in the private markets. To achieve this flexibility, farmers continued to systematically underdeclare yields.[33]

The government's decision to pay higher prices for farming output in 2002 could not contribute to major increases in productivity. Disincentives remained for cooperative farms to grow anything more than that which would cover basic farm needs and guarantee constituent members enough surplus to sell in markets to provide a better standard of living for their families. Massive increases in output would have achieved less than optimal gains. The government still paid lower prices than those obtained on the market, but expenditure would have to be made on necessary inputs such as labor, fuel, and fertilizer—the last two at more or less real international market prices. At the same time, excessive sales of under-declared yields in local markets could trigger a punitive response from local authorities.

Economic enterprises that succeeded in selling goods abroad and obtaining foreign currency continued to pay workers in the almost worthless *won*. Economic entities therefore could obtain only marginally more benefits for their members, and this only if they were profitable. In addition, even when enterprises were profitable, benefits to workers remained limited. The law did not permit payment to individuals of the hard currency that they needed to purchase many goods, including food and clothing.

Another barrier to economic expansion was the absence or obsolescence of infrastructure in transport, communications, the power sector, and industry. Roads, bridges, and tunnels were either decayed or made literally by hand with inadequate materials, causing rapid deterioration on use. Power stations and the electricity grid functioned imperfectly due to inadequate materiel, technology, and management skills. Telecommunications networks operated poorly, with few telephone lines, little maintenance, and antiquated technology. Mines and power stations operated without appropriate safety equipment and with inefficient and inadequate technology. Those factories left operating after the massive closures of the early and mid-1990s had insufficient fuel, out-of-date technology, and management approaches that continued to rely on ideological exhortation rather than economic reward to encourage productivity.

Other government policies indicated that the state had not abandoned a highly interventionist role in the economy. In the early 2000s, for instance, planned relocations of the population continued. The northern province of Ryanggang, where the population density was relatively low and in which some counties, such as Daehongdan, have a reasonable amount of arable land, became a target of government-sponsored migration, often of demobilized soldiers and their families.[34] The high flat plains of Ryanggang, despite a short growing season due to the extreme winter temperatures, provided suitable land for potato cultivation, in which the government, with the help of foreign donors including the Swiss government, heavily and systematically invested.[35] The new free-trade zone of

Sinuiju was also premised on moving large sections of the population away from the proposed new central hub of the city and relocating them in a walled-off residential development.[36]

Systemic Barriers to Foreign Investment

Many systemic barriers to foreign investment remained, including a controlled labor market and a domestic legal system that did not provide a reliable regulatory and legal structure in which foreign business could operate.[37] Foreign businesses still had to employ labor allocated by government, and in practice a local employee could not be dismissed for any reason.[38] Domestic legislation to regulate market transactions remained rudimentary and the legislative process opaque. The legal system continued to discriminate structurally against foreign nationals in the sense that North Korean legal norms were privileged over foreign norms and procedures. DPRK law, for instance, continued to assume that "trial parties' equality is a fraudulent slogan in capitalist countries to make working-class people obey the bourgeois court."[39]

The Absence of a Social Policy

When government began to retake control of economic policy in late 1998, it concentrated its efforts at the macrolevel. In direct contrast to the Kim Il Sung era, the government of Kim Jong Il abandoned social policy management, giving up on the policy of balancing and mediating the different interests of various social groups. There was also little sign of serious policies designed to respond to the needs of disadvantaged social groups or to direct national resources to social sectors such as health, education, or child care.

Large sectors of the population, including formerly privileged industrial workers, farmers living on less productive cooperative farms, and those party officials without access to foreigners, had no means of benefiting from the meager economic expansion of the early 2000s. Per capita national income in 1998, according to DPRK estimates and at official exchange rates, was just $446.[40] Real exchange rates would take this figure even lower—probably nearer $20 to $100 a year. A Canadian source indicates gross domestic product per capita at $760 in 2002.[41] These figures, inexact though they are, indicated a nation in poverty.

Disadvantaged groups suffered further hardship as the government offered insignificant resources to rebuild the decrepit health services, relying instead on local production of "Koryo," or herbal, medicine and international assistance for supplies and inputs.[42] International humanitarian health assistance was not large, and what was available was very often directed by government priorities. These priorities sometimes coincided with humanitarian community assessment of need—for instance, the vaccination and tuberculosis programs—but not always. International agencies were frequently asked to support the Pyongyang Maternity Hospital —the best-equipped maternity hospital in the country—and to support sophisticated medical procedures such as transplant surgery, at a time when most of the population did not have ready access to basic antibiotics or rudimentary painkillers such as aspirin.

The only sign by government of a realization that the food and economic crisis had disproportionately affected women was the move to support pregnant and nursing women. Policies developed included insisting that pregnant women spend two weeks in the hospital after birth and trying to ensure food allocations were sufficient to allow for a healthy mother and baby. Women often avoided staying in the hospital for any length of time, however. The buildings were not heated, water was dangerously contaminated, and food, medicines, and medical equipment were either nonexistent or in short supply. Doctors could give advice but could not offer much practical assistance to a hungry or sick mother. Government policy was ill thought through and designed primarily to counter the decreasing birthrate rather than to alleviate suffering. The neglect of women's health was evidenced in the 2002 nutrition survey, which showed that a third of mothers with children aged under two were suffering from malnutrition.[43]

The government's strategy for responding to the needs of the poor was not made explicit but in practice seemed limited to relying on humanitarian assistance to deliver a basic food ration to the most vulnerable groups—pregnant and nursing women and children. The government attempted to ensure some redistribution of basic grains from food-surplus counties to food-deficit counties, although local authorities then allocated food according to competing priorities. Local authorities balanced food needs of nonearning residents, including children, the sick, the elderly, and the unemployed, with those of working adults in strategic sectors, including miners and those in the power sector.[44]

The Army: A Mixed Contribution to the Economy

The military was the only social group to which the Kim Jong Il government gave systematic attention; it channeled resources to the army and increased its political status in the domestic polity. The military simultaneously contributed to economic activity and drained economic resources. On the one hand, its superior organization skills and privileged access to resources made it well placed to make use of economic investments that came its way. On the other hand, its enormous outlays in feeding, clothing, and managing the million-person army, along with the civilian defense activities that enjoined almost the entire population, greatly constrained the rational use of economic resources for development.

Defense spending was protected somewhat, but defense could not be isolated from the effects of inflation and hard-currency shortages. Defense spending averaged out at just under $20,000 per soldier at official rates of exchange in 2000.[45] Given that the real rate of exchange in late 2000 ranged from 10 to almost 300 *won* to one U.S. dollar, these figures indicate that the DPRK government could afford to spend only between $66 and $2,000 per soldier.[46]

Available data relating to military activities in civilian sectors of the economy, for instance in agriculture, construction, and production, is very speculative—even more so than the already sparse and tentative information on other sectors of the economy. Thus it needs to be used with extreme caution. One widely circulated estimate was that half of the army of about 1 million was engaged in nonmilitary production.[47] Even if the numbers cannot be confirmed, there was some evidence from observers and those doing business with the DPRK that the military remained active in civilian sectors of the economy. Official news bulletins also occasionally mentioned Korean People's Army (KPA) involvement in civilian sectors of the economy.[48] Insufficient funding propelled the military into a new economic role. During the Kim Il Sung period it had assisted the population with necessary but non-hard-currency-generating labor, such as transplanting and harvesting. Its new priority was developing export industries for hard-currency earnings.

The government permitted and encouraged the KPA to engage in both production and foreign trade. Production for export by the military included "nonmilitary" commodities as well as the more classical military products of arms and missile technology.[49] Of the latter, the South Korean press estimated that the DPRK exported 540 missiles between 1980 and 2003.[50] Credible figures related to earnings from arms sales are, however, nonexistent. Even so, U.S. government and military sources in particular point to arms sales' continued importance to the DPRK economy as of 2001.[51] What is known for certain is that missile spare parts and technological expertise were still exported by the DPRK in 2002 and, in a period when export earnings opportunities were scarce and the country desperate for hard currency, incentives for such exports remained.

The "Army First" policy had unintended effects other than its encouragement of entrepreneurial activities within the military. As the army was strengthened and its size maintained, feeding all the soldiers continued to be difficult. Both soldiers and their families experienced hunger and privation. Regular reports of soldiers stealing livestock and crops for food showed that the military did not remain exempt from food shortages and hunger.[52] One dissident, in a sober report that was probably exaggerated but also probably contained a large element of truth, stated that in late 2000, the military was

> losing discipline badly. Though they are better off compared with others, still they themselves don't have enough to eat. So they go out of their units, steal and rob as they please wherever they find easy targets either on the streets or on train even during the daytime. They steal rice and they steal food. At night, they hide by the road and steal the bags of passers-by. Nobody could complain about their arrogance and behavior because they just beat them up if anyone tells them to stop. There are a large number of weak and ill among the soldiers, and military hospitals are packed with them. There aren't [*sic*] enough medicine even at the military hospitals and often patients are sent to perform hard labor instead of receiving treatment. Many die or become disabled.[53]

As far as the government was concerned, its large army provided its main security guarantee against unrest domestically and threat from abroad. Indeed, as relations worsened with the Bush administration in 2003, the "Army First" policy was consolidated, with efforts made to increase and institutionalize civilian support for military activities nationwide.[54]

The New Human Security Patchwork

By 2003 the government had made a start to economic reform, but there was insufficient realization of the scale of systemic change that would be needed to attract foreign public or private investment. No major efforts were made to scale back corruption, and there was no sign of efforts toward rethinking and reconstituting internal regulatory and legal frameworks that would have been necessary to institutionalize market reforms.

Negative consequences of the new socioeconomy included the fact that the population could no longer, officially, rely on the state for help with the basic necessities of life. One longtime visiting aid worker noted in September 2002 that "individuals in the whole country are, for the first time, given more responsibility and thus feel more in charge of their own destiny. [But] the cradle-to-grave security has disappeared."[55]

Increases in wages brought some short-term relief to workers in that they could purchase goods from traders who were prepared to accept the *won* in exchange for their goods. Given the underlying weakness of the economy, however, increases in wages did not increase real purchasing power. The already weak *won* simply inflated against the dollar, and those who could obtain hard currency continued to do so.[56] Freedoms to sell and buy were, however, accompanied by growing social inequalities.[57] Those who could produce or buy food were in the minority. Most had precarious access to food and little in the way of hard currency, which was the only other guarantee of food accessibility. For those with access to few assets apart from their labor and with little hope of employment, the ability of self-help to produce economic rewards was likely to be minimal. On the other hand, the state had not been able systematically to assist the poorest with the basic necessities of life for at least a decade, and the legislative changes of 2002 at least permitted individuals to legally do what they had been doing outside the law for nearly a decade.

Contradictory changes took place in terms of the freedom-from-fear aspects of human insecurity. Some improvements in personal choice and freedoms were institutionalized in the economic reforms of 2002, as individuals and families were given the power and responsibility to take charge over their own budgets and, by extension, permitted a huge increase in personal decision-making authority. The limited moves toward decentralized economic management also supported trends toward decreased state control over the individual's daily life. Dissent was still punished but often sporadically and inconsistently—one indicator that by 2002 the Kim Jong Il regime had still not worked out a coherent strategy to deal with the socioeconomic restructuring that was taking place around it.

As had happened in the economic sector, because of the exigencies of survival, transformation of political practice took place as individuals made more decisions themselves and operated outside party and state strictures. The difference between the political and the economic sectors was that nationwide de jure policy change did not occur in the former and individual freedoms were not enshrined in new legislation. Neither was this likely when external security threats, actual or perceived, could be used as an excuse (as far as North Korean lawmakers are concerned, a reason) to restrict personal freedoms. In spring 2002, reacting to international human rights activism on behalf of North Korean migrants/refugees in China, the North Korean state clamped down on unauthorized migration across the China border, after what had been de facto acceptance of border crossings as a way to alleviate food shortages. This was one example of how the state would still not tolerate what it considered too great a breach of its self-determined security policies.[58] Kim Jong Il's insurance policy against insurrection was also manifest in the reinforcement of the repressive apparatus of the state through the pursuit of the "Army First" policy.

The Human and National Security Nexus

The freedom from want that had characterized life for most in the Kim Il Sung period was replaced in the Kim Jong Il era by a pervasive human insecurity involving threats to all aspects of individuals' lives. Governmental policy came to be built on an economistic and technocratic strategy that promoted aggregate economic growth by encouraging marketization but failed to offer ways of meeting the interests of formerly influential groups. It institutionalized inequality at the same time that it no longer provided a viable safety net for the nation's poor majority. These were not just questions of assuring that the population would not starve, although this was a serious enough issue. This was also a question of how Kim Jong Il could maintain political legitimacy and national capability to prevent domestic unrest or to stave off an opening for successful "regime change" from outside. Overcoming human insecurity at home became directly implicated with a fundamental reconstruction of national security priorities abroad.

A New Diplomacy
The Humanitarian Transmission Belt

B Y THE 2000S, given the manifest inability of the state to secure resources from domestic sources or from former allies, the DPRK government's only alternative was to seek assistance from the economically developed states with which it had a history of hostile relations. The DPRK government recognized that assistance on the scale it required would not be forthcoming unless a settlement was reached on the issues of concern to those states, especially concerning missiles and nuclear proliferation. Thus economic imperatives forced a radical reorientation of foreign policy toward interaction and negotiation with former and current adversaries.

Reoriented DPRK foreign policy demanded a new type of diplomacy —a proactive engagement with the world based on compromise and dialogue rather than unilateral ultimatums and bellicosity. The DPRK was able to draw on its experiences of working with humanitarian organizations to acquire some of the skills and know-how necessary to undertake these new and more conventional interventions in international negotiations. The decade-long partnership with the humanitarian agencies, in addition to providing concrete humanitarian assistance, had provided a safe framework for learning about the norms, principles, and modalities of acceptable international activity and behavior. Although the DPRK had increasingly regular contact with foreign business, the most profound of its contacts with the West came through its continuous interaction with humanitarian agencies in-country as well as with visiting representatives of donor governments, some at very senior level indeed, and with private organizations associated with the humanitarian work. It was this necessitous and prolonged relationship with the humanitarian organizations that the DPRK, consciously and unconsciously, was able to use to provide a transmission belt into the wider world.

The government did not abandon its suspicions of the West. It retained a deeply ambivalent attitude to international humanitarian agencies, as it did to all its new global partners. Nevertheless, its increasing openness and approachability in the 2000s was made possible partly because the DPRK learned, through its relationships with the humanitarian agencies, that compromise and negotiation as means to resolve conflict were possible and even productive. This experience also demonstrated to DPRK foreign policymakers, albeit in a relatively microlevel manner, that relationships with Western countries might be changed from automatic hostility and suspicion to a more nuanced relationship of some form of collaboration.

This chapter traces the development of DPRK foreign policy and negotiating objectives in respect to major external partners and adversaries. It shows how DPRK national security policy developed to encompass meeting human security priorities for the population as a fundamental objective of all its postfamine foreign policy negotiations. The chapter also traces the intersection of DPRK relationships with humanitarian agencies and the governments of its major interlocutors to demonstrate both the advantages and dangers for DPRK foreign policymakers of the inevitable humanitarian entanglement with major national (for the DPRK) and international (for the rest of the world) security issues.

From Forced Opening to a New Foreign Policy

DPRK international policymakers dealt with faltering growth in the 1970s by attempting to diversify sources of economic support and borrowing from the West, even as they continued to rely on barter, swap, and subsidized trade arrangements with the former Soviet Union, China, and the Communist bloc.[1] This strategy failed. Intending to pay for increased Western imports with sales of minerals and Western loans, the DPRK could not afford to repay debt when commodity prices fell and interest rates increased in the 1970s.[2] Many economically developing countries, the most famous being Mexico, faced a similar situation. Unlike these countries, however, the DPRK and its creditors did not work out a deal for repayment, and the DPRK simply defaulted on its obligations. When the DPRK lost its former allies at the end of the 1980s, it was left with no significant sources of alternative international economic support. Apart from the extant political conflicts with the West that made economic support unlikely, economic relationships were blocked by the experience of the DPRK's cavalier treatment of Western banks and economic institutions in the not-too-distant past.

In the early 1990s the DPRK again tried to establish foreign policy links with capitalist countries. These contacts were mostly with Asian neighbors—some of which, such as Indonesia, it had worked with in the Non-Aligned Movement (NAM) since the 1970s.[3] The DPRK also renewed its efforts to enter into relations with the major Western powers —inviting Western journalists from CNN and the BBC, for example, to visit the country. These efforts did not result in increased understanding or improved links, however, as the DPRK was still not prepared to enter into interchange that would involve an admission that it was a supplicant or dependent partner. Conversely, the major Western countries would have been prepared to enter into political or economic relationships with the DPRK only through a process of tough negotiations about outstanding economic, political, and security concerns. They would have refused to allow the DPRK to negotiate only on its own terms. The DPRK's refusal to admit weakness or to enter into substantial policy dialogue meant that it did not seek help at the onset of the food crisis in the early 1990s. It took the acute food crisis of 1994 and 1995 for the government to publicly admit that it could no longer manage even the basics— human survival—on its own.

The DPRK approached the major UN humanitarian agencies—the World Food Program (WFP), UNICEF, and the UNDP—and NGOs in the United States, Europe, and Asia for help throughout 1995. At the same time, the government began a concerted policy to encourage foreign business to invest in the DPRK, again concentrating on Western sources of support. Accompanying the moves to obtain humanitarian assistance and foreign investment was a major diplomatic offensive toward former adversaries, including the Western European states and, much more importantly, the Republic of Korea, Japan, and the United States. This push to the West happened because, by the early 2000s, the government realized that the scale of foreign investment required for economic redevelopment would come only from wealthy states or from multilateral institutions like the World Bank, which would not lend to the DPRK until U.S. sanctions were lifted. Economic imperatives propelled the DPRK diplomatic offensive toward the West in the early 2000s.

Humanitarian Agencies—the Transmission Belt

All UN agencies, as multilateral intergovernmental agencies, are, by definition, funded by governments. The United States was an important supplier of food surpluses for WFP operations worldwide and also gave food to the WFP operations in the DPRK. In addition, many U.S. and European NGOs received large amounts of financial assistance from their governments and the European Union. Only a small number of NGOs operating in the DPRK could operate without financial support and consequently some supervision of their activities from governmental donors. The two major exceptions to this rule were the Red Cross movement and Caritas, the Catholic confederation of aid agencies. Governmental donors generally accepted the principle of noninterference with the impartiality and neutrality of the Red Cross movement, and Caritas was mainly funded by private donations.

The principle of accountability to the providers of humanitarian assistance meant that UN agencies and NGOs funded by governments had to provide regular reports on their work to donors. In carrying out their standard operating procedures, the humanitarian agencies provided information on DPRK society and economy to the country's major donors—the United States, South Korea, and Japan. These were the same countries with which the DPRK was locked in tense political conflict. The DPRK was thus drawn by default into a process of opening up and interacting with major Western states, albeit sometimes indirectly, and could not help but develop linkages of some sort with what it considered to be enemies.

NGOs and the UN humanitarian agencies were initially welcomed as a source of inputs. Less welcome at first was NGO and UN insistence on engaging in dialogue about broader policy issues, for instance on health or agricultural priorities. This the DPRK government initially viewed as interference in its sovereign right to decide domestic policy. Conflicts over the appropriate realm and responsibility of humanitarian agencies as compared to the exclusive rights of government took place at the level of individual and collective agency relations with the government. The highest-profile of these conflicts was the continuing dispute over the quality of agency access to the aid beneficiary population.[4] The DPRK government was forced to respond to donor concerns that unacceptable restrictions were being placed on humanitarian agency freedoms of movement—expressed vocally through the international media—in order to try to deal with the threat of the cutoff of aid. The government's response was to gradually improve humanitarian conditions. Although the agencies recognized the improvements, the remaining constraints on operational activities continued to be a source of friction between the government and the humanitarian agencies.

Many practical, technical, and policy negotiations—other than on the highly politicized issue of humanitarian access—took place between international agencies and the government over almost a decade, on a daily basis, inside and outside the country. Such negotiations more often than not resulted in compromise that was not wholly satisfactory to both parties but that did enable implementation of agreements.

A More Realistic Approach to Foreign Business

European, Asian, Australian, Canadian, and South Korean business was at first welcomed into the country only hesitantly. By the turn of the millennium, however, the government demonstrated more concerted efforts to attract foreign business, underpinned by more realistic and less ideological approaches. Some legislation was introduced to accommodate the requirements of foreign investors.[5] Delegations were sent abroad to reinforce the new approach. The Pyongyang Chamber of Commerce, for instance, which visited Hong Kong in September 2001, went armed with a list of projects in which the government was encouraging foreign investment, ranging from heavy industry to food processing.[6] The delegation made some efforts to stress the new DPRK realism, emphasizing that "the DPR Korean government is further developing the external economic relations in accordance with the national economic progress and *the newly changed situation in the international arena.*"[7]

A New Diplomatic Practice

Until the mid-1990s the DPRK had little experience of diplomacy other than the formal negotiations of Socialist bloc diplomacy or state-to-state rituals of high diplomacy with small states, conducted multilaterally through the Non-Aligned Movement or bilaterally, involving heavily orchestrated and highly ritualistic state visits. In the former case, Communist diplomatic relations were conducted at the government-to-government level, involved closed and secret negotiations, and excluded domestic affairs from the agenda. In the latter case, many of the states were beneficiaries of military, agricultural, or technical assistance from the DPRK, including Burkina Faso, Sierra Leone, and Guinea-Conakry, and these negotiated as dependents.[8] In addition, it was a rule of Non-Aligned Movement diplomacy that no state interfered in the domestic affairs of another member-state.

The DPRK had no experience of complex diplomacy in which a state might have disagreements with other states or organizations and yet achieve compromise through diplomatic trade-offs. The DPRK also had no history of accepting input from foreigners into the direction of domestic policy and practice. Its own aid projects abroad in agriculture and construction were more or less unconditional—informally requiring nothing more than the setting up of a local study group, funded by the DPRK government, to help promote the DPRK's national ideology of *Juche*.

Prior to the mid-1990s, when foreigners had disagreed with it or tried to intervene domestically, the DPRK had reacted by threatening war or withdrawing from negotiations. The nuclear crisis of 1993–94, which brought the DPRK into direct negotiations with U.S. officials, although involving significant contact with the West, did not compromise the DPRK's control over domestic policy or precipitate any overall reconsideration of national security policy. In contrast, the food crisis and its aftermath forced the DPRK to rethink national security policies, to negotiate compromise, and to accept limited change in domestic policy.

Negotiating Style

DPRK anxiety to improve relations with former adversaries and old allies was genuine enough, but the government's fifty-odd years of solipsistic policy management left it ill-equipped to make the compromises necessary for effective diplomacy. Diplomatic initiatives were a mixture of the well judged and the naive, always underpinned by a fierce jealousy of national sovereignty, and often clumsy in execution. Very often they displayed a counterproductive lack of comprehension and perception of international norms and expectations.

Its goal-oriented actions in negotiations often contradicted the belligerence, verging on abuse, that emanated from official pronouncements. This was partly a result of public pronouncements being geared to a domestic audience. It was also partly because the DPRK's news agency, like all the DPRK's bureaucratic agencies, did not operate in a horizontally coordinated manner with other agencies. This meant that foreign policy and political negotiators would have little regular contact with communications agencies except on the very major issues—such as the North-South Summit, for instance—when instructions from the very top would determine how relations were handled and portrayed. For lesser events, the communications agencies would not necessarily have effective mechanisms for coordinating with those actually involved in external affairs, leaving a large amount of leeway as to how those events would be reported for both the domestic and international audience.[9] The DPRK had no conception of the modern art of "spin" and did not calibrate its propaganda announcements as part of a diplomatic strategy. One result was the sometimes extreme ranting of the official news agency, the KCNA, which elicited both apprehension and derision in international listeners.

DPRK diplomacy was too unsophisticated to foster meaningful dialogue with global actors who lacked patience or trust in DPRK willingness to make and implement binding agreements. Diplomatic objectives of improved and intensified cooperation had a chance of success only if partners had the patience to distinguish the verbiage from the substance and were prepared to accept incremental improvements in relationships, believing that progress was possible through engagement. States such as South Korea and Switzerland were prepared to engage in this long-term process of confidence building and incremental improvement. Others, such as Japan and the United States, were often more reluctant.

Promise and Paralysis: The United States

Until the 1990s, the DPRK had a narrowly focused policy toward the U.S. government, aiming to secure a peace treaty to replace the armistice that ended the 1950–53 Korean War. The DPRK had also insisted on bilateral negotiations. It refused to accept South Korea as a legitimate negotiating partner, arguing that the South was not a signatory to the 1953 armistice and that only the United States had the power and authority to conclude a peace treaty. The United States flatly refused to engage in direct negotiations, arguing that the DPRK must talk to the South about the shape of a future peace before the United States would become involved.

The 1993–94 nuclear crisis, in which the United States accused the DPRK of developing nuclear weapons, almost resulted in war. Instead, after last-minute diplomacy from former U.S. president Jimmy Carter, it ended with the 1994 Agreed Framework.[10] The Agreed Framework, also known as the Geneva Agreement, created the multilateral Korean Peninsula Energy Development Organization (KEDO), designed to ensure that nuclear power in the DPRK was put to only peaceful use.[11] The DPRK thus achieved its objective of engaging the United States in direct negotiations—in the efforts to both secure and implement the agreement. The KEDO framework also locked the DPRK into an institutionalized multilateral dialogue with the United States and South Korea on the issue of nuclear power cooperation.[12] The North Koreans thus developed substantial direct and indirect experience of negotiating with the United States, and channels were opened up for formal and informal contacts between the two states.

Hungry for Peace

From the inception of the new negotiating relationship with the United States, DPRK objectives included trying to obtain help to deal with food shortages. As early as 1994, during the nuclear negotiations, DPRK officials approached U.S. officials to request food assistance.[13] The North Koreans used personal contacts they developed with U.S. officials to continue to raise food aid requests through 1995 and 1996 and offered to cut back or end missile exports in exchange for food.[14] The DPRK focused entirely on the food crisis through 1997. It agreed to participate in the four-party talks on peace and security, proposed by the United States and South Korea and designed to include China as well as the DPRK, only on the condition that it would receive food assistance.[15] These four-party talks, however, made little headway, although they continued sporadically up until 2000. They were sidelined by bilateral arms control negotiations between the DPRK and the United States.[16]

In 1998 the DPRK announced that it would negotiate an end to its missile development program and repeated its willingness to make a deal that would end its missile exports.[17] In return, the DPRK wanted the implementation of the normalization of relations between itself and the United States, as agreed in the 1994 Geneva Agreement. It also wanted reimbursement for the cash it would lose by ending arms exports.[18] Bilateral negotiations resulted in some progress in meeting DPRK and U.S. objectives. The DPRK agreed to a U.S. inspection of an underground site in 1999 that U.S. analysts suspected of being a nuclear installation, in return for food aid.[19] The Korean People's Army also agreed to give the U.S. Department of Defense regular access to the DPRK to search for the remains of U.S. soldiers missing in action (MIA) in the Korean War.[20] In return the DPRK received financial transfers from the U.S. government.

DPRK foreign policy achievements with respect to the United States during the Clinton administration included reductions in U.S. sanctions toward the DPRK, a reconsideration of the official U.S. designation of the DPRK as a "terrorist state," and the diplomatic triumph of a visit by U.S. secretary of state Madeleine Albright to Pyongyang in October 2000.[21] A missile agreement seemed near, and in November 2000 there was serious consideration of a state visit by President Clinton to the DPRK. It was eventually ruled out, as much because of the domestic constitutional controversy over the voting irregularities in the U.S. presidential elections of 2000 as for lack of confidence that a deal would be secured.[22] The DPRK viewed these improvements in relations as steps toward the normalization of relations envisaged in the 1994 Agreement.

Coping with the Bush Administration

Relations deteriorated after incoming Bush administration officials told North Korean negotiators they were not committed to upholding previously agreed-on communiqués between the two countries.[23] U.S. president George W. Bush cited the DPRK as one-third of the "axis of evil"—along with Iraq and Iran—in January 2002, and the United States, in a change of policy, asserted its right to make preemptive nuclear strikes, using Korea as an example of where this could be necessary. Bilateral talks were attempted in 2002 but broke down after U.S. negotiators informed the DPRK in a meeting in Pyongyang that they had evidence that the DPRK possessed high-energy uranium enrichment technology that could only mean that the DPRK was developing a clandestine nuclear weapons program.[24] U.S. negotiators insisted that the DPRK had admitted that the charge was true. DPRK spokespersons hotly denied both having such a program and admitting to the U.S. allegations.[25] As of May 2004 DPRK spokespersons continued to maintain that, when Jim Kelly made his accusation, their chief negotiator had replied, "We have more powerful weapons than that." This reply many experienced DPRK analysts would take as a reference to the strength of the party and the ability to mobilize the entire population in self-defense.

In response to the Pyongyang meeting, the United States abandoned its commitments under the 1994 Agreed Framework to supply annually 500,000 tonnes of crude oil to the DPRK. Given the DPRK's chronic lack of energy resources, the DPRK argument that it needed to reopen its nuclear reactors in order to compensate for the U.S. oil cutoff assumed some plausibility.[26] Whatever the justifications for each side's actions, the outcome was a spiral of potentially dangerous action and counteraction. The DPRK withdrew from the Nuclear Non-Proliferation Treaty and reopened unsafe nuclear facilities that it had shut down a decade previously and whose by-products were material that could be used to make nuclear bombs.[27]

By 2003 the DPRK was proclaiming its right to develop a "nuclear deterrent" and using the threat of nuclear development as a bargaining chip in the continuing talks with the United States, which were transferred into multilateral fora in 2003. The DPRK engaged in six-party talks with the United States, China, Russia, South Korea, and Japan in

2003 and 2004 in Beijing but remained convinced that the Bush administration intended to attack the country militarily. The DPRK responded
by continuing to try to engage with the United States on the margins of
the talks, but unlike the Japanese delegation, which used the talks as a way
to explore improved bilateral relations, the United States refused to enter
into bilateral dialogue. DPRK negotiators said they had the impression
that U.S. negotiators had been instructed not to have any form of interchange with their DPRK counterparts; U.S. delegates rejected even informal overtures.[28]

The Humanitarian Channels—Making a Difference?

The DPRK encountered U.S. NGOs as both indirect—as funders of
the IFRC, through the American Red Cross and Caritas, by way of the
Catholic Relief Service—and direct aid-givers. Korean American individuals and groups, the most important of which was the Korean-American
Sharing Movement, spearheaded initial humanitarian assistance.[29] The
DPRK government had some direct contact with Korean Americans but,
in the main, did not attempt to use Korean American individuals or organizations as a conduit to the U.S. government. This was partly due to
Korean Americans' lack of receptivity to such a role. They maintained a
low profile and cautious involvement in the DPRK. From the beginning,
they were aware of the complex and inevitable political and diplomatic
overtones of humanitarian assistance to the DPRK, designated as a "terrorist nation" by the U.S. government and with which South Korean legislation prohibited direct contact.[30]

The DPRK government did not approve residence for U.S. NGOs,
although in practice U.S. NGO representatives stayed in-country for
many months at a time between 1997 and 2000, monitoring food aid
projects on behalf of a consortium of U.S. NGOs—the Private Voluntary
Organizations' Committee (PVOC).[31] The PVOC had been formed to
monitor U.S. government food aid, which was operationally under the
control of the UN World Food Program.[32] The DPRK saw little added
value from the PVOC in terms of additional assistance from NGO resources that would not otherwise have come to the DPRK from U.S. food
aid donated through the multilateral institution of the WFP. The DPRK
view was that the presence of PVOC food monitors decreased overall food

resources. The PVOC carried out the same monitoring as WFP monitors, but it had to be logistically supported by the WFP and the DPRK government, thus causing a duplication of scarce resources. There was some sympathy for this view within the WFP and the other agencies, as the PVOC did not routinely integrate its monitoring findings into WFP program evaluations or regularly share its findings with the rest of the humanitarian agencies.

The lack of operational logic may not have mattered much if some of the U.S. NGOs had not operated so closely with the U.S. government that they were viewed in Pyongyang at best as operational agents and at worst as spies.[33] Both views had some validity. The PVOC did, by and large, act as a monitoring agent for U.S. Department of Agriculture food donations. It was also true that PVOC monitors and NGO leaderships were in direct and regular contact with the U.S. State Department and other agencies of the U.S. government.[34] Most of this contact was not hidden from the DPRK. Some within the PVOC believed that information sharing with government officials in Washington might encourage the U.S. government to provide more assistance and might help open confidence-building channels between the two countries. Some agencies indicated to DPRK officials that they did indeed have privileged contacts within the U.S. government and that this could be useful to promote improved bilateral diplomatic relations.

The difficulty for DPRK decision makers in distinguishing PVOC activity from U.S. government activity was strengthened when Mercy Corps, one of the leading NGO members of the PVOC, appointed to a senior position someone known to Pyongyang mainly because of his former activities in the DPRK as a medium-level U.S. State Department official working on the nuclear agreement between the two countries.[35] In this particular case, the credibility of both the NGO and the U.S. government was brought into question after the official was arrested, charged, and found guilty of taking kickbacks from a U.S.-based businessman who had been doing business with the DPRK.[36] The overpoliticization of PVOC agency operations was combined with what USAID and U.S. Department of Agriculture officials, in a report published by the United States Government Accounting Office (GAO), described as weak and bureaucratic management of DPRK projects.[37]

The DPRK experience of U.S. NGOs that operated independently—raising their own funds and taking a low-key political approach—was more positive. The DPRK worked closely, for instance, with Americares, whose patron was President George H.W. Bush, and whose operations in the DPRK were led by the fluent Korean-speaking international officer Aimee Gilbert. Other independent NGOs operating in the DPRK included the Friends Service Committee, the Eugene Bell Foundation, and the Christian Friends of Korea. The latter two were faith-based organizations whose leading members were the children of Christian missionaries who had worked in Korea, some in northern Korea before partition, and who were also fluent Korean speakers. The DPRK government also maintained relations with individual PVOC members, engaging in some small bilateral projects.

The combined effect of relatively small volumes of assistance, contentious in-country relations, poor management of projects, and over-politicization of U.S. humanitarian activity militated against U.S. NGOs providing a vehicle for dialogue or a trust-building mechanism for an always-suspicious DPRK government. By 2001 the DPRK distinguished between privately funded U.S. aid, which it understood as strictly humanitarian, and U.S. government–funded assistance, whether the latter was operationalized by NGOs or multilateral agencies, which it understood as more directly an instrument of U.S. foreign policy. Nevertheless, it remained leery of using NGOs as a vehicle for informal diplomacy with the United States. When formal diplomatic contacts were frozen, as they were during the early part of the Bush administration, the DPRK organized its "back-track" diplomatic efforts, not through the NGOs, but through overt political contacts, including U.S. political grandees Democrat Bill Richardson and Republican Donald Gregg.[38]

Shifting National Security Policies

Beginning in the mid-1990s, restoring human security at the level of basic survival for the population was the absolute priority of DPRK policymakers. The government had even been prepared to negotiate away the classic national security instruments of armaments in return for humanitarian assistance, economic aid, and improved political relations with the United States. DPRK negotiators engaged seriously with U.S. policymakers in the talks that continued from the near war of mid-1994 throughout the rest of the Clinton administration. DPRK policy toward the Bush administration was guided initially by a naive belief that the incoming administration would adopt a slightly harder tone than the Clinton administration but would essentially continue with negotiations and a similar policy.

The Bush team's antipathy to both the Clinton-brokered 1994 agreement and to doing business with Kim Jong Il, combined with accusations from each side that the other had broken the 1994 agreement, ended the thaw in U.S.-DPRK diplomatic relations. Both sides had some right on their side. The DPRK had probably investigated the feasibility of a uranium enrichment program, even if it had not been as active and developed a research program as the United States alleged. Conversely, the United States had not fulfilled its promise to normalize relations with the DPRK.[39]

One outcome of the increased tension between the two countries was that DPRK policy discernibly shifted back toward "hard" security objectives of maintaining territorial security and securing a peace deal with the United States after 2002. Post–September 11, 2001, and the attack on the World Trade Center in New York, the invasion of Afghanistan, and the war against Iraq, the DPRK's foreign policy toward the United States became primarily motivated by fear of invasion and military attack. The securing of food, energy, and support for economic redevelopment remained important global goals but, in the relationship with the United States, the overwhelming priority became to provide for defense against military attack.

From "Puppet" to Partner: The Republic of Korea

DPRK relations with South Korea changed dramatically in June 2000 after South Korean president Kim Dae Jung took the historically unprecedented step of going to Pyongyang to meet directly with Kim Jong Il, his northern counterpart. In a dramatic shifting of international relations on the peninsula, the DPRK rapidly moved from an official and actual position of deepest hostility toward the South to one where, just two years later, the South became its major provider of economic support and quasi interlocutor with the United States, its feared enemy.

Prehistory

Up until the late 1990s, the DPRK's stance toward the Republic of Korea remained relatively static. It was encapsulated in the often-repeated charge that the ROK was a "puppet regime" of the United States.[40] After the Korean War ended in 1953, in an armistice but not a peace treaty, contacts between the two countries were sporadic and superficial. In 1972 and 1991 the two sides issued joint statements of intent to try to resolve their differences, but these statements did not displace underlying enmity.[41] They were not accompanied by any substantial societal contact, so the population of each country held the most extreme mirror-image visions of their neighbors as demonic, nonhuman, and evil.[42]

DPRK national security policy toward the South was led first by a desire for unification on its own terms and second by a policy of constant war-readiness. DPRK policy mirrored the South's policy toward the North. The 1993–94 nuclear crisis brought North and South Korea literally to the brink of war and occurred in the context of this "old" foreign policy.[43] The outcome, that South Korea would effectively take the lead in helping the DPRK plan energy developments for the future, was not willingly accepted but instead grudgingly accommodated on the basis that the Geneva Agreement would contribute to the "normalization" of relations with the United States.[44]

Humanitarian Need—the Impulse for Policy Change

In the mid-1990s, after they became aware of famine conditions in the North, South Korean NGOs and religious groups began to make indirect contacts with the North Korean government—via third parties like the Red Cross or Caritas—to provide food and other emergency assistance. North Korean contact with the South had hitherto taken place almost entirely via formal and sometimes clandestine intergovernmental negotiations. Thus these contacts with nongovernmental organizations, although at first very tentative, brought a new dynamic to relations with the South. These new relations were not without problems. Five decades of the DPRK's extreme negative stereotyping of its southern neighbor meant, for instance, that an early aid shipment containing medicines with South Korean markings had to have the labels carefully stripped, one by one, in

1997. Reasons given included the allegation that ordinary North Koreans would refuse to accept South Korean medicines, thinking they were being poisoned. Perhaps a more salient factor was the government's reluctance to admit to its people just how dependent it had become on outside aid—including from the demonized neighbor to the south.

From the late 1990s on, the DPRK's relations with South Korean NGOs accelerated because of the continuing need for humanitarian assistance. DPRK suspicions continued but did not prevent the intensification of relations with South Korean nongovernmental organizations, mainly because the South Korean partners had enormous patience in dealing with their often ungrateful and sometimes cynical counterparts in the DPRK. South Korean NGO assistance was also high compared to U.S. and European NGO input, although it was only a small portion of the total humanitarian aid into the DPRK, which came largely through the UN agencies.[45]

North Koreans also worked, albeit more indirectly, with South Koreans through multilateral institutions, given that the South remained a major funder of UN efforts to provide agricultural and humanitarian aid to the DPRK.[46] In addition, from as early as 1997, South Korean business conglomerates such as Hyundai provided some humanitarian aid as well as pursuing the better-known investment ventures.[47]

In addition to high volumes of assistance, the DPRK also benefited from the philosophy and methods of operation of South Korean NGOs. These NGOs were consistent in their contact and involvement with the DPRK, choosing to weather conflict, not by withdrawing assistance as a few European NGOs did, but by intensifying their involvement. From 1999 through 2000, including the period before the North-South summit officially warmed relations between the two states, South Korean NGOs were visiting the DPRK on average once a week—by air (Beijing to Pyongyang), land (Dandong, China, to Sinuiju), and sea (Inchon to Nampo).[48] South Korean NGOs argued for aid relations as confidence-building channels as much as for their intrinsic value. From the beginning the South Korean NGO perspective was that humanitarian assistance could provide a forum for dialogue between North and South and help encourage reconciliation and peaceful change on the Korean peninsula.

The Normalization of North-South Diplomatic Relations

As late as 1998, an official publication from Pyongyang's Foreign Languages Publishing House reported, "The United States and south Korea, upon [*sic*] 1998, are seeking military confrontation with the north more frantically than ever before."[49] In 1999 the *Pyongyang Times,* the English-language newspaper that reproduced articles from the state-controlled Korean-language North Korean daily press, was still referring to the unnamed "chief executive" of South Korea, that is, President Kim Dae Jung, as the "traitor to the nation."[50] As early as 1998, however, the DPRK was also showing signs of a new openness toward the South. A DPRK-approved publication reported that the DPRK was receiving food and agricultural aid from the South, that Hyundai and Samsung were negotiating with the DPRK government on inter-Korean business cooperation, that the first South Korean airline flew over North Korean airspace after authorization was given by the DPRK, that cultural exchanges were taking place between the two capitals, and that talks continued about the reunification of separated families.[51]

North Korean negotiators met with South Korean officials from the late 1990s on, in the context of KEDO, in the four-party talks, and bilaterally in the context of resolving humanitarian problems such as reuniting families divided since the Korean War and the subsequent hermetic partition of the peninsula. North Koreans also met privately with South Koreans, sometimes discovering that the common culture and language forged over the previous five thousand years made communicating surprisingly easy.[52]

North Korean dealings with South Korean organizations increased dramatically after President Kim Dae Jung's engagement policy made it easier for South Koreans to have more direct links with the North. In the first-ever summit between North and South Korean leaders, held in June 2000, Kim Jong Il met with Kim Dae Jung, the "traitor to the nation," in Pyongyang. North Korean television widely covered this milestone event.[53] The DPRK government placed a further seal of approval on its warming relations with South Korea by issuing a special commemorative stamp depicting the two leaders shaking hands.[54] It also placed photos of Kim Jong Il greeting the South Korean leader in public buildings throughout the country—side by side with Kim Jong Il meeting other world leaders, including Russia's Vladimir Putin.[55]

After the summit, the highly controlled official press and media began to report regularly on North-South cooperation. The summit legitimated the explosion of contacts that were being made. In the first eleven months of 2002, for instance, about 1,000 North Koreans visited the South. In the same period, some 12,300 South Koreans—not counting the Kumgang tourists—visited the North for economic, business, sports, cultural, or political purposes.[56] North Koreans, in other words, were now entering into relatively substantial interpersonal contact with their South Korean compatriots, unhampered by language barriers.

Humanitarian and economic cooperation between North and South was not without conflict. The North intermittently delayed and suspended interministerial meetings and the family reunions that were a centerpiece of North-South engagement.[57] Arguments took place over the scope and scale of economic support—most publicly over the reduction in payments from Hyundai for the Kumgang tourism project in 2001.[58] After the 2000 summit, however, in a very different manner from that of previous North-South exchanges, disagreements were negotiated and compromise both sought and often achieved. The DPRK did not, as it had in the past, withdraw from any of the various levels of talks with its Southern counterparts. Instead it intensified collaboration and continued to engage with the South—even when, during the nuclear crisis of 2002–5, the DPRK declared itself prepared for war should it be attacked by the Republic of Korea's major ally, the United States.

Relations with the South were reconstituted such that in June 2002, when the ships of both navies clashed in Korea's West Sea, causing loss of life on both sides, both sides' reaction was more of embarrassment that local military activity might derail the fast-developing relationship than of bellicosity.[59] Though some foreign analysts predicted the "end" of engagement policy, the incident caused hardly a blip in the relationship.[60] The first direct flight between North and South was delayed for just one week, taking place on July 21, three weeks after the incident, and the DPRK's expression of "regret" on July 25 brought discussion of the military clash to an end.[61] By 2004 the North was talking to Southern counterparts on almost a daily basis, on humanitarian, economic, and political issues.

Foreign Policy Reorientation toward the South

The DPRK's shift toward accommodation with the South was accompanied by a substantive reorientation of its attitude toward the different axes of the United States–Republic of Korea alliance. The DPRK government had long proclaimed a policy of negotiating only with the United States, arguing that South Korea was merely a junior partner in the U.S.-ROK alliance and had no independent foreign policy toward the North. This policy was maintained throughout the Clinton administration, which left office in January 2001. With the failure to establish a negotiating relationship with the Bush administration of 2001 on, however, the DPRK government turned increasingly to solidify its relationship with the South. The call for bilateral negotiations with the United States was not abandoned, but this was no longer seen as mutually exclusive of establishing a functioning relationship with the South.

Through the slow process of political negotiation, the North Koreans developed a relationship with the South Koreans such that, by the early 2000s, the South was parting company with the United States on how to deal with the DPRK. The South refused to accept U.S. hard-line approaches to the 2002–5 nuclear crisis and engaged in intensive efforts to try to persuade the United States and the DPRK to try to find diplomatic solutions to the crisis.[62] Partly because of the buttress provided by improved relations with the South, the North did not retreat into isolationist policies in the wake of this second nuclear crisis. Nor did it withdraw from KEDO. Instead it continued with intergovernmental, business, and nongovernmental links with the South. It moved ahead with the implementation of sensitive projects, including the opening of road links between the two countries, even as the nuclear crisis escalated.[63] Years before, in the nuclear crisis of 1993–94, the DPRK had been totally isolated globally. A decade later the South had become the new mediator for the North with the United States and Japan—an amazing turnaround of diplomatic relations. In the space of a decade, DPRK policy toward the South had been transformed. The South was seen no longer as a "puppet" but instead as a partner.

Conflict remained between North and South, but diplomatic negotiation largely replaced the saber rattling of military threat as a way to resolve disputes.[64] It would not be overstating the case to argue that the process of interaction with the South on humanitarian and human security issues forced the DPRK to reconsider the utility of its hitherto preferred foreign policy instruments. One lesson for the DPRK was that international negotiations could be conducted on sensitive matters. Another was that military instruments were not the only means to deal with national security threats. Instead, effective threat-reduction measures could be promoted through a process of cooperation.

The Japanese Debacle

For the DPRK, the legacy of Japanese colonialism remained unresolved. (South Korea had already come to a formal agreement with Japan in 1965, including the payment of reparations.)[65] The DPRK kept historic grievances alive through a national mythology that posited, in education, culture, and political discourse, a nation-building symbolism that had at its heart the notion of a triumphant victory of a morally pure cause, of anti-imperial North Koreans over an exploitative, rapacious, and evil Japanese colonialism.[66] The founding myths of the DPRK glorified and aggrandized the role of the late president Kim Il Sung as leader of the "anti-Japanese" guerrillas.[67] DPRK national symbolism thus kept historical conflict alive and visible.[68] Repeated, high-profile references to Japanese crimes—in the media, on television, at exhibitions, and in political rhetoric—reinforced anti-Japanese feeling as the "common sense" of public and private discourse.[69] This anti-Japanese climate provided an overall context of poisonous confrontation.

All parties, including Japan, recognized that the DPRK would be entitled to Japanese development assistance as some compensation for the colonial past (as the South had been granted) once a political settlement was agreed on. The DPRK did enter into normalization talks in the 1990s, but little progress was achieved.[70] The DPRK government was angry and disappointed when the agreements of the early 1990s with senior Japanese politician Shin Kanemaru resulted in little tangible progress. The Kanemaru delegation made a number of promises to the DPRK, including offers of a substantial financial settlement. These promises were not kept by the Japanese government, which made it clear that Kanemaru had gone beyond his mandate. For the DPRK, this was another sign of Japanese duplicity and untrustworthiness.

The DPRK had real and substantial grievances, including human rights claims against the Japanese government for recognition of and compensation for Korean so-called comfort women forced into sexual slavery during the war.[71] In addition, the DPRK had concerns about the treatment of the 700,000 Koreans resident in Japan. Though many of them were born in the country and had little direct connection with Korea other than cultural heritage, they were still denied voting rights under Japanese law and discriminated against in public-sector employment and admission to university.[72]

The DPRK itself still had to answer for human rights abuses against Japanese, particularly the abduction of Japanese civilians in the 1970s and 1980s. The DPRK government also showed scant respect for Japanese public opinion in 1998 when it launched a rocket into space. Ostensibly designed to put into orbit a satellite broadcasting songs about Kim Il Sung, the rocket flew over Japan before crashing into the sea. The DPRK rocket launch failed in its stated objective. Instead, it demonstrated to a frightened Japanese population that the DPRK had ballistic technology capable of sending a missile to the Japanese mainland.

Humanitarian Bonds—a Lost Opportunity

With the advent of the food crisis in the mid-1990s, the DPRK used the contacts it had with Japan through the Association of Korean Residents in Japan, the Chosen Soren, and other sympathetic individuals and groups to solicit food aid from Japan. The Japanese government responded generously with 200,000 tonnes of rice aid between 1995 and early 1996, making it the largest recorded food aid donor in that period.[73] The 1998 DPRK rocket launch interrupted but did not put a halt to food aid, and Japan continued to deliver food assistance, including an enormous 500,000 tonnes of rice in 2001.[74] Japanese NGOs also supported the DPRK, although their volume of aid was relatively small compared to South Korean inputs.[75]

DPRK bitterness toward Japan was not assuaged by generous food assistance. The DPRK felt it was owed the assistance because of the Japanese colonial past, and it made little attempt to hide this perspective. Representatives of the Japanese government visited the DPRK as humanitarian donors, although DPRK authorities also routinely blocked, denied, or delayed visas for Japanese donor missions, from the government and from

NGOs alike.[76] NGOs aiding children in nurseries were forbidden to send any toys printed with Japanese characters.[77] Despite these obstacles Japanese NGOs maintained aid to the DPRK, visiting when permitted and providing assistance in the food, agricultural, and energy sectors.[78] The Japanese government was not so forgiving. After several years of what it saw as DPRK intransigence, Japan decided to end humanitarian assistance after 2001.

The DPRK did not use the links created through humanitarian negotiations to try to improve relations with Japan. Instead it chose to view aid as an "entitlement." Its justification for this approach was the history of colonialism for which reparations had not yet been negotiated.[79] This rationale, although based on a substantial grievance, was inappropriate and in the end irrelevant, as it would have taken negotiations to determine the shape of any political deal of which aid would be a component. While in receipt of Japanese governmental food assistance, the DPRK refused to consider the channels of communication that were opened through the aid links as potential channels for informal political dialogue. It therefore reduced the possibility of a negotiated political settlement.

Learning from Mistakes

The DPRK's realization of its mistakes and a reconsideration of old attitudes toward Japan brought it back to the negotiating table in 2002. The DPRK admitted that state agents had abducted Japanese citizens, and Kim Jong Il apologized directly to Japan's prime minister, Junichiro Koizumi, who visited Pyongyang in September 2002. The DPRK also sent back to Japan relatives of the four Red Army Faction members who had been living in Pyongyang since 1970 after hijacking a Japanese Airlines jet in an attempt to reach Cuba.[80] The relatives of the hijackers were put on the same flight as the returned abductees in September 2002, in an effort by the DPRK to take concrete steps toward reconciliation with Japan.[81] The DPRK's attempts to resolve the abductee issue by admitting responsibility and apologizing only inflamed Japanese public opinion further, however, especially after it reported that a number of the kidnapped persons had died, yet it could not fully account for their deaths.

In 2003, the hopes of rapprochement raised by the groundbreaking meeting between Prime Minister Koizumi and Kim Jong Il foundered.

Tension was exacerbated when the DPRK asserted its right to develop an independent nuclear arms development program. Although the DPRK had recognized that old approaches were antithetical to its new national interest based on human security requirements as well as territorial defense, it still had not developed a sophisticated enough diplomatic approach to Japan. It had not taken the abductee issue seriously or sufficiently addressed the genuine concerns of the Japanese public after the 1998 missile test.

By 2004, however, the DPRK was again showing signs that it was on an upward diplomatic learning curve. The government took advantage of the opportunities offered for ongoing bilateral dialogue at the Beijing multilateral talks on the nuclear crisis to conclude negotiations that resulted in another visit by Koizumi to Pyongyang, in May 2004. This time the children of four of the abductees returned to Japan with Koizumi, and the DPRK was promised renewed humanitarian assistance. The family of the remaining abductee were reunited in Japan later that same year. The DPRK demonstrated continued diplomatic flexibility, which helped it achieve its objective of the renewal of humanitarian assistance. Continuing DPRK structural, historical, and cultural antagonism to Japan, however, combined with Japanese skepticism about DPRK intentions, also made for powerful barriers to significant improvements in cooperation.

Donors and Sometime Foreign Policy Interlocutors: The Rest of the West

The DPRK had existing diplomatic relations with a number of capitalist states before the crisis of the mid-1990s. These included Western countries like Sweden and Australia as well as Asian states such as India, Pakistan, and Indonesia. Sweden, for instance, had had an embassy in Pyongyang since 1973 and acted as the representative for U.S. interests in the country. The food and economic crisis forced the DPRK government into more intensive negotiating relationships with capitalist states with which it had historic ties. The crisis also propelled the government into new relations with Western countries, some of which resulted in the establishment of diplomatic relations in the late 1990s. From 1991 to 2001, the DPRK established diplomatic relations with an astonishing forty-two states.[82] Some of these were the new states created from the breakup of the

Soviet Union, but others included thirteen of the European Union states and oil-rich Brunei, Qatar, Oman, and Kuwait.[83] The DPRK pursued active engagement with countries it saw as influential—welcoming, for instance, the setting up of a British embassy in Pyongyang in 2000 and establishing its own embassy in the United Kingdom in 2003.

The DPRK found the European Union and its member-states easier to deal with than the United States, although the government never expected that the EU could replace South Korea or the United States as a key political dialogue partner. It had high expectations, however, of economic as well as humanitarian assistance from EU states. Initially it was also confident that it could engage in productive political dialogue with the European Union and its member-states. The DPRK government's approach to the European Union—displaying a mix of trust, hope, suspicion, and innocence as well as pragmatism and sometimes cynicism—was vividly demonstrated in its approach to human rights dialogue.

The DPRK was pressured into human rights dialogue with the European Union, but once begun, the dialogue became more than just a paper exercise. DPRK officials produced reports that were then jointly discussed with visiting EU officials.[84] The DPRK also sent officials to Sweden and the UK for human rights training.[85] The DPRK government was, however, shocked when the European Union sponsored a resolution to the United Nations Human Rights Commission in 2003 criticizing DPRK human rights practices without informing the government in advance of its intentions. The European Union saw part of its mission as publicly condemning human rights abuses as well as negotiating to end them. The DPRK authorities viewed this unilateral EU resolution, which had not been raised in the framework of the human rights dialogue, as a rejection of the DPRK's good-faith efforts to move toward change. In response the government attacked the EU's own record on human rights, especially in the areas of racial discrimination, what it termed "national chauvinism," and widespread unemployment. The DPRK's official comment was that

> the EU brought up the "draft resolution" for discussion at the meeting without any consultation with the DPRK, its dialogue partner, backtracking from dialogue and cooperation with the DPRK though they are getting brisk. This only arouses disillusion with the EU. Cooperation can never go with confrontation.[86]

The Humanitarian Foundation

The most substantial of DPRK relationships with the capitalist countries developed through the humanitarian and economic assistance provided by those states. Donor approaches ranged from the hands-off—not seeking to link economic support to any political agenda—to the hands-on, where donors tried to encourage domestic policy change. An important project of the former variety was the $20 million contribution from the Kuwait Fund for Arab Economic Development to the costs of modernizing the water and drainage supply to Pyongyang.[87] This project was effectively managed and implemented by the DPRK government with the advice of Australian engineers but without policy input from the donors.[88]

EU-supported projects, in contrast, were managed in an intervention-ist manner. The Commission insisted on transparency, accountability, and efficiency in the implementation of economic and humanitarian assistance, and rigorous financial monitoring and accounting standards were imposed. DPRK officials engaged in continuous, often acrimonious in-country negotiations with Commission representatives on everything from conditions of access to hospitals for monitoring purposes to tendering procedures for inputs paid for by EU funds.[89] As a result of these inten-sive and continuing negotiations, however, the DPRK was introduced to the conventional requirements of international financial transfers and to the norms of accountability and transparency.

Unappreciated Benefits: The Spillover Effects

The DPRK benefited from humanitarian and related economic activity through its increasing exposure to international conventions and methods of doing business.[90] Some local officials resented what they saw as undue interference in internal affairs. DPRK leaders, however, increasingly began to perceive the possibilities of using links with the EU and other countries, for instance through the Swiss Agency for Development and Cooperation based in Pyongyang, as a means of training officials in good economic practice. The Ministry of Foreign Trade accepted with alacrity the EU offer of conducting training for its personnel abroad from 2000 on.[91] Even the notoriously conservative Ministry of Foreign Affairs—once the bas-tion of opposition to the necessity for foreign training—changed its out-look. When asked by the British Foreign Office in 2002 how many scholarships it could use, the ministry indicated that a thousand would be preferred (two were finally offered).[92]

On the whole, however, DPRK officials remained ambivalent about cooperation with the European Union and other capitalist countries. On the one hand, the benefits of cooperation were increasingly appreciated. On the other hand, DPRK decision makers were irritated by the access that Western humanitarian and economic development organizations and donor governments had to information about the DPRK. In some cases, they viewed it as a potential infringement of sovereignty.

Rekindling Old Flames: Russia and China

Up until the late 1980s and early 1990s, the DPRK had depended on hidden subsidies from China and the former Soviet Union in the form of cheap oil imports, barter trade, cheap transfers of technology and spare parts, and preferential market access for DPRK exports. Like the rest of the world, the DPRK did not anticipate or plan for the end of the Cold War. Unlike most of the rest of the world, however, the DPRK was highly vulnerable to economic shocks after these two states renounced the privileging of the DPRK in economic relations. Russia and China diverted their export and import sectors toward developed capitalist country markets and also insisted that, beginning in 1991, goods be paid for in hard currency, with both countries insisting on international market prices for exports.[93]

Loss of economic support was accompanied by diplomatic distancing as both the Soviet Union and China established diplomatic relations and sought to develop trade and economic relations with the Republic of Korea. The DPRK reacted with anger and dismay, warning Soviet foreign minister Eduard Shevardnadze that if it could not rely on the Soviet Union, it might have to develop further its own security capacities.[94] This was widely interpreted as a threat to develop nuclear weapons.

DPRK relations with Russia under Yeltsin remained antagonistic. Relations warmed politically under Putin but never returned to the Cold War days of substantial economic support and technology transfers.[95] The DPRK owed Russia over $4 billion, and although it promised to pay, it had little likelihood of doing so while the economic crisis of the 2000s persisted.[96] The most substantive relations with Russia were the cross-border economic links with Russia's Far East, where about 20,000 North Koreans worked in logging, agriculture, fishing, and construction in the late 1990s.[97] The DPRK was also accused of sponsoring illicit economic activities in the Russian Far East, including currency counterfeiting, drug trafficking, and money laundering.[98]

Diplomatic relations with China waned in the early 1990s but later improved. In July 1996, for instance, Chinese warships visited DPRK ports to mark the thirty-fifth anniversary of the 1961 DPRK-China treaty on friendship, cooperation, and mutual assistance.[99] Nevertheless, relations with China remained distant. The DPRK did not consult China before embarking on major foreign or domestic policy initiatives, remaining jealous of what it saw as its independence in its relations with China. It did not consult China before it launched the 1998 rocket/satellite over Japan.[100] Nor did it consult China before it announced its decision in 2002 to establish a free-trade zone in Sinuiju, the main China-DPRK border town. It also did not engage substantially with China concerning its nuclear weapons programs.

Kim Jong Il made a number of visits to Russia and China in the early to mid-2000s and showed interest in how economic reforms had taken place in those countries.[101] Economically, the ongoing process of restructuring in China and Russia provided opposing lessons for the North Koreans. While the DPRK was impressed by rapid Chinese economic development, it was less persuaded by the Russian example, which it understood as having brought poverty to its people and having diminished a former Great Power in world affairs.

The government consolidated military ties with China, inviting the Chinese military to visit the DPRK in 2000, the same year that it hoped to close the ultimately unsuccessful missile deal with the Clinton administration.[102] The DPRK also signed a new treaty of cooperation with Russia in 2000.[103] Unlike the 1961 treaty that it replaced, the 2000 agreement did not promise Russian military aid to the DPRK if it were attacked. Its signing and ratification, however, reassured the DPRK that Russia was no longer the hostile neighbor it had become during Yeltsin's rule.

The DPRK initially showed little enthusiasm for Russian or Chinese involvement in the nuclear crisis of 2002 on, maintaining that it needed to resolve security problems bilaterally with the United States. Nevertheless, the DPRK hedged its bets in security terms. It resuscitated friendly links with both China and Russia that had fallen into desuetude in the 1990s. The government finally accepted Chinese good offices as the facilitator for what became known as the Beijing six-party talks, so that by 2003 and 2004, it was participating actively in the forum established by the Chinese government. This did not mean that China assumed a privileged role as confidant for the DPRK government. Instead the government maintained its policy of independence. It pursued strong ties with both China and Russia in order to strengthen its capacity to prevent and, if necessary, respond to national security threats. But at the same time it stubbornly refused to defer to the policy direction of either Great Power. The outcome of these consolidated diplomatic ties with two of the veto-holding members of the United Nations Security Council was some assurance for the DPRK that the United States would be unlikely to receive UN support for economic sanctions or for military attacks against the DPRK.

The Absence of Humanitarian Influence

The DPRK did not receive humanitarian assistance from Russia until 2003, when grain shipments were channeled through the World Food Program to Pyongyang. The government received food aid from the government of China, some of which was accounted for in UN records, although much more probably remained unrecorded.[104] Chinese-Korean NGOs and churches based in the Korean autonomous region of Yanbian, in Jilin province, gave food and other basic humanitarian assistance to North Korean migrants and refugees in China and channeled food into the northern counties of the DPRK.[105] Chinese governmental assistance was bilateral and donated directly to the DPRK government. The DPRK could thus distribute Chinese aid according to its own procedures and therefore did not need to accept new forms of negotiating practice or accommodations with partners with different interests and values. On the other hand, NGO assistance was clandestine and controversial. Both Chinese and DPRK governments linked Chinese-Korean NGO humanitarian work, sometimes for good reason, with political activities designed to overthrow and undermine both governments. These NGOs therefore had no influence on DPRK negotiating practice. Given the overall paucity of nongovernmental contacts with Russia and China, the DPRK had no reason to engage in any form of diplomacy with China and Russia other than that of formal state-to-state contacts, with which all three states felt most comfortable.

The Foundations of a New Foreign Policy

From the late 1990s on, DPRK diplomacy was characterized by global proactivity to respond to economic imperatives while simultaneously maintaining national defense capabilities. The DPRK began a dialogue with the United States, established strong cooperative relations with the Republic of Korea, and opened serious negotiations with Japan. It also succeeded in gaining recognition for the state and the government from a number of Western governments, including, as of May 2004, fourteen of the fifteen states of the European Union (excluding France) and the Union itself. Diplomatic relations were not without conflict. Unlike in previous decades, however, the dialogue with partners was substantial—indicating governmental recognition that the future of the DPRK was no longer in autarky but instead in international collaboration. The DPRK achieved the most success in its new relationship with South Korea and, until the advent of the Bush administration, with the United States. It had the least success with former colonial power and neighbor Japan. The DPRK developed relatively intensive interaction with European, Asian, and Australasian capitalist states and rekindled relations with former partners China and Russia.

The DPRK learned a new practice of negotiating, some of which was reflected in its more nuanced and less dogmatic approach to the West. At the same time, the DPRK remained paranoid about contact with the outside world and suspicious about the motivations of partners as well as enemies. On balance, though, from the late 1990s on, the DPRK demonstrated an increasingly visible persistence and willingness to engage in substantial dialogue with former adversaries on difficult issues, most successfully in its diplomacy with the Republic of Korea and the European Union, but also, intermittently, with the United States and Japan.

National security conceptions remained founded in territorial integrity and regime stability. The major change to national security policy was that, beginning in the mid-1990s, regime stability was understood as being about potential threats to the regime from the human security crisis as much as from threats from outside. The government displayed signs of intent to tackle some freedom-from-fear issues—for instance, in the acceptance of a human rights dialogue with the European Union and Switzerland. These were intermittent efforts, however, that, as of 2004, fizzled out, as they were subordinated to old priorities of national defense.

The DPRK's efforts to establish normalization with the West, as well as its intent to maintain an independent military capacity, should be understood as two sides of the same coin—of intent to cooperate at the same time as preparation for war. The proactive diplomatic policy of the late 1990s on laid the foundations for a long-term diplomatic reorientation toward peaceful and cooperative relations with the West, particularly the ROK, the United States, and Japan. This policy did not entirely replace national security policies that were focused on maintaining the DPRK's ability to fend off attacks from those same states, until and unless the DPRK government received cast-iron national territorial security guarantees. The dramatic difference for DPRK foreign policy in the 2000s in terms of the entire history of the state was the rapprochement with South Korea. This would make military action against the DPRK very difficult indeed, even if pursued with the fervor and single-mindedness that marked the foreign policy ventures of the administration of George W. Bush.

7

International Security and Humanitarian Assistance

UMANITARIAN ASSISTANCE to and intervention in the DPRK were designed to respond to the pressing needs of the population for food and medical care. Although not initially intended to respond to national security priorities of external interlocutors, in practice, humanitarian strategies were not entirely separate from national security policies. They could not be, given that the major aid donors were also the DPRK's main political adversaries with which it had been in constant conflict, not just since the 1990s, but since partition of the peninsula in the 1940s.

All the major external actors responded to some extent to the human security emergency of the mid-1990s. All except Japan, which suspended assistance between 2001 and 2004, and Russia, which only began food aid donations in 2003, continued assistance throughout the serious international tension of the early 2000s. Only South Korea (after Kim Dae Jung assumed the presidency), Switzerland, and to a certain extent the European Union practiced a "joined-up" strategy. They responded to the human security imperatives of the North Korean people and integrated these into a diplomatic strategy designed to ameliorate tension and contribute to resolving the Korean conflict, which by the early 2000s had become a global international security concern.

This chapter reviews and analyzes the security priorities and strategies of the major states that made and implemented policy toward the DPRK.

The chapter also considers how these states responded to the urgent human security imperatives of the North Korean people. It does this by investigating the nature of the relationship between humanitarian and economic assistance policies and the diplomacy designed to increase international security—in the classical sense of reducing military threat and the risk of war. Those states that consciously integrated a human security perspective into the classical national security, or securitized, approach to the DPRK were able to push forward the peacemaking agenda, to a greater or lesser extent. Those that did not were unable to achieve either their own national security objectives or the broader goal of consolidating a stable international security regime in and around the Korean peninsula.

The United States

After the Korean War ended in stalemate in 1953, the United States had little bilateral or multilateral contact with the DPRK. Its geopolitical strategic concerns during the Cold War were in managing conflict with both the Soviet Union and China. The DPRK was viewed as an irritant but not a player of global significance in the same class as the two Communist giants of Northeast Asia. The major change in the type and frequency of contact by the United States with the DPRK came after the 1993–94 nuclear crisis that brought the two countries literally to the brink of war.[1]

A Paucity of Contact, 1953–93

Direct contact between the United States and the DPRK had come about either as the result of accidental and trivial intercourse in third-country diplomatic functions where both stationed embassies or, more substantially, through the periodic meetings of the militaries of the two sides under the aegis of the Military Armistice Commission (MAC).[2] The commission was established in 1953, at the end of the Korean War. Although multilateral in form, involving input from South Korea as well as others involved in the UN coalition that had fought in Korea, in practice the MAC provided a channel for bilateral dialogue between the United States and the DPRK. This channel remained open through the 2000s, providing a negotiating forum for the return of the remains of Americans miss-

ing in action as well as for the return of those from the North or South
who had accidentally strayed across the border. Contacts through the
MAC were formal and often highly conflictual. For instance, protracted
negotiations took place in 1968 over the release of the crew of the USS
Pueblo, held for eleven months by DPRK authorities, who accused the
espionage ship of entering DPRK waters.[3] The MAC meetings did not
spill over from the highly functional remit of necessary military cooperation into political confidence-building mechanisms.

Multilateral relations were also sparse. The DPRK did not join the
United Nations until 1991. U.S. sanctions precluded the DPRK from
joining major international financial institutions such as the IMF, the
World Bank, and the Asian Development Bank. Nongovernmental links
were infinitesimal, although the DPRK did host a small number of
Korean-Americans trying to make contact with family members, church
groups such as the Quakers, and a few U.S. academics.[4]

The Clinton Administration: Learning through Doing

The 1993–94 nuclear crisis, in which the Clinton administration made
a credible threat of war should the DPRK develop a nuclear weapons program, was resolved through U.S. bilateral negotiations with the DPRK.
The outcome of negotiations was the 1994 Geneva Agreement, which
established both an institution for nuclear cooperation and, through the
process of negotiation, a bank of knowledge and experience of negotiating with North Koreans that had not previously existed within U.S.
administrations.

Further direct experience of negotiating with the North Koreans was
obtained through the substantial negotiations with the DPRK during the
late 1990s, through the four-party talks with China and South Korea as
well as the North, and the sustained bilateral negotiations to try to achieve
a deal on the production and export of DPRK missiles.[5] In 1999 President
Clinton appointed a special DPRK coordinator, ex–secretary of defense
William Perry, to review U.S. policy.[6] Perry was succeeded as DPRK policy coordinator by State Department official Wendy Sherman, appointed
at ambassadorial level specifically to ensure an integrated policy within the
administration.[7] All of these high-level officials, as well as their midlevel
colleagues, engaged in direct contact with North Korean officials.

Crises buffeted but did not derail the relationship, which remained strained yet nevertheless deepened qualitatively. The worst such crisis was the DPRK launch of a rocket in 1998, ostensibly to put a satellite in space. The rocket ended up flying over mainland Japan before crashing, causing political anger and consternation in the United States as well as Japan.[8] The United States used the channels it had opened up with the DPRK to defuse this crisis and others, however. In 1999, for instance, the United States negotiated inspections of a suspected nuclear site, which in the end turned out to have no trace of nuclear activity.[9] The relationship developed to the extent that Secretary of State Albright visited Kim Jong Il for direct negotiations in October 2000, discussing the fine points of a missile deal, including exports, testing, development, production, and deployments.[10] North Korean inability to respond in a timely manner meant the deal was not wrapped up before Clinton and the Democrats left office in January 2001.[11]

Government officials and ex-officials subsequently disseminated and analyzed their negotiating experiences through the numerous policy and research institutes that characterize semiofficial Washington, D.C., and that have the capacity to influence government policy on the DPRK.[12] Although the DPRK was still considered opaque and still detested as a regime, for the first time in official Washington, negotiation with the DPRK came to be seen as possible and sometimes desirable. It came to be seen as a way of reducing tension and securing a peace deal that could respond to the U.S. national security priority of reducing the military threat from an armed and unpredictable DPRK.[13]

The "Washington Consensus" on the DPRK

The Clinton administration was both generous and ambivalent in its aid policies to the DPRK. Over half a billion dollars of food assistance, although mainly consisting of agricultural surpluses that could not be sold on open markets, was sent to the DPRK.[14] Although food aid was largely grain surplus, Clinton did not have to donate the food to the DPRK; other humanitarian emergencies around the globe could have been recipients of these food allocations. Washington's financial contribution to the U.S.-led KEDO, although half that of South Korea, was substantial.[15] The United States, however, was slow to deliver on its commitments under the 1994

Geneva Agreement to supply 500,000 tonnes of crude oil a year. Deliveries often arrived behind schedule.[16] The speculation, denied by Clinton administration negotiators, was that little thought was given to the long-term United States obligations specified in the 1994 agreement as the dominant assumption was that the DPRK would "collapse" before very long.[17] Such a development would have obviated the need for the United States and its partners to make substantial progress on the installation of light water nuclear reactors by 2003, the date specified in the agreement, and would have given rise to a new government with which they hoped it would be easier to work.

The Clinton administration only tentatively engaged in linkage diplomacy with the DPRK. Although aware of the severity of the food and economic crisis and that economic inducements might have a role in diplomacy, the administration was deeply skeptical about North Korean willingness to engage in meaningful talks that could link food and economic assistance to broader political and security dialogue.[18] The administration also did not recognize the depth of socioeconomic change that had taken place since the mid-1990s. Thus it did not seek concrete ways to build on the pressure points provided by such knowledge to encourage steps toward increased economic freedoms. The small exception was U.S. officials' reiterated rhetorical commitment to markets at occasional multilateral meetings to discuss humanitarian assistance. Neither did it take advantage of the thaw in North-South diplomatic relations to try to channel emerging economic linkages in such a way as to encourage good governance in the DPRK. This would have meant targeted investment along with continued and extensive dialogue with the DPRK—the option chosen by the South as a means of encouraging peace and stability after the 2000 summit.

Instead of recognizing an opening for tying the DPRK into a globalized economic system, the Clinton administration chose to focus on securing an arms deal.[19] Some negotiators recognized that a major security deal would encourage subsequent investment from Japan and South Korea and allow the lifting of the U.S. veto on DPRK membership in the international financial institutions, but no major efforts were made to overtly link security and economic negotiations.

Clinton's policy of concentrating on securing an arms deal, backed up by continuing humanitarian assistance along with cautious engagement, received broad support among the Washington diplomatic and think tank community, particularly those with knowledge of the Korean peninsula. The Council on Foreign Relations, an influential foreign policy think tank representing a cross-party spectrum of Washington establishment opinion, published two task force reports on U.S. relations with the DPRK, in 1998 and again in 1999. The reports could more or less be seen as a "Washington consensus" on how U.S. policy toward the DPRK might be handled.[20] Although critical of some aspects of the Clinton approach, the reports endorsed Clinton policies of negotiation and the policy of cautious engagement and urged close coordination with South Korea and Japan.[21] The ex-ambassadors and officials heading the council's task force on Korea understood the consequences of a U.S. military intervention, even in the form of a targeted "surgical strike" on any part of the DPRK. Seoul, home to about half of the Republic of Korea's 44 million people, is only a few miles from the border and highly vulnerable to even a low-technology North Korean retaliation.

The nongovernmental humanitarian sector also more or less supported Clinton's agenda. Humanitarian NGOs worked closely with the State Department, monitoring U.S. government food donations in the DPRK. The salaries and costs of U.S. food monitors, resident in the DPRK intermittently between 1998 and 2000, were paid by USAID, to which they also directly reported.[22]

The Clinton administration faced dissent by members of Congress who thought he had given too much away to the North Koreans and who saw the 1994 agreement as nothing but appeasement of an evil regime.[23] Congressional critics were supported by conservative think tanks such as the American Enterprise Institute and the Heritage Foundation. Both remained deeply critical of both the DPRK and the Clinton administration but operated within, if on the uneasy edge of, the new consensus.[24] Their lack of influence within the Clinton administration was partly due to a lack of clear policy alternatives and partly because, with the advent of the Kim Dae Jung presidency, they lost critical support from South Korea that had hitherto provided funding and legitimacy for hard-line approaches to the DPRK.[25]

A Fragile Consensus

U.S. policy under Clinton opened up substantial channels of dialogue between the two adversaries but did not establish a systematic strategy to link economics, human rights, and humanitarian assistance sectors to the all-important U.S. goal of obtaining an agreement on DPRK chemical, biological, and nuclear weapons. Wider constituencies, including Congress, did not share the consensus that had been forged over intense negotiations by Clinton officials with DPRK representatives that the two countries could do business, albeit in a sometimes strained manner. This always fragile consensus was not embedded enough in the body politic to remain unchallenged by those who lacked the experience of the Clinton administration in dealing with the DPRK.

The Paralysis of the Bush Administration

The administration of President Bush came to office with a commitment to review U.S. policy toward North Korea. The review began after a strained meeting with South Korean president Kim Dae Jung in Washington in March 2001 in which President Bush seemed publicly to rebuff Kim. In June 2001 the review was completed. Formally the review decided that

> [U.S.] North Korea policy will emphasize seven themes: 1) Supporting South Korea's engagement with the North; 2) Strengthening U.S. alliances with South Korea and Japan; 3) Improving implementation of the 1994 Agreed Framework; 4) Moving U.S.-North Korean contacts to a lower working level; 5) Addressing missile issues (both missile development and export); 6) Reducing North Korean conventional force levels; and 7) Emphasizing humanitarian issues (e.g., food aid and human rights).[26]

U.S. aims remained, therefore, more or less the same as under the Clinton administration, with the exception of the additional and not unreasonable addition of considering how to reduce the excessive military forces in the DPRK. In practice, implementation of policy was dogged by what President Bush himself termed a visceral reaction against Kim Jong Il. Bush went on record as saying he "loathed" the DPRK leader.[27] The Bush administration abandoned the security deal brokered by Clinton's officials and conducted its public demarches toward the DPRK in language that was anything but diplomatic. This reinforced to an already suspicious DPRK government that the new administration was not serious about negotiating an agreement between the two states. President Bush's January 2002 speech categorizing the DPRK as part of an "axis of evil," along with Iraq and Iran, was perhaps the most famous of these verbal attacks.[28] These high-profile presidential speeches were also accompanied by similarly belligerent public utterances from senior officials such as John Bolton that kept hostility high throughout the Bush administration.

Superficially, the Bush speech of 2002 marked a reversal of U.S. policy to that of the early, also tough-talking days of the Clinton administration. The new administration was, however, anxious to distance itself from the later Clinton policies that had undertaken rapprochement with Kim Jong Il. Washington insiders, both Democratic and Republican, regularly and publicly joked that Bush had adopted an ABC policy—Anything But Clinton. The substantial influence of neoconservative administration officials such as Paul Wolfowitz, Donald Rumsfeld, and Dick Cheney, who leaned toward an aggressive interventionism toward the DPRK, combined with the predilection to denigrate Clinton administration policy, severely limited the pursuit of serious diplomacy to resolve conflict.[29]

In practice, no alternative policies were either promulgated or implemented. As a result, the policy instruments used by the Clinton administration in its later days were retained, albeit in a diluted form. Humanitarian aid was maintained, if significantly reduced. In late 2002, the administration abandoned its commitment from the 1994 Agreed Framework to supply heavy fuel oil to the DPRK, but it did not withdraw completely from participation in KEDO.[30] The Missing in Action program of cooperation between the U.S. Department of Defense (DoD) and the Korean People's Army (KPA) was also maintained. U.S. and DPRK militaries continued to work together inside the DPRK to search for and recover the bodies of U.S. soldiers killed in the Korean War.[31]

Those who would have preferred a policy of aggressive interventionism vis-à-vis the DPRK were strengthened by the September 11, 2001, attacks on the United States and the subsequent popular support for interventionism abroad, in Afghanistan and Iraq. Nevertheless, they were not able to implement such a policy in Northeast Asia. Even as the United States adopted its new global policy of military preemption, worried Northeast Asian allies, who did not relish hot conflict that would inevitably spill over into their territories, stressed dialogue as a means of resolving the Korean conflict. Some in the United States floated the idea of asking the United Nations to impose economic sanctions, in addition to the sanctions already implemented by the United States on the DPRK. Recognition of the impossibility of gaining Russian and Chinese Security

Council votes prevented the vigorous pursuit of this option. Sanctions would also have had little impact in terms of curtailing trade, since DPRK trade volumes with the rest of the world remained minimal.

After continued dialogue with Northeast Asian allies, particularly South Korea but also Japan, as well as China and Russia, the Bush administration agreed to negotiations with the DPRK. At the same time the bar was set so that substantial talks faced insurmountable difficulties. The U.S. wanted the DPRK government to acquiesce to a series of demands before negotiations could take place, thus making an oxymoron of the concept of diplomatic negotiations.[32] Formal talks between the United States and the DPRK first took place in Pyongyang, where U.S. representative Jim Kelly, operating on a minutely scripted set of instructions from Washington, aggressively instructed the North Koreans on what they should and should not be doing to fulfill their nuclear obligations. Kelly accused the DPRK of having a nuclear weapons program, yet he seemed taken aback when the North Koreans appeared to admit to possessing a uranium-enrichment program, a necessary part of nuclear weapons development.

Inexplicably, the United States did not announce these DPRK revelations until twelve days after the meeting.[33] The delay may have been caused in part by the ambiguity of the DPRK's admission; it denied ever having admitted to being engaged in nuclear weapons development based on highly enriched uranium. Another reason was the Bush administration's anxiety to avoid the appearance of inconsistency. In the interim it had been trying to secure approval for a war in Iraq on the basis of a suspected (rather than, as with the DPRK, an allegedly admitted) capacity to launch weapons of mass destruction.

The next set of talks in Beijing, with a Chinese diplomatic presence, took on a further appearance of farce. Kelly announced that the DPRK had admitted to possessing nuclear bombs, but he also reported that this admission had not taken place at the negotiating table, but later, in an informal conversation, presumably through an interpreter.[34] A skeptical international audience might have queried why normal diplomatic practice was not followed and the informal admission brought back to the table for confirmation. Instead talks broke up a day early with the United States ignoring the DPRK proposal to return to the status quo ante, that is, to the stage in diplomatic relations between the two achieved toward the end of the Clinton administration, through a series of graduated and reciprocal steps.

In 2003 and 2004, the United States sent a team of officials to participate in the Chinese-brokered multilateral talks with China, Russia, Japan, South Korea, and North Korea. The U.S. position was that it would not engage in negotiation until the DPRK agreed to what became known in political shorthand as CVID—complete verifiable and irreversible dismantling of nuclear weapons programs.[35] This position was accompanied by a presidential statement denying that the United States had any intention of militarily attacking the DPRK. The DPRK view was that the United States was proposing unilateral disarmament and therefore found the Bush position unacceptable.

In June 2004, however, the Bush administration engaged in what the *New York Times* called a "turnabout" in policy.[36] The United States offered to discuss potential benefits for North Korea, including shipments of heavy fuel oil, should the DPRK agree "to fully disclose its nuclear activities, submit to inspections and pledge to begin eliminating nuclear programs after a 'preparatory period' of three months."[37] Again according to the *New York Times,* "China, South Korea and Japan . . . all urged the United States to bring a concrete proposal to the latest round [of multilateral talks] or risk being seen as recalcitrant."[38]

Domestically, Congress maintained a high-profile campaign critical of the DPRK, citing the presence of North Korean refugees in China as evidence of DPRK human rights abuses. Congress focused on the brutal conditions in prisons, the large numbers of political prisoners, and the lack of religious freedom.[39] Congressional critics also criticized the DPRK for not permitting adequate monitoring of humanitarian assistance. Congressional committees held numerous hearings, receiving testimony from reputable human rights organizations and humanitarian organizations such as Human Rights Watch and the World Food Program, whose concerns centered on the opacity in DPRK society such as to cause uncertainty and suspicion of DPRK government motivations and actions.[40] Congress also repeatedly invited more questionably representative figures, whose funding, accountability, and organizational structures were less than transparent.[41] The "evidence" given by these persons was characterized by deliberate exaggeration of their own knowledge and what amounted to active deception through distortion of evidence.[42]

From late 2002 to mid-2004, Bush administration foreign policy toward the DPRK was in a state of paralysis. One part of the administration, clustered around Vice President Dick Cheney, could not garner enough support for the vigorous options it preferred to take against the DPRK.[43] At the same time, both allies and more moderate U.S. government officials could not ensure that U.S. diplomatic engagement with the DPRK achieved the level of genuine negotiations. After engaging in two wars, in Afghanistan and Iraq, and with campaigning beginning for the 2004 presidential election in mid-2003, the administration showed signs of downgrading the DPRK as a foreign policy priority. A deep distrust of the DPRK, stoked by vigorous ideological interventions by congressional Republicans, combined with policy stasis, made innovative diplomatic initiatives difficult. By mid-2004, however, the Bush administration was demonstrating some signs of more profound engagement as it worked with allies to present more nuanced proposals to the multilateral talks.

Humanitarian Linkages and Political Strategies

The United States continued to give humanitarian food assistance to the DPRK through the Clinton and Bush administrations. Most governmental assistance was channeled through the UN World Food Program, with some assistance organized via NGOs. During the Clinton years there were some attempts to gain strong bilateral controls over humanitarian food donations. The intention was to ensure food was distributed to targeted beneficiary groups and to obtain more information about DPRK society.[44] In contrast, under the Bush administration, food aid became more divorced from the political strategy toward the DPRK. In other words, food aid became more "humanitarian" during the Bush administration and less "political" than it had been under the Clinton administration.

During the Bush administration nongovernmental actors continued minor attempts to develop linkages between the two countries through support for training and capacity-building projects that might lead to confidence building. Training projects were developed by Syracuse University with the DPRK's prestigious Kimchaek University for Technology. Additionally, the California-based Nautilus organization continued its support for small-scale energy development as well as its important information-dissemination activities on the DPRK via its globally respected website.[45] These activities were insufficient in scope and scale to affect government attitudes toward the DPRK. Their very existence, however, showed that alternative foreign policy conceptions and practice could emerge after the period of paralysis. Such foreign policy conceptions might combine more nuanced analysis, along with the previous experience of Clinton administration officials at achieving a toughly negotiated settlement, with an imaginative and balanced diplomacy that could promote the human security of the North Korean population as well as the national security objectives of the U.S. government.

The Republic of Korea

South Korean diplomacy toward the DPRK underwent a massive shift in 1998 with the presidency of Kim Dae Jung, a former dissident who had spent six years in prison for campaigning for democracy. Kim came to office determined to seek reconciliation with the North and a real, not nominal, rapprochement between the two adversaries. President Kim's objective was to end the division of a great and ancient nation that traced its roots back five thousand years. The almost hermetic sealing of one state from the other had cut off even basic communication between Koreans on different sides of the border. After the Korean War ended in 1953, the brutality of the division meant that families did not know if their closest kin were alive or dead. Inter-Korean telephone and postal communication remained impossible even after the 2000 summit.

A History of Failed Diplomacy

President Kim inherited a history of failed diplomacy between South and North. The two societies had minimal interaction other than through the formal and strained contacts that continued by way of the 1994 KEDO agreement. The two diplomatic demarches previously signed between South and North Korea, the last in 1991, had not resulted in any substantial amelioration of the conflictual relations between the two. If anything, the tone and atmosphere of exchanges had become more hostile since the death of Kim Il Sung in 1994. Kim Young Sam, Kim Dae Jung's predecessor, had grossly offended the North Koreans by not extending condolences after the late North Korean president's death, and relations remained tense, punctuated by small-scale military conflict. One notorious incident in

1996 involved a nationwide hunt and the eventual death of eleven North Korean submariners whose midget submarine had drifted ashore in South Korea.[46] Although the previous South Korean president had jointly proposed four-party talks with the DPRK along with the United States, diplomatic efforts were not awarded much of a priority. Kim Young Sam assumed that the DPRK would collapse under the weight of the economic crisis of the 1990s, the starvation that killed so many of the Northern population in the mid-1990s and the subsequent chronic food shortages and continued economic devastation.[47]

The Humanitarian Bridge to Peace

Many South Koreans, appalled by the increasingly visible starvation of the mid-1990s, had sought ways to make contact with the North so as to deliver aid to people that they saw not just as desperate individuals but as desperate Koreans to whom the South had national as well as humanitarian obligations, irrespective of the conflictual relations between the two governments. Some groups, like Caritas–South Korea, supported famine relief through an international relief agency, in this case Caritas-Internationalis, headquartered in the Vatican. Others attempted direct contacts through feeding hungry North Koreans on the China border. Others, such as World Vision South Korea, made direct visits to Pyongyang.

Churches, NGOs, and individuals were sometimes concerned that they would face penalties under the National Security Law that forbade contacts with North Koreans. By the 1990s, however, South Korea was a functioning democracy. Despite some efforts to control and direct nongovernmental aid, especially under the Kim Young Sam administration, South Korean governments did not try to prevent civil society organizations from helping starving North Koreans.[48] Not all economic transactions were of a direct humanitarian nature in that their primary objective was to relieve humanitarian need. Between 1992 and 1997, for instance, South Korean business began to make business investments in the North—in sectors including clothing manufacture, food processing, and television assembly. The best-known investment, initiated in 1997, was Hyundai's large-scale tourism project to develop one of the peninsula's most ancient and revered scenic areas, Mount Kumgang, in the southeast of the DPRK.[49] Chung Ju Yung, the president of Hyundai, visited the DPRK several times in

1998, donating cattle for humanitarian purposes and drawing up terms for economic cooperation projects. All of these business ventures helped bring some semblance of economic reconstruction, itself a fundamental part of responding to the chronic and complex humanitarian emergency that characterized the DPRK's socioeconomic crisis.

Humanitarian and business representatives traveled around the country to visit the projects in which they were engaged, seeing for themselves the conditions of life outside Pyongyang, without the handicap of having to mix with North Koreans through interpreters. The people-to-people and societal contacts that were initiated for humanitarian and business reasons had an unanticipated outcome. They provided, almost for the first time, factual information on the North to a South that had been exposed to only highly colored propaganda about the North for fifty years. These civil society contacts helped demystify the North in the South and provided a social base within South Korea, beyond the radical pro-Pyongyang left, of opposition to isolationist, belligerent policies toward the North.

Changing the Paradigm: Kim Dae Jung's Profound Legacy

The presidency of Kim Dae Jung explicitly rejected prior policies of belligerence and sought to resolve the conflict with the North through engagement. Kim Dae Jung most substantially articulated the engagement, or "sunshine," policy in March 2000, in a speech made in Berlin, symbolic of successful national reunification after a similar bitter experience of post–World War II division.[50] The "Berlin declaration" formally renounced absorption as a goal of policy. Instead the South Korean president announced his government's intention to enter into intergovernmental economic cooperation with the DPRK. This was by no means an appeasement policy. In the same speech, President Kim reiterated what he had been saying since the start of his presidency. Engagement would take place side by side with a policy of military deterrence. The president's speech acknowledged the contribution of nongovernmental actors to the engagement policy and encouraged other international actors to support South Korea in its new diplomacy. The president stated,

> We do not want another war with North Korea. We want to coexist with it and intend to help it. Whenever we witness the tragic scene of hungry North

Koreans on TV, we are devastated. We want to help North Korea feed their citizens adequately. We want to help it recover from the deep economic slump and improve its standard of living. Currently, there is no government-to-government dialogue because of Pyongyang's reluctance. But my Administration is aggressively encouraging private sector cooperation and exchanges. We welcome and encourage all international efforts to increase exchanges with Pyongyang.[51]

In June 2000, any excitement generated by the Berlin declaration was superseded by the historically astonishing sight of the South Korean president flying into Pyongyang to receive a welcome hitherto accorded only to Communist North Korea's closest allies. The Pyongyang Summit was the beginning of a series of negotiations between the two countries—on subjects ranging through the reunion of separated familes, the rebuilding of rail and road links, economic cooperation, and humanitarian assistance.[52] Concrete outcomes resulted from these meetings, which, among other things, enjoined the two countries' militaries in the logistics of mine clearing along the border.[53] Conflict was still endemic to the relationship, but what quickly became an institutionalized relationship of cooperation between the two parties allowed channels for conflict to be resolved peacefully. These peacemaking efforts were internationally recognized when President Kim Dae Jung was awarded the Nobel Peace Prize in 2000.[54]

An average of 7,000 South Koreans visited the North every year between 1998 and 2002, on aid, economic, cultural, and political trips. This compared to an average of merely 270 between 1989 and 1997, when it first became possible for South Koreans to visit Pyongyang.[55] These figures do not include the numbers of South Korean tourists who made the boat trip to Mount Kumgang, which by 2002 amounted to nearly half a million people.[56] Building on the information base provided by South Korean NGOs, South Korean visitors in this next wave were thus able to make judgments for themselves instead of having to rely on the highly skewed perspective that dominated outside accounts of the DPRK. This intensified interaction contributed to a reformulation of a national attitude toward the DPRK. In 2002 South Koreans rejected the front-running presidential candidate, whose main plank had been to take a tougher line on the DPRK. Instead they elected Roh Moo Hyun, whose key promise was to maintain and intensify the policy of engagement.[57]

South Korea's New Role: Interlocutor for the DPRK

The impact of the post-2000 South Korean government assumption of leadership in peacebuilding with the DPRK was felt in the domestic and international arenas. Domestically, the NGOs that had hitherto acted as de facto peacemakers, as a result of their provision of channels of communication with the DPRK, were able to focus more on their role as technical providers of aid and less on their contribution to peacebuilding. Humanitarian assistance became just one more instrument in the panoply of governmental instruments designed to achieve overall foreign policy goals rather than, as it had been prior to the summit, an inadvertent substitute for foreign policy activity. Internationally, South Korea persuaded other states to support the policy of engagement. Its most notable success was in persuading the European Union and its member-states, excepting (as of July 2004) France, to diplomatically recognize the DPRK if they had not already done so and to enter into a critical dialogue with the DPRK as well as to provide humanitarian and development assistance.

The South Korean government maintained formal and informal contact with the DPRK throughout the international tension that accompanied the worsening of U.S.-DPRK relations from 2002 on. Ten meetings were held at interministerial level between June 2000 and April 2003, with talks often taking place more or less simultaneously with public threats of war and aggressive intervention from both the DPRK and the United States.[58] The South continued in the sometimes thankless role of mediator as the presidencies of Kim Dae Jung and his successor, Roh Moo Hyun, continued to work patiently toward a diplomatic resolution.

The Roh Moo Hyun Presidency: Engaging the United States as Well as the DPRK

The new presidency of Roh Moo Hyun was more adept at working with the United States than its predecessor. It engaged with Bush administration concerns about international terrorism while simultaneously continuing the policy of engagement with the DPRK. President Roh offered to send troops to Iraq in 2003 as a symbol of its commitment to the "war on terrorism" and the United States–South Korea alliance. This action contrasted sharply with Kim Dae Jung's refusal of the U.S. request the previous year to send combat troops to Afghanistan.[59] President Roh appointed as

U.S. ambassador Han Sung-Joo, a scholar and previous ROK foreign minister who was well known and respected in Washington and not known for being overly sympathetic to the DPRK.[60] The new South Korean administration benefited in turn from a reappraisal by the Bush administration of its previous clumsy dealings with South Korea.[61] The U.S. administration, for instance, had appeared to snub President Kim Dae Jung when he visited Washington, six weeks after the inauguration of the new U.S. president in 2001, when policy toward Korea had not been fully formulated.[62] It had also engaged in eventually counterproductive efforts to embrace the conservative candidate in the 2002 South Korean elections.

President Roh vigorously pursued negotiations with the DPRK but, at the same time, demonstrated a tougher approach than his predecessor. Much-needed humanitarian assistance continued, as did construction on rail and road links between the two countries. At the same time the ROK refused to accept verbal provocations from DPRK officials. In one instance in 2003, after a DPRK negotiator threatened the South with "unimaginable disaster" should the United States engage in actions that the DPRK found "aggressive," ROK negotiators refused to continue discussion on economic assistance until the DPRK explained in writing what was meant by this outlandish statement.[63]

Prior to winning the presidency, Roh had been widely considered a liberal outsider to politics who might have difficulties working with the United States, given his overriding commitment to engagement as the way to resolve the Korean conflict. Roh's new realism toward the DPRK and the United States, however, combined to make South Korea a more comfortable negotiating partner for the United States than his predecessor. Roh's continued commitment to tripartite coordination with Japan and the United States, along with improved relationships with the United States, made for smoother allied relationships with respect to the DPRK than many had anticipated.

Japan

The "securitized" approach to national security policy, that is, territorial defense through military means combined with a strong anti-Communist ideological agenda, shaped Japanese policy toward the DPRK. The securitized approach reflected a more or less shared perspective among the Japanese political establishment, although the Foreign Ministry sometimes attempted to engage in negotiations to try to break what many considered was the dangerous state of Japan-DPRK relations.

Most Japanese governments maintained a mirror-imaging of the DPRK government, viewing them as beyond the pale and leaving policy direction to the U.S. government.[64] Hard security concerns about the DPRK's large armed forces and ideological antipathy toward a Communist regime were not the only factors making for poor relations between Japan and the DPRK. Specific bilateral concerns included the questions of Japanese civilians abducted by the DPRK in the 1970s and 1980s, permission for home visits by Japanese women who had married North Koreans and emigrated to the DPRK, and the North Korean harboring of Red Army Faction terrorists.[65]

Roadblocks along the Normalization Highway

From the late 1980s on, senior Japanese political figures attempted the "normalization" of relations with the DPRK. In 1989 Prime Minister Takeshita Noboru expressed a desire for improved relations with the DPRK.[66] Between 1990 and 1992, eight rounds of talks were held with the DPRK, initially led by respected Liberal Democratic Party (LDP) statesman Shin Kanemaru and subsequently conducted by Foreign Ministry officials.[67] In 1992 the Japanese representative at the secret normalization talks with the North Koreans in Beijing apologized for the treatment of the women who had been forced into sexual slavery during the war.[68] Talks broke down in 1992 because of the lack of progress on the nature of compensation for the colonial period, the refusal by the DPRK to open up nuclear sites for inspection, and the denial that Japanese civilians had been kidnapped and taken to the DPRK.[69]

As well as providing a resolution to the nuclear conflict, the 1994 Geneva Agreement allowed for the resumption of normalization talks that had taken place in 1995.[70] Limited progress ensued, however, with DPRK officials continuing to deny the existence of Japanese abductees. Relations were not helped when, in 1997, Japanese authorities found and interdicted a drug-smuggling operation that used a North Korean ship. The nadir of relations between the two came in August 1998 after what the DPRK called a satellite launch and Japan and the United States termed a missile test. Whatever the terminology, the technology displayed an ability by the DPRK to manufacture a medium-range ballistic missile rocket. That, plus the fact that the satellite/missile malfunctioned and shot over the center of Japan, caused widespread fear and anger in the Japanese public as well as the political establishment. Both Houses of the Diet unanimously condemned the rocket launch as an "unforgivable act."[71]

Some positive developments occurred during the late 1990s. In 1997 and 1998 Japanese women married to North Koreans were given permission to visit Japan, and in 1999 former prime minister Tomiichi Murayama visited Pyongyang.[72] The Murayama visit opened up Red Cross channels between the two countries, but what facilitated the resumption of normalization talks in 2000, five years after the agreement to renew them, was the impetus provided by South Korean and North Korean proactive diplomacy toward Japan.[73] South Korea was anxious that Japan support the engagement policy that it considered the only viable option for dealing with the DPRK. The lack of credible alternatives, combined with U.S. encouragement of the South's engagement policy during the Clinton administration, ruled out any strategic risk in terms of potential damage to its primary alliance with the United States. Japanese policy thus inched back toward increased normalization efforts.[74]

The Abrogation of Political Leadership

In late 2001, senior Japanese diplomats began a series of secret talks with their North Korean counterparts, making these public only in August 2002, three weeks prior to the surprise visit by Prime Minister Koizumi to Pyongyang in mid-September.[75] Koizumi's visit was intended to clear away some of the major obstacles to normalization, which for Japan primarily meant clarifying the abductee issue, resolving the nuclear problem, and coming to an agreement on compensation for colonial occupation.[76] Koizumi's decision to visit Pyongyang was extraordinarily popular with the Japanese public. Polls showed over 80 percent approval ratings.[77]

The summit resulted in the Pyongyang Declaration—essentially a commitment to seek normalization between the two countries.[78] The summit also produced an admission from Kim Jong Il that DPRK agents had abducted thirteen Japanese civilians and that eight had died.[79] Apologies

were given by Kim Jong Il along with a statement that the people responsible had been punished. The DPRK leader also dropped claims to "reparations" from Japan for the colonial past.[80] On Japan's part, Prime Minister
Koizumi apologized for the "damage and suffering to the people of Korea"
wreaked through the years of colonialism.[81] The Japanese government
negotiated an agreement whereby the five remaining abductees should
return to Japan for two weeks and then return to the DPRK pending further negotiations. According to one reputable scholar of Japanese foreign
policy, Pyongyang's offer to allow the abductees' children to go to Japan with
them was rejected.[82]

Relations deteriorated on Koizumi's return to Japan in the wake of public anger about the fate of the abductees. Once in Japan the two married
couples and one woman (the latter of whom had also left her husband
behind in Pyongyang, a deserter from the U.S. Army who faced immediate
arrest if he traveled outside the DPRK) were the focus of a national campaign by a variety of groups, including very vocal right-wing anti-DPRK
political groups, to allow them to stay in Japan and to force them to stay
if necessary.[83] These groups explicitly called for the overthrow of the
DPRK government and the renunciation of peaceful means to achieve that
objective.[84] They demanded that the children of the abductees be sent to
Japan but refused to support negotiations that might achieve that end.
Furthermore, a demand was raised that the child of one of the Japanese
abductees who had died be sent to Japan to live with her grandparents.
This child could not speak a word of Japanese and was living with her
Korean father and family in a Korean home, as a Korean child, within her
own culture and country. In a bizarre mirror-imaging of DPRK crimes,
the Japanese groups formed ostensibly to support the abductees were de-
manding that the situation be rectified by forcibly taking Korean children
to Japan and not allowing them to return to their homes in the DPRK.

The domestic political atmosphere was underpinned by an anti-Korean
mentality that permeated majority Japanese discourse on the DPRK.
Genuine human rights–based criticism of the DPRK abductions was
drowned in the outpouring of organized anti-DPRK activity that omitted
to mention past Japanese human rights crimes against Koreans or sought
to exculpate Japan from blame for those crimes. (Incidentally, South
Korea had also used abduction as a tool of foreign policy, the most famous

case being the kidnapping of Kim Dae Jung from a Tokyo hotel room by South Korean CIA agents in 1973.)[85] A minority of Japanese commentators recognized that Japan had yet to acknowledge its own responsibilities toward Korea, particularly to the Korean women who were forced to act as sex slaves for the Japanese army during the war and who were still seeking recognition for the abuse they had faced.[86] The majority perspective, however, was still influenced by colonialist views on Korea, as exemplified in June 2003 when a senior figure in the ruling party, Taro Aso, offended South and North Koreans by stating that, during the colonial period, Koreans had actively welcomed the Japanese practice of forcing Koreans to take Japanese names.[87]

The Japanese political leadership did not initially attempt to engage in leadership in terms of arguing for a resolution to the various outstanding conflicts between the two countries through negotiation. Instead it used the fear of the DPRK, whipped up through the media, to support its efforts to give the Japanese military, the Self-Defense Forces, more ability to use its considerable weaponry. (According to the London-based military think tank the International Institute of Strategic Studies, Japan was the third-biggest military spender in the world, after the United States and China but before the United Kingdom and France.)[88] Laws adopted in June 2003 gave the government a freer hand to use military forces, which ratcheted up tension in East Asia. Japan's neighbors, all former victims of Japanese militarism, reacted with what the South Korean president, on his first visit to Tokyo in that same month, voiced as "anxiety and suspicion."[89]

The economic sanctions that were touted by hard-liners were not supported by the South Korean government. Since Japan had pledged to coordinate activity toward the DPRK with the South Koreans, it was left without a credible policy alternative to negotiation. The disinclination to follow through with the tough and necessarily complicated negotiations that had commenced in 2002 effectively denied Japanese political leaders a role in resolving the security crisis that threatened the stability of all of Northeast Asia. With the Japanese political leadership succumbing to a populist chauvinism as a substitute for hard political bargaining, it was left to the South Koreans and the United States to look for ways to negotiate a resolution to the regional conflict.[90]

Prime Minister Koizumi continued to be under intense domestic political pressure to "do something" to reunite the abductees with their families left behind in Pyongyang. In May 2004 Koizumi made his second visit to the DPRK, returning with all of the children except those fathered by the U.S. military deserter, who also stayed behind. Normalization was again on the agenda, made possible by the opportunities for bilateral dialogue with the North Koreans provided by the umbrella of the six-party nuclear talks in Beijing. The multilateral framework had also made dialogue with the DPRK more acceptable to Japanese public opinion, which had hitherto been reluctant to accept renewed bilateral engagement with Pyongyang.

The Humanitarian Window Closed . . . and Reopened

Japanese Foreign Ministry officials received approaches from the DPRK to help with food assistance as early as 1994 and again in 1995.[91] Japan had responded to what was becoming an internationally visible humanitarian crisis with generous and large shipments of rice aid. The Japanese government had agreed to humanitarian assistance to the DPRK for its own sake and because it had hoped that such assistance would provide a way to encourage the resuscitation of normalization talks that had started and then stalled in the early 1990s without any substantial progress.[92] Pyongyang, however, did not take this opportunity to revive political dialogue. Because of the lack of goodwill or any show of reciprocity, Japan decided to end food assistance in 2001.[93]

The decision to cut off humanitarian food aid for political reasons, despite the attested need for humanitarian assistance, aroused virtually no domestic controversy. Japan had not disputed that its food aid was helping to prevent hungry women and children from dying, particularly weaning-age babies who relied solely on Japanese rice. Japan also held millions of tonnes of surplus rice in its warehouses, some of which it had to destroy because of limited storage capacity and all of which it had paid subsidies to farmers to produce. Japan's position was quite unlike that of the United States. From Reagan through to the second Bush administration, the United States had argued that humanitarian assistance should be separate from political leverage. Thus it had maintained food aid to hungry North Koreans in the midst of the tense political and security crises of the early 2000s.

Japanese NGOs maintained small but symbolic assistance. They were, however, unable to change the climate of opinion in Japan. From 2002 on, Japanese increasingly viewed DPRK policy as a humanitarian issue only in terms of the crimes committed against Japanese abductees and, to a lesser extent, as a national security issue. The continuing humanitarian crisis in the DPRK was barely reported in the Japanese media. The large multilateral agencies such as UNICEF that operated in Japan mainly to raise funds from the public and private sectors judged that the political climate in Japan was so hostile to the DPRK that they refrained from calling for funding for the DPRK despite the fact that their country operations in the DPRK were badly underfunded. The rationale was that if UNICEF made an issue of the DPRK in Japan, it would impair the ability of UNICEF to raise funds for field operations in other parts of the world.

Another reason for the dearth of humanitarian links with the DPRK was that the conduit for much of the NGO humanitarian assistance was the General Association of Korean Residents in Japan (Chochongryun in Korean; Chosen Soren in Japanese). This institution, which represented Korean residents with links to Pyongyang, carried out many legitimate activities in Japan, including welfare and schooling. Chosen Soren was shunned by the Japanese media, however, partly for the very fact of its association with the DPRK and also because its members were the source of financial remittances to individuals and to the DPRK government.[94] Guilt through association was reinforced by Chosen Soren's control of over 30 percent of Japan's popular *pachinko,* or pinball, halls, whose management and ownership were alleged to be linked to organized crime, run by the Japanese equivalent of the mafia, the *yakuzas.*[95] The organization was also vilified because some of its members had been found involved in drug smuggling, and the suspicion was that such illegal activities were directly organized by the DPRK government.[96] With Chosen Soren viewed with such hostility, this main channel of nongovernmental assistance to the DPRK could not provide an opening for humanitarian diplomacy between Japan and the DPRK.

The Rest of the West

Of the remaining Western countries, only those acting collectively as the European Union attempted to play a diplomatic role in the outstanding areas of international conflict involving the DPRK. The European Union had only modest political objectives. It recognized that it had lesser interests in the region than the United States or the regional powers. It also acknowledged that, as a major economic power, consisting of member-states that also had diplomatic clout in world affairs, it could not afford to remain passive in a potential crisis with implications for global security. The European Union saw itself in a subsidiary role as a diplomatic actor and saw its function as acting in support of inter-Korean reconciliation and the engagement policy of South Korea.[97]

The European Union's intervention in the DPRK was based on a clear set of foreign policy guidelines derived from its own experience of dealing with Communist states during the Cold War. The European Union considered that its patient diplomacy in venues such as the Organization for Security and Cooperation in Europe had helped bring about peaceful change in Eastern Europe and Russia. Thus it emphasized engagement and careful dialogue as instruments of peaceful change even for the most apparently rigid of political structures.[98] In the case of the DPRK, European Union strategy was similar and analogous to that which drove its comprehensive approach toward the consolidation of democratic transition in Eastern Europe. The Union argued that "assistance . . . for sustainable economic and social development must go hand in hand with respect for democratic principles and human rights and prospects of regional peace and stability."[99] The instruments chosen to implement this strategy were humanitarian and development assistance and regularized dialogue.

From the start of its involvement in the DPRK in 1997, Switzerland also adopted a policy of engagement. The Swiss gave humanitarian assistance but had a long-term goal of encouraging and supporting increased DPRK openness to the outside world. They provided support for training and study for DPRK officials as well as engaging in economic and political dialogue with the government. The aim was to help lay the foundations for peaceful transformation on the Korean peninsula.

Helping the Diplomatic Sun Shine In

The European Union displayed a high-level interest in the DPRK. It sent its governing troika, consisting of the president of the Council of Ministers, the high representative for the Common Foreign and Security Policy

(CFSP), and the commissioner for external relations for consultations with Kim Jong Il in May 2001.[100] The European Union attempted a series of cautious interventions designed to support inter-Korean reconciliation through economic support, for instance in contributions toward KEDO, at the same time that it engaged in dialogue on the tougher areas of human rights, nonproliferation, and general security concerns.[101]

An implicit benefit of the regular contact that the DPRK had with European aid officials was the improved ability of European Union and member-state diplomats to assess DPRK political and economic developments. The opacity of DPRK governmental activity diminished, although it did not disappear, and European diplomats had access to useful and reliable information from the extensive activities of the humanitarian organizations. More informed European diplomatic activity resulted in better and more informed dialogue with Washington, aiding the demystification of the DPRK and partially contributing to normalization efforts. The EU was able to develop an improved knowledge base because of the member-states' resident embassies and missions (Sweden, Germany, the United Kingdom, and the Italian Development Corporation) and because, since 1997, it had established a resident presence in Pyongyang to handle humanitarian assistance.

EU-DPRK diplomatic relations, like their relations in the field of humanitarian assistance, were not always harmonious. The European Union's insistence on a meaningful human rights dialogue brought it into conflict with DPRK authorities, especially after it sponsored a resolution condemning DPRK human rights practices at the United Nations Human Rights Commission in 2003.[102] It also showed itself prepared to sanction the DPRK by withdrawing promised development assistance, for instance when it suspended economic training programs pending a resolution of the nuclear conflict of 2002–3.[103]

The European Union continued to maintain that a peaceful solution to the Korean conflict was possible and that dialogue contributed to confidence building and increased awareness of all sides' priorities and interests. Subsequent to the election of the new South Korean president in 2002 and the renewed outbreak of tensions in 2002–3, it reasserted the policy of supporting engagement, welcoming and supporting efforts toward a multilateral resolution of conflict.[104]

Of the individual member-states, Sweden remained pivotal given its additional role of representing U.S. interests in the DPRK. With a resident presence since the 1970s, the Swedes were active even prior to the flurry of European diplomatic engagement from 2000 on. They helped organize the links between the Korean People's Army and the U.S. Department of Defense that brought about the remains-recovery operations. They also prepared the way for Madeleine Albright's October 2000 visit to Pyongyang and organized the high-level European Union troika visit in May 2001. The Swedish embassy benefited from the in-country presence of an experienced diplomat, chargé d'affaires Svante Kilander. His organizational and diplomatic achievements were all the more impressive given that the embassy operated with two international staff members, one phone, one fax machine, and no e-mail or Internet connection.

Humanitarians as "Ice-Breakers"

The European Union did not argue that humanitarian aid should be provided for any other reason than to alleviate humanitarian needs. Its analysis, however, was that the consistent interaction between EU officials, the NGOs that it funded, and DPRK officials, arising out of negotiations over the transfer of humanitarian assistance, could act "as an ice-breaker in the opening process of the country."[109] Interaction on humanitarian assistance, in other words, could contribute in a small way to the transfer of international good practice, including norms of transparency, accountability, and efficiency. These interactions formed part of a confidence-building process that the European Union hoped would facilitate "spill-over," providing the foundation for a substantial dialogue on more controversial topics, including human rights and economic reform. To this end, the European Union had a strong policy of encouraging NGO operations in the DPRK, only funding those that agreed to set up an office in the country.[106]

Development aid programs were designed to bridge the gap between humanitarian need and economic reconstruction but were also aimed at institution building in the sense of providing familiarization with and training to DPRK officials on good economic and social practices. Social development and combating poverty should be "based on a close integration of the political, economic, social and environmental dimensions of development."[107] To this end the European Union funded training programs in economic reform. It also funded human rights training, in which DPRK officials attended courses in Stockholm, Sweden, and at the University of Essex in the United Kingdom.[108]

The process of dialogue did not eradicate conflict. Mistakes were made on both sides. EU policy was sometimes undermined by difficulties in the European NGOs it funded. The biggest disaster was when Children's Aid Direct—a British NGO—went bankrupt in 2002, leaving substantial debts to the DPRK government. The process of dialogue, however, provided a forum in which the many conflicts that emerged in the day-to-day relationships as well as over the larger strategic issues could be played out and negotiated—albeit very often to the total satisfaction of neither side. Writing in 2001, the resident representative in Pyongyang of the European Union's humanitarian office (ECHO) commented on the "see-saw pattern" of relations.

> The road . . . remains, uphill; a good many set-backs have also occurred. Progress vis-à-vis the initial conditions in 1995–6 has undoubtedly taken place but the good cooperation spirit that seemed to prevail in 1998, was replaced in 1999 by an icily cold, negative and confrontational policy. Then, last year, there has been a partial thaw and . . . some small signs of progress.[109]

The most visible conflicts arose when four European NGOs left the DPRK between 1998 and 2000, citing irreconcilable differences with the government over the conditions under which they were permitted to operate.[110] The EU strongly supported NGO calls for better and increased access for monitoring, reporting, and evaluation purposes but did not advocate a policy of aid withdrawal. Instead, the EU response to conflict was to negotiate with the government within the framework of an overall approach under the aegis of the UN humanitarian coordinator—supporting the "Statement of Humanitarian Principles" that came to form the basis of negotiations on all humanitarian operations with the DPRK government.[111]

Strategically, the response was to identify the reasons for noncooperation, which, the European Union argued, came about mainly from ignorance of standard operating procedures of international transfers. The conclusion was that progress could be made only "through a process of mutual

patience and slow development of understanding about the constraints
and requirements of all parties."[112] To this end, the European Union reoriented its technical assistance programs toward what it called "institution-
building." Training, or "capacity-building," was to be "the first pillar of an
EC-DPRK co-operation strategy."[113] The explicit purpose was to

> provide the DPRK with the necessary capacity to prepare a policy blueprint
> on its future development. It entails the need to strengthen the capacity of key
> institutions and human resources, in particular as regards their ability to
> define a path of economic and *democratic* development and to implement
> poverty reducing policies.[114]

The underlying philosophy of EU analysis was that economic reform
in the direction of more openness, predictability, and stability would have
to occur for economic development to take place. The logical corollary,
although never directly enunciated in policy documents, was that if DPRK
policymakers could be persuaded that economic development could come
about only through more openness, then future dialogue could encourage institutional reform, including a free labor market and an independent judiciary. Such institutional change would necessarily imply decreased
control by the state over individual actions and increased political freedom. Given that by 2002 the DPRK had finally been persuaded of the
necessity of economic reform, the European Union had some hopes that,
with continued engagement and some assistance, the DPRK could be
helped along the road to democracy and peace.

The Swiss Contribution

The Swiss more or less shared European Union analysis but went much
further in implementing a linkage policy that funded projects designed to
increase human security in the food and agriculture sector as well as providing training in institutional reform. The approach was termed "aid for
self-help."[115] The Swiss Agency for Development and Cooperation (SDC)
systematically engaged in an integrated policy that funded agronomists,
resident in the DPRK, who were based on the same farms as when the
program began in 1997. Officials at the local and national level were
identified for technical training in agriculture, as well as in the fields of

diplomacy and economics. The SDC, which is part of the Swiss Foreign Ministry, regularly reported back to the Swiss government on economic and political developments in the DPRK, thus providing another source of information to the outside world.

China and Russia

China and Russia shared a common approach to the DPRK. Both maintained intergovernmental diplomatic links with the DPRK and at the same time worked to block hard-line proposals to induce changed international behavior from Pyongyang, for instance via economic sanctions or the use of military force. As permanent members of the United Nations Security Council, both had veto power and could therefore prevent the imposition of UN sanctions on the DPRK. Russia and China shared an analysis that a resolution to conflict on the peninsula and any hope for economic growth in the DPRK would require that country to come to some form of peace deal with South Korea and the United States and that this should come about through peaceful means. Both were also opposed to any North Korean development of nuclear weapons.[116] China and Russia supported international proposals for negotiations to find a peaceful solution to conflict, using the diplomatic capital they had with Pyongyang to urge compromise and with the United States to stress patience and restraint.

Russia and China based their diplomatic policies on government-to-government links, with both countries eschewing interference in the domestic affairs of the DPRK. Chinese and Russian business links, the main nongovernmental contact with the DPRK, were not integrated by either government into diplomatic policy. Humanitarian aid from China was bilateral and unconditional; the government had direct control over its allocation and distribution. In 2003, Russia became a global World Food Program donor for the first time, and 40,000 tonnes of wheat was allocated to the DPRK.[117] Russia did not, however, insist on any specific or additional donor conditions, over and above the normal WFP requirements of transparency and accountability.

China, and to a lesser extent Russia, had local conflicts with the DPRK, mainly centering on cross-border issues. China reacted strongly to the

DPRK proposal to establish a free-trade zone at Sinuiju in 2002. It arrested the Dutch-Chinese entrepreneur who the DPRK government had, without consultation, announced would be the area's governor and in 2003 sentenced him to eighteen years in prison.[118] The reason given for the arrest was tax fraud. The larger reason was Chinese concern that unregulated trade into its increasingly prosperous border province of Liaoning would have brought a grave threat of economic destabilization. Chinese government officials were well aware that the DPRK had little internal regulation of market transactions and no substantial plans to build the economic institutions that would be necessary to prevent the growth of illicit as well as legal trade. The criminalized capitalism that the Chinese government was attempting to stamp out elsewhere would have been encouraged to gravitate to this area.

China also had to respond to the influx of migrants and refugees that crossed the DPRK's northeastern border in search of food from the 1990s on.[119] Chinese reaction was mixed. Publicly it reaffirmed its treaty commitments with the DPRK and sent back what it identified as economic migrants to the DPRK. In practice, the Chinese government veered between ignoring the issue of North Korean migrants and permitting Chinese-Korean authorities and NGOs to provide humanitarian assistance and taking a tougher line, insisting on returning those without authorization to stay in the country.

Russian border irritations were generally left to local authorities to handle. These included the criminality associated with some DPRK nationals, including those caught smuggling drugs. The murder of a South Korean diplomat in 1996 in Vladivostok, whose murderer was never found, brought to the fore concern over illegal immigration from the DPRK and allegations that, of the North Koreans legally resident, many were actually DPRK intelligence agents.[120] Russia associated DPRK nationals with increasing crime in its Far Eastern region, but given the overall problems of the country of dealing with gangster capitalism in the transition to democracy, these were relatively minor incidents in a region far away from Moscow and had little impact on the overall Russia-DPRK relationship. Instead the Russian leadership focused on the economic benefits that might be obtained for Russia from peaceful transition in the peninsula, particularly from the construction of a Russia–South Korea natural gas pipeline through the DPRK and the trans-Korea railroad being constructed by the DPRK and South Korea.[121]

The Primacy of National Security Perspectives

For China and Russia, the priority was to achieve stability in Northeast Asia, and the means chosen was mediatory diplomacy. Humanitarian assistance and nongovernmental links with the DPRK were not included as instruments of a diplomatic strategy. This was partly a question of political choice and partly a reflection of the overwhelming priority of resolving human security and economic development problems in their own countries. Politically, the obverse side of Russian and Chinese resentment of interference in their own domestic affairs was a strong commitment to noninterference in the domestic affairs of other nations. Economically, both countries were too preoccupied with their own restructuring and institution building to view such activities as a priority in relations with the DPRK.

International Security and Humanitarian Assistance

South Korea, the European Union, and Switzerland were successful in building relationships in the humanitarian and economic sectors such that "spillover" gains were made in the security sectors. South Korea's policy of economic engagement brought rapprochement, sharply reducing the perceived threat from the DPRK. The European Union devised a strategy, built around the provision of humanitarian and development assistance, that eventually allowed it to re-engage in frank political dialogue with the DPRK, on human rights as well as nuclear nonproliferation. Switzerland, a very minor diplomatic actor in the Korean conflict, nevertheless involved its most senior Foreign Ministry officials and politicians in its strategy to develop confidence building side by side with humanitarian economic assistance. In this way it sought to encourage the opening that it saw as a necessary part of bringing peace to the peninsula.[122]

A Strategy of "Intelligent Intervention"

The comprehensive engagement, or what could be called "intelligent intervention," of South Korea and the European Union did not reflect military carelessness or a reduced concern for hard-security conflict resolution. Instead, in the case of the ROK, military deterrence was maintained at the same time that very substantial economic engagement and dialogue continued. National defense was not considered separately from human security engagement. Instead, national defense was considered enhanced by a strategy that integrated a response to the human security crisis in the North, confidence-building measures through dialogue, and a strong military defense capability. Similarly, the European Union's dialogue with the DPRK and its policy of humanitarian and technical support was seen as the obverse side of engagement based on frank discussions about, among other things, the practicalities and modalities of aid transactions, and also about the diplomatically sensitive issues of human rights and nuclear nonproliferation.

The Limits and the Obstacles

There were limits to the strategy of "intelligent intervention." Engagement as confidence building could not substitute for the tough task of reaching agreements on hard security, including nuclear and other armaments issues. It could only facilitate the confidence-building dynamics necessary to build the trust that had been missing from previous negotiations and that would be necessary to reach an eventual peace deal that could satisfy all parties. Implementation of a strategy of "intelligent intervention" was in turn sometimes constrained by both the DPRK's unwillingness to engage and the domestic politics of the external actors themselves.

The DPRK was often enough its own worst enemy. This was most clearly shown in its attitude to the Japanese, which up until the withdrawal of Japanese humanitarian assistance in 2001 was distrusting, ungrateful, and contemptuous. The DPRK had some grounds to be suspicious of Japan, given the nonimplementation of the Kanemaru agreement, but it also showed itself unable to build on the potential for increased dialogue provided by Japanese humanitarian engagement. This intensely suspicious attitude colored all its dealings with humanitarian assistance providers, but the strategic approach of South Korea and the European Union was to view this suspicion as symptomatic of fifty years of global isolation. The conclusion of South Korea and the European Union was that this distrust was part of the problem, to be addressed in much the same way that the substantive problems of economic collapse needed to be addressed.

Reconstituting International Security Strategies

The process of confidence building through sustained engagement based on human security concerns as well as the classical issues of national security, including nuclear weapons proliferation and arms control, had mixed results. Comprehensive engagement worked best where there was strong political leadership committed to a long-haul involvement, backed up by a willingness to offer practical assistance, as in the case of South Korea and the European Union. Reductions in tension were most dramatic in the case of changed perceptions by South Koreans of the DPRK—from the demonized enemy to the pitiable neighbor. Even for those states that were not ready to engage in a sustained process of comprehensive engagement with the DPRK, particularly the United States and Japan, humanitarian and other international activity abated the security dilemma to a certain extent through increasing transparency with respect to the DPRK's capacities and objectives.

Conflict did not disappear from the relationships between the DPRK and those countries that implemented a policy of intelligent intervention. Conflict was, however, channeled into fora whereby solutions could be found through peaceful means and negotiations. The challenge for the major actors was to use the lessons learned from engagement to inform and reorient their strategies to help build an active and stable peace on the peninsula.

8

Intelligent Intervention for a Stable Peace

F ROM THE END OF THE KOREAN WAR in 1953 until the 1980s, the population of the DPRK gained security in freedom from want at the expense of insecurity in terms of freedom from fear. The population more or less accepted this trade-off. Freedom from want increased visibly, and benefited almost all individuals, while losses in freedom from fear were, for most, more insidious and applied less to day-to-day living. Freedom-from-fear human security needs were met in the external sphere in that the population did not experience war after 1953. The benefits of the human security trade-off were the increasing strength of the nation and the economic and social welfare gains that accrued to new postwar generations. This was never a secure trade-off. It had to be continually reinforced by a deliberate socialization process implemented through the state's educational and cultural apparatus and based on a glorification of the Kim Il Sung family (the personality cult). This, in turn, was backed up by systemic repression involving self-censorship and, when necessary, the coercive instruments of the security forces.

Beginning in the mid-1990s, when famine hit the country, most of the population faced insecurity in the most basic of living conditions—in their ability to secure enough food to stay alive. In the Kim Jong Il era, human insecurity became an everyday condition for most people, lacking freedom from want and fearing threats to life and personal security from malnutrition and increased lawlessness. In the external sphere, given the volatile international relations of the peninsula, the freedom from fear of war was only precariously retained. The human security crisis also brought, unexpectedly, a significant socioeconomic structural transformation. The country moved from a planned, centrally directed economy toward a market economy, although not yet a free-market economy. Such a transformation provided new national security threats to DPRK policymakers, but it also forced changes in policy that otherwise would not have been contemplated.

Humanitarian Assistance and Human Security

From the mid-1990s on, basic human security needs—for health support, clothing, emergency supplies, and, most of all, food—were met to a significant degree by international humanitarian agencies. Indirectly and inadvertently, the international agencies also provided a transmission belt for alternative ideas and social practices. This was because the prerequisites for humanitarian assistance included the provision of information to donors (accountability and transparency); regular and regulated financial transactions through the banking system (transparency); and the drawing up and implementing of contracts, memorandums, and letters of understanding that could not be arbitrarily interpreted by either side (rule of law). These were brought into the DPRK and consolidated by way of day-to-day practice and constant negotiations through the process of humanitarian aid transfers.

The impact of humanitarian work in the freedom-from-fear sphere should not be overstated. It was not part of the remit of humanitarian agencies to promote political freedoms. On the other hand, it should not be ignored. The DPRK food aid operation was the world's largest, directly feeding some 8 million people in 2001, making for contact with foreigners by hundreds of different institutions and individuals in DPRK society. It would be as unrealistic to argue that humanitarian operations could or should move the society toward more individual freedom as it would be to imagine that humanitarian agency norms, principles, and decision-making procedures did not have some impact on the many institutions within the society with which the agencies were negotiating and collaborating for nearly a decade.

Humanitarian agencies were thus in a position to respond to freedom-from-want aspects of human security from the late 1990s on. They contributed in a small way to providing an environment where freedom-from-fear human security needs could be addressed. At the same time, the negotiating practice of the agencies provided a model of conflict resolution through patient diplomacy and confidence building. Humanitarian agencies could not go further. Nor were the humanitarian agencies, with the partial exception of the UNDP, able to respond to the new threats to human security from the increasingly visible inequitable distribution of resources in the new and unregulated semimarketized DPRK of the early 2000s.[1] Humanitarian intervention was not and is not a diplomatic strategy in itself.

The Reconstitution of DPRK National Security Priorities

Since the creation of the state, DPRK national security doctrine had been based on a conventional understanding of what constituted national security—the defense of national territorial integrity. The complicating factor was that the DPRK government understood national territory to include South and North Korea. (Likewise, the Southern government understood national territory to include North Korea.) This conceptualization allowed for both defense of the DPRK territory and military aggression against South Korea (justified as reclaiming Korean territory for the nation). DPRK national security doctrine was not expansionist beyond the bounds of what it understood as constituting Korea—even toward the Korean-speaking territories in China and northeast Russia. Nor did it include ideas that could justify aggression against non-Koreans outside the DPRK. This was one reason why the state could not publicly admit to or justify the kidnapping of Japanese civilians during the Cold War. This was also why, when Kim Jong Il eventually admitted DPRK responsibility in 2002, the blame was assigned to "out-of-control" individuals, not to state policy.

After the 1990s, the need to secure regime maintenance as well as defend the national territory forced a reconstitution of national security doctrine. It became an absolute priority for DPRK foreign policymakers to help find ways to reinvigorate the economy. Gaining food supplies and economic assistance became just as important an objective of national policy as defending the territory. Many commentators argued that the DPRK used its pivotal position as a key source of Western security anxiety to coerce foreign governments into offering food assistance. Whether the correct term is "coercion" or "diplomacy," the outcome was that the government demonstrated a new priority of placing the human insecurity of the population, at least in the realm of freedom from want, at the center of its national security policies.

With the new cooperative relationship with the ROK that emerged in the late 1990s, DPRK policymakers abandoned national security conceptions that could include military aggression against the South. The naval clashes of the next few years were not justified in DPRK official discourse by any inherent "right" by the DPRK to make incursions into the South but as "self-defense." By the time of the Roh Moo-Hyun presidency in South Korea, the DPRK had abjured any such conceptions of national security policy. Indeed, in 2003, after a DPRK spokesperson momentarily relapsed into the old diplomacy of threats toward the South, Northern negotiators were forced by their Southern counterparts to explain themselves. The DPRK's rather meek compliance signified a very new approach to the South. All in all, the DPRK government's ongoing intensification of inter-Korean interaction made it much more likely that negotiation, rather than military force, would be used to resolve conflict.

One consequence of the normalization of North-South relations was that DPRK state boundaries, as opposed to the national territorial area of the Korean peninsula, were for the first time accepted as the limit of national security concerns. The mishandled admission of culpability and apology for the abduction of Japanese civilians was a sign of policy ineptitude but also a sign of attempts at normalization of relations with neighbors and adversaries. The deterioration in DPRK-Japan relations, as opposed to the thaw hoped for by foreign policy officials on both sides, arose partly from the DPRK's total inability to gauge the potential reaction of Japanese public opinion and its lack of comprehension of the role and power of the media in modern polities.[2] The public admissions were designed to indicate to the world that the DPRK now accepted limits on its methods of foreign policy action. They also inadvertently demonstrated the DPRK's lack of skills in managing complex foreign policy processes.

The Reasons for Political Stability

The government faced threats to its domestic legitimacy, as its threadbare policies had not been able to deliver basic requirements for the population for at least a decade. The weakened socialization process, which had previously inculcated Kim Il Sungism from the cradle to the grave, was no longer efficient or effective. It could no longer provide the cultural cement that had, under the Kim Il Sung regime, bound the building blocks of economic development into a sustainable national edifice. Reduced political legitimacy, even though combined with the deterioration in state capacity of the 1990s, was not, however, translated into political instability.

This was the case for at least five reasons. The first was that most people's time and energy were taken up with ensuring personal and family survival. Few hours were left in the day for oppositional political organization. Second, despite the susceptibility of the security apparatus to bribery, the repressive apparatus of the state was reinforced by the "Army First" policy that shored up Kim Jong Il's authority at home. A third and powerful barrier to the articulation or organization of dissent was that most people lacked knowledge of the existence of alternative and more successful ways of organizing society. Fourth, community-based social solidarity provided a mechanism for social cohesion, not around economic development, but around the necessity to struggle for survival. Fifth, rapid increases in human insecurity consolidated a sense of national integrity or national feeling. North Koreans reinforced their sense of Korean national identity and social bonds with each other to help weather the crises and the hardships.

New Dilemmas

The reconfigured social landscape brought new pressures on the DPRK government. The "Army First" policy, for instance, while acting as insurance against foreign attack and domestic political opposition, created a new set of difficult institutional problems. The military's institutional interests were not well met by the "Army First" policy. It directed basic resources to a large army but could not sustain a reasonable quality of living for soldiers and their families or provide adequate military material.

The marketized economy, with its generation of losers as well as winners, also had the potentially destabilizing effect of creating dissatisfaction from the formerly privileged and loyal industrial working class. This group did not benefit from the socioeconomic reconstitution of the country toward the commercial activities in the Nampo/Pyongyang/Sinuiju northwest corridor. Their leadership—in the North and South Hamgyong party—had historically had a disproportionately powerful voice in party structures. It remained to be seen for how long the still powerful and well-organized provincial political leadership in the northeast would continue to tolerate the contrast between the relatively comfortable lifestyle of the Pyongyang nouveau riche and the misery of its constituents.

Differentiated pressures from different provinces, social groups, and institutions brought conflicting demands on the DPRK government (which social groups to feed—the most vulnerable or the most necessary for defense and economic reconstruction; and where to direct national priorities—to rehabilitate agriculture or to try to resuscitate heavy industry). The DPRK government thus juggled diverse priorities at a time of very scarce resources available to meet demands.

International Security: Policies for Peace and Stability

Contrary to mythology, the DPRK government and the state it leads are as intelligible as most others. In the international security sense, the DPRK can be understood as a rational actor with conventional interests that assure some predictability in its international behavior. Its imperatives for action come from both national society and the international context. International strategies that do not understand the "facts on the ground" and, most importantly, how these have so dramatically changed in the DPRK over the past decade are probably doomed to failure. Conversely, strategies of intelligent intervention need to recognize the reconstituted national security imperatives of the DPRK that guide its actions both domestically and internationally.

A Mixed Record for International Actors

South Korean and EU analysis held that the DPRK's lack of understanding of international norms and lack of trust of global actors could be overcome through patient diplomacy. This underpinned South Korea's and the European Union's decisions to continue negotiations with the DPRK, even when the DPRK appeared gratuitously offensive. A strategy designed to address the underlying problem of absence of access to global norms, procedures, and conventions was developed by South Korea and the European Union. This strategy was supported by the use of the whole range of available policy instruments—diplomatic dialogue, economic and humanitarian assistance, and in the case of South Korea, military deterrence.

In the United States, distrust was mitigated, although never entirely dissipated, as a by-product of the Clinton administration's negotiations to try to achieve a missile deal. The DPRK's reconceptualization of its national security to include as a major priority economic development and human security in terms of freedom from want, and its understanding that substantial foreign economic assistance would not be forthcoming until "normalization" with the rest of the world had occurred, continued to propel the government toward seeking a peace deal with the United States. Its inability to convince the Bush administration of the seriousness of its intent, as well as divisions within the Bush administration, militated against serious progress.

The dominant perspective within the United States, despite the mild thaw in relations during the later period of the Clinton administration, was to maintain United States sanctions on the DPRK. This approach ruled out significant consideration of increasing and reorienting humanitarian aid toward capacity-building programs that would have allowed more sustained interaction between U.S. and DPRK officials and provided economic assistance as a mechanism for building peace. For the United States, such assistance was viewed as a reward that might come after a peace and security deal had been concluded. To promise or give economic assistance before such a deal would be tantamount to "blackmail" or "appeasement"—the two most common pejoratives used to assail such a strategy.

In Japan domestic politics prohibited a constructive response to the pressing humanitarian needs of the North Korean people and prevented negotiations toward a peace and security agreement. In late 2002 the North Korean government admitted that its agents had kidnapped Japanese citizens in the 1970s and that nine of them had since died. This revelation stoked justifiable popular anger, preventing the consolidation of Prime Minister Koizumi's substantial breakthrough in DPRK-Japan relations. Only in 2004, after Japanese and North Korean officials were able to meet under cover of the Beijing multilateral talks, could the normalization process resume, as symbolized by Koizumi's second visit to Pyongyang in May 2004.

A More Productive Alternative

International policies should be designed to address DPRK governmental dilemmas even as they promote the political freedom and economic redevelopment that should top the list of international objectives. The model of humanitarian diplomacy could be an example for broader conflict negotiation processes in the search for a stable peace in Korea. International policy proposals should place international objectives in a negotiating context that recognizes the government's dilemmas and the new socioeconomic context in which it operates and should be negotiated in a way that demonstrates both firmness and patience. These are much more likely to be successful than those generated and countenanced by the securitization paradigm.

Hope for a Change?

The overt rationale for the "Army First" policy was that the "special national security situation" of the DPRK—lacking a peace treaty after the Korean War and threatened by the most powerful nation on earth, the United States—required a heightened state of security consciousness, increased military capacity, and constant mobilization. If this rationale were demonstrably eviscerated and the army downsized and returned to its appropriate place as the guarantor against external threats, then some space could be opened for political change in the DPRK. The government has considered reducing conventional forces—probably a reflection that a small professional army could be more sustainable for the DPRK economy in the long term.[3] Major reductions in the armed forces remain unlikely, however, prior to a security agreement that will reassure the DPRK that it is not going to be attacked by its enemies.

Should a security deal be agreed on, a proposal that replaced a direct U.S. presence on the peninsula with a NATO-led peacekeeping force of U.S. and other troops could help promote international security in the classical sense: stability between states. Another proposal that could find supporters in all camps would be to include the DPRK in a security and cooperation pact for East Asia along with the United States, Japan, South Korea, Russia, and China. This could be welcomed by the DPRK as being in its interests if it were accompanied by economic assistance. Military cooperation could take place within the aegis of an East Asian security pact, with the eventual objective of creating a new Korean peninsula integrated army.

Arms deals, including on conventional weapons, may find a more welcome reception in the Korean People's Army than has hitherto been recognized. They would enable the military to scale down its armed forces as well as provide financing that could be pumped into the economy to benefit the population as a whole. The size and turnover of military personnel means that the military has been integrated in a very pragmatic way into the society. This would not have been the case if the military were a small elite professional force. Instead it shares the interests of the wider population in the necessity for economic development. If economic reform brought growth and improved human security for the population as a whole, and did not challenge the fundamental raison d'être of the armed forces, that of national defense, there is a strong possibility of such change being supported by at least some sections of the military.

The Special Role of South Korea

In helping the DPRK out of its self-imposed isolation and toward a more collaborative future, South Korea can play a crucially important role. North Koreans do not see themselves as possessing a specifically *North* Korean identity. They are proud of their Korean identity, which is understood as shared with all South Koreans, irrespective of political differences. South Korean policies that allowed North Koreans a sense of personal and national dignity, within the context of a Korean identity that included them but did not seek to deride or humiliate them, could provide a framework for substantial confidence building between the DPRK and the ROK and a "safe haven" for the DPRK's dealing with the non-Korean capitalist world.

Rapid and complete social and political unification would be an unwelcome policy option in the short term for most in the South and the North alike. As of 2005 South Korea was not prepared for the wholesale incorporation of North Koreans in a single state and society, economically or sociologically. The North Korean economy requires billions of dollars to bring it to anywhere near the South's level of development. In addition, the vast majority of North Koreans have absolutely no familiarity with the culture of advanced capitalist societies. They would inevitably be "second-class citizens" if integration with the South should come about without adequate planning and preparation.

Instead, pragmatic policy recommendations should aim at providing practical help for projects that will bridge the economic, social, and political divide. One suggestion would be for ROK policymakers to initiate the creation of a light multilateral framework, conceived as a technical organization that could provide a source of project-based financing for North Korean development projects. Such an organization would be somewhat similar in function to the post–World War II European Coal and Steel Community, set up in 1951.[4] This ostensibly nonpolitical institution permitted the revival of German industries within a multilateral organization of six member-states: France; Germany; the small states of Holland, Belgium, and Luxembourg; and Italy, the other defeated European power. Each member possessed equal voting rights and hence, officially, equal status. In practice, France assumed the leadership role, but the institution allowed Germany to save face. It circumvented the loss of German sovereignty that would have occurred if France had been granted direct control over the defeated country's key industries. It also permitted U.S., French, and English policymakers to channel investment into the industrial sector of what, just six years before, had been the hated enemy, without causing a public backlash in their own countries.

Such an institution could provide a vehicle for the Japanese investment that will come in the wake of a peace settlement. It would also allow multilateral public oversight to make sure that capital transfers do not end up in the gray economy that proliferated in the train of the marketization without liberalization that characterized the DPRK economy from the late 1990s on. It would allow DPRK policymakers to save face in accepting the very substantial and intrusive international intervention that would be needed to ensure that economic inputs were put to best use. Technical help would be required, as would policy inputs to help build the institutions of a liberal capitalist economy. Without such institutions, increased economic inputs would feed only the growing shadow economy, running the risk of fueling the growth of transborder crime and dissuading legitimate business from investing in Korea—North and South.

Policies for Peace

The alternatives are too costly not to continue to engage in comprehensive engagement that includes military deterrence, diplomatic endeavor, and economic and humanitarian assistance—in other words, a policy of "intelligent intervention." This is the optimal policy to both secure prosperity and freedom for North Koreans and bring a stable peace to the Korean peninsula.

The Costs of Alternatives

Alternative policies on the Korean security conflicts include the use of the military option, economic sanctions, further isolation, and nonengagement. The use of the military option would undoubtedly bring chaos and disorder to the Korean peninsula and its neighbors. The North Korean population would suffer further. Global economic sanctions would likewise punish the population. Further isolation would, by definition, end the process of engagement through which the DPRK gradually learns more about the practice and conventions of economic and political reform.

Nonengagement, either from policy paralysis or as a policy of "active neglect," would most likely lead to an already defensive and suspicious DPRK consolidating its military defense in whatever way it thought would prevent an attack from the United States. It would also mean the closure of economic and political openings, as the DPRK would continue to channel resources into military spending and would place the population under a state of permanent mobilization readiness. In these circumstances there would be attempts to strengthen the political control that partially disintegrated in the 1990s and, probably, to roll back economic and political freedoms that have emerged through the incipient moves toward a market economy.

Nation Building as Prevention, Not Cure

The pursuit of a military option would bring further threats to the human security of the North Korean people. They would be unlikely to benefit in the aftermath of even a "successful" or "humanitarian" war with the West because of the chaos and disorder that would inevitably occur. Substantial political and economic commitment to nation building on the Korean peninsula would be needed in the aftermath of any military conflict. In the light of competing claims in Bosnia, Kosovo, Afghanistan, and Iraq, where orderly states still have to be built in the wake of post–Cold War military interventions, it is unlikely that Korea would be much of a priority except for South Korea, which, in a postwar scenario, would itself require economic and physical reconstruction.

The way to create a stable security and peace regime on the Korean peninsula is to engage in substantial nation building in the North without waiting for a war to take place. Nation building of a modern, liberal, and democratic state should take place as a preemptive security strategy. This would require a comprehensive, coordinated strategy of intelligent intervention that would build on the examples provided by South Korea, the European Union, and Switzerland, of building peaceful channels for conflict resolution, at the same time as helping to relieve the immediate human insecurity of the North Korean population, which has, by now, suffered enough.

Bringing Peace and Security to Korea

Conventional national security analysis has not been fruitful as a source of theoretical insights, a framework for empirical investigations, or a foundation for successful policy responses to Korean security dilemmas. This book suggests that a perspective that takes human security as an analytical focus can be productive in deciphering the animus of DPRK domestic and foreign policies. Understanding the human/national/international security nexus provides both a theoretically powerful explanatory device and a framework for analyzing the empirical material available on the DPRK. It allows for an ethically supportable policy of peaceful negotiations, practical assistance, and political dialogue as an effective means of securing peace and responding to pressing human and international security concerns. Last, but not least, it provides a useful guide for those whose job it is to develop workable, feasible, and appropriate policies in the quest for a stable peace on the Korean peninsula.

Notes

Introduction

1. For a very accessible review of the Korean War, see Jon Halliday and Bruce Cumings, *Korea: The Unknown War* (London: Viking, 1988). For the definitive account of the background to the war, see Bruce Cumings, *The Origins of the Korean War*, vol. 1, *Liberation and the Emergence of Separate Regimes, 1945–1947* (Princeton, NJ: Princeton University Press, 1981); and Bruce Cumings, *The Origins of the Korean War*, vol. 2, *The Roaring of the Cataract, 1947–1950* (Princeton, NJ: Princeton University Press, 1990).

2. A good account of relations between the DPRK and the ROK is Don Oberdorfer, *The Two Koreas: A Contemporary History* (London: Warner Books, 1997).

3. This is, of course, also true of the South Korean population, but given that this book is about assessing the prospects for peace and stability from the perspective of the DPRK and its population, that would have to be the subject of another study.

4. For discussion of the historical development of penal, policing, and judicial systems in the DPRK and the possible contribution of external actors to transformation of these institutions, see Hazel Smith, "Brownback Bill Will Not Solve North Korea's Problems," *Jane's Intelligence Review*, February 2004, 42–45.

5. Hazel Smith, "North Korean Foreign Policy in the 1990s: The Realist Approach," in *North Korea in the New World Order*, ed. Hazel Smith et al. (New York: St. Martin's Press, 1996).

6. For an account of economic reform plans, drawing on an early UNDP mission to the DPRK by two British consultants, see Frederick Nixson and Paul Collins, "Economic Reform in North Korea," in *North Korea in the New World Order*, ed. Smith et al.

7. UNICEF/Institute of Child Nutrition, "Working Paper on Pilot Survey in Kangwon Province," mimeo, Pyongyang, June 1988.

8. An exception is the useful analysis from Tony Michell. See, for example, Anthony R. Michell, "The Current North Korean Economy," in *Economic Integration of the Korean Peninsula,* ed. Marcus Noland (Washington, DC: Institute for International Economics, 1998).

9. See the KEDO website at http://www.kedo.org. For discussion, see Mitchell B. Reiss, "KEDO and North Korea: Problems and Prospects on the Road Ahead," in *Solving the North Korean Nuclear Puzzle,* ed. David Albright and Kevin O'Neill (Washington, DC: Institute for Science and International Security Press, 2000).

10. The U.S. Department of Defense operates a website where it periodically provides information about its activities in the DPRK. For a summary of initial activities, see http://www.af.mil/news/May1998n-19980527_980737.html. See also http://www.defenselink.mil/news/May2001/b05022001_bt192-01.html for news of the twenty-eight-member team being sent to the DPRK that year. The author has frequently seen the U.S. soldiers in Pyongyang—once on the evening of September 9, 2001, dancing, along with other foreigners, in Kim Il Sung Square with young Korean men and women on the occasion of a Korean national holiday.

11. Much of this is posted on the excellent Reliefweb website. Its entry for the DPRK contains an enormous cache of reports from governmental, nongovernmental, and multilateral institutions going back as far as 1995. See http://www.reliefweb.int/w/rwb.nsf/vCD/Democratic+People's+Republic+of+Korea?OpenDocument&StartKey=Democratic+People's+Republic+of+Korea&ExpandView.

12. I reviewed this problem while researching and writing UNICEF, *An Analysis of the Situation of Children and Women in the Democratic People's Republic of Korea, 2000* (Pyongyang: UNICEF, DPRK, December 1999). See ibid., 12–14.

13. Communication to the author by Umberto Greco, Food Aid Liaison Unit, Pyongyang, April 2002.

14. For discussion, see Hazel Smith, *Overcoming Humanitarian Dilemmas in the DPRK,* Special Report no. 90 (Washington, DC: United States Institute of Peace, July 2002).

15. For discussion of the concept and empirical illustrations, see Robert O. Keohane and Joseph S. Nye, *Power and Interdependence,* 2nd ed. (Glenview, IL: Scott, Foresman, 1989).

1. Preventing War and Forging Peace

1. For a readable introduction to the academic discipline of international relations theory and to key theories, see Michael Nicholson, *International Relations: A Concise*

Introduction (Basingstoke, UK: Macmillan, 1998). For a critique of the underconceptualization of the state in international relations theorizing, see Hazel Smith, "Why Is There No International Democratic Theory?" in *Democracy and International Relations Theory: Critical Theories/Problematic Practices*, ed. Hazel Smith (New York: St. Martin's Press, 2000).

2. A key textbook that has influenced two generations of international relations scholars and practitioners worldwide and that explicitly models international relations as a structure and system of unit (state) interreactions is Kenneth Waltz, *Theory of International Politics* (New York: Random House, 1979).

3. For the classic study of the "bureaucratic politics" approach to understanding international relations, see Graham T. Allison, *Essence of Decision: Explaining the Cuban Missile Crisis* (Boston: Little, Brown, 1971). For a discussion of international politics informed by the "great men" approach, see Henry Kissinger, *A World Restored: Metternich, Castlereagh, and the Problems of Peace, 1812–1822* (London: Weidenfeld, 1957).

4. See Nicholson, *International Relations.* For another useful review, particularly concerning social-constructivist approaches to international relations theory, see John Baylis and Steve Smith, eds., *The Globalization of World Politics: An Introduction to International Relations*, 2nd ed. (Oxford: Oxford University Press, 2001).

5. For background on the concept of rogue state and critique of the notion, see Robert S. Litwak, *Rogue States and U.S. Foreign Policy: Containment after the Cold War* (Washington, DC: Woodrow Wilson Center Press/Johns Hopkins University Press, 2000).

6. For a discussion of DPRK foreign policy from 1945 to the mid-1990s, see Smith, "North Korean Foreign Policy." See also Byung Chul Koh, "Foreign Policy Goals, Constraints and Prospect," in *North Korea: Ideology, Politics, Economy*, ed. Han S. Park (Englewood Cliffs, NJ: Prentice-Hall, 1995).

7. For DPRK sources, see the plethora of books published in various foreign languages, but particularly in English, from the Foreign Languages Publishing House in Pyongyang. See, for example, Hwan Ju Pang, *Korean Review* (Pyongyang: Foreign Languages Publishing House, 1987). For the CIA view, see Helen-Louise Hunter, *Kim Il-Song's North Korea* (Westport, CT: Praeger, 1999). Hunter's work as a CIA analyst on the DPRK was widely available in mimeo form prior to publication in 1999. See Stephen J. Solarz, "Foreword," in Hunter, *Kim Il-Song's North Korea.*

8. From 2002 on, in a dramatic change of policy toward the battlefield use of nuclear weapons agreed upon in the U.S. Nuclear Posture Review, the United States arrogated to itself the right to engage in a preemptive nuclear attack on the DPRK. See Morton Abramowitz, James T. Laney, and Eric Heginbotham, *Meeting the North Korean Nuclear Challenge* (Washington, DC: Council on Foreign Relations, 2003), reproduced on http://www.cfr.org/publication.php?id=5973, 16.

9. For paradigmatic and widely quoted positions underpinned by the securitization perspective, see Nicholas Eberstadt, "Hastening Korean Reunification," *Foreign Affairs* 76, no. 2 (1997); and Marcus Noland, "Why North Korea Will Muddle Through," *Foreign Affairs* 76, no. 4 (1997). Eberstadt is a researcher with the American Enterprise Institute. Noland is a senior fellow at the Institute for International Economics. Neither is a political scientist.

10. This argument is developed in detail in Hazel Smith, "Bad, Mad, Sad, or Rational Actor? Why the 'Securitisation' Paradigm Makes for Poor Policy Analysis of North Korea," *International Affairs* 76, no. 3 (July 2000). This chapter draws on this essay.

11. One example of the sidelining of research findings: there has been a general lack of receptivity to Sigal's thesis that cooperation is an option with North Korea, despite the fact that he draws on meticulously researched work. See Leon V. Sigal, *Disarming Strangers: Nuclear Diplomacy with North Korea* (Princeton, NJ: Princeton University Press, 1998). Marcus Noland calls into question the merits of a position that directly challenges the dominant view in his "Introduction" in Noland, *Economic Integration of the Korean Peninsula*, 5, commenting on K. A. Namkung, "US Leadership in the Rebuilding of the North Korean Economy," in the same work, 223–235.

12. Thomas S. Kuhn, *The Structure of Scientific Revolutions*, 2nd ed. (Chicago: University of Chicago Press, 1970). For a full discussion as to how Kuhnian theory can be applied to understanding the way political and social theory has sought to interpret the DPRK, see Smith, "Bad, Mad, Sad, or Rational Actor?"

13. Litwak, *Rogue States*.

14. United States Institute of Peace, *Mistrust and the Korean Peninsula: Dangers of Miscalculations*, Special Report no. 38 (Washington, DC: United States Institute of Peace, November 1998). Previous publications on the DPRK were more qualified. See, for instance, United States Institute of Peace, *A Coming Crisis on the Korean Peninsula? The Food Crisis, Economic Decline, and Political Considerations*, Special Report no. 19 (Washington, DC: United States Institute of Peace, October 1996).

15. After a U.S. State Department visit to Pyongyang, spokesperson James P. Rubin announced on June 25, 1999, that "the [suspected nuclear] site . . . does not contain a plutonium reactor or reprocessing plant either completed or under construction." See http://nautilus.org/napset/dr/index.html, Daily Report, 3.

16. For discussion, see Hazel Smith, "'Opening Up' by Default: North Korea, the Humanitarian Community, and the Crisis," *Pacific Review* 12, no. 3 (1999).

17. Scholar David Kang argues that DPRK military and security policy is essentially defensive and realist. See Kang, "North Korea's Military and Security Policy," in *North*

Korean Foreign Relations in the Post–Cold War Era, ed. Samuel S. Kim (Oxford: Oxford University Press, 1998), 182.

18. Center for Nonproliferation Studies of the Monterey Institute of International Studies and the Center for Contemporary International Problems at the Russian Diplomatic Academy, "DPRK Report," no. 16 (January–February 1999), in "North East Asia Peace and Security Network Special Report," http://www.natilus.org/napset/dr/index .html, 2. See also Hazel Smith, "The Koreas: Threat or Opportunity?" in *World Today* 58, no. 1 (January 2002).

19. Patrick M. Morgan, "New Security Arrangements between the United States and North Korea," in *North Korea after Kim Il Sung,* ed. Dae-Sook Suh and Chae-Jin Lee (London: Lynne Rienner, 1998), 171.

20. Kang, "North Korea's Military and Security Policy," 172.

21. Ibid.

22. Edward A. Olsen, "The Conventional Military Strength of North Korea: Implications for Inter-Korean Security," in *North Korea after Kim Il Sung,* ed. Suh and Lee, 147.

23. For detailed quantitative analysis of DPRK military capacity, see International Institute for Strategic Studies (hereafter IISS), *The Military Balance 2001/2002* (Oxford: Oxford University Press/IISS, 2001), 196–197.

24. Ibid., 196.

25. Ibid.

26. The IISS estimates the DPRK's population at 24.5 million for 2001/2002. The Food and Agriculture Organization (FAO) and the World Food Program (WFP) cite a figure of 23.5 million for 2001/2002. See ibid. and FAO/WFP, "Crop and Food Supply Assessment Mission to the Democratic People's Republic of Korea," mimeo, Rome, October 26, 2001.

27. IISS, *Military Balance 2001/2002,* 196–197.

28. Dong-won Lim, "North Korean Policy under the Kim Dae-Jung Government," speech at breakfast meeting with National Reconciliation Council, March 11, 1999, 3, quoted in Chung-in Moon, "Understanding the DJ Doctrine: The Sunshine Policy and the Korean Peninsula," paper sent by e-mail to author, September 1999, 5–6.

29. For numbers of those in each armed service and their terms of service, see IISS, *Military Balance 2001/2002,* 196–197.

30. Marcus Noland, for instance, speaks of a "parallel" military economy and states that "half of the army is engaged in what elsewhere would be civilian economic activities." See Noland, "Prospects for the North Korean Economy," in *North Korea after Kim Il Sung,* ed. Suh and Lee.

31. U.S. Department of State, Bureau of Democracy, Human Rights and Labor, "Democratic People's Republic of Korea Country Report on Human Rights Practices for 1998" mimeo, February 26, 1999, published on http://www.reliefweb.int, 1.

32. The report does not cite sources, although it is probably based on reports from defectors. A basic problem with unsourced reporting is that it is impossible to assess what is fact and what is interpretation. For a thoughtful discussion based on interviews with North Korean defectors, see Roy Richard Grinker, *Korea and Its Futures: Unification and the Unfinished War* (Basingstoke, UK: Macmillan, 1998).

33. Bureau of Democracy, Human Rights and Labor, "Democratic People's Republic of Korea Country Report," 2.

34. From author's discussions with Kathi Zellweger, director of international cooperation, Caritas–Hong Kong representative, Pyongyang, Hong Kong, Rome, and Geneva 1998–2001, and Han Il Son, secretary general of Korean Council of Religionists, Korean Catholics Association, Pyongyang, September 2001.

35. I visited several orphanages throughout the country between 1998 and 2001. The DPRK and the majority of international agency officials agreed that the increase in numbers was a direct result of the food crisis, but a detailed analysis was not undertaken. For the UNICEF position, see UNICEF, *Situation of Children and Women* (1999), 89–90.

36. Médecins Sans Frontières (MSF) intimated that this was a possibility. See Marie Rose Pecchio, *Identification of an At Risk Group: Socially Deprived Children* (Pyongyang: MSF, September 11, 1998).

37. United Nations Office for the Coordination of Humanitarian Assistance (hereafter UNOCHA), database on children's residential institutions in the DPRK, Pyongyang, 2001.

38. Eberstadt, "Hastening Korean Reunification," 88, emphasis original.

39. Ibid., 88, 89.

40. The message is not new. In May 1950, just prior to the outbreak of the Korean War, a U.S. reporter wrote that John Foster Dulles was "militantly for the unification of Korea. Openly says it must be brought about soon." Quoted in Halliday and Cumings, *Korea: The Unknown War*, 65.

41. Pedro Almeida and Michael O'Hanlon, "Impasse in Korea: A Conventional Arms-Accord Solution?" *Survival* 41, no. 1 (Spring 1999).

42. Ibid., 69.

43. Ibid., 60.

44. One commentator noted that if North Korea had behaved as "a rational regime" in its negotiations with Japan, it could have achieved desirable outcomes in terms of economic support. See Aidan Foster-Carter, *North Korea: Peace, War, or Implosion* (Seoul: Jardine Fleming Securities Ltd, June 1997), 20. Another warned that North Korea should "choose [its] policies rationally." See Kyongmann Jeon, "The Likelihood and Implications of a North Korean Attack on the South," in *Economic Integration of the Korean Peninsula*, ed. Noland, 20.

45. *Economist*, July 10–16, 1999.

46. Ibid., "The Koreas Survey," 14.

47. Marcus Noland, "Why North Korea Will Muddle Through," 105, 107. Perhaps Noland exaggerates here to make the point. That this might be so is borne out by his own research, where he uses available data in a rigorous manner to draw conclusions about the North Korean economy. See Marcus Noland, Sherman Robinson, and Tao Wang, *Famine in North Korea: Causes and Cures*, Working Paper no. 99-2 (Washington, DC: Institute for International Economics, 1999). What he may be trying to argue is that the data is sometimes unsatisfactory and he would like more of it, something that could, however, be said about many countries of the world.

48. Robert A. Scalapino, "Introduction," in *North Korea after Kim Il Sung*, ed. Suh and Lee, 1.

49. Richard Buckley, ed., *North and South Korea: The Last Ideological Frontier* (Cheltenham, UK: Understanding Global Issues, 1998).

50. Quotations in this paragraph are from Nicholas Eberstadt, "North Korea's Unification Policy: 1948–1996," in *North Korean Foreign Relations in the Post–Cold War Era*, ed. Kim, 236–239. For an authoritative and succinct account of the outbreak of the Korean War, see Bruce Cumings, *Korea's Place in the Sun: A Modern History* (New York: Norton, 1997), 260–264. The North Koreans have yet another view. See Ho Jong Ho, Sok Hui Kang, and Thae Ho Pak, *The US Imperialists Started the Korean War* (Pyongyang: Foreign Languages Publishing House, 1993).

51. Eberstadt, "North Korea's Unification Policy," 237.

52. Morgan, "New Security Arrangements," 171.

53. A very well-researched, thoughtful, and informative book, whose value in understanding the DPRK goes far beyond that implied by its title, is James Clay Moltz and Alexandre Y. Mansourov, eds., *The North Korean Nuclear Program: Security, Strategy, and New Perspectives from Russia* (London: Routledge, 2000). For an example of recent literature underpinned by Cold War assumptions, see Robert Dujarric, *Korean Unification and After* (Indianapolis: Hudson Institute, 2000). Another takes an essentialist perspective— that DPRK negotiating behavior has been unchanged through the Cold War and post–Cold War period: it is "a relatively weak, rogue state . . . [maximizing] its negotiating advantage by pursuing unconventional tactics." See Scott Snyder, *Negotiating on the*

Edge: North Korean Negotiating Behavior (Washington, DC: United States Institute of Peace Press, 1999), 144.

54. Hwang Jang Yop, the architect of the DPRK's ruling *Juche* ideology, who defected to Seoul in February 1997, insisted in a meeting with the author in August 1991 that the DPRK would not permit political liberalization. For further discussion, see Hazel Smith, "Defecting to Snatch Victory from Defeat," *World Today* 53, no. 3 (March 1997).

55. Sharing the assumptions of the securitization perspective but differing from it in its methodological rigor is the excellent analysis of Korean economic options by Marcus Noland, *Avoiding the Apocalypse: The Future of the Two Koreas* (Washington, DC: Institute for International Economics, 2000).

56. Noland, "Why North Korea Will Muddle Through," 110.

57. See the United Nations Development Program (hereafter UNDP) and DPRK government, "Thematic Roundtable Meeting on Agricultural Recovery and Environmental Protection," mimeo, Pyongyang, May 1998. Many of the donor governments attributed responsibility for the food crisis to DPRK policies, but all, even the harshest critics, acknowledged that lack of material resources was a problem and that furthermore, since the crisis emerged in 1995, there had been evidence of change in DPRK policies. See UK Presidency Report, "European Union Technical Mission to the Democratic People's Republic of Korea, 9–16 May 1998," mimeo, undated.

58. FAO/WFP, "Crop and Food Supply Assessment," October 26, 2001.

59. Eberstadt, "North Korea's Unification Policy," for example.

60. This problem is exemplified in Snyder, *Negotiating on the Edge*. For a contrasting view, in an article written prior to the emergence of the food crisis, I argued that there had been clearly discernible changes in DPRK foreign policy orientation and practices since the inception of the DPRK as a state. See Smith, "North Korean Foreign Policy."

61. Hazel Smith, "Policy Reforms in the DPRK: Limits and Opportunities" (Rome: World Food Program, 1999).

62. Noland, "Why North Korea Will Muddle Through," 105–106.

63. Ibid., 105.

64. See Robert A. Manning, "The United States in North Korean Foreign Policy," in *North Korean Foreign Relations in the Post–Cold War Era*, ed. Kim, 153–155.

65. Allison, *Essence of Decision*.

66. Ibid., 10–38.

67. For an accessible and scholarly introduction to North and South Korean politics and society, see Cumings, *Korea's Place in the Sun*.

68. Sigal, *Disarming Strangers.*

69. Carter interrupted a White House "Council of War" discussing military action against the DPRK in a telephone call from Pyongyang outlining the deal that had been agreed with Kim Il Sung. See Sigal, *Disarming Strangers*, 157. For Harrison's position, see Selig S. Harrison, "Promoting a Soft Landing in Korea," in *Foreign Policy* 106 (Spring 1997).

70. Sigal outlines a list of North Korean diplomatic moves as direct and logical responses to U.S., ROK, and International Atomic Energy Agency actions between 1991 and 1994. See Sigal, *Disarming Strangers*, 257–259.

71. The major source of funding for the new nuclear power reactors was the Republic of Korea. Other funders included the United States, Japan, and the European Union. South Korea agreed to provide some $4 billion for the actual construction of the light-water reactors, although most of the spending was intended to take place in the ROK on materials and inputs for the North Korean reactors. See Joel Wit, response to policy forum online (#23B), NAPSNet@nautilus.org, December 9, 1998. Japan promised $1 billion to help build the light-water reactors. The United States agreed to provide funding "not to exceed" $35 million. See excerpts from the House-Senate Conference report for HR4328 (Omnibus Appropriation Bill), October 19, 1998, Congressional Record, obtained from NAPSNet@nautilus.org, October 29, 1998.

72. For this perspective, see Sigal, *Disarming Strangers.* This is also the message of Michael J. Mazarr, *North Korea and the Bomb: A Case Study in Nonproliferation* (Basingstoke, UK: Macmillan, 1995).

73. A useful introduction to different approaches to "human security" as a theory of international peace can be found in Edward Newman, "Human Security and Constructivism," *International Studies Perspectives* 2, no. 3 (August 2001).

74. UNDP, "An Agenda for the Social Summit," available at http://www.undp.org/hdro/e94over.htm.

75. For a thorough discussion of human security, see Caroline Thomas, *Global Governance, Development and Human Security* (London: Pluto, 2000).

76. For the foundation of Rawlsian ideas, see John Rawls, *A Theory of Justice* (Cambridge, MA: Belknap Press of Harvard University, 1971). For a succinct introduction to historical materialism, see Karl Marx and Friedrich Engels, *The German Ideology*, ed. S. Ryazanskaya (London: Lawrence and Wishart, 1965).

77. Quoted in Thomas, *Global Governance*, 12.

78. United Nations Conference on Trade and Development (hereafter UNCTAD), *The Least Developed Countries Report 2002: Escaping the Poverty Trap* (New York: United Nations, 2002), 57–59.

2. The Human Security Trade-off

1. A useful outline of the educational system is in Pang, *Korean Review,* 160–166. A description of the basic structures of health, education, and food distribution can be found in UNICEF, "Draft Situation Analysis, DPR Korea 1997," revised and edited mimeo, Pyongyang, June 13, 1997; and Lola Nathanail, *Food and Nutrition Assessment of the DPRK* (Rome: World Food Program, 1996).

2. DPRK literature geared toward tourists describes the social and economic achievements of the DPRK. The description is idealized but still provides a useful review of major achievements as the country moved from great poverty in the mid-1950s to the universal provision of a range of welfare and educational services. See, for example, Pang, *Korean Review.*

3. For discussion of how Kim Il Sung consolidated his rule over the Korean Workers' Party and the state, see Callum MacDonald, "The Democratic People's Republic of Korea: An Historical Survey," in *North Korea in the New World Order,* ed. Smith et al., 1–13. On the purges of the 1960s, see Charles K. Armstrong, "The Nature, Origins, and Development of the North Korean State," in *The North Korean System in the Post–Cold War Era,* ed. Kim, 53.

4. For the latter point, see David I. Steinberg, "On Patterns of Political Legitimacy in North Korea," in *The North Korean System in the Post–Cold War Era,* ed. Kim, 93.

5. Ibid.

6. A useful, if self-serving, account of Japanese investment in economic infrastructure in Korea can be found in Bank of Chosen, *Economic History of Chosen* (Seoul: Bank of Chosen, 1920), 101–103.

7. A standard account of Korean society during the Japanese occupation of Korea is Andrew J. Grajdanzev, *Modern Korea* (New York: The John Day Company, 1944). See also Carter J. Eckert, Ki-baik Lee, Young Ick Lew, Michael Robinson, and Edward W. Wagner, *Korea Old and New: A History* (Cambridge, MA: Harvard University Press, 1990), 269–273.

8. For review of how the system of Japanese colonialism operated within Korea, see Grajdanzev, *Modern Korea.*

9. A study published in 1931 illustrates the cultural coexistence of Confucian hierarchy and some modern notions of individual freedom in pre–World War II Korea. See Ellasue Wagner, *Korea: The Old and the New* (New York: Fleming H. Revell, 1931).

10. The state-created fabrications and myths of later years were nevertheless grounded in some historical accuracy. Kim Il Sung was a significant guerrilla leader but not the only one. For evaluation, see Gavan McCormack, "Mists Clearing: Forecasts for the Past and

Future History of the DPRK" (paper presented at the First Pacific Basin International Conference on Pacific Studies, HI, 1992).

11. The point about North Korea being an independent nation "despite the many difficulties" is almost always mentioned in formal meetings with officials at any level in the hierarchy in any part of the country. This is always said not to deny help given by foreign states and organizations but to stress the country's independence in making its own decisions.

12. See Hazel Smith, *WFP DPRK Programmes and Activities: A Gender Perspective* (Pyongyang: World Food Program, December 1999).

13. Joseph Sang-hoon Chung, *The North Korean Economy: Structure and Development* (Stanford: Hoover Institution Press, 1974), 10–14.

14. Ellen Brun and Jacques Hersh, *Socialist Korea: A Case Study in the Strategy of Economic Development* (New York: Monthly Review Press, 1976), 131.

15. Ibid.

16. Chung, *North Korean Economy*, 14.

17. Marian Cadogan, *Distribution and Use of Inputs for the 1998 Double Crop Programme, DPRK* (Caritas–Hong Kong/Trócaire, July 1998, 9).

18. Roberto Christen and Gamal M. Ahmed, "Agriculture in DPRK," mimeo, Pyongyang, undated but 2002, 1. Roberto Christen was the senior UNDP agronomist working and resident in the DPRK, 1999–2003.

19. Woon-Keun Kim, "The Agricultural Situation of North Korea," September 1, 1999, reproduced on http://www.agnet.org/library/article/eb475.html.

20. Number of state farms from Nathanail, *Food and Nutrition Assessment*, 10.

21. The number of cooperative farmers and their families is from FAO/WFP, "Crop and Food Supply Assessment Mission to the Democratic People's Republic of Korea," Special Alert no. 267 (mimeo, May 16, 1996), 2. The figure of 3,800 cooperative farms comes from Christen and Ahmed, "Agriculture in DPRK." Nathanail, in 1996, gives a figure of 3,220. See Nathanail, *Food and Nutrition Assessment*, 10. On the contribution of cooperative farms to the agricultural economy, see Cadogan, *Distribution and Use of Inputs*, 8.

22. In 1998 one agricultural consultant reported that all homes in the 44 farms visited in breadbasket provinces and in more marginal areas were connected to the electricity grid. See Cadogan, *Distribution and Use of Inputs*, 9.

23. A useful map of North and South Hamgyong provinces that shows the mountainous topography in relationship to main centers of population can be found on the *Korea Today* website at http://www.korea-np.co.jp/pk/080th_issue/99020301.htm.

24. Author's observations in Chongjin, Kimchaek, Hamhung, Tanchon, and Musan, 2000.

25. Nathanail, *Food and Nutrition Assessment*, 24.

26. "Flickers of Unrest Dog the North" on "Out There News" on http://www .megastories.com/nkorea/glossary/unrest.htm.

27. Data on composition of Central Committee by province of origin in Sung Chul Yang, *The North and South Korean Political Systems: A Comparative Analysis*, revised ed. (Elizabeth, NJ: Hollym, 1999), 278–279.

28. The former interpretation is offered in the excellent and comprehensive survey of North and South Korean politics by Sung Chul Yang in ibid., 279.

29. Andrew C. Nahm, *Introduction to Korean History and Culture* (Seoul: Hollym, 1993), 255.

30. Terms of service in 2001 were 5–8 years in the army, 5–10 years in the navy, and 3–4 years in the air force. See IISS, *Military Balance 2001/2002*, 196.

31. For an extremely useful guide to how food distribution systems in the DPRK operated before the crisis of the 1990s, see Nathanail, *Food and Nutrition Assessment*, 24–27.

32. Pang, *Korean Review*, 77–78.

33. Jiangcheng He, "Educational Reforms," in *North Korea: Ideology, Politics, Economy*, ed. Park, 33–50.

34. For positive and negative impact of DPRK policies on women, see Kyung Ae Park, "Ideology and Women in North Korea," in *North Korea: Ideology, Politics, Economy*, ed. Park, 71–85.

35. On the content of education and its relationship to the socialization process, see He, "Educational Reforms."

36. For essays on various aspects of the DPRK's *Juche* philosophy, see *North Korea in the New World Order*, ed. Smith et al.

37. For a succinct but pertinent discussion of the family cult, see Armstrong, "North Korean State," 54.

38. Ibid.

39. On education under the Japanese occupation, see Nahm, *Korean History and Culture*, 189. For a very detailed review of the extension of the educational system under the Kim Il Sung regime, see He, "Educational Reforms."

40. Author's observations between 1990 and 2002 in travel throughout the country.

41. On the unavailability of alternatives to DPRK images and representations of the world, see Hazel Smith, "Living with Absences: A Foreigner's Sojourn in Pyongyang," *Korea Society Quarterly* (Winter 2001/2002).

42. On the lack of information and disinformation promulgated by the state, see Jon Halliday, "The North Korean Enigma," in *Revolutionary Socialist Development in the Third World,* ed. Gordon White et al. (Brighton, UK: Wheatsheaf, 1983), 137–140.

43. Armstrong, "North Korean State," 54.

44. UNICEF, *Situation of Children and Women* (1999), 27–29.

45. For discussion on collective organizations and the *Juche* philosophy, see ibid., 28.

46. For membership number in the 1980s, see Pang, *Korean Review,* 85. In 1999 secondary school children amounted to 2.14 million. Calculated from UNICEF, *Social Statistics: DPRK* (UNICEF: Pyongyang, undated but 2000), 5.

47. Jeong-Ho Ro, "Making Sense of the DPRK Legal System," in *The North Korean System in the Post–Cold War Era,* ed. Kim, 142.

48. See Vasily Mikheev, "Politics and Ideology in the Post–Cold War Era," in *North Korea: Ideology, Politics, Economy,* ed. Park, 95.

49. It is not quite accurate to argue that the DPRK essentially took over Japanese colonial structures of community surveillance. First of all, these were never as developed in Korea as they were in other parts of the Japanese empire, particularly Taiwan. Second, we simply have insufficient information on how these institutions functioned to judge the degree of similarity to Japanese methods of social control in northern Korea (as opposed to generic methods). For discussion on Japanese methods of community surveillance in the colonial period and how these varied according to colony, see Ching-chih Chen, "Police and Community Control Systems in the Empire," in *The Japanese Colonial Empire, 1895–1945,* ed. Ramon H. Myers and Mark R. Peattie (Princeton, NJ: Princeton University Press, 1984).

50. Mikheev, "Politics and Ideology," 95.

51. Details on the workings of the legal system can be found in the useful Ro, "DPRK Legal System."

52. Amnesty International reported that it was not able to verify reports of "serious and hidden patterns of human rights violations." See Amnesty International, "Report 2001 on the DPRK," reprinted in *Republic of Korea Newsletter,* Circular no. 77 (Amnesty International United Kingdom, November 2001). This is because these reports, which come from defectors, are not always reliable. An unsourced account is Bureau of Democracy, Human Rights and Labor, "U.S. Department of State." For the DPRK view on its human rights record, see DPRK government, "Second Periodic Report of the Democratic People's Republic of Korea on Its Implementation of the International Covenant on Civil and Political Rights 25 December 1999," reproduced in United Nations International Covenant on Civil and Political Rights, Human Rights Committee, CCPR/C/PRK/2000/2, mimeo, May 4, 2000.

53. DPRK government, "Second Periodic Report," 31.

54. Chol-Hwan Kang and Pierre Rigoulot, *Aquariums of Pyongyang: Ten Years in the North Korean Gulag,* trans. Yair Reiner (New York: Basic Books, 2001).

55. A North Korean analysis can be found in Pang, *Korean Review.* A detailed discussion is in Eui-Gak Hwang, "North and South Korean Economies Compared," in *The Korean Peninsula in Transition,* ed. Dae Hwan Kim and Tat Yan Kong (London: Macmillan, 1997). Another useful survey is Shenying Shen, "Politics and Strategies for Economic Development," in *North Korea: Ideology, Politics, Economy,* ed. Han. A hagiographic and uncritical review of North Korean economics and politics, but useful because it is the only book-length study in English based on field research in the DPRK in the early 1970s, is Brun and Hersh, *Socialist Korea.*

56. United Nations Human Rights Committee, *Second Periodic Report of the Democratic People's Republic of Korea on Its Implementation of the International Covenant on Civil and Political Rights,* GE.00-41814 (E), May 4, 2000, 12.

57. For an examination of the data, see Hwang, "North and South Korean Economies," 68–75.

58. For discussion of the Soviet and Russian economic relationship with the DPRK, see Natalya Bazhanova, "Economic Forces and the Stability of the North Korean Regime," in *The North Korean Nuclear Program: Security, Strategy and New Perspectives from Russia,* ed. James Clay Moltz and Alexandre Y. Mansourov (New York: Routledge, 2000); and James Clay Moltz, "The Renewal of Russian–North Korean Relations," in ibid.

59. Noland, *Avoiding the Apocalypse,* 99.

60. On efforts to decrease dependence on oil imports, see Halliday, "North Korean Enigma," 129.

61. An introduction to the "agri-milieu" that discusses, among other things, the intensive nature of agriculture in the DPRK, levels of urbanization, and the DPRK development strategy that had concentrated on heavy industry can be found in UNDP and DPRK government, "Documents Prepared for the Thematic Roundtable Meeting on Agricultural Recovery and Environmental Protection," mimeo, Pyongyang, May 1998.

62. Bank of Korea via *South China Post,* reproduced in the very thorough analysis by Tim Beal, *The Waters of Prosperity Will Fill the Han and Taedong Rivers: Economic Recovery and Business Prospects for the DPRK after the Summit,* undated and reproduced on http://www.vuw.ac.nz/~caplabtb/dprk/waters%20of%20prosperity.htm.

63. Data from "Table 7: Estimates of Foreign Trade of DPRK 1946–1999," in ibid.

64. Ibid.

65. Ibid.

66. The 15 percent figure is from UNDP and DPRK government, "Thematic Round-table Meeting on Agricultural Recovery." The 20 percent figure is from Christen and Ahmed, "Agriculture in DPRK," 2.

67. Christen and Ahmed, "Agriculture in DPRK," 2.

68. For thorough discussion of the agricultural sector in the DPRK, see UNDP and DPRK government, "Documents Prepared for the Thematic Roundtable Meeting on Agricultural Recovery and Environmental Protection."

69. DPRK (1946–97) and FAO (1961–97) official figures for grain production are tabulated in Suk Lee, "Food Shortages and Economic Institutions in the Democratic People's Republic of Korea" (doctoral thesis, Department of Economics, University of Warwick, January 2003), 151. See also "Table 3.3: Table of Selected Products," in Hwang, "North and South Korean Economies," 71; and "Table 3: Production Index Numbers for Agriculture, DPRK and ROK, 1961–1999," in Beal, *Waters of Prosperity.*

70. DPRK figures show a reduction in grain production starting in 1990; the FAO shows reductions starting in 1994. In this instance the DPRK figures are probably more reliable than those of the FAO. For figures on grain production, see Lee, "Food Short-ages," 151. See also Beal, "Table 3: Production Index Numbers for Agriculture, DPRK and ROK, 1961–1999," in *Waters of Prosperity;* and "Table 5.1: Food Balance Estimates," in Noland, *Avoiding the Apocalypse,* 173.

71. Kim, "Agricultural Situation of North Korea."

72. Author interviews with farmers in Kangwon province in September 2001. See Hazel Smith, *Caritas Five-Year Evaluation of Programmes and Projects in the DPRK,* Hong Kong, 2001.

73. For thorough discussion, see Lee, "Food Shortages."

74. The national emblem and a brief description of the country's development strategy can be found in Pang, *Korean Review.*

75. Data in this paragraph is from UNICEF, *Situation of Children and Women* (1999), 22.

76. For details, see Shen, "Politics and Strategies."

77. Chung, *North Korean Economy,* 97.

78. The most visible example of homemade hospital equipment was the extensive use of intravenous transfusion equipment made from old beer bottles and rubber piping. See UNICEF, "DPRK Mission Report," mimeo, Pyongyang, 1997; Milton Amayun, Christopher Arthen, and Barney Smith, "Trip Report: PVO Consortium Short-Term Monitoring Visit to the Democratic People's Republic of Korea 18 April–2 May 1998," mimeo, May 1998, 11. Another example of "make do and mend" and creative recycling was the hospital mattresses "stuffed with the husks of grain—releasing dust into sensitive TB patients' lungs every time they change position." See Christian Friends of Korea, "Activity Report," mimeo, July 2002.

79. Marina Ye Trigubenko, "Economic Characteristics and Prospect for Development: With Emphasis on Agriculture," in *North Korea: Ideology, Politics, Economy*, ed. Han, 147–151.

80. On the creation of the unified grid, see Valentin I. Moiseyev, "The North Korean Energy Sector," in *The North Korean Nuclear Program*, ed. Moltz and Mansourov, 55.

81. International evaluations of the rural energy sector in 2001 commented that electricity was used in rural areas for domestic purposes such as lighting and refrigeration. See James H. Williams, David Von Hippel, and Peter Hayes, "Fuel and Famine: Rural Energy Crisis in the DPRK," Policy Paper no. 46 (University of California, Institute on Global Conflict and Cooperation, 2001), reproduced on http://www-igcc.ucsd.edu/publications/policy_papers/pp46.html#ftn2.

82. IISS, *Military Balance 2001/2002*, 196.

83. The official media reported the physical efforts made by large sectors of the population. Commenting on a dam built on the River Kumjin, for instance, a state-run magazine comments that "county officials and people . . . disdaining to turn to the country for help when it was going through difficulties . . . decided to carry out the project on their own. The whole county turned out to complete the works at all costs . . . overcoming all difficulties . . . all the projects were finished after days of hardships." See "The River Kumjin Changes Its Appearance," *Korea* 557 (January 2003), *Juche* 92, 16–17.

84. The DPRK official press reported deaths from these construction efforts—stating, for example, "The country and the people will always remember the exploits of the comrades-in-arms who died while building the Kumgangsan Power Station." See "KPA Supreme Commander's Telegraphic Order no. 001," *Pyongyang Times*, July 6, 1996.

85. Michell, "Current North Korean Economy," 144. This author came across reference to the "eat two meals a day campaign" on posters in Pyongyang in May 1990 and August 1991.

86. Quotation from Oberdorfer, *The Two Koreas*, 370.

87. Background to the agricultural crisis can be found on the WFP website at http://www.wfp.org/country_brief/index.asp?country=34. For details of the grain shortages of 1997, see FAO/WFP, "Crop and Food Supply Assessment Mission to the Democratic People's Republic of Korea," Special Alert no. 275, mimeo, June 3, 1997.

88. UN Department of Humanitarian Affairs, "United Nations Consolidated UN Inter-Agency Appeal for Flood-Related Emergency Humanitarian Assistance to the Demo-

cratic People's Republic of Korea (DPRK) 1 July 1996–31 March 1997," April 1996, reproduced on http://www.reliefweb.int/ocha_ol/pub/appeals/96appeals/dprk/prk_atx1 .html#top.

89. Ian Davies, former UN director of industrial development for China and the DPRK, quoted in Beal, *Waters of Prosperity.*

90. UN Department of Humanitarian Affairs, "Consolidated UN Inter-Agency Appeal, 1 July 1996–31 March 1997."

91. Ken Quinones, draft, chapter 2, "The American NGO Experience in North Korea," mimeo sent to author, March 12, 2002.

92. UN Department of Humanitarian Affairs, "Consolidated UN Inter-Agency Appeal, 1 July 1996–31 March 1997."

93. Centers for Disease Control and Prevention, "Status of Public Health— Democratic People's Republic of Korea, April 1997," reproduced on http://www.cdc.gov/ mmwr/preview/mmwrhtml/00048030.htm#top.

94. Ibid.

95. Although there are no figures for the consumption of "alternative foods" in this period, I interviewed Koreans throughout the country between 1999 and 2001 who stated that their chronic illness was caused by the consumption of this type of food. The counties institutionalized the preparation and distribution of "alternative food"; when the harvest ran out and there was no international food or food from other sources, county authorities tried to mix the last of grain supplies with this nonnutritious "food" to provide something to eat for people who had nothing else.

96. UN Department of Humanitarian Affairs, "Consolidated UN Inter-Agency Appeal, 1 July 1996–31 March 1997."

97. Ibid.

98. See, for example, Marie-France Bourgeois, "Nutrition in the DPRK—a Field View," reproduced on http://www.ennonline.net/fex/05/fa21.html. UNICEF notes "the worst cases of malnutrition [are seen] in children's centres." See UNICEF, "Emergency Situation Analysis for DPRK," Pyongyang, undated but 1996 or 1997.

99. Marie Staunton, report of conversation with Mr./Ms. (not clear from text) Kim, UNICEF officer, Huichon, August 5, 1997, recorded in "Trip Diary DPRK," mimeo, August 6, 1997.

100. See, for example, Bourgeois, "Nutrition in the DPRK."

101. UNICEF, "Section 6, Interview Transcripts," in Emergency Fundraising Kit, mimeo, Pyongyang and London, August 1997.

102. Save the Children, "DPRK Assessment Report," mimeo, August 18–31, 1997, 14; and UNICEF, "Draft Situation Analysis," June 13, 1997, 14.

103. The figure of 85 percent is taken from the overview of the DPRK energy sector by David F. Von Hippel and Peter Hayes, "North Korean Energy Sector: Current Status and Scenarios for 2000 and 2005," in *Economic Integration of the Korean Peninsula*, ed. Noland, 89.

104. Quinones, "American NGO Experience"; and UNICEF, *Situation of Women and Children* (1999), 61.

105. UNICEF, *Situation of Women and Children* (1999), 61.

106. South Korean intelligence sources identified the outbreak of cholera, reported by Reuters, July 5, 1996, reproduced on http://www.reliefweb.int.

107. Ian Davies, quoted in Beal, *Waters of Prosperity.*

108. Lee, "Food Shortages," 120–138.

109. UNICEF/Institute of Child Nutrition, "Working Paper."

110. For a discussion of the nutritional and health conditions of children in Kangwon province in 2001 inter alia, see Smith, *Caritas Five-Year Evaluation of Programmes and Projects in the DPRK*, 33–37.

111. UNICEF, "Draft Situation Analysis," June 13, 1997, 10.

112. UNICEF, "DPRK Mission Report."

113. World Health Organization South-East Asia Region, "Emergency and Humanitarian Assistance Programme" (mimeo, January–February 1998), 7.

114. For MOPH figure, see UNICEF, *Situation of Children and Women* (1998), 14. For WHO figures, see WHO, "Health Situation Acute in North Korea" (press release, October 2, 1997), reproduced on http://www.who.int/archives/inf-pr-1997/en/pr97-71.html.

115. Centers for Disease Control and Prevention, "Status of Public Health— Democratic People's Republic of Korea, April 1997."

116. Ibid.

117. FAO/WFP, "Food and Crop Assessment Mission to the DPRK," Rome, December 10, 1997.

118. On the DPRK government's lack of transparency and its inability to provide meaningful nutritional data, see Save the Children, "DPRK Assessment Report," 3, 11.

119. A very thorough piece of research undertaken on famine deaths is Lee, "Food Shortages." Another, based on research applicable to families from North Hamgyong province in the mountainous northeast of the country, is W. Courtland Robinson, Myung Ken Lee, Kenneth Hill, and Gilbert M. Burnham, "Mortality in North Korean Migrant

Households: A Retrospective Study," *Lancet* 354, no. 9175 (July 24, 1999). A professional review is Daniel Goodkind and Loraine West, "The North Korean Famine and Its Demographic Impact," *Population and Development Review* 27, no. 2 (June 2001).

120. Lee, "Food Shortages." The figure of 220,000 is cited in an OCHA bulletin of 1998/1999 (undated) that states: "Government announced the mortality rate has increased from 6.8 per 1000 in the early 1990s to 9.3 per 1000 in 1998, indicating a 37% increase, bringing the total number of famine-related deaths to 220,000 over the last four years." See UNOCHA Field Co-ordination Unit DPR-Korea, "Basic Facts," mimeo, undated, probably 1998/1999. A WFP "DPRK Update" announced that "the Government has informed WFP that the mortality rate has increased from 6.8 per 1000 prior to 1995, to 9.3 per thousand in 1998. During the same period the rate of increase of the population of the DPRK has reduced from 1.5% to 0.9%." See WFP, "DPRK Update," Pyongyang, April 1999. The government never gave a specific figure of deaths that could be attributed to the economic and food crisis. For discussion, see Goodkind and West, "North Korean Famine." See also John Owen-Davies, "North Korea's Public Health Pays the Price of Isolation" (mimeo, undated but June 2000), 2, and John Owen-Davies, "North Korea Says It with Flowers," *Financial Times*, June 24, 2000.

121. For details, see UNDP and DPRK government, "Thematic Roundtable Meeting on Agricultural Recovery."

122. UNICEF, *Situation of Women and Children* (1999), 21–24.

123. Ian Davies, quoted in Beal, *Waters of Prosperity*.

3. Human Insecurity and Socioeconomic Reconstitution

1. See report on a meeting held at the Jenam coal mine, in "Increased Coal Output Called For," *Pyongyang Times*, January 12, 2002, *Juche* 91, 4.

2. "Joint Editorial Published on New Year," *Bulletin d'Information*, DPRK Delegation in France, mimeo, Paris, January 1, 1999.

3. Detailed description and analysis of the changes in agricultural policy can be found in Woon-Keun Kim and Tae-Jin Kwon, "Food Situation and Agricultural Reform in North Korea," *Journal of Rural Development* 21 (Summer 1998): 73–88.

4. On changes to the subwork team system, see ibid., 83–84.

5. Tae-Jin Kwon and Woon-Keun Kim, "Assessment of Food Supply in North Korea," *Journal of Rural Development* 22 (Winter 1999): 61–62.

6. Young Whan Kihl, "The DPRK and Its Relations with the ROK," in *Korea Briefing 1997–1999: Challenges and Change at the Turn of the Century*, ed. Kongdan Oh (New York: M. E. Sharpe and Asia Society, 2000), 125.

7. For discussion of the "Army First" policy, see ibid., 132–137.

8. Smith, "Defecting to Snatch Victory."

9. The agencies with long-term involvement in the DPRK have been making the point since their arrival that individuals fared differently depending on a variety of factors, including age, occupation, geographic location, etc. See, for example, World Food Program, "Recovery Assistance for Vulnerable Groups in DPR Korea," draft, mimeo, Pyongyang, undated but 1999, 8.

10. Christen and Ahmed, "Agriculture in DPRK."

11. FAO/WFP, "Special Report: Crop and Food Supply Assessment Mission to the Democratic People's Republic of Korea" (mimeo, December 22, 1995), 5.

12. FAO/WFP, "Crop and Food Supply Assessment Mission," May 16, 1996, 2.

13. Ibid., and see section "Food Aid Required until the 1996 Harvest," in UN Department of Humanitarian Affairs, "Consolidated UN Inter-Agency Appeal, 1 July 1996–31 March 1997."

14. From November 1995 to March 1996, the Japanese government donated between 39,000 and 44,000 tonnes of rice a month. See "Annex Three: Deliveries of Food Aid to the DPRK 1995/1996," in UN Department of Humanitarian Affairs, "Consolidated UN Inter-Agency Appeal, 1 July 1996–31 March 1997."

15. Center for Contemporary International Problems, "The DPRK Report no. 8 July–August 1997" (Moscow, reproduced as "North East Asia Peace and Security Network Special Report), accessed from NAPSNet website, September 30, 1997. See also Young-Hoon Kim, "The AREP Program and Inter-Korean Agricultural Cooperation," *East Asian Review* 13, no. 4 (Winter 2001): 96.

16. Center for Contemporary International Problems, "DPRK Report no. 8." One agricultural consultant noted after an assessment visit that markets were held "every ten days or so." It seems likely that their frequency was underreported to her. See Cadogan, *Distribution and Use of Inputs*, 8.

17. World Food Program, "Recovery Assistance for Vulnerable Groups," 3.

18. Center for Contemporary International Problems, "DPRK Report no. 8."

19. The farm run by KPA Unit 549, for instance, was inspected by Kim Jong Il on November 7, 2000. Another, Chicken Farm no. 112, "built by servicemen" and with "a total floor space of more than 25,000 square metres," was similarly inspected on November 2, 2000. Army units were told "to show deep concern in the supply service." See "Leader Kim Jong Il Gives On-the-Spot Guidance to Newly-Built Units," in *Korea Today* 530 (December 2000): 1–2.

20. The DPRK state news agency reported that Song UnPak's unit of the KPA carried out land rezoning in Haeju. KCNA website (http://www.kcna.co.jp), accessed April 24, 2001.

21. The DPRK news agency reported that as well as contributing to resolving the food problem, land rezoning in North Pyongan province was a way of "totally eradicating the remnants of the feudal ownership of land in rural areas." See KCNA website (http://www.kcna.co.jp), April 21, 2000.

22. Observations from visiting humanitarian workers, who also noted an absence of factory output in Hamhung, one of the major industrial cities in the DPRK. See Amayun et al., "Trip Report," 6.

23. Hazel Smith, "Desperate Times in North Korea," *Far Eastern Economic Review*, February 14, 2002.

24. Robinson et al., "Mortality in North Korean Migrant Households."

25. World Food Program, "Recovery Assistance for Vulnerable Groups," 2.

26. World Food Program, "Alternative Foods," information sheet on "WFP in DPRK," Pyongyang, December 1999.

27. World Food Program, "Recovery Assistance for Vulnerable Groups," 3.

28. FAO/WFP, "Crop and Food Supply Assessment Mission to the Democratic People's Republic of Korea," June 25, 1998, 2; and FAO/WFP, "Special Report: Crop and Food Supply Assessment Mission to the Democratic People's Republic of Korea," June 29, 1999, 7.

29. For a review of North Korean migrants and refugees in China, see Hazel Smith, "North Koreans in China," in *Human Flows across National Borders in Northeast Asia*, ed. Tsuneo Akaha with the assistance of Anna Vassilieva and Shizu Naruse, seminar proceedings, United Nations University, Tokyo, November 2002 (Monterey: Center for East Asian Studies, Monterey Institute of International Studies, January 2003).

30. From one of the few pieces of credible research on North Korean migration into China. See Robinson et al., "Mortality in North Korean Migrant Households," 293.

31. *NK Chosun Ilbo*, May 26, 2002, http://nk.chosun.com/english/news/news.html?ACT=detail&res_id=5530.

32. Hazel Smith, "La Corée du Nord vers l'économie de marché: Faux et vrais dilemmas," in *Critique Internationale* (Paris) (April 2002).

33. In 1998 a team of three PVOC workers was based in UNICEF. Their specific brief was to focus on health, and they were assigned orphanages in Nampo, South Pyongan, and North Hwanghae to monitor. The team leader repeatedly expressed concerns about the poor nutritional status of the Nampo children, even compared to the malnourished children in other provinces. See, for instance, PVOC, "Field Trip: Nampo City Baby Home," mimeo, Pyongyang, April 8, 1998. This point was repeated in the author's discussions with PVOC team leader, Pyongyang, April 1998. See also Private Voluntary Organization Consortium in Democratic People's Republic of Korea, "Interim Report," mimeo, Pyongyang, April 1998.

34. Central Bureau of Statistics, DPRK, "Report on the DPRK Nutrition Assessment, 2002," mimeo, Pyongyang, November 20, 2002, *Juche* 91.

35. Quotation from FAO/WFP, "Crop and Food Supply Assessment Mission to the Democratic People's Republic of Korea," Rome, July 24, 2000, 11.

36. North Korean workers earned money through employment in Vladivostok as construction workers and in logging camps. See Anatoly Medetsky, "News. 26 May. North Korean Workers—and Their Government—Earn Money in Russian Far East," distributed by OCHA, Pyongyang, via direct e-mail to author, May 26, 2002.

37. Reports of the Onsong riot in "Chinese Influence on the Rise in Pyongyang," November 5, 1999, Stratfor.com Global Intelligence Update, http://www2.gol.com/users/coynerhm/chinese_influence_on_pyongyang.htm; NAPSNet Daily Report, November 2, 1999, http://www.nautilus.org/napsnet/dr/9911/NOV02.html#item7. See also Bradley Martin, "The Koreas: Pyongyang Watch: The Riot Act?" November 3, 1999, http://www.atimes.com/koreas/AK03Dg01.html.

38. John Powell, "Testimony to the Sub-committee on East Asia and the Pacific of the US House of Representatives, 2 May 2002," reproduced as "Special Report, North East Asia Peace and Security Network," May 20, 2002.

39. International FIDES Service no. 4144, "Hell on Earth: The Church Must Wipe the Tears," April 23, 1999, http://www.fides.org/English/1999/e19990423.html.

40. For description of safety net breakdown and its effects on women and children, see UNICEF, *Situation of Children and Women* (1999).

41. This paragraph and the following one draw on Smith, *WFP DPRK Programmes*.

42. For full discussion of the gender implications of the crisis, see ibid.

43. I interviewed a brother and sister in the mountains northeast of Yanji City in China in September 2002 who had migrated from the DPRK in February 2002 because they had had no food for the three days before they left. Their mother had died from eating "wild mushrooms" at the height of the food crisis.

44. See UNDP, "Annex K: Labour Force and Employment," in UNDP and DPRK government, "Documents Prepared for the Thematic Roundtable Meeting on Agricultural Recovery and Environmental Protection," mimeo, Pyongyang, May 1998.

45. UNICEF, *Situation of Children and Women* (1999).

46. Dilawar Ali Khan, "Democratic People's Republic of Korea: Improving the Quality of Basic Social Services for the Most Vulnerable Children and Women," mimeo, UNICEF Pyongyang, April 2001, 2.

47. Abortions continued to be performed throughout the country as the food crisis continued, despite the government's efforts to try to encourage women to have children. Author's interviews with international humanitarian medical workers, Pyongyang, 2000–2001.

48. For analysis of children's multiple deprivation, see UNICEF, *Situation of Children and Women* (1999).

49. "Winter Set to Be Cruel in North Korea," *ABC World Today,* November 23, 2001, on http://www.abc.net.au/worldtoday/s424241.htm. Statistics for 1993 from UNICEF, *Situation of Children and Women* (1999), 41.

50. UNICEF, *Situation of Children and Women* (1999).

51. Severe malnutrition affected 35 percent of little boys and 25 percent of little girls in 1998. See EU, UNICEF, and the WFP in partnership with the government of the DPRK, "Nutrition Survey," mimeo, November 1998. UNICEF infant mortality rates were based on the pre-crisis 1993 census and must greatly understate infant mortality rates. See UNICEF, *Situation of Children and Women* (1999), 41.

52. Infant formula was occasionally seen in the hard-currency shops in Pyongyang but was not reported as available in the nurseries, hospitals, or orphanages. South Korean NGOs have occasionally provided infant formula to orphanages. Author's observations, Pyongyang baby home, 1999.

53. UNICEF, *Situation of Children and Women* (1999), 72–73.

54. DPRK OCHA Situation Bulletin, March 2002, http://www.reliefweb.int/w/ rwb.nsf/a94094ac73e84191c125671c002fcbbc/52e0c11ac4ef989bc1256b9800444f3f? OpenDocument.

55. Khan, "Democratic People's Republic of Korea," 6.

56. Ibid.

57. The DPRK national media recognizes the "arduous march" necessary to reconstruct the DPRK economy and regularly runs articles telling how different groups of the population have managed to overcome "difficulties" to increase production. See, for example, "We Will Advance Confidently," "We Will Increase Power Production," and "We Will Hit Coal Target Ahead of Others," in *Korea Today* 547, no. 1 (2002), *Juche* 91, 3–4.

58. Where funding could not be obtained for international assistance for school feeding, there was evidence of decreased school attendance. See section titled "Consequences of Underfunding" in United Nations Office for the Coordination of Humanitarian Assistance, *Consolidated Agency Appeal for the DPRK January–December 1999*, December 1998, 15.

59. One of the findings documented in Smith, *WFP DPRK Programmes*. See section "Women Workers in the Children's Institutions."

60. For description of how the PDS operated prior to the crisis, see Nathanail, *Food and Nutrition Assessment*, 24–27.

61. The UN World Food Program stated in a 2003 information leaflet that 3,600 PDCs "were operational." This is a highly speculative figure, given that very few WFP monitoring visits were made to PDCs when they were actually distributing food. Furthermore, those that did take place were more likely to reflect PDC distribution for a special program, such as to distribute international food in a food-for-work project. See the World Food Program, "DPR Korea: The Public Distribution System," mimeo, Pyongyang, undated but obtained by author from WFP Pyongyang, February 2003.

62. A July 1997 appeal for food assistance for the DPRK discusses the changes to the PDS but states that "the same low allocation [of food is given] to everyone independent of type of work." It is, however, unlikely that all citizens continued to receive food rations at this time. See World Food Program, "Emergency Operation DPR Korea no. 5710.02: Emergency Food Assistance Following Floods," in World Food Program, *WFP Operations in DPR Korea as of 14 July 1999* (Rome: WFP, undated but 1999), 4.

63. A December 1997 WFP appeal for the DPRK noted that food distribution through the PDS was "irregular." See World Food Program, "Emergency Operation DPR Korea no. 5959: Emergency Food Assistance for Vulnerable Groups," in World Food Program, *WFP Operations in DPR Korea as of 14 July 1999*, 2.

64. FAO/WFP, "Special Report: Crop and Food Supply Assessment Mission to the Democratic People's Republic of Korea," November 25, 1997, 3.

65. The FAO/WFP twice-yearly food and agriculture surveys repeatedly mentioned the vulnerability of nonfarmers to food shortages. See, for example, FAO/WFP, "Crop and Food Supply Assessment Mission," June 25, 1998, 2; FAO/WFP, "Special Report: Crop and Food Supply Assessment Mission," June 29, 1999, 7.

66. Michell, "Current North Korean Economy," 4. While working in the DPRK, particularly from September 2000 to September 2001, this author regularly observed local officials engaging in petty trade, for instance in fruit, vegetables, and alcohol, with visiting officials from Pyongyang.

67. For connivance by local officials, see Center for Contemporary International Problems, "DPRK Report."

68. While not mentioning the humanitarian agencies specifically, the *Pyongyang Times* carried a long editorial attacking the importation of capitalist political, economic, and cultural ideas. The article was first published in the party newspaper *Rodong Sinmun* and translated. See "Reject Imperialists' Ideological and Cultural Poisoning," *Pyongyang Times*, June 12, 1999.

69. In 1996 individual farmers were warned that land distributed to them to grow food could be taken away from them in the future. See Center for Contemporary International Problems, "DPRK Report."

70. "Korea Is Making a Forced March," *Korea Today*, April 1998, *Juche* 87, 11.

71. A very common sight in the lower floors of apartments in small semi-urban settlements in rural areas, as well as in urban areas, is grills and gratings covering windows and balconies—presumably as protection against theft.

72. See, for example, the plausible account in the interview by Dong-Ho Park (anonymous researcher) titled "A Peek into Life in the Labor Training Camps" on http://www.nknet.org/enknet/ekeys/ekeys-frame.htm. See also letter from Ed Evanhoe on Internet "chat" site, http://www.ku.edu/~ibetext/korean-war-1/2001/12/msg00072.html.

73. See Park, "A Peek into Life," on http://www.nknet.org/enknet/ekeys/ekeys-frame.htm.

74. Mikheev, "Politics and Ideology," 100–101.

75. Moltz, "Russian–North Korean Relations," 207.

4. Humanitarian Assistance and Human Security

1. I have written extensively on the subject of humanitarian assistance to the DPRK, and some of this chapter is drawn from those published texts. See, for example, Hazel Smith, "'Opening Up' by Default: North Korea, the Humanitarian Community and the Crisis," in *Pacific Review* 12, no. 3 (1999). See also my UNICEF-commissioned piece: UNICEF, *Situation of Children and Women* (1999). For an extensive survey of humanitarian involvement in the DPRK, see Hazel Smith, "Minimum Conditions for Humanitarian Action in the DPRK: A Survey of Humanitarian Agency Involvement and Perspectives" (paper to workshop organized by the Centre for Humanitarian Dialogue, Geneva, December 2001). See also Smith, *Overcoming Humanitarian Dilemmas*.

2. The common humanitarian strategy toward the DPRK can be found in the annual UN-coordinated common humanitarian appeals for the DPRK. See, for example, United Nations Office for the Coordination of Humanitarian Assistance, "Consolidated Agency Appeal 2002 for the DPRK," mimeo, Pyongyang, 2002.

3. UNDP, "1998 Annual Report of the United Nations Resident Co-ordinator in DPR Korea," mimeo, Pyongyang, January 31, 1999, 7–8.

4. United Nations Office for the Coordination of Humanitarian Assistance, "Consolidated Agency Appeal 2002."

5. UNDP Pyongyang publishes detailed accounts of agricultural activities in the DPRK giving the implementing agency, funding source, amount of funding, duration of project, location, types and numbers of beneficiaries, etc. See, for example, UNDP/AREP, "Status of Agricultural Activities," mimeo, Pyongyang, 2001.

6. UNDP and DPRK government, "Thematic Roundtable Meeting," May 1998, 20.

7. The joint UNDP/DPRK government progress report on the Agricultural Recovery and Environmental Protection (AREP) plan of 2000 strongly intimates, for example, that food security will not be attainable without increased foreign exchange and a revived export sector. See "Section 2.2.1: Macroeconomic Stability" in UNDP, "Documents Prepared for the Second Thematic Roundtable Meeting on AREP for the DPRK," mimeo, Pyongyang, 2000.

8. Humanitarian Development Working Group, "Position Paper on Rehabilitation and Development in DPR Korea," mimeo, Pyongyang, June 26, 2001.

9. The jointly developed (government/UNDP) UNDP Country Cooperation Framework 2001–3 recognizes, for instance, that food security cannot be envisaged for the DPRK without the reconstruction of the export sector and foreign investment. See UNDP, *Second Country Cooperation Framework for the DPRK (2001–2003)* (New York: UNDP, June 2001). It does not, however, touch on what domestic economic and political change would be necessary to encourage foreign investment.

10. UNDP, "1998 Annual Report," 2.

11. I have discussed the initial engagement of the humanitarian agencies with the DPRK government as providing both aid and confidence building in Smith, "'Opening Up' by Default."

12. UNICEF figures calculated from CAP appeal documents for 2000, 2001, and 2002. See under "United Nations Office for the Coordination of Humanitarian Assistance" in the bibliography for full details.

13. For numbers of WFP staff, see "Report on Humanitarian Principle no. 8," in United Nations Office for the Coordination of Humanitarian Assistance, "Consolidated

Agency Appeal 2002," 140. UNICEF staff number is in "Annex VII: Agency Staffing in DPR Korea," United Nations Office for the Coordination of Humanitarian Assistance, *Consolidated Agency Appeal for the DPRK January–December 2001* (New York: UNOCHA, 2000), 101. It is unlikely UNICEF staffing would have increased as of 2001 or 2002, as the program could not attract sufficient funding.

14. United Nations Office for the Coordination of Humanitarian Assistance, "Consolidated Agency Appeal for the DPRK January–December 1998," mimeo, 1998, available on http://www.reliefweb.int.

15. Office for the Coordination of Humanitarian Assistance, *Consolidated Agency Appeal 2000* (New York: UNOCHA, 1999), 19.

16. Appendix 5, in UN Department of Humanitarian Affairs, "Consolidated UN Inter-Agency Appeal, 1 July 1996–31 March 1997."

17. "Table V: Major Donors of Humanitarian Assistance for the Democratic People's Republic of Korea in 1998," in United Nations Office for the Coordination of Humanitarian Assistance, *Consolidated Agency Appeal 1999* (1998), 89.

18. "Table V: Major Donors of Humanitarian Assistance for the Democratic People's Republic of Korea in 1999," in United Nations Office for the Coordination of Humanitarian Assistance, *Consolidated Agency Appeal 2001* (2000), 130.

19. Ibid., 117.

20. "Table VI: Total Humanitarian Assistance to Korea, Democratic People's Republic of," in United Nations Office for the Coordination of Humanitarian Assistance, "Consolidated Agency Appeal 2002," 123.

21. Ibid.

22. See "Farewell Interview with Mr. Lemaire," in UNDP, *Interagency Quarterly* 1, Pyongyang (Autumn 1999): 5–7.

23. See Smith, "North Korean Foreign Policy," 99.

24. World Food Program, "Outline for EMOP Submission: Emergency Operation DPR Korea no. 5710.00: 'Emergency Food Assistance for Flood Victims,'" in *WFP Operations in DPR Korea as of 14 July 1999*, by WFP (Rome: WFP, undated but 1999), no page numbers.

25. For detail on agencies resident in 1998, see United Nations Office for the Coordination of Humanitarian Assistance, *Consolidated Agency Appeal 1999* (1998).

26. WFP information from World Food Program, "Emergency Operation DPR Korea no. 5710.01: 'Emergency Food Assistance for Flood Victims and Children under Five,'" in *WFP Operations in DPR Korea as of 14 July 1999*, by WFP (Rome: WFP, undated but 1999), no page numbers. UNICEF information from UNICEF, "UNICEF Revised

Funding Requirements: United Nations Consolidated Inter-Agency Appeal for the Democratic People's Republic of Korea: April 1997–March 1998," mimeo, undated but 1998, 1.

27. For details of numbers of international and national staff of UN agencies, bilaterals, and NGOs in 2000, see "Annex VII: Agency Staffing in DPR Korea," in United Nations Office for the Coordination of Humanitarian Assistance, *Consolidated Inter-Agency Appeal 2001* (2000), 101.

28. United Nations Office for the Coordination of Humanitarian Assistance, *Consolidated Agency Appeal 1999* (1998), 93.

29. See "Annex 5: Bilateral, Multilateral and Non-Governmental Organisations," in United Nations Office for the Coordination of Humanitarian Assistance, "Consolidated Agency Appeal 2002."

30. Ibid.

31. Information on initial work by Children's Aid Direct and International Federation of the Red Cross is from United Nations Office for the Coordination of Humanitarian Assistance, *Consolidated Agency Appeal 1999* (1998), 93–100. The first Caritas food shipment reached the DPRK in November 1995. Kathi Zellweger, e-mail to author, August 18, 2002.

32. A review of South Korean NGO activity in the DPRK is in Jae-Shik Oh, "Reports on the Humanitarian Assistance to North Korea: South Korean Non-governmental Organizations," prepared for the Third International NGO Conference on Humanitarian Assistance to North Korea, mimeo, Seoul, June 2001. Japanese NGO activity is briefly reviewed in Kiyomi Yoshida, "Supporting Activities of Japanese NGOs," in *International NGO Conference on Humanitarian Assistance to DPRK, June 30–July 2, 2000, Conference Proceedings,* by Executive Committee of the International NGO Conference on Humanitarian Assistance to DPRK (Tokyo: National Christian Council in Japan, 2000), 37–39. On U.S. NGOs, see Victor W. C. Hsu, "The Role of Non-governmental Organizations in the USA," in *International NGO Conference on Humanitarian Assistance to DPRK, June 30–July 2, 2000,* 26–33. A summary of activity by a consortium of Canadian faith-based NGOs can be found in "Annex V: Non-resident NGOs Working through the Food-Aid Liaison Unit (FALU)," in United Nations Office of the Coordination of Humanitarian Assistance, *Consolidated Inter-Agency Appeal 2001* (2000), 97.

33. Office for the Coordination of Humanitarian Affairs, Field Coordination Unit, Democratic People's Republic of Korea, untitled list and description of NGOs, Pyongyang, 1998, 1–5.

34. Ibid.

35. Details on Cap Anamur, Oxfam, and ACF in United Nations Office for the Coordination of Humanitarian Assistance, *Consolidated Agency Appeal 1999* (1998), 93–97. Details on Help Age International from author's interviews with Help Age International representatives, Pyongyang, April–May 1998.

36. Pecchio, "Identification of an At Risk Group"; Action against Hunger, "Action against Hunger's Withdrawal from North Korea, Press Dossier," mimeo, London, March 2000. See also NAPSNet Daily Report, March 9, 2000, on http://www.nautilus.org/napsnet/dr/0003/MAR09.html; the Oxfam withdrawal is discussed in General Accounting Office, *US Bilateral Assistance to North Korea Had Mixed Results* (Washington, DC: USGAO, June 2000), 55; information on Help Age International from author's interviews, Help Age International, Pyongyang, 1998.

37. For detail on ADRA and PMU-Interlife, see United Nations Office for the Coordination of Humanitarian Assistance, *Consolidated Agency Appeal 2000* (1999), 102–105. Information on Triangle and Handicap International in United Nations Office for the Coordination of Humanitarian Assistance, "Consolidated Agency Appeal 2002," 138 and 6, respectively.

38. See website of Hungarian Baptist Aid, www.hbaid.org/aa_north.html. See also "Section IV. NGOs in DPRK" in Food Aid Liaison Unit, "Annual Report 2001," mimeo, Pyongyang, undated but 2002.

39. Pyongyang Square, on http://www.pyongyangsquare.com/aid/.

40. For summary of the role of FALU, see John O'Dea, "Experience of the FALU," in *International NGO Conference on Humanitarian Assistance to DPRK, June 30–July 2, 2000*, 17–19.

41. A detailed history and evaluation of the PVOC activities in the DPRK can be found in Hsu, "Non-governmental Organizations," 26–33.

42. Kathi Zellweger, e-mail to author, August 18, 2002.

43. Draft FALU information sheet, e-mailed from Kathi Zellweger, mimeo, August 2002.

44. These were the core members, although some joined and left at different times. Except for World Vision, member NGOs cited are listed in General Accounting Office, *US Bilateral Assistance*, note 1, 3. World Vision is cited in reports from a PVOC monitoring mission to the DPRK in April 1998. See PVOC, "Field Trip: First Visit," April 24, 1998.

45. Amayun et al., "Trip Report"; PVO Consortium, "Interim Report." PVOC cooperation with WFP is discussed in Hsu, "Non-governmental Organizations," 26–33.

46. The GAO reports two Korean speakers employed in-country by the PVOC. See General Accounting Office, *US Bilateral Assistance*, 37. There were, in fact, three PVOC staff in-country who were fluent Korean speakers: two were food monitors and one was the project administrator. See Hsu, "Non-governmental Organizations," 31.

47. NAPSNet Daily Report, April 6, 2000, on http://www.nautilus.org/napsnet/dr/0004/APR06.html.

48. See, for example, American Red Cross, "Food Crisis Worsens in North Korea: American Red Cross Sends Food, Medicine," press release, September 18, 1998, reproduced on www.reliefweb.int (section "Complex Emergencies," subsection "DPR Korea," subsection "American Red Cross"); and Smith, *Caritas Five-Year Evaluation*.

49. Jong-Moo Lee, "Humanitarian Assistance toward North Korea in South Korea: Historical and Current Overview for South Korean Context," in Oh, "Reports on the Humanitarian Assistance to North Korea," 13.

50. Ibid.

51. See section "World Vision Korea" in International Organizing Committee for the International NGO Conference, "Listing of the NGO Activities," in a set of documents prepared for the Third International NGO Conference on Humanitarian Assistance to North Korea, mimeo, Seoul, June 2001.

52. Information on Mercy Corps and American Friends Service Committee from Hsu, "Non-governmental Organizations," 26; data on AmeriCares from author interviews, AmeriCares representatives, New York, May 2002 and UNOCHA Office in the DPRK, "DPR Korea: Situation Bulletin, no. 06/02," June and July 2002.

53. Yoshida, "Supporting Activities of Japanese NGOs," 37–39.

54. Ibid., 37.

55. Lee, "The Situation of and the Agenda for the Humanitarian Aid to the DPRK," in *International NGO Conference on Humanitarian Assistance to DPRK, June 30–July 2, 2000*, 28. Information on Caritas-Coreana from interview with Kathi Zellweger, Caritas–Hong Kong, September 2001.

56. A list of these eighteen and their activities is in International Organizing Committee for the International NGO Conference, "Listing of the NGO Activities." There were certainly other South Korean NGOs working to support the DPRK that were not included on this list. One was Caritas-Coreana.

57. See "Farewell Interview with Mr. Lemaire," 5–7; UNICEF, *Situation of Children and Women 2000* (1999), 11; World Food Program, "Basic Agreement between the United Nations FAO World Food Program and the Government of the Democratic People's Republic of Korea Concerning Assistance from the World Food Program," mimeo, June 9, 1986; and Smith, *Caritas Five-Year Evaluation*, 16.

58. Data from "Annex 3: Deliveries of Food Aid to the DPRK 1995/1996," in UN Department of Humanitarian Affairs, "Consolidated UN Inter-Agency Appeal, 1 July 1996–31 March 1997."

59. UN Department of Humanitarian Affairs, "Consolidated UN Inter-Agency Appeal, 1 July 1996–31 March 1997."

60. Information on appeals in International Federation of the Red Cross and Red Crescent Societies, "Evaluation Mission to North Korea 15–31 May 1997," mimeo, 9. Data on IFRC food deliveries in "Annex 3: Deliveries of Food Aid to the DPRK 1995/ 1996," in UN Department of Humanitarian Affairs, "Consolidated UN Inter-Agency Appeal, 1 July 1996–31 March 1997."

61. See "Appendix Four: Caritas Assistance to the DPRK by Year and Sector," in Smith, *Caritas Five-Year Evaluation*, 51.

62. Oh Jae-Shik, "A Call for the Reassessment of NGO Humanitarian Activities in DPRK," in *International NGO Conference on Humanitarian Assistance to DPRK, June 30–July 2, 2000*, 119. Information on Korea Food for the Hungry in International Organizing Committee for the International NGO Conference, "Listing of the NGO Activities."

63. UN Department of Humanitarian Affairs, "Consolidated UN Inter-Agency Appeal, 1 July 1996–31 March 1997." Data on amount of assistance requested from United Nations Office for the Coordination of Humanitarian Assistance, "Consolidated Agency Appeal 1998."

64. UN Department of Humanitarian Affairs, "Consolidated UN Inter-Agency Appeal, 1 July 1996–31 March 1997."

65. United Nations Office for the Coordination of Humanitarian Assistance, "Consolidated Agency Appeal 1998." There is no complete information as to how much of the assistance went to food aid or other sectors. From the available information, it is likely that the vast majority of aid in the first appeal went to food aid, with some assistance being directed to the reclamation of flood-damaged land and the health sector.

66. United Nations Office for the Coordination of Humanitarian Assistance, "Consolidated Agency Appeal 1998."

67. Ibid.

68. Ibid.

69. There is some contradiction among the UN documents as far as the figures are concerned. The 1998 appeal document cites the figures used in the text. The 1999 appeal, in its discussion of the "previous CAP in review," states that the previous appeal was for $383,242,336, of which $345,801,900, or 90 percent, was for food assistance.

Either way, a very large amount of funding was required, and most of it was for food assistance. See United Nations Office for the Coordination of Humanitarian Assistance, "Consolidated Agency Appeal 1998"; United Nations Office for the Coordination of Humanitarian Assistance, *Consolidated Agency Appeal 1999* (1998), 1.

70. United Nations Office for the Coordination of Humanitarian Assistance, *Consolidated Agency Appeal 1999* (1998), 1.

71. "Table 1: Funding to the 1998 UN Consolidated Inter Agency Appeal for the DPRK," in ibid., 82.

72. United Nations Office for the Coordination of Humanitarian Assistance, *Consolidated Agency Appeal 1999* (1998), ix.

73. Ibid.

74. Ibid.

75. "Table 1: Funding to the 1999 UN Consolidated Inter Agency Appeal for the DPRK," in United Nations Office for the Coordination of Humanitarian Assistance, *Consolidated Agency Appeal 2000* (1999), 126.

76. United Nations Office for the Coordination of Humanitarian Assistance, *Consolidated Agency Appeal 2000* (1999), xii–xiii.

77. Ibid., 5. See also "Table 1: Funding to the 2000 UN Consolidated Inter Agency Appeal for the DPRK," in United Nations Office for the Coordination of Humanitarian Assistance, *Consolidated Agency Appeal 2001* (2000), 110.

78. Ibid., 110.

79. "Table 1: UN Consolidated Inter Agency Appeal for the DPR of Korea 2001," in United Nations Office for the Coordination of Humanitarian Assistance, "Consolidated Agency Appeal 2002," 111.

80. United Nations Office for the Coordination of Humanitarian Assistance, "Consolidated Agency Appeal 2002," 11.

81. "Table 1: UN Consolidated Inter Agency Appeal for the DPR of Korea 2001," in ibid., 111.

82. United Nations Office for the Coordination of Humanitarian Assistance, "Consolidated Agency Appeal 2002," 10.

83. Ibid.

84. Ibid.

85. For the 2003 figures, see United Nations Office for the Coordination of Humanitarian Assistance, *Consolidated Agency Appeal for Democratic People's Republic of Korea 2003*, November 19, 2002, on Reliefweb, http://www.reliefweb.int/w/rwb.nsf/

437a83f9fa966c40c12564f2004fde87/96b6c5fc02925530c1256c6f003815ce?Open-Document. For 2004 figures, see United Nations Office for the Coordination of Humanitarian Assistance, *Consolidated Agency Appeal 2004 for the DPRK* (Geneva: UNOCHA, 2003), 11, reproduced on http://ochadms.unog.ch/quickplace/cap/main.nsf/h_Index/CAP_2004_DPRK/$FILE/CAP_2004_DPRK_SCREEN.PDF?OpenElement.

86. For the 2003 figures, see United Nations Office for the Coordination of Humanitarian Assistance, *Consolidated Agency Appeal 2003* (2002). For 2004 figures, see United Nations Office for the Coordination of Humanitarian Assistance, *Consolidated Agency Appeal 2004* (2003), 11.

87. For details of activities of six resident NGOs, see "Resident NGOs in DPR Korea Involved in the CAP," information leaflet, November 2001.

88. Data taken from "Appeals/Operations Coordinated by the International Federation 1919–2002," reproduced on http://www.ifrc.org/cgi/pdf_statistic.pl?allaps.pdf.

89. Smith, *Caritas Five-Year Evaluation*, 51.

90. Ibid., 52.

91. For an account of Caritas aid priorities, see ibid.

92. Giorgio Maragliano, untitled paper presented to the Third International NGO Conference on Humanitarian Assistance to North Korea, Seoul, mimeo, June 2001; and European Commission, "The EC–Democratic People's Republic of Korea (DPRK) Country Strategy Paper 2001–2004," 25, reproduced on http://europa.eu.int/comm/external_relations/north_korea/csp/01_04_en.pdf.

93. United Nations Office for the Coordination of Humanitarian Assistance, "Consolidated Agency Appeal 2002," 3.

94. The summaries of nongovernmental assistance to the DPRK provided every year in the UN CAP documents (1998–2002) do not report significant contributions from U.S. or Japanese NGOs. The Eugene Bell Foundation, although run by Americans, received the bulk of its funding from South Korea.

95. Data on South Korean NGO expenditure from Dong-Won Lim, "Prospects for Inter-Korean Relations and South Korean Policy on Assistance to North Korea" (paper prepared for the Third International NGO Conference on Humanitarian Assistance to North Korea, mimeo, Seoul, June 2001), 8. It is difficult to obtain financial data from or on U.S. NGO expenditure in the DPRK. The PVO Consortium was largely funded by the U.S. government, with the NGO contribution amounting to about $1.2 million; data derived from General Accounting Office, *US Bilateral Assistance*, 12–13. A previous GAO report states that the USDA, "beginning in 1996, [has] given approximately $4.5 million to allow a consortium of US private voluntary organizations to monitor portions of US donations provided through WFP to North Korea." See General

Accounting Office, *North Korea Restricts Food Aid Monitoring* (Washington, DC: GAO, October 1999), 7. Japanese NGO assistance is not quantified but summarized qualitatively in Yoshida, "Supporting Activities of Japanese NGOs."

96. This was the author's task when she was employed by the WFP for 11 months in 2000–2001.

97. UNICEF, "Draft Report on the Multiple Indicator Cluster Survey in the Democratic People's Republic of Korea, 1998," mimeo, Pyongyang; and EU, UNICEF, and WFP, "Nutrition Survey."

98. Action contre la Faim (ACF) carried out an extremely detailed nutritional survey in the nurseries it assisted in 1999. See Action contre la Faim, "Nutritional Programme: North Hamgyong Province DPR of Korea, November 1999," mimeo. See also EU, UNICEF, and WFP, "Nutrition Survey."

99. See, for example, FAO/WFP, "Crop and Food Supply Assessment," October 26, 2001.

100. The regular reports of the Food Aid Liaison Unit (FALU) provide accounts of how NGOs complemented the multilateral donors in providing "niche" commodities such as sugar and oil, in their focus on the most remote provinces (FALU NGOs work primarily in the northeast), and in their ability to target additional vulnerable groups (for example, industrial workers in the northeast). See, for instance, Food Aid Liaison Unit, "Activity Report to FALU Steering Committee," mimeo, Pyongyang, April 1999; and Food Aid Liaison Unit, "Annual Report 2001."

101. The scale of the operation is noted in General Accounting Office, *North Korea Restricts Food Aid Monitoring,* 5.

102. The UNOCHA reported that 807,327 metric tons of food was distributed between January and September 2001. See United Nations Office for the Coordination of Humanitarian Assistance, "Consolidated Agency Appeal 2002," dated 2002 but written in late 2001. WFP DPRK reported that 1 million tons of aid was distributed in 2001. Author's interviews, DPRK logistics staff, January 2002.

103. I have discussed the "data gap" in a number of places. See, for instance, Smith, "'Opening Up' by Default," 465–470.

104. In October 1999, for instance, WFP made 404 visits, including to 78 families, 14 schools, 25 food-for-work sites, 1 farm, 49 nurseries, 53 kindergartens, 42 hospitals, and 142 counties or public distribution centers. See World Food Program, "DPR Korea Update no. 10," Pyongyang, October 1999. In May 2002, 410 visits were completed— to the same range of locations but also including ports, orphanages, and local food production factories. See World Food Program, "DPR Korea Update no. 40," Pyongyang, May 2002.

105. United Nations Office of the Coordination of Humanitarian Assistance, *Consolidated Inter-Agency Appeal 2001* (2000), 23.

106. World Food Program in DPR Korea, "Access to Counties," December 1999.

107. World Food Program, "DPR Korea Update no. 41," Pyongyang, June 2002.

108. The WFP made assessment visits and evaluations of vulnerability after every new county was made accessible. In 1999, after five counties were made accessible to the humanitarian community, the WFP produced a short report that identified some commonalities among them. They were in remote, mountainous areas; were industrialized; had little agricultural land; and had relatively high levels of child malnutrition. See World Food Program, "Special Update: Newly Accessible Counties," mimeo, Pyongyang, July 5, 1999.

109. WFP interviews with named beneficiaries discussed the impact of aid. See World Food Program, "Stories from DPR Korea: Emergency Officers Talk to Beneficiaries" (Pyongyang: WFP, 2000).

110. Collected quantitative data is in UNICEF, *Social Statistics: DPRK.*

111. EU, UNICEF, and WFP, "Nutrition Survey."

112. Percentage figure from ibid.

113. Ibid.

114. United Nations Office for the Coordination of Humanitarian Assistance, "Consolidated Agency Appeal 2002," 7; and Central Bureau of Statistics, DPRK, "DPRK Nutrition Assessment."

115. Data in this paragraph from Central Bureau of Statistics, DPRK, "DPRK Nutrition Assessment." See also Central Bureau of Statistics, DPRK, "DPRK 2004 Nutrition Assessment," mimeo, Pyongyang, 2005, for more recent trends toward reduction in malnutrition levels.

116. David Morton, e-mail to author, October 2001.

117. UNDP and DPRK government, "Thematic Roundtable Meeting."

118. UNDP, *Second Country Cooperation Framework.*

119. An assessment of the double-cropping initiative is in Cadogan, *Distribution and Use of Inputs.*

120. FAO/WFP, "Crop and Food Supply Assessment Mission," October 26, 2001.

121. "UN Calls for 221 Million Dollars in Aid for North Korea in 2004," November 19, 2003, ClariNews, http://quickstart.clari.net/qs_se/webnews/wed/bz/Qnkorea-un-food-china.R2HG_DNK.html.

122. UNDP Pyongyang lists details of 230 agricultural projects undertaken by various international agencies in the DPRK between 1996 and 2001. See UNDP/AREP, "Status of Agricultural Activities."

123. "Annex VI: Statement by David Morton, UN Resident Coordinator," in UNDP/ AREP, *Report of the Second Thematic Round Table Conference for the Democratic People's Republic of Korea* (Geneva: UNDP, June 2000), 29–31.

124. United Nations Office for the Coordination of Humanitarian Assistance, "Consolidated Agency Appeal 2002."

125. The Republic of Korea supplied over $53 million worth of fertilizer between May and June 2000. For details of ROK and World Vision assistance in 2000, see "Table IV: 2000 Additional Humanitarian Assistance to the Democratic People's Republic of Korea," in United Nations Office of the Coordination of Humanitarian Assistance, *Consolidated Inter-Agency Appeal 2001* (2000), 115–116. See also Soon-Kwon Kim, "NGO's Activity for the South and the North Korean Cooperation on Agriculture" (paper prepared for the Third International NGO Conference on Humanitarian Assistance to North Korea, Seoul, mimeo, June 2001).

126. Quoted in Omawale Omawale, "An Exercise in Ambivalence: Negotiating with North Korea," *Harvard Asia Pacific Review* 3, no. 2 (summer 1999).

127. A comprehensive, though not exhaustive, survey of capacity-building projects undertaken by DPRK officials is in Park, "Track-Two Foreign Contact."

128. Khan, "Democratic People's Republic of Korea." Training/study visits reported in UNICEF, "UNICEF Humanitarian Action, DPR Korea: Donor Update." New York, February 4, 2002.

129. UNOCHA Office in the DPRK, "DPR Korea: Situation Bulletin, no. 06/02," June and July 2002.

130. Ibid.

131. Author's telephone interview with Fiona Terry, MSF research director, November 2001, discussed in Smith, "Minimum Conditions for Humanitarian Action."

132. The 2001 consensus statement is reproduced as "Annex IX" in United Nations Office for the Coordination of Humanitarian Assistance, *Consolidated Agency Appeal 2004* (2003), 11.

133. An Oxfam Hong Kong representative visited the DPRK in May 2002 as part of a Caritas-led delegation. See Caritas, "Trip Report," mimeo, May 14–21, 2002.

134. Pecchio, "Identification of an At Risk Group."

135. On MDM funding constraints, see Smith, "'Opening Up' by Default," 464.

136. CARE press release, April 4, 2000, on http://www.careusaorg/newsroom/ pressreleases/2000/apr/northkorea0404.asp.

137. Marv Frey, director of Program Service, Canadian Foodgrains Bank, e-mail to author, November 2001.

138. Ibid.

139. General Accounting Office, *US Bilateral Assistance*, 38.

140. The humanitarian principles and the three consensus statements with all the signatory organizations are reproduced in Smith, "Minimum Conditions for Humanitarian Action." The humanitarian principles and the detailed benchmarking for each principle for 2001 can be found in United Nations Office for the Coordination of Humanitarian Assistance, "Consolidated Agency Appeal 2002."

141. United Nations Office for the Coordination of Humanitarian Assistance, "Consolidated Agency Appeal 2002."

142. Ibid.

143. March 2001 consensus statement reproduced in Smith, "Minimum Conditions for Humanitarian Action."

144. For 2002 figures, see World Food Program, "DPR Korea Update no. 41."

145. The first significant nutrition survey after 1995 took place in 1997 and was conducted by the WFP in collaboration with FAO, UNICEF, and Save the Children. Although the survey provided some interesting data, the sampling was not carried out randomly and was therefore limited in its utility. See World Food Program in collaboration with FAO, UNICEF, and Save the Children, *Nutritional Assessment to the Democratic People's Republic of Korea* (Pyongyang/Rome: World Food Program, November 1997).

146. An account of the gains made in the direction of increased transparency by the senior negotiator for the humanitarian agencies, the UNICEF special representative, is Omawale, "An Exercise in Ambivalence," 60–62.

147. United Nations Office for the Coordination of Humanitarian Assistance, "Consolidated Agency Appeal 2002."

148. For discussion on living conditions for humanitarian workers, see Smith, "Living with Absences."

149. Information in this paragraph from "Annex B: The Preparation Process," in UNDP and DPRK government, "Thematic Roundtable Meeting."

150. "Annex XXII: Statement by Mr. David Hagen, Director of USAID," in UNDP/AREP, *Report of the Second Thematic Round Table Conference*, 72–73.

151. "Annex XXVII: Summary of Comments Made by H.E. Mr. Choe Su Hon, Vice-Minister, Ministry of Foreign Affairs, DPR Korea, on Points Raised by Participants," in UNDP/AREP, *Report of the Second Thematic Round Table Conference*, 81.

152. See "Annex VII: Statement by H.E. Mr. Lee Jae-Gil, Republic of Korea, Ambassador, Permanent Mission, Geneva," in UNDP/AREP, *Report of the Second Thematic Round Table Conference*, 33.

153. KEDO was not totally opaque, as it produced some reports on its activities. See KEDO, *Annual Report 2000/2001* (New York: KEDO, 2001).

5. The New Human Security Patchwork

1. For longer discussion, see Smith, "La Corée du Nord."

2. Author's observations, 1998–2001, around the country.

3. Author's observations, 1998 onward.

4. The DPRK computing industry dates back to the establishment of the Pyongyang Informatics Center in 1986. See "Pyongyang Informatics Centre," *Pyongyang Times,* September 14, 1996, 5. See also "Scientists in Their Twenties," *Korea* 530 (December 2000), *Juche* 89, 10–11.

5. "2002 Be a Year of a New Surge," *Pyongyang Times,* January 5, 2002, *Juche* 91, 1–2.

6. Ibid., 2.

7. Foreign Languages Publishing House, *Socialist Constitution of the DPRK* (Pyongyang: Foreign Languages Publishing House, 1998).

8. Noland is right to report the mixed signals from the DPRK in 1998. At the same time that changes to the constitution were promulgated, party newspapers condemned economic "reform." What is significant in retrospect is that the government felt compelled to introduce any modification of the planned economy, given the antipathy to economic policy change. See Noland, *Avoiding the Apocalypse,* 86–87.

9. "Annex V, Statement by Choe Su Hon, Vice-Minister, Ministry of Foreign Affairs, DPR Korea," in *Report of the Second Thematic Round Table Conference,* 27–28.

10. By 2002 there were many official references to "the principle of profitability" as a principle of economic development. See KCNA, "Spectacular Achievements in Construction," February 15, 2002, at http://www.kcna.co.jp/calendar/frame.htm. A KCNA article dated January 29, 2002, reports that profitability should be a part of "Juche-based socialist economic construction." See ibid.

11. Daily Report, July 23, 2002, http://www.nautilus.org/napsnet/dr/0207/JUL23 .html#item9.

12. For details, see "NK Unveils 'Shinuiju Special Law,'" *Korea Times,* September 27, 2002.

13. Key sections of the statute granting autonomy to Sinuiju in "Basic Law of Sinuiju Special Administrative Region," *Pyongyang Report* 4, no. 4 (October 2002), available at http://www.vuw.ac.nz/~caplabtb/dprk/. On Yang Bin, see James Kynge and

Andrew Ward, "Beijing Raises Wall of Silence over N Korea's Capitalist King," *Financial Times* (London), Japan edition 1, September 27, 2002.

14. For details of how the state previously engaged in detailed and highly interventionist economic management in the area of price setting, see "Price Assessment in Korea," *Pyongyang Times*, April 20, 1996, 5.

15. Quotation from Cadogan, *Distribution and Use of Inputs*, 8.

16. From *Joosong Ilbo*, June 4, 2001, reported in NAPSNet Daily Report, June 5, 2001, http://www.nautilus.org/napsnet/dr/0106/JUN05.html.

17. Pyongyang Chamber of Commerce, "Country Report," September 2001. The Economist Intelligence Unit reports an average per capita income in 2000 of $757, which seems rather high given the observable poverty throughout the country. See Economist Intelligence Unit, "The Koreas," in *Business Asia*, March 11, 2002. The black market *won*:dollar rate changed from 10:1 in September 2000 to 26:1 in July 2001 while the author was living in the DPRK.

18. Author's observations, Kangwon and North Hwanghae provinces, early September 2001.

19. Author's observations, throughout the country, 1999–2001. This practice is also observed in Pyongyang.

20. The discussion in this and following sections draws on Smith, "La Corée du Nord." Much of this paragraph draws on the experience of the author while living and working in the DPRK.

21. Michell, "Current North Korean Economy," 152.

22. For an excellent summary and analysis of South Korean business activity in the DPRK, see Joseph A. B. Winder, *Promoting Economic Cooperation between North and South Korea* (Washington, DC: Korea Economic Institute, October 19, 2001).

23. For discussion of the critique within South Korea of the way that Hyundai operated the Kumgang tourist venture, including the practice of cash transfers, see Norman Levin and Yong-Sup Han, "The South Korean Debate over Policies toward North Korea: Issues and Implications" (Santa Monica, CA: Rand, 2002), mimeo, 28–29.

24. For analysis of conditions throughout the country in health, nutrition, education, and water and sanitation, see UNICEF, *Situation of Children and Women 2000* (1999).

25. FAO/WFP, "Crop and Food Supply Assessment Mission," October 26, 2001.

26. The term "Stone Age" is used literally here. In 1999, 2000, and 2001, I traveled, worked, and interviewed North Koreans in these areas. There were no tools for mending bridges, roads, and houses, apart from roughly fashioned homemade instruments, many of which could literally have been a product of Stone Age technology. This was in an area that had been the industrial hub of the DPRK, building machine tools and producing fertilizer and pharmaceuticals for the entire country.

27. Kwon and Kim, "Assessment of Food Supply," 51. Quotation from FAO/WFP, "Special Report: Crop and Food Supply Assessment Mission," November 16, 2000, 7.

28. Quoted in Jeremy Page, "U.N. Agency Seeks Immediate Food Aid for North Korea," April 10, 2002, reproduced on asia.news.yahoo.com/020410/reuters/asia-99461.html.

29. For discussion on problems for human development in DPRK, see UNDP, *Second Country Cooperation Framework*.

30. For description of the type and extent of humanitarian need and resources required, see United Nations Office for the Coordination of Humanitarian Assistance, *Consolidated Inter-Agency Appeal 2001* (2000).

31. The DPRK had sought help from the UNDP to encourage foreign investment as early as 1992, but at that time it made clear to the two British consultants who carried out the assessment that it did "not intend to reform, restructure nor liberalize its economy and indeed does not appear to accept that such changes are neither necessary or desirable." In contrast, by the early 2000s, DPRK encouragement of foreign investment was paralleled by an acceptance in principle of the need for reform (even if that reform was not yet for full-blown capitalism). Quotation from Paul Collins and Frederick Nixson, "The Changing Global Economic Environment and the Centrally Planned Economy: The Case of the Democratic People's Republic of Korea," (paper presented at a conference on "Management Development of Centrally-Planned Economies in a New Global Environment 1–3 April 1992," mimeo, UNDP/ODI, London, undated but 1992), 17.

32. For harvest and food deficit figures for 2001–2, see FAO/WFP, "Crop and Food Supply Assessment Mission," October 26, 2001.

33. Interviews with agronomists in the DPRK 2000, 2001, and 2002.

34. The report of Kim Jong Il's visit to Ryanggang province in November 2000 specifically describes his visit to "a village of discharged soldiers" and comments on the building of "hundreds of modern houses." For report, see http://www.kcna.co.jp/item/2000/200011/news11/28.htm. This author also observed these timber-built new houses while traveling in Ryanggang in October 2000.

35. See report of Kim Jong Il's visit to Ryanggang dated August 12, 1999, on http://www.kcna.co.jp/item/1999/9908/news08/12.htm. For summary of the Swiss work in Ryanggang, see UNOCHA, DPR Korea: *Humanitarian Situation Information Bulletin December 2000–January 2001*, January 31, 2001, reproduced on http://www.reliefweb.int.

36. Barbara Demick, "Forced Migration Is Key to N. Korean Trade Zone," *Los Angeles Times*, September 26, 2002.

37. For discussion of legal barriers to foreign trade, see Pilho Park, "A Review of Major Legal Issues along the Foreign Investment Road to North Korea" (paper presented at "Symposium on North Korea's Engagement with the Global Economy: Prospects and Challenges," University of Wisconsin–Madison, April 12–13, 2002).

38. The humanitarian organizations, for instance, had no control over who was employed, the duration of employment, or in what capacity the employee worked. Firing an unsatisfactory staff member was impossible, occasionally resulting in difficult relations between local and international staff.

39. Park, "A Review of Major Legal Issues," 8.

40. Pyongyang Chamber of Commerce, "Country Report," 3.

41. From the website of the Canadian International Development Agency (CIDA). See http://www.acdi-cida.gc.ca/CIDAWEB/webcountry.nsf/0/7D484015AB33312E 85256C04007DC8A9?OpenDocument.

42. World Health Organization, Office of WHO Representative to DPR Korea, "Briefing on Health Situation in DPR Korea November 2002," mimeo, February 12, 2003. On the use of Koryo medicines, see Chris Dammers et al., *Review of the Red Cross Health and Care Programme, Democratic Peoples' [sic] Republic of Korea*, mimeo, October 2001, 11.

43. Central Bureau of Statistics, DPRK, "DPRK Nutrition Assessment," 28.

44. I interviewed North Korean migrants/refugees in northeast China in September 2002. One elderly woman from Onsong county in North Hamgyong province informed me that miners had been fed 20 kilograms a month until the previous January, after which their ration was cut to 10 kilograms. She also said that nurseries, kindergartens, and pregnant women had not received food from the state for several years.

45. Figures from IISS, *Military Balance 2001/2002*, 196.

46. Lower exchange rates observed by author, Pyongyang, 2000. Higher rates reported by Chinese traders to author in Pyongyang. A 210:1 rate was reported in the free-trade zone of Rajin-Sonbong, and the currency was reportedly made legally convertible at that rate, in 1997. See Michell, "Current North Korean Economy," 156. The 300:1 (and higher) rate was reported to the author by traders in Pyongyang in 2000 and 2001.

47. For summary of available evidence, see Noland, *Avoiding the Apocalypse*, 71–73.

48. Some glimpses of the civilian activities of the military can be found in the DPRK official news agency reports of Kim Jong Il's regular inspection visits to army units throughout the country. See, for example, reference to a chicken farm built by the KPA, in "Kim Jong Il Sees Servicepersons in Training," March 12, 2002, in http://www.kcna.co.jp/

calendar/frame.htm. A February 6, 2002, report from the same source notes that DPRK "soldiers are tenaciously and assiduously managing their economic life at every unit . . . this proud feature can be found only in the heroic KPA." A May 20, 2001, report from the same source notes the reforestation activities of one KPA battalion. Not all reports of visits mention the economic activities of KPA units, which may indicate that not all KPA units are engaged in nonmilitary activities.

49. The Federation of American Scientists reported the existence of a "Second Economic Committee," which reported to the Party Central Committee and which was in charge of the defense industry, but the FAS does not present information on volumes or cash amounts of production.

50. Yonhap, Seoul, December 11, 2002, quoted in *Vantage Point* 26, no. 1 (January 2003): 56.

51. Few specific instances of DPRK missile technology sales are reported. One exception is the report of suspected arms sales to Iran, in *JoonAng Ilbo*, "N.K. Reaping Profit out of Missile Proliferation, Says Washington Times," April 19, 2001, reproduced on http://english.joins.com/article.asp?aid=20010419112430&sid=E00. For detailed review of DPRK exports and imports, which does not include earnings from weapons sales, see W. J. Jung, "North Korea's Foreign Trade in 2000," reproduced on the website of the Korea Trade Investment Promotion Agency (KOTRA). The KOTRA website on the DPRK in English can be found at http://www.kotra.or.kr.main/info/nk/eng/main.php3.

52. "North Korean Society Today," on http://www.keepingapace.org/html/archives/war/nkorea.htm.

53. "The True Situation inside North Korea after the Summit Meeting," undated, http://www.bekkoame.ne.jp/ro/renk/en/anessay.htm. International aid workers did not report marauding gangs of youths around the country, and their personal safety was not threatened anywhere in the country, even in the most remote areas. International aid workers did not travel with armed or any other guards and were very visible but were not, as in other countries, targets for attack. This was also the case when aid workers were stranded by typhoons or flooding and had to stay overnight in locations where they were not expected and had no means of communication with Pyongyang. It is unlikely that foreigners would be attacked, given the definite repercussions from the security apparatus.

54. "National Meeting of Support-Army Activists," *Korea* 557 (January 2003): 8–10.

55. Kathi Zellweger, "DPRK Trip Report 6 August to 3 September 2002," mimeo, Hong Kong, September 30, 2002.

56. Barbara Demick, "Inflation Hits 600% as Reforms Fail," *The Age*, February 6, 2003, http://www.theage.com.au/articles/2003/02/05/1044318668734.html.

57. FAO/WFP, "Special Report: Crop and Food Supply Assessment Mission," November 16, 2000, 2.

58. Smith, "North Koreans in China."

6. A New Diplomacy

1. In 1974, 54 percent of DPRK imports originated in the West, according to a European Parliament report. See European Parliament, "On the Community's Trade Relations with North Korea," mimeo, July 17, 1985, 15. For discussion, see Smith, "North Korean Foreign Policy," 98.

2. This section draws from Smith, "North Korean Foreign Policy."

3. The DPRK played an active part in the Non-Aligned Movement. See Kim Il Sung, "'Non-Aligned Information Must Contribute to the People's Cause of Independence,' speech at the Fourth Conference of Ministers of Information of Non-Aligned Countries," Pyongyang, June 15, 1993, reproduced in *Bulletin d'Information,* DPRK Delegation in France, mimeo, Paris, June 15, 1993.

4. For detailed discussion, see Smith, *Overcoming Humanitarian Dilemmas.*

5. In December 2000, North-South ministerial talks ended with the signing of agreements preventing double taxation, enabling the settling of financial accounts, and encouraging dispute settlement in investment and economic matters, both sides agreeing to implement these domestically. See "Eight Point Joint Communiqué," circulated on the website of "The People's Korea" at www.korea-np.co.jp/pk/153th_issue/2000122122.htm.

6. Pyongyang Chamber of Commerce, "Country Report."

7. My emphasis. From ibid.

8. See, for example, "Housing Aid for Guinea," *Pyongyang Times,* July 13, 1996, 6. See also "Agricultural Research Centre in Africa," *Pyongyang Times,* January 18, 1997, 8.

9. My experience of living and working in the country was that most of the time KCNA announcements about domestic events had little or no relationship to what were considered the important issues of the day for North Koreans. The KCNA did not have anywhere near the status of central news agencies or operations in other states—for instance, the BBC in the UK, NHK in Japan, or Xinhua in China. My (completely subjective) impression was that this was where they put out to grass the party hacks who could not fit into real jobs in the fast-changing new socioeconomy of the DPRK.

10. Sigal, *Disarming Strangers.*

11. Ibid.

12. For the best account of the negotiations, see ibid.

13. Oberdorfer, *The Two Koreas*, 372.

14. Quinones, "American NGO Experience," 2; and Oberdorfer, *The Two Koreas*, 386.

15. Oberdorfer, *The Two Koreas*, 397.

16. For content of the talks, see Robert A. Scalapino, "China and Korean Reunification—a Neighbor's Concerns," in *Korea's Future and the Great Powers*, ed. Nicholas Eberstadt and Richard J. Ellings (Seattle: University of Washington Press, 2001), 115–116.

17. Leon V. Sigal, "Mr. Perry's New Course on Korea," in *Solving the North Korean Nuclear Puzzle*, ed. David Albright and Kevin O'Neill (Washington, DC: Institute for Science and International Security, 2000), 200.

18. Ibid., 201.

19. Holly Higgins, "The Foundation Is Shaken," in *Solving the North Korean Nuclear Puzzle*, ed. Albright and O'Neill, 172–174.

20. The MIA deal was initiated in an agreement between the KPA and the U.S. DoD on August 24, 1993. See "The US Blocks the Way to Resolving GI Remains Issue," in *Pyongyang Times*, November 18, 1995, 8. The MIA deal is mentioned in Manning, "North Korean Foreign Policy," 157, and Joel Wit, "Clinton and North Korea: Past, Present and Future," in *Solving the North Korean Nuclear Puzzle*, ed. Albright and O'Neill, 206.

21. "US Lifts Economic Sanctions against DPRK," *Pyongyang Times*, October 2, 1999. In practice the United States delayed implementing the sanctions reductions agreements; thus they did not come into force before Clinton left office, and the Bush administration refused to implement them.

22. The DPRK government certainly believed that President Clinton would visit the DPRK. The ultra-cautious DPRK official media reported that one of the reasons for Madeleine Albright's visit to Pyongyang was to "prepare for Clinton's visit." See "Leader Kim Jong Il Meets US State Secretary," *Korea* 530 (December 2000), *Juche* 89, 3.

23. Those communiqués included an agreement that the United States would not use nuclear weapons against the DPRK. See "North Korean Nukes," posted on January 8, 2003, PBS Newshour Extra website, March 24, 2003, http://www.pbs.org/newshour/extra/features/jan-june03/nkorea.html.

24. For chronology of events, see "Timeline: North Korea Nuclear Crisis," BBC News World Edition, February 24, 2004, http://news.bbc.co.uk/2/hi/asia-pacific/2604437.stm.

25. For the DPRK account of the meeting with James Kelly in Pyongyang, see "J. Kelly Failed to Produce 'Evidence' in Pyongyang; Framed Up Admission Story," *People's Korea*, January 19, 2003, on http://www.korea-np.co.jp/pk/188th_issue/2003013001.htm. For U.S. perspective, see "Peaceful Solutions First," *Korea Now*, November 30, 2002, 7.

26. Relevant excerpts from the DPRK statement on the reopening of the old nuclear reactor at Yongbyon are quoted in "Urgent Diplomacy," *Korea Now* 31, no. 26 (December 28, 2002): 12.

27. "Timeline: North Korea Nuclear Crisis."

28. DPRK diplomat, London, May 2004.

29. For a description of initial Korean-American humanitarian assistance, see Quinones, "American NGO Experience," 3–4.

30. Ibid., 5.

31. For description of PVOC activity in the DPRK, see ibid., 20–31.

32. A detailed discussion of the operational aspects of PVOC activity in the DPRK is in General Accounting Office, *US Bilateral Assistance*.

33. Quinones, "American NGO Experience," 23–25.

34. The PVOC were formed under the aegis of Interaction, a Washington-based coordinating mechanism for NGOs. Interaction's regular special meetings on the DPRK were commonly attended by State Department officials, for two-way reporting. The author attended two of these, the first in 2000 and the second in 2001. State Department officials attended both meetings.

35. Quinones's account of his own early involvement in the aid effort can be found in Quinones, "American NGO Experience."

36. The person involved was Kenneth Quinones, former DPRK desk officer at the State Department. For details, see Allison R. Hayward, "Passing the Torch: What Bob Torricelli Did Wrong," *National Review*, September 30, 2002, reproduced on http://www.nationalreview.com/comment/comment-hayward093002.asp.

37. General Accounting Office, *US Bilateral Assistance*, 44.

38. Former congressman Bill Richardson, later secretary of energy and then governor of New Mexico, visited the DPRK on a number of occasions. See, for instance, "Foreign Delegations' Visit to DPRK," *Pyongyang Times*, December 7, 2003, 5. Donald Gregg also visited the DPRK.

39. For DPRK perspective on U.S. abrogation of the 1994 Agreement, see "DPRK FM Spokesman: US's Logic of Unilateralism Not Workable," *Pyongyang Times*, November 23, 2002, *Juche* 91, 1.

40. A guidebook for foreigners, published in 1989 but still circulated in the DPRK as of 2002, makes explicit use of the phrase. See Foreign Languages Publishing House, *Korea Guidebook* (Pyongyang: Foreign Languages Publishing House, 1989), 157.

41. For discussion of the 1972 and 1991 statements see, respectively, Oberdorfer, *The Two Koreas*, 24–25 and 260–262.

42. Grinker provides an excellent analysis of South Korean perceptions of North Koreans, with one particularly useful chapter on images conveyed through school textbooks. See Grinker, *Korea and Its Futures*. Similar work on North Korean perceptions is being attempted by the Carnegie Council on Ethics and International Affairs. There is more information on the project at http://www.carnegiecouncil.org/page.php/prmID/99 and a midterm report at www.carnegiecouncil.org/media/MidprojBleiker.pdf. The project is about both South and North Korean textbooks.

43. For information on KEDO, see KEDO, *Annual Report 2001*. See also KEDO, *KEDO Fact Sheets 1–9*, New York, November 2001.

44. KEDO was U.S. led in the sense that its first two directors, Stephen Bosworth and Charles Kartman, were American. Its most substantial funding and technical support, however, came from the ROK. See "B. Total Financial Support by Country," KEDO, *Annual Report 2001*, 14.

45. It is difficult to account for all the aid received by the DPRK, especially from NGOs. One attempt at systematic comparison of assistance is "Annex: Donor Assistance to the DPRK 1995–2000," in European Commission, "EC–Democratic People's Republic of Korea." Oknim Chung notes that in 1999 the ROK NGOs gave food and fertilizer assistance worth $358.7 million, compared to a 2000 total of $106.07 million. See Oknim Chung, "South Korean Assistance to the DPRK," unpublished paper (Washington, DC, 2002), 49.

46. An account of the Geneva meeting where North and South Korean governmental representatives met to discuss the UN's Agricultural Recovery and Environmental Protection (AREP) plan is in UNDP, "Report of the First Thematic Round Table Conference for the Democratic People's Republic of Korea," Geneva, May 1998.

47. Chung, "South Korean Assistance to the DPRK," 49.

48. See ibid., 17.

49. Takashi Nada, *Korea in Kim Jong Il's Era* (Pyongyang: Foreign Languages Publishing House, 2000), 101. The Japanese author gives a slavish interpretation of the DPRK's version of domestic and world events, even by the standards of the DPRK's official literature. Nevertheless, this publication would not have been distributed in the DPRK if it did not represent official policy, at least when the book was written in November 1998.

50. KCNA, "Remarks Worthy of Pro-U.S. Lackey," *Pyongyang Times*, October 23, 1999.

51. List of activities from a publication published and disseminated by the DPRK government. See Jon Chol Nam, *A Duel of Reason between Korea and U.S.: Nuke, Missile and Artificial Satellite* (Pyongyang: Foreign Languages Publishing House, 2000), 208–213.

52. In the late 1990s North and South Koreans could increasingly be seen at the same conferences—organized by institutions such as the British Wilton Park and the International Institute of Security Studies—where cautious interchange took place. In 2002 a South Korean diplomat based at the ROK embassy in Washington told me that at a similar conference held in the United States he was surprised to feel that he "could read the mind" of the North Koreans there because of the strong cultural commonality.

53. North Koreans throughout the DPRK were made aware of the visit by the state media.

54. These stamps are available from the tourist hotels in the DPRK and can also be obtained from the DPRK's philatelic services, Korea Stamp Corporation, Pyongyang, DPRK, Telex: 5503UP KP.

55. Observed by the author throughout the country in 2000, 2001, and 2002.

56. Young-ho Park, "Inter-Korean Relations," in *Vantage Point* 26, no. 1, 26.

57. Chung-in Moon, "Sustaining Inter-Korean Reconciliation: North-South Korea Cooperation," *Joint U.S.-Korea Academic Studies* 12 (2002): 235–236.

58. Ibid., 237–238.

59. "North/South Korea: Naval Clash Threatens Dialogue," *Oxford Analytica*, July 1, 2002.

60. Ibid.

61. "North Korea Has Expressed 'Regret' for a Lethal Naval Clash with the South—BBC, 25 July 2002," reproduced from BBC website in UN OCHA DPRK e-mail, July 26, 2002.

62. "Presidents' Resolutions" and "Agenda: New Government Unveils Priorities," in *Korea Now*, January 11, 2003, 5 and 6, respectively.

63. "Inter-Korean Talks: Fifth Reunion Planned," *Korea Now*, December 28, 2002, 14.

64. North Koreans remained cautious in dealings with the South, but this did not prevent steady progress (compared to the previous decades of stalemate). For an illustration of both the conflicts and the cooperation, see the account of both at working-level meetings to discuss practical implementation of agreed-on projects: "Inter-Korean Talks: Fifth Reunion Planned," *Korea Now*, December 28, 2002, 14.

65. On the Japan-ROK normalization agreement of 1965, see Chae-Jin Lee, "Conflict and Cooperation: The Pacific Powers and Korea," in *Korea's Future and the Great Powers,* ed. Eberstadt and Ellings, 56–57. Not all grievances with South Korea were resolved, but after 1965 dialogue began to replace confrontation as a means of resolution of outstanding conflicts. Relations also warmed to the extent that South Korea and Japan were joint hosts of the World Cup soccer tournament in 2002. For review of Japan-ROK conflicts, see Michael H. Armacost and Kenneth B. Pyle, "Japan and the Unification of Korea: Challenges for U.S. Policy Coordination," in *Korea's Future and the Great Powers*, ed. Eberstadt and Ellings, 131–134.

66. This Manichean view remained current as of 2005. It is set out in standard form in "Japan Must Take a Correct Option," *Korea Today* 12, no. 523 (December 1999): 45–46.

67. The twenty-seven rooms of the "Hall for the Period of the Anti-Japanese Revolutionary Struggle display relics and materials which are associated with President Kim Il Sung's revolutionary family, his early revolutionary activity and the brilliant history of the anti-Japanese armed struggle." From Editing Committee of the Album of the Korean Revolution Museum, *The Korean Revolution Museum*, vol. 2 (Tokyo: Miraisha, 1975), 4.

68. The elaborate Revolutionary Martyrs Cemetery on Mount Taesong in Pyongyang is dedicated to more than 100 leaders of the anti-Japanese struggle and is a national monument to which Koreans from all over the DPRK visit to pay their respects. See Foreign Languages Publishing House, *Pyongyang Review* (Pyongyang: Foreign Languages Publishing House, 1995), 71–72.

69. See, for instance, articles titled "Japan Should Dismantle US Military Bases," "A-Bomb Photo Show," and "The Japanese Government Should Apologize and Compensate," *Korea* 516 (October 1999), *Juche* 88, 30–31.

70. Information in this paragraph is from Armacost and Pyle, "Japan and the Unification of Korea," 136–139.

71. For the DPRK view on the "comfort women" issue, see "The Japanese Government Must Apologize for Their Past Crimes of Sexual Slavery and Make State Compensation," *Korea Today* 12, no. 523 (December 1999): 47–48. The "comfort women" came from other Asian countries as well as Korea. For discussion by a Japanese activist leading the campaign for an apology, reparations, and prosecution of perpetrators, see Yayori Matsui, "How to End Impunity for Wartime Sexual Violence? The Meaning of Women's International War Crimes Tribunal 2000 on Japanese Military Sexual Slavery," mimeo, July 2002. A thorough study is in George Hicks, *The Comfort Women: Japan's Brutal Regime of Enforced Prostitution in the Second World War* (New York: Norton, 1997). The DPRK perspective is mentioned in ibid., 232–236.

72. Armacost and Pyle, "Japan and the Unification of Korea," 133.

73. "Appendix III: Deliveries of Food Aid to the DPRK 1995/6," in UN Department of Humanitarian Affairs, "Consolidated UN Inter-Agency Appeal, 1 July 1996–31 March 1997."

74. Toshimasa Yamamoto, "New Developments in Japan on Humanitarian Assistance to DPRK since the Summit of June 2000" (paper presented at the Third International NGO Conference on Humanitarian Assistance to North Korea, mimeo, Seoul,

June 2001). For mention of the 500,000 tonnes of rice donated by Japan in 2001, see Food Aid Liaison Unit, "Annual Report 2001," 2.

75. Yamamoto, "New Developments in Japan."

76. For comment on refusal of the DPRK to issue visas to representatives of Japanese NGOs that were donating assistance, see ibid. My personal experience of working at the WFP during 2000–2001 was that securing visas for donor missions from Japan always required tough negotiations with DPRK authorities. Officials also put up obstacles to WFP HQ staff of Japanese origin visiting the DPRK in a professional capacity.

77. Yoshida, "Supporting Activities of Japanese NGOs," 38–39.

78. UN Office for the Coordination of Humanitarian Affairs (OCHA), "DPR Korea OCHA Situation Bulletin April 2002," reproduced on http://www.reliefweb.int.

79. Hong Nack Kim, "Japan in North Korean Foreign Policy," in *North Korean Foreign Relations in the Post–Cold War Era,* ed. Kim, 126.

80. Shane Green, "North Korean Welcome Wears Out for Hijackers," *Age,* September 10, 2002, on http://www.theage.com.au/articles/2002/09/09/1031115997300.html.

81. Ibid.

82. Cankor #64 at http://www.pcaps.iar.ubc.ca/pubs.htm. The total would be forty-three if the resumption of diplomatic relations with Australia in the year 2000 were included.

83. Ibid.

84. Information from a serving EU member-state government official to author, 2002. (The methodological premise of this book has been not to use anonymous sources that cannot be corroborated through public sources to support substantial claims. This reference is one of the few exceptions because of my inability to access written sources on this issue.)

85. European Commission, "EC–Democratic People's Republic of Korea," 4. Conversations with Swedish and British diplomats, Pyongyang; Washington, DC; and London, 2000–2003.

86. "EU Proposed Anti-DPRK 'Resolution' Assailed," *Korean News,* April 19, 2003, *Juche* 92, reproduced on http://www.kcna.co.jp/index-e.htm.

87. UN Office for the Coordination of Humanitarian Affairs (OCHA), "DPR Korea OCHA Situation Bulletin April 2002," reproduced on http://www.reliefweb.int.

88. The Australian engineering firm was the Snowy Mountains Engineering Corp. See ibid.

89. In 2003 the ECHO representative in Pyongyang informed me that DPRK officials had refused to allow tenders from one long-established Chinese trading firm with the aim of forcing ECHO to purchase from a specific DPRK business. ECHO refused to allow the tendering procedures to be distorted and was prepared to withdraw the aid if the DPRK did not retreat from its position. Author's interview, Pyongyang, February 2003. The previous ECHO representative in Pyongyang summarized his skeptical view of DPRK willingness to change in Maragliano, untitled paper.

90. For the DPRK view on the economic foundations of EU relations, see "Booming DPRK-EU Ties," *Foreign Trade of the Democratic People's Republic of Korea*, April 2002, *Juche* 91, 9.

91. I led a foreign-trade training and exchange project on behalf of the University of Warwick that trained Ministry of Foreign Trade officials in the UK and the DPRK, which started in 1999. I have an archive of written material on this project. See also European Commission, "The EC–Democratic People's Republic of Korea," 21–22.

92. Author interviews, Foreign Office diplomats, London, 2002.

93. Jane Shapiro Zacek, "Russia in North Korean Foreign Policy," in Kim, ed., *North Korean Foreign Relations in the Post–Cold War Era,* 81; Ilpyong J. Kim, "China in North Korean Foreign Policy," 91.

94. Alexander Platkovskiy, "Nuclear Blackmail and North Korea's Search for a Place in the Sun," in Moltz and Mansourov, eds., *North Korean Nuclear Program,* 97.

95. The DPRK press reported the renewal of DPRK-Russian relations "on a fresh basis" in April 1996. See "DPRK FM Spokesman: Russian Govt. Delegation's Visit," *Pyongyang Times,* April 27, 1996. See also "Korea-Russia Friendship House," *Korea* 557 (January 2003), *Juche* 92, 27.

96. Moltz, "Russian–North Korean Relations," 202, 204.

97. Ibid., 203.

98. Ibid., 206.

99. "DPRK-China Treaty on Friendship, Cooperation and Mutual Assistance: 35 Years," *Pyongyang Times,* July 13, 1996, 4.

100. Evgeniy P. Bazhanov and James Clay Moltz, "China and the Korean Peninsula," in Moltz and Mansourov, eds., *North Korean Nuclear Program,* 177.

101. For details on the outcome of Kim Jong Il's visit to Moscow in August 2001, see "Russia, N. Korea Leaders Sign Pact," *NKChosun.com,* http://nk.chosun.com/english/news/news.html?ACT=detail&key=1&res_id=4805. For details of China visits in 2000 and 2001, see Zhu Jianrong, "Traditional Beijing-Pyongyang Ties Revived," http://www.korea-np.co.jp/pk/174th_issue/2002013103.htm.

102. Conspicuously juxtaposed in the same edition of the state-run publication that celebrated Madeleine Albright's visit to the DPRK was an article on a visit to the DPRK of a "Chinese high-ranking military delegation." See "Korea-China Friendship Will Be Constantly Cemented," *Korea* 530 (December 2000), *Juche* 89, 4–5.

103. Vasily Mikheev, "Russian Policy towards North Korea," CSIS PacNet Newsletter 38, September 2, 2000, on http://www.csis.org/pacfor/pac0038.html.

104. The DPRK official press reported that China promised to deliver 20,000 tonnes of food in June 1996 and in October 1996 reported that China had delivered 100,000 tonnes of food aid in 1996. See respectively, "International Food Aid to DPRK," *Pyongyang Times,* June 1, 1996, and "China's Total Food Aid Arrives," *Pyongyang Times,* October 5, 1996, 6.

105. Smith, "North Koreans in China."

7. International Security and Humanitarian Assistance

1. Sigal, *Disarming Strangers.*

2. William T. Harrison, "Military Armistice in Korea: A Case Study for Strategic Leaders" (strategy research report written for the U.S. Army War College, Pennsylvania, mimeo, 2002), available on http://www.urbanoperations.com/harrison.pdf.

3. The excellent website of the USS Pueblo Veterans Association provides a comprehensive account with links to other sites and materials. See http://usspueblo.org/v2f/incident/incidentframe.html.

4. Quinones, "American NGO Experience," 3–4.

5. The four-party talks are evaluated in Scalapino, "China and Korean Reunification," 115–116. See also David Albright and Holly Higgins, "The Agreed Framework: Status Report," in *Solving the North Korean Nuclear Puzzle,* ed. Albright and O'Neill, 46.

6. Perry recommended continued diplomacy in conjunction with U.S. allies and other interested powers, particularly China. For discussion, see Morton Abramowitz and James T. Laney, *U.S. Policy toward North Korea: A Second Look* (Washington, DC: Council on Foreign Relations, 1999), 7–9, reproduced on http://www.cfr.org/publication.php?id=3205.

7. "New US DPRK Policy Coordinator Appointed," NAPSNet Daily Report, September 27, 2000, http://www.nautilus.org/napsnet/dr/0009/SEP27.html#item7.

8. Abramowitz and Laney, *U.S. Policy toward North Korea,* 7.

9. On U.S.-DPRK negotiations on the suspected nuclear site, see Higgins, "The Foundation Is Shaken," 172–174. See also Abramowitz and Laney, *U.S. Policy toward North Korea,* 6.

10. Morton Abramowitz, James T. Laney, and Robert A. Manning, *Testing North Korea: The Next Stage in U.S. and ROK Policy* (Washington, DC: Council on Foreign Relations, 2001), 16, reproduced on http://www.cfr.org/pdf/Korea_TaskForce2.pdf.

11. Ibid., 17. Madeleine Albright confirms that timing was an issue. See "Former Secretary of State Speaks Out on Korean Experience," *Chosun Ilbo*, March 11, 2001, http://srch.chosun.com/cgi-bin/english/search?did=34429&OP=5&word=BUSH%20 KIM%20DAE%20JUNG%20WASHINGTON%20&name=english/National&dtc=20 010311&url=http://english.chosun.com/w21data/html/news/200103/200103110164.h tml&title=Former%20Secretary%20of%20State%20S.

12. Ambassador Robert L. Gallucci, former lead official in the nuclear negotiations with the DPRK, became dean of the School of Foreign Service at Georgetown University. Robert Einhorn, former assistant secretary for nonproliferation at the Department of State, became senior adviser at the Center for Strategic and International Studies (CSIS). Joel Wit, former coordinator for the 1994 U.S.–North Korea Agreed Framework, became a senior fellow at CSIS.

13. The policy of encouraging negotiation was made explicit in the influential 1999 Council on Foreign Relations task force report that recommended that "the United States, Japan and South Korea should continue to engage Pyongyang on all fronts while taking steps to deter a second ballistic missile launch." See Leslie Gelb, "Foreword," in Abramowitz and Laney, *U.S. Policy toward North Korea,* 2, report reproduced on http:// www.cfr.org/publication.php?id=3205.

14. Mark Manyin and Ryun Jun, "U.S. Assistance to North Korea" (report for Congress received through CRS Web, mimeo, Washington, DC, March 17, 2003), 7–9.

15. The numbers vary. A Congressional Research survey shows total U.S. aid to KEDO between 1995 and 2003 at $406 million. See "Table 1. U.S. Assistance to North Korea, 1995–2003," in ibid., 1. KEDO's own figures report larger sums, probably including large indirect costs. KEDO reports that between March 1995 and December 2001, the United States funded KEDO to the tune of $3 billion, compared to $6 billion from the ROK. See "Total Financial Support by Country," KEDO, *Korean Peninsula Energy Development Organization, Annual Report 2001* (New York: KEDO, 2001), 14. Irrespective of the differences between the various figures, the relative proportions of U.S./ROK aid remain about the same.

16. On oil deliveries, see Albright and Higgins, "The Agreed Framework," 31.

17. For both speculation and denial by the State Department official responsible for U.S. policy on the 1994 Agreed Framework, see Wit, "Clinton and North Korea," 206–207.

18. The dominant view was expressed in a 1999 Council on Foreign Relations report that stated, "Pyongyang has established a pattern in which it agrees to dialogue in order to receive food aid but then scuttles the dialogue with provocations before it is forced to make any significant concessions of its own." See Abramowitz and Laney, *U.S. Policy toward North Korea*.

19. "Instead of the collapse or reform of North Korea, the Perry policy seeks a complete end to its nuclear and missile programs." See Sigal, "Mr. Perry's New Course," 199.

20. Michael Green, *Managing Change on the Korean Peninsula* (Washington, DC: Council on Foreign Relations, 1998), reproduced on http://www.cfr.org/publication .php?id=119; and Abramowitz and Laney, *U.S. Policy toward North Korea*.

21. Green, *Managing Change*.

22. For residency dates, see Quinones, "American NGO Experience," 21. For information on salaries, see ibid., 26.

23. Republican congressman Benjamin Gilman, chair of the House International Relations Committee, was representative of this approach, commenting in 1998 that the United States was "paying for bad behavior by rewarding North Korean brinkmanship." Quote from Higgins, "The Foundation Is Shaken," 169.

24. Nicholas Eberstadt of the American Enterprise Institute expounds the appeasement perspective in Eberstadt, *The End of North Korea* (Washington, DC: American Enterprise Institute Press, 1999), 22–24.

25. The Korea Foundation, for instance, financially supported Eberstadt, *The End of North Korea*. See ibid.

26. Committee on International Relations, News Advisory, "What's Next for North Korea and U.S.?" July 25, 2001, reproduced on http://wwwc.house.gov/international_ relations/107/na072501.htm.

27. Bob Woodward, *Bush at War* (New York: Simon and Schuster, 2002), 339–340.

28. Abramowitz et al., *North Korean Nuclear Challenge*, 15.

29. On the divisions within the U.S. administration, although without naming names, see ibid., 24.

30. "KEDO Executive Board Meeting Concludes—November 14, 2002," http://www.kedo.org/news_detail.asp?NewsID=10.

31. See, for example, "U.S., North Korea Conclude POW/MIA Talks in Bangkok," press release, Embassy of the United States of America, Bangkok, October 7, 2002, http://www.usa.or.th/news/press/2002/nrot102.htm.

32. I have discussed this approach to diplomacy in Hazel Smith, "Korea: Gobbledygook," *World Today* 59, no. 2 (February 2003): 15–16.

33. For the timelines of meeting and announcement, see Abramowitz et al., *North Korean Nuclear Challenge*, 13.

34. "Diplomacy on N.K. Nukes," *Korea Now* 32, no. 9 (May 3, 2003).

35. Ralph Cossa, "Do All Parties Agree on CVID?" *Japan Times Online*, May 10, 2004, reproduced on http://www.japantimes.co.jp/cgi-bin/geted.pl5?eo20040510rc.htm.

36. David E. Sanger, "About-Face on North Korea: Allies Helped," *New York Times*, June 24, 2004, A13.

37. Joseph Kahn, "North Korea Is Studying Softer Stance from the U.S.," *New York Times*, June 24, 2004, A13.

38. Ibid.

39. "North Korea: Humanitarian and Human Rights Concerns, Hearing before the Sub-committee on East Asia and the Pacific," May 2, 2002, reproduced on http://wwwa.house.gov-international_relations-107-79392.pdf.

40. See, for instance, Powell, "Testimony to the Sub-committee."

41. Research that identifies and analyzes the various groups operating to support North Korean migrants and/or refugees, and their funders and backers, does not exist. I refer to this motley group in Smith, "North Koreans in China." In congressional testimony, one of these organizations, "Helping Hands Korea," stated that it was not a registered charity in South Korea, where it was based. Its chairman, Timothy Peters, informed the committee that it had arranged for a ten-year-old North Korean boy to make the arduous journey from China into Mongolia, during which the boy died. The chairman expressed no sense of shame for the child's death, instead calling on Congress to fund more of these types of adventures. See "North Korea: Humanitarian and Human Rights Concerns, Hearing before the Sub-committee on East Asia and the Pacific," May 2, 2002, reproduced on http://wwwa.house.gov-international_relations-107-79392 .pdf. Peters's web sites for his "Ton a Month" organizations can be found on http://ton-a-month.tripod.com/ and for his "Helping Hands Korea" project on http://www .familycare.org/network/p01.htm. There is no indication as to who funds Peters and his family (members of which also work for these organizations) and how much of the money raised through donations go to Peters's expenses, to buy the small amount of food aid donated, and to fund people-smuggling of North Koreans to Mongolia.

42. A favorite of congressional committees was Norbert Vollertsen, who worked for a German NGO in the DPRK from 1999 to 2000. In numerous interviews he claims to have been expelled from the DPRK, to have had unique access to the countryside, to have been given a driving license because he unselfishly donated some of his skin for a burn victim, and to have visited hospitals in which no food was available. The truth is a little more prosaic. Vollertsen was not expelled, but his home organization did not renew his contract, and he left the DPRK when his contract, and therefore his visa, expired in December 2000. Vollertsen visited a limited number of hospitals in a small number of counties, as these were where the Cap Anamur projects were based, always with a North Korean interpreter. UNICEF, IFRC, and WFP officials, in contrast, have visited hundreds of hospitals, clinics, and other medical institutions nationwide on a regular basis since 1995. Like all humanitarian workers, Vollertsen could take the DPRK driving test and drive independently in Pyongyang and as far down the coast as Nampo (I also took the driving test, obtained a DPRK driver's license, and drove independently in the city and nearby areas) but would not be permitted to drive outside these areas. Vollertsen never drove outside Pyongyang without an interpreter. The burn story is told in reverse. A factory worker suffered severe burns, and hundreds of his colleagues donated a square quarter-inch of their skin. Vollertsen, visiting the hospital at the time, was so impressed with the gesture of the factory workers that he offered to do the same. DPRK hospitals do not generally provide food; as in many poor countries, families provide food and nursing care. The WFP provided food for hospitals for a short time, but its monitoring showed that food allocated to hospitals was being allocated to families of patients. As they could not guarantee it would not be shared, the WFP ceased allocating food to hospitals in 2000. For interviews that repeat these untruths, see "View from the Axis," March 9, 2002, http://www.worldmag.com/world/issue/03-09-02/cover_1.asp. It's not clear how much Vollertsen believes his own revamping of history. See "Interview with Norbert Vollertsen," in *Chosun Journal*, where he insists he was "expelled" from the DPRK, on http://www.chosunjournal.com/vollertseninterview.html. My data comes from intensive interviews with all Cap Anamur staff, including Vollertsen, who left the DPRK while I was still working and living there (in the same apartment block as he).

43. Sanger, "About-Face on North Korea."

44. See chapter 4 for discussion.

45. http://www.nautilus.org/.

46. James Cotton, "The Rajin-Sonbong Free Trade Zone Experiment: North Korea in Pursuit of New International Linkages," in *North Korean Foreign Relations in the Post–Cold War Era*, ed. Kim, 229. See also Eberstadt, "North Korea's Unification Policy," 251.

47. Sigal, "Mr. Perry's New Course," 205.

48. President Kim Young Sam had tried to implement a "one-channel" policy for South Korean NGO aid to the DPRK via the Korean Red Cross. It was never wholly successful and was abandoned by President Kim Dae Jung when he came to power in 1998 in favor of a "multichannel" policy. See Chung, "South Korean Assistance."

49. South Korean businesses and the projects in which they were engaged from 1992 to 2001 are listed in "Companies Approved for South-North Korean Economic Cooperation," Korea Trade Investment Promotion Agency, reproduced on http://crm.kotra.or.kr/main/info/nk/eng/sntrade/cooperative.php3.

50. All material in this paragraph taken from "Address by President Kim Dae-jung of the Republic of Korea at the Free University of Berlin March 9, 2000," reproduced on http://russia.shaps.hawaii.edu/fp/korea/berlin_declaration.html.

51. Ibid.

52. "Koreas Agree on Rice, Rail Links," *Korea Now* 32, no. 11 (May 31, 2003): 10.

53. Keith Feigenbaum, "Korea United: North & South Set Aside Differences to Demine," report published on website of James Madison University, http://maic.jmu.edu/journal/5.1/Focus/Keith_F/keith.html.

54. "The Nobel Peace Prize 2000," http://www.nobel.se/peace/laureates/2000/.

55. Se-Hyun Jeong, *Sunshine Policy for Peace and Cooperation* (Seoul: Ministry of Unification, May 2002), 25.

56. Ibid.

57. The text of President Roh's post-election victory press conference is reproduced as "New Chapter Begins to Unify 70 Million People," *Korea Now*, December 28, 2002.

58. Front page, *Chosun Ilbo*, April 28, 2003, http://srch.chosun.com/cgi-bin/english/search?did=58787&OP=5&word=INTER%20MINISTERIAL%20MEET INGS%20&name=english/Today%20in%20PHotos&dtc=20030427&url=http:// english.chosun.com/w21data/html/news/200304/200304270018.html&title=Front%2 0Page%20-%20April%2028%.

59. "ROK Rejects U.S. Call to Send Combat Troops to Afghanistan," *Korea Economic Report* 17, no. 6 (June 2002): 10.

60. "Ex-Foreign Minister Han Named New Envoy to U.S.," *Korea Now,* online edition, April 5, 2003, http://kn.koreaherald.co.kr/SITE/data/html_dir/2003/04/05/ 200304050003.asp.

61. *Chosun Ilbo,* May 18, 2003, on http://srch.chosun.com/cgi-bin/english/ search?did=59338&OP=5&word=BUSH%20KIM%20DAE%20JUNG%20 WASHINGTON%20&name=english/Columns&dtc=20030518&url=http://english .chosun.com/w21data/html/news/200305/200305180003.html&title=.

62. "Kim Fails to Get Full Support from Bush," *Chosun Ilbo*, March 8, 2001, http:// srch.chosun.com/cgi-bin/english/search?did=34346&OP=5&word=BUSH%20KIM% 20DAE%20JUNG%20WASHINGTON%20&name=english/National&dtc=200103 08&url=http://english.chosun.com/w21data/html/news/200103/200103080187.html &title=%3Cfont%20color%3Dblue%3E%3Cb%3E%3C.

63. Min-cheol Kim, "Threat Mars North-South Meeting," *Chosun Ilbo*, May 21, 2003, http://srch.chosun.com/cgi-bin/english/search?did=59433&OP=5&word= INTER%20KOREAN%20TALKS%20&name=english/National&dtc=20030521&ur

l=http://english.chosun.com/w21data/html/news/200305/200305210011.html&title= Threat%20Mars%20North-South%20Meeting; and Min-chul Kim, "Pyongyang Repeats 'Disaster' Threat," *Chosun Ilbo*, May 26, 2003, http://srch.chosun.com/cgi-bin/english/ search?did=59547&OP=5&word=INTER%20KOREAN%20TALKS%20&name= english/National&dtc=20030526&url=http://english.chosun.com/w21data/html/news/ 200305/200305260008.html&title=Pyongyang%20Repeats%20%27Disaster%27% 20Threat.

64. Armacost and Pyle, "Japan and the Unification of Korea," 128–129.

65. For discussion written prior to DPRK admission of kidnapping Japanese citizens, see Yamamoto, "New Developments in Japan."

66. Kim, "Japan in North Korean Foreign Policy," 118.

67. Armacost and Pyle, "Japan and the Unification of Korea," 138–139.

68. Hicks, *The Comfort Women*, 235.

69. Kim, "Japan in North Korean Foreign Policy," 119–122.

70. Ibid., 122–125.

71. Quoted in Armacost and Pyle, "Japan and the Unification of Korea," 129.

72. Ibid., 137–139.

73. On the resumption of the normalization talks in April 2000, see "Tokyo-Pyongyang Talks Yield Little, Rescheduled," *Japan Times Online*, April 8, 2000, http:// www.japantimes.co.jp/cgi-bin/getarticle.pl5?nn20000408a2.htm. For the three-point agreement concluded at the end of Prime Minister Murayama's visit to the DPRK, see "Joint Press Statement of WPK [Workers' Party of Korea] and Japanese Delegation," December 3, 1999, http://www.korea-np.co.jp/pk/122nd_issue/99120402.htm.

74. Kim Dae Jung briefed Japanese prime minister Yoshiro Mori in Tokyo a week before his groundbreaking summit meeting with Kim Jong Il in Pyongyang and was asked by the Japanese leader to convey to the North Korean leader Japan's commitment to the normalization process. See "Mori, Kim Vow Efforts to Engage Pyongyang," *Japan Times Online*, June 9, 2000, http://www.japantimes.co.jp/cgi-bin/getarticle.pl5? nn20000609a2.htm.

75. Haruki Wada, "Recovering a Lost Opportunity: Japan–North Korea Negotiations in the Wake of the Iraqi War," May 3, 2003, reproduced on ZNet, http://www .zmag.org/content/showarticle.cfm?SectionID=44&ItemID=3569, 2.

76. Ibid.

77. Ibid.

78. For text of the declaration, see "News. Japan-DPRK Pyongyang Declaration [Govt of Japan]," circulated on UNOCHA e-mail, September 18, 2002.

79. For a list of the abductees, along with the details known about their fate, see Gavan McCormack, "North Korea in the Vice," *New Left Review* 18 (November–December 2002): 4, reproduced on http://www.newleftreview.net/NLR25201.shtml.

80. Ibid., 3.

81. Ibid., 2.

82. Gavan McCormack, "North Korea: Coming in from the Cold?" December 14, 2002, 4, ZNet, http://www.zmag.org/content/showarticle.cfm?SectionID=44&ItemID=2749.

83. A thorough discussion of the pressures placed upon the abductees by various political groups is in ibid.

84. Explicit calls for the overthrow of Kim Jong Il were made by Katsumi Sato, the chair of the National Association for the Rescue of Japanese Kidnapped by North Korea (NAR). See Wada, "Recovering a Lost Opportunity," 6–7. For criticism of the use of peaceful means to achieve a resolution of the abductees issue, see "Returnees, Kin Welcome G-8 Stand on Abductions," *Asahi Shimbun,* English edition, June 5, 2003, 20.

85. On Kim Dae Jung's abduction, see McCormack, "Coming in from the Cold?" 2.

86. Ibid., 6.

87. "Taro Aso Should Apologize to Koreans / North Korea's Intentional Provocation," *Korea Times,* June 2, 2003, http://times.hankooki.com/lpage/opinion/200306/kt2003060215325811300.htm.

88. "Table 26: International Comparisons of Defence Expenditure and Military Manpower 1985, 2000 and 2001," in IISS, *Military Balance 2002–2003,* 332–337.

89. "Roh Urges Japan to Face Up to War-Time History," *Japan Today,* June 9, 2003, http://www.japantoday.com/e/?content=news&cat=9&id=262475&page=2.

90. On October 14, 2002, Prime Minister Koizumi announced that the DPRK was "a disgraceful state that abducts and kills people." See McCormack, "Coming in from the Cold?" 6.

91. Kim, "Japan in North Korean Foreign Policy," 125.

92. On the Japanese government rationale for humanitarian assistance, see Yamamoto, "New Developments in Japan"; on the talks of the early 1990s, see Armacost and Pyle, "Japan and the Unification of Korea," 138.

93. I was told on a number of occasions by senior Japanese officials from the Washington and London embassies in 2002 that the DPRK had given Japan "nothing" in return for massive food aid.

94. On remittances, see Kim, "Japan in North Korean Foreign Policy," 126.

95. Mary Jordan and Kevin Sullivan, "Pinball Wizards Fuel North Korea," *Washington Post Foreign Service*, June 7, 1996, reproduced on http://kimsoft.com/korea/jp-nk1.htm. See also "General Association of Korean Residents in Japan (Chosen Soren)," *FAS Intelligence Resource Program*, December 22, 1997, http://www.fas.org/irp/world/dprk/chosen_soren/. On the DPRK's alleged links to the *yakuzas*, see "Yakuza Cash Is Funding Pyongyang's WMD: U.S.," *Japan Times Online*, June 6, 2003, http://www.japantimes.co.jp/cgi-bin/getarticle.pl5?nn20030606a1.htm.

96. Kim, "Japan in North Korean Foreign Policy," 132.

97. European Commission, "EC–Democratic People's Republic of Korea," 7.

98. For review of EU approaches to the transition from Communism to liberal democracy in Eastern Europe and Russia, see Hazel Smith, *European Union Foreign Policy: What It Is and What It Does* (London: Pluto, 2002), 224–266.

99. European Commission, "EC–Democratic People's Republic of Korea," 18.

100. I was present at the press conference of the troika at the Koryo Hotel in Pyongyang after their meeting with Kim Jong Il. Chris Patten, the external relations commissioner, made a short intervention but nevertheless reiterated the Union's commitments to engaging the DPRK on human rights, among other things. This was a remarkable intervention in the context of Pyongyang politics and indicated to DPRK officials and humanitarian workers present at the meeting that the EU intended to take human rights seriously. See also European Commission, "EC–Democratic People's Republic of Korea," 4.

101. European Commission, "EC–Democratic People's Republic of Korea." The contributions to KEDO were relatively small—some 15 million euro annually and a one-time donation of 75 million euro—compared to the estimated total cost of the program of $4.6 billion. The contribution was more significant for its demonstration of political support for KEDO.

102. "UN Commission on Human Rights Passes Resolutions on North Korea and Turkmenistan for the First Time," *Human Rights Watch Monthly Update*, April 2003, http://www.hrw.org/update/2003/04.html#5.

103. "19 November 2002: Korean Peninsula—Council Conclusions," reproduced on http://europa.eu.int/comm/external_relations/north_korea/intro/gac.htm#nk140403.

104. See, for example, General Affairs and External Relations Council, "14 April 2003: North Korea," reproduced on http://europa.eu.int/comm/external_relations/north_korea/intro/nk140403.

105. European Commission, "EC–Democratic People's Republic of Korea," 14.

106. Maragliano, untitled paper, 6.

107. European Commission, "EC–Democratic People's Republic of Korea," 5.

108. Reference to the Stockholm training is in European Commission, "EC–Democratic People's Republic of Korea," 9. Information on the human rights training from Jim Hoare, UK chargé d'affaires to the DPRK, March 2003.

109. Maragliano, untitled paper, 6–7.

110. For review and discussion, see Smith, *Overcoming Humanitarian Dilemmas.*

111. On the humanitarian principles, see ibid., 7. See also chapter 4 of this book.

112. European Commission, "EC–Democratic People's Republic of Korea," 17.

113. Ibid., 21.

114. Ibid. The italics and emphasis are mine.

115. Joachim Ahrens, "Humanitarian Aid in North Korea," Swiss Agency for Development and Cooperation, February 13, 2003, posted on Reliefweb, http://www .reliefweb.int/w/rwb.nsf/0/ca57b6a0cfc9757bc1256cd1003f4df7?OpenDocument.

116. Jing-Dong Yuan, "China and the North Korean Nuclear Crisis," CNS Monterey Institute of International Studies, January 2003, http://cns.miis.edu/research/ korea/chidprk.htm.

117. World Food Program, "DPR Korea Update no. 52," Pyongyang, May 2003.

118. "China through a Lens," on http://www.china.org.cn/english/2003/Jul/69917.htm.

119. For discussion of points raised in this paragraph, see Smith, "North Koreans in China." See also Human Rights Watch, *The Invisible Exodus: North Koreans in the People's Republic of China* (New York: Human Rights Watch, 2002), reproduced on http:// www.hrw.org/reports/2002/northkorea/#P164_32652.

120. Lara V. Zabrovskaya, "The Korean Peninsula and the Security of Russia's Primorskiy Kray (Maritime Province)," in *The North Korean Nuclear Program,* ed. Moltz and Mansourov, 192–193.

121. James Clay Moltz, "Russian Policy on the North Korean Nuclear Crisis," CNS Monterey Institute of International Studies, May 2003, http://cns.miis.edu/research/ korea/ruspol.htm.

122. "Swiss Envisages Role in Nuclear Dispute," *Korea Now* 32, no. 11 (May 31, 2003): 11.

8. Intelligent Intervention for a Stable Peace

1. Smith, "La Corée du Nord."

2. It would take a separate exegesis to evaluate the relationship between the Western media and the DPRK. After having read, listened to, and watched accounts and been myself interviewed by print, radio, and TV journalists from all over the world for over a decade on the DPRK, it's always fascinating to me to see how individual journalists have tackled reporting on the DPRK. Over the decade I have read dozens of "I was the first journalist to do this, that, or the other" accounts, usually about visiting Panmunjom, the border area, and talking to whichever general is on duty. Hundreds of accounts have generalized about the history, politics, and society of the country on the basis of a five-day visit to the Koryo Hotel (the main hotel in Pyongyang). And one particularly well-known U.S. TV journalist seemed highly exercised about DPRK iniquities more because he was not permitted a personal interview with Kim Jong Il than because of much else. It's also interesting to watch the recycling of fantasy as news in even the "quality" press. A favorite one used to be that Kim Il Sung drank pints of virgins' blood to keep him healthy. This died with the late president, but I was amused to see the story reemerging in the *Asian Wall Street Journal,* this time applied to Kim Jong Il. This story was referred to in the U.S. talk show hosted by David Letterman: see http://www.newsmax.com/showliners.shtml?a=2003/1/23/31026. There are, of course, also wonderful and professional journalists doing their best in a difficult area to cover—including Libby Rosenthal of the *New York Times,* scholar and journalist Selig Harrison, Jon Watts at the *Guardian* (UK), and many others.

3. "News. 16 October. North Korea Said to Begin Scaling Down Armed Forces (Korea Herald)," circulated on UNOCHA e-mail, October 18, 2002.

4. For discussion, see Smith, *European Union Foreign Policy,* 42–43.

Bibliography

Books and Articles

Abramowitz, Morton, and James T. Laney. *U.S. Policy toward North Korea: A Second Look*. Washington, DC: Council on Foreign Relations, 1999. Reproduced on http://www.cfr.org/publication.php?id=3205.

Abramowitz, Morton, James T. Laney, and Eric Heginbotham. *Meeting the North Korean Nuclear Challenge*. Washington, DC: Council on Foreign Relations, 2003. Reproduced on http://www.cfr.org/publication.php?id=5973.

Abramowitz, Morton, James T. Laney, and Robert A. Manning. *Testing North Korea: The Next Stage in U.S. and ROK Policy*. Washington, DC: Council on Foreign Relations, 2001. Reproduced on http://www.cfr.org/pdf/Korea_TaskForce2.pdf.

Action contre la Faim. "Action against Hunger's Withdrawal from North Korea, Press Dossier." Mimeo, London, March 2000.

———. "Nutritional Programme: North Hamgyong Province DPR of Korea, November 1999." Mimeo.

Albright, David, and Holly Higgins. "The Agreed Framework: Status Report." In *Solving the North Korean Nuclear Puzzle*, edited by David Albright and Kevin O'Neill. Washington, DC: Institute for Science and International Security, 2000.

Allison, Graham T. *Essence of Decision: Explaining the Cuban Missile Crisis*. Boston: Little, Brown, 1971.

Almeida, Pedro, and Michael O'Hanlon. "Impasse in Korea: A Conventional Arms-Accord Solution?" *Survival* 41, no. 1 (Spring 1999).

Amayun, Milton, Christopher Arthen, and Barney Smith. "Trip Report: PVO Consortium Short-Term Monitoring Visit to the Democratic People's Republic of Korea 18 April– 2 May 1998." Mimeo, May 1998.

Amnesty International. "Report 2001 on the DPRK." Reprinted in *Republic of Korea Newsletter*, Circular no. 77, Amnesty International United Kingdom, November 2001.

Armacost, Michael H., and Kenneth B. Pyle. "Japan and the Unification of Korea: Challenges for U.S. Policy Coordination." In *Korea's Future and the Great Powers*, edited by Nicholas Eberstadt and Richard J. Ellings. Seattle: University of Washington Press, 2001.

Armstrong, Charles K. "The Nature, Origins, and Development of the North Korean State." In *The North Korean System in the Post–Cold War Era*, edited by Samuel Kim. New York: Palgrave, 2001.

Bank of Chosen. *Economic History of Chosen*. Seoul: Bank of Chosen, 1920.

Baylis, John, and Steve Smith, eds. *The Globalization of World Politics: An Introduction to International Relations*. 2nd ed. Oxford: Oxford University Press, 2001.

Bazhanov, Evgeniy P., and James Clay Moltz. "China and the Korean Peninsula." In *The North Korean Nuclear Program: Security, Strategy, and New Perspectives from Russia*, edited by James Clay Moltz and Alexander Y. Mansourov. New York: Routledge, 2000.

Bazhanova, Natalya. "Economic Forces and the Stability of the North Korean Regime." In *The North Korean Nuclear Program: Security, Strategy and New Perspectives from Russia*, edited by James Clay Moltz and Alexandre Y. Mansourov. New York: Routledge, 2000.

Beal, Tim. *The Waters of Prosperity Will Fill the Han and Taedong Rivers: Economic Recovery and Business Prospects for the DPRK after the Summit*. Undated and reproduced on http://www.vuw.ac.nz/~caplabtb/dprk/waters%20of%20prosperity.htm.

Bourgeois, Marie-France. "Nutrition in the DPRK—a Field View." Reproduced on http://www.ennonline.net/fex/05/fa21.html.

Brun, Ellen, and Jacques Hersh. *Socialist Korea: A Case Study in the Strategy of Economic Development*. New York: Monthly Review Press, 1976.

Buckley, Richard, ed. *North and South Korea: The Last Ideological Frontier*. Cheltenham: Understanding Global Issues, 1998.

Bureau of Democracy, Human Rights and Labor. "U.S. Department of State: Democratic People's Republic of Korea Country Report on Human Rights Practices for 1998." Mimeo, February 26, 1999. Reproduced on http://www.reliefweb.int.

Cadogan, Marian. *Distribution and Use of Inputs for the 1998 Double Crop Programme, DPRK*. Ireland: Caritas-Hong Kong/Trócaire, July 1998.

Caritas. "Trip Report." Mimeo, May 14–21, 2002.

Center for Contemporary International Problems. "The DPRK Report no. 8 July–August 1997." Moscow. Reproduced as "North East Asia Peace and Security Network Special Report." Mimeo but copied from NAPSNet website, September 30, 1997.

Central Bureau of Statistics, DPRK. "Report on the DPRK Nutrition Assessment, 2002." Mimeo, Pyongyang, November 20, 2002, *Juche* 91.

———. "DPRK 2004 Nutrition Assessment." Mimeo, Pyongyang, 2005.

Chen, Ching-chih. "Police and Community Control Systems in the Empire." In *The Japanese Colonial Empire, 1895–1945*, edited by Ramon H. Myers and Mark R. Peattie. Princeton, NJ: Princeton University Press, 1984.

Christen, Roberto, and Gamal M. Ahmed. "Agriculture in DPRK." Mimeo, Pyongyang, undated but 2002.

Christian Friends of Korea. "Activity Report." Mimeo, July 2002.

Chung, Joseph Sang-hoon. *The North Korean Economy: Structure and Development.* Stanford: Hoover Institution Press, 1974.

Chung Oknim. "South Korean Assistance to the DPRK." Unpublished paper, Washington, DC, 2002.

Collins, Paul, and Frederick Nixson. "The Changing Global Economic Environment and the Centrally Planned Economy: The Case of the Democratic People's Republic of Korea." Paper presented at conference on "Management Development of Centrally-Planned Economies in a New Global Environment 1–3 April 1992." UNDP/ODI, London. Mimeo, undated but 1992.

Cossa, Ralph. "Do All Parties Agree on CVID?" *Japan Times Online*, May 10, 2004. Reproduced on http://www.japantimes.co.jp/cgi-bin/geted.pl5?eo20040510rc.htm.

Cotton, James. "The Rajin-Sonbong Free Trade Zone Experiment: North Korea in Pursuit of New International Linkages." In *North Korean Foreign Relations in the Post–Cold War Era,* edited by Samuel Kim. Oxford: Oxford University Press, 1998.

Cumings, Bruce. *Korea's Place in the Sun: A Modern History.* New York: Norton, 1997.

———. *The Origins of the Korean War.* Vol. 1, *Liberation and the Emergence of Separate Regimes, 1945–1947.* Princeton, NJ: Princeton University Press, 1981.

———. *The Origins of the Korean War.* Vol. 2, *The Roaring of the Cataract, 1947–1950.* Princeton, NJ: Princeton University Press, 1990.

Dammers, Chris, et al. "Review of the Red Cross Health and Care Programme, Democratic Peoples' [*sic*] Republic of Korea." Mimeo, October 2001.

Democratic People's Republic of Korea Government. "Second Periodic Report of the Democratic People's Republic of Korea on Its Implementation of the International

Covenant on Civil and Political Rights 25 December 1999." Reproduced in United Nations International Covenant on Civil and Political Rights, Human Rights Committee, CCPR/C/PRK/2000/2. Mimeo, May 4, 2000.

Dujarric, Robert. *Korean Unification and After.* Indianapolis: Hudson Institute, 2000.

Eberstadt, Nicholas. *The End of North Korea.* Washington, DC: American Enterprise Institute Press, 1999.

———. "Hastening Korean Reunification." *Foreign Affairs* 76, no. 2 (1997).

———. "North Korea's Unification Policy: 1948–1996." In *North Korean Foreign Relations in the Post–Cold War Era*, edited by Samuel S. Kim. Oxford: Oxford University Press, 1998.

Eckert, Carter J., Ki-baik Lee, Young Ick Lew, Michael Robinson, and Edward W. Wagner. *Korea Old and New: A History.* Cambridge, MA: Harvard University Press, 1990.

Economist Intelligence Unit. "The Koreas." *Business Asia,* March 11, 2002.

Editing Committee of the Album of the Korean Revolution Museum. *The Korean Revolution Museum.* Vol. 2. Tokyo: Miraisha, 1975.

European Commission. "The EC–Democratic People's Republic of Korea (DPRK) Country Strategy Paper 2001–2004." Reproduced on http://europa.eu.int/comm/external_relations/north_korea/csp/01_04_en.pdf.

European Union, United Nations Children's Fund, and World Food Program, in partnership with the government of the Democratic People's Republic of Korea. "Nutrition Survey." Mimeo, Pyongyang, November 1998.

Feigenbaum, Keith. "Korea United: North & South Set Aside Differences to Demine." Report published on website of James Madison University. http://maic.jmu.edu/journal/5.1/Focus/Keith_F/keith.html.

Food Aid Liaison Unit. "Activity Report to FALU Steering Committee." Mimeo, Pyongyang, April 1999.

———. "Annual Report 2001." Mimeo, Pyongyang, undated but 2002.

Foreign Languages Publishing House. *Korea Guidebook.* Pyongyang: Foreign Languages Publishing House, 1989.

———. *Pyongyang Review.* Pyongyang: Foreign Languages Publishing House, 1995.

———. *Socialist Constitution of the DPRK.* Pyongyang: Foreign Languages Publishing House, 1998.

Foster-Carter, Aidan. "North Korea: All Roads Lead to Collapse—All the More Reason to Engage Pyongyang." In *Economic Integration of the Korean Peninsula*, edited by Marcus Noland. Washington, DC: Institute for International Economics, 1998.

————. *North Korea: Peace, War or Implosion*. Seoul: Jardine Fleming Securities Ltd, June 1997.

————. "North Korea in Retrospect." In *The Korean Peninsula in Transition*, edited by Dae Hwan Kim and Tat Yan Kong. Basingstoke, UK: Macmillan, 1997.

Gelb, Leslie, "Foreword." In Morton Abramowitz and James T. Laney, *U.S. Policy toward North Korea: A Second Look*. Washington, DC: Council on Foreign Relations, 1999, 2. Reproduced on http://www.cfr.org/publication.php?id=3205.

General Accounting Office. *North Korea Restricts Food Aid Monitoring*. Washington, DC: GAO, October 1999.

————. *U.S. Bilateral Assistance to North Korea Had Mixed Results*. Washington, DC: GAO, June 2000.

Goodkind, Daniel, and Loraine West. "The North Korean Famine and Its Demographic Impact." *Population and Development Review* 27, no. 2 (June 2001).

Grajdanzev, Andrew J. *Modern Korea*. New York: John Day, 1944.

Green, Michael. *Managing Change on the Korean Peninsula*. Washington, DC: Council on Foreign Relations, 1998. Reproduced on http://www.cfr.org/publication.php?id=119.

Grinker, Roy Richard. *Korea and Its Futures: Unification and the Unfinished War*. Basingstoke, UK: Macmillan, 1998.

Halliday, Jon. "The North Korean Enigma." In *Revolutionary Socialist Development in the Third World*, edited by Gordon White et al. Brighton, UK: Wheatsheaf, 1983.

Halliday, Jon, and Bruce Cumings. *Korea: The Unknown War*. London: Viking, 1988.

Harrison, Selig S. "Promoting a Soft Landing in Korea." *Foreign Policy* 106 (Spring 1997).

Harrison, William T. "Military Armistice in Korea: A Case Study for Strategic Leaders." Strategy research report written for the U.S. Army War College, Pennsylvania. Mimeo, 2002. Reproduced on http://www.urbanoperations.com/harrison.pdf.

He, Jiangcheng. "Educational Reforms." In *North Korea: Ideology, Politics, Economy*, edited by Han S. Park. Englewood Cliffs, NJ: Prentice Hall, 1996.

Hicks, George. *The Comfort Women: Japan's Brutal Regime of Enforced Prostitution in the Second World War*. New York: Norton, 1997.

Higgins, Holly. "The Foundation Is Shaken." In *Solving the North Korean Nuclear Puzzle*, edited by David Albright and Kevin O'Neill. Washington, DC: Institute for Science and International Security, 2000.

Ho Jong Ho, Sok Hui Kang, and Thae Ho Pak. *The US Imperialists Started the Korean War*. Pyongyang: Foreign Languages Publishing House, 1993.

Hong Song Un. *Economic Development in the Democratic People's Republic of Korea*. Pyongyang: Foreign Languages Publishing House, 1990.

Hsu, Victor W. C. "The Role of Non-Governmental Organizations in the USA." In Executive Committee of the International NGO Conference on Humanitarian Assistance to DPRK, *International NGO Conference on Humanitarian Assistance to DPRK June 30–July 2, 2000, Conference Proceedings.* Tokyo: National Christian Council in Japan, 2000.

Human Rights Watch. *The Invisible Exodus: North Koreans in the People's Republic of China.* New York: Human Rights Watch, 2002. Reproduced on http://www.hrw.org/reports/2002/northkorea/#P164_32652.

Humanitarian Development Working Group. "Position Paper on Rehabilitation and Development in DPR Korea." Mimeo, Pyongyang, June 26, 2001.

Hunter, Helen-Louise. *Kim Il-Song's North Korea.* Westport, CT: Praeger, 1999.

Hwang, Eui-Gak. "North and South Korean Economies Compared." In *The Korean Peninsula in Transition,* edited by Dae Hwan Kim and Tat Yan Kong. London: Macmillan, 1997.

International Federation of the Red Cross and Red Crescent Societies. "Evaluation Mission to North Korea 15–31 May 1997." Mimeo.

International Institute for Strategic Studies. *The Military Balance, 2001–2002.* London: Oxford University Press, 2001.

———. *The Military Balance, 2002–2003.* London: Oxford University Press, 2002.

International Organizing Committee for the International NGO Conference. "Listing of the NGO Activities." In a set of documents prepared for the Third International NGO Conference on Humanitarian Assistance to North Korea. Mimeo, Seoul, June 2001.

Jeon, Kyongmann. "The Likelihood and Implications of a North Korean Attack on the South." In *Economic Integration of the Korean Peninsula,* edited by Marcus Noland. Washington, DC: Institute for International Economics, January 1998.

Jeong, Se-Hyun, *Sunshine Policy for Peace and Cooperation.* Seoul: Ministry of Unification, May 2002.

"Joint Editorial Published on New Year." *Bulletin d'Information,* DPRK Delegation in France. Mimeo, Paris, January 1, 1999.

Jon Chol Nam, *A Duel of Reason between Korea and U.S.: Nuke, Missile and Artificial Satellite.* Pyongyang: Foreign Languages Publishing House, 2000.

Jordan, Mary, and Kevin Sullivan. "Pinball Wizards Fuel North Korea." *Washington Post Foreign Service,* June 7, 1996. Reproduced on http://kimsoft.com/korea/jp-nk1.htm.

Kang, Chol-Hwan, and Pierre Rigoulot. *Aquariums of Pyongyang: Ten Years in the North Korean Gulag.* Translated by Yair Reiner. New York: Basic Books, 2001.

Kang, David. "North Korea's Military and Security Policy." In *North Korean Foreign Relations in the Post–Cold War Era*, edited by Samuel S. Kim. Oxford: Oxford University Press, 1998.

Keohane, Robert O., and Joseph S. Nye. *Power and Interdependence*. 2nd ed. Glenview: Scott, Foresman, 1989.

Khan, Dilawar Ali. "Democratic People's Republic of Korea: Improving the Quality of Basic Social Services for the Most Vulnerable Children and Women." Mimeo, UNICEF Pyongyang, April 2001.

Kihl, Young Whan. "The DPRK and Its Relations with the ROK." In *Korea Briefing 1997–1999: Challenges and Change at the Turn of the Century*, edited by Kongdan Oh. New York: M. E. Sharpe and Asia Society, 2000.

Kim, Hong Nack. "Japan in North Korean Foreign Policy." In *North Korean Foreign Relations in the Post–Cold War Era*, edited by Samuel Kim. Oxford: Oxford University Press, 1998.

Kim Il Sung. "Non-Aligned Information Must Contribute to the People's Cause of Independence." Speech at the Fourth Conference of Ministers of Information of Non-Aligned Countries, Pyongyang, June 15, 1993. Reproduced in *Bulletin d'Information*, DPRK Delegation in France. Mimeo, Paris, June 15, 1993.

Kim, Ilpyong J. "China in North Korean Foreign Policy." In *North Korean Foreign Relations in the Post–Cold War Era*, edited by Samuel S. Kim. Oxford: Oxford University Press, 1998.

Kim, Soon-Kwon. "NGO's Activity for the South and the North Korean Cooperation on Agriculture." Paper prepared for the Third International NGO Conference on Humanitarian Assistance to North Korea, Seoul. Mimeo, June 2001.

Kim, Woon-Keun. "The Agricultural Situation of North Korea." September 1, 1999. Reproduced on http://www.agnet.org/library/article/eb475.html.

Kim, Woon-Keun, and Tae-Jin Kwon. "Food Situation and Agricultural Reform in North Korea." *Journal of Rural Development* 21 (Summer 1998).

Kim, Young-Hoon. "The AREP Program and Inter-Korean Agricultural Cooperation." *East Asian Review* 13, no. 4 (Winter 2001).

Kissinger, Henry. *A World Restored: Metternich, Castlereagh and the Problems of Peace 1812–1822*. London: Weidenfeld, 1957.

Koh, Byung Chul. "Foreign Policy Goals, Constraints and Prospect." In *North Korea: Ideology, Politics, Economy*, edited by Han S. Park. Englewood Cliffs, NJ: Prentice Hall, 1995.

Korean Peninsula Energy Development Organization. *Annual Report 2000/2001.* New York: KEDO, 2001.

———. *KEDO Fact Sheets 1–9.* New York, November 2001.

Kuhn, Thomas S. *The Structure of Scientific Revolutions.* 2nd ed. Chicago: University of Chicago Press, 1970.

Kwon, Tae-Jin, and Woon-Keun Kim. "Assessment of Food Supply in North Korea." *Journal of Rural Development* 22 (Winter 1999).

Lee, Chae-Jin. "Conflict and Cooperation: The Pacific Powers and Korea." In *Korea's Future and the Great Powers,* edited by Nicholas Eberstadt and Richard J. Ellings. Seattle: University of Washington Press, 2001.

Lee, Jong-Moo. "Humanitarian Assistance toward North Korea in South Korea: Historical and Current Overview for South Korean Context." In Jae-Shik Oh, "Reports on the Humanitarian Assistance to North Korea: South Korean Non-governmental Organizations." Prepared for the Third International NGO Conference on Humanitarian Assistance to North Korea, Seoul. Mimeo, June 2001.

———. "The Situation of and the Agenda for the Humanitarian Aid to the DPRK." In *Executive Committee of the International NGO Conference on Humanitarian Assistance to DPRK, International NGO Conference on Humanitarian Assistance to DPRK June 30–July 2, 2000, Conference Proceedings.* Tokyo: National Christian Council in Japan, 2000

Lee, Suk. "Food Shortages and Economic Institutions in the Democratic People's Republic of Korea." Unpublished doctoral thesis, Department of Economics, University of Warwick, January 2003.

Levin, Norman, and Yong-Sup Han. "The South Korean Debate over Policies toward North Korea: Issues and Implications." Mimeo, Santa Monica, RAND, 2002.

Lim, Dong-won. "North Korean Policy under the Kim Dae-Jung Government." Speech at breakfast meeting with National Reconciliation Council, March 11, 1999, 3. Quoted in "Prospects for Inter-Korean Relations and South Korean Policy on Assistance to North Korea." Paper prepared for the Third International NGO Conference on Humanitarian Assistance to North Korea. Mimeo, Seoul, June 2001.

Litwak, Robert S. *Rogue States and U.S. Foreign Policy: Containment after the Cold War.* Washington, DC: Woodrow Wilson Center Press, 2000.

MacDonald, Callum. "The Democratic People's Republic of Korea: An Historical Survey." In *North Korea in the New World Order,* edited by Hazel Smith et al. New York: St. Martin's Press, 1996.

Manning, Robert A. "The United States in North Korean Foreign Policy." In *North Korean Foreign Relations in the Post–Cold War Era*, edited by Samuel S. Kim. Oxford: Oxford University Press, 1998.

Manyin, Mark, and Ryun Jun. "U.S. Assistance to North Korea." Report for Congress received through CRS Web. Mimeo, Washington, DC, March 17, 2003.

Maragliano, Giorgio. Untitled paper presented to the Third International NGO Conference on Humanitarian Assistance to North Korea. Mimeo, Seoul, June 2001.

Marx, Karl, and Friedrich Engels. *The German Ideology.* Edited by S. Ryazanskaya. London: Lawrence and Wishart, 1965.

Matsui, Yayori. "How to End Impunity for Wartime Sexual Violence? The Meaning of Women's International War Crimes Tribunal 2000 on Japanese Military Sexual Slavery." Mimeo, July 2002.

Mazarr, Michael J. *North Korea and the Bomb: A Case Study in Nonproliferation.* Basingstoke, UK: Macmillan, 1995.

McCormack, Gavan. "Mists Clearing: Forecasts for the Past and Future History of the DPRK." Paper presented at the First Pacific Basin International Conference on Pacific Studies, Hawaii. Mimeo, 1992.

———. "North Korea: Coming in from the Cold?" December 14, 2002, Znet. http://www.zmag.org/content/showarticle.cfm?SectionID=44&ItemID=2749.

———. "North Korea in the Vice." *New Left Review* 18 (November–December 2002). Reproduced on http://www.newleftreview.net/NLR25201.shtml.

Michell, Anthony R. "The Current North Korean Economy." In *Economic Integration of the Korean Peninsula*, edited by Marcus Noland. Washington, DC: Institute for International Economics, 1998.

Mikheev, Vasily. "Politics and Ideology in the Post–Cold War Era." In *North Korea: Ideology, Politics, Economy*, edited by Han S. Park. Englewood Cliffs, NJ: Prentice Hall, 1996.

———. "Russian Policy towards North Korea." *CSIS PacNet Newsletter* 38, September 2, 2000. http://www.csis.org/pacfor/pac0038.html.

Moiseyev, Valentin I. "The North Korean Energy Sector." In *The North Korean Nuclear Program: Security, Strategy and New Perspectives from Russia,* edited by James Clay Moltz and Alexandre Y. Mansourov. New York: Routledge, 2000.

Moltz, James Clay. "The Renewal of Russian–North Korean Relations." In *The North Korean Nuclear Program: Security, Strategy and New Perspectives from Russia,* edited by James Clay Moltz and Alexandre Y. Mansourov. New York: Routledge, 2000.

———. "Russian Policy on the North Korean Nuclear Crisis." CNS Monterey Institute of International Studies, May 2003. http://cns.miis.edu/research/korea/ruspol.htm.

Moltz, James Clay, and Alexandre Y. Mansourov, eds. *The North Korean Nuclear Program: Security, Strategy, and New Perspectives from Russia.* London: Routledge, 2000.

Moon, Chung-in. "Sustaining Inter-Korean Reconciliation: North-South Korea Cooperation." *Joint U.S.-Korea Academic Studies* 12 (2002).

———. "Understanding the DJ Doctrine: The Sunshine Policy and the Korean Peninsula." Mimeo, September 1999.

Morgan, Patrick M. "New Security Arrangements between the United States and North Korea." In *North Korea after Kim Il Sung,* edited by Dae-Sook Suh and Chae-Jin Lee. London: Lynne Rienner, 1998.

Nahm, Andrew C. *Introduction to Korean History and Culture.* Seoul: Hollym, 1993.

Namkung, K. A. "U.S. Leadership in the Rebuilding of the North Korean Economy." In *Economic Integration of the Korean Peninsula,* edited by Marcus Noland. Washington, DC: Institute for International Economics, 1998.

Nathanail, Lola. *Food and Nutrition Assessment of the DPRK.* Rome: World Food Program, 1996.

Newman, Edward. "Human Security and Constructivism." *International Studies Perspectives* 2, no. 3 (August 2001).

Nicholson, Michael. *International Relations: A Concise Introduction.* Basingstoke, UK: Macmillan, 1998.

Nixson, Frederick, and Paul Collins. "Economic Reform in North Korea." In *North Korea in the New World Order,* edited by Hazel Smith et al. New York: St. Martin's Press, 1996.

Noland, Marcus. *Avoiding the Apocalypse: The Future of the Two Koreas.* Washington, DC: Institute for International Economics, 2000.

———, ed. *Economic Integration of the Korean Peninsula.* Washington, DC: Institute for International Economics, 1998.

———. "Prospects for the North Korean Economy." In *North Korea after Kim Il Sung,* edited by Dae-Sook Suh and Chae-Jin Lee. London: Lynne Rienner, 1998.

———. "Why North Korea Will Muddle Through." *Foreign Affairs* 76, no. 4 (1997).

Noland, Marcus, Sherman Robinson, and Tao Wang. *Famine in North Korea: Causes and Cures.* Working Paper no. 99-2. Washington, DC: Institute for International Economics, 1999.

Oberdorfer, Don. *The Two Koreas: A Contemporary History.* London: Warner Books, 1997.

O'Dea, John. "Experience of the FALU." In Executive Committee of the International NGO Conference on Humanitarian Assistance to DPRK, International NGO Conference on Humanitarian Assistance to DPRK June 30–July 2, 2000, conference proceedings. Tokyo: National Christian Council in Japan, 2000.

Oh, Jae-Shik. "A Call for the Reassessment of NGO Humanitarian Activities in DPRK." In Executive Committee of the International NGO Conference on Humanitarian Assistance to DPRK, International NGO Conference on Humanitarian Assistance to DPRK June 30–July 2, 2000, conference proceedings. Tokyo: National Christian Council in Japan, 2000.

———. "Reports on the Humanitarian Assistance to North Korea: South Korean Non-Governmental Organizations." Prepared for the Third International NGO Conference on Humanitarian Assistance to North Korea. Mimeo, Seoul, June 2001.

Olsen, Edward A. "The Conventional Military Strength of North Korea: Implications for Inter-Korean Security." In *North Korea after Kim Il Sung*, edited by Dae-Sook Suh and Chae-Jin Lee. London: Lynne Rienner, 1998.

Omawale, Omawale. "An Exercise in Ambivalence: Negotiating with North Korea." *Harvard Asia Pacific Review* 3, no. 2 (Summer 1999).

Owen-Davies, John. "North Korea Says It with Flowers." *Financial Times*, June 24, 2000.

———. "North Korea's Public Health Pays the Price of Isolation." Mimeo, undated but June 2000.

Pang, Hwan Ju. *Korean Review*. Pyongyang: Foreign Languages Publishing House, 1987.

Park, Kyung Ae. "Ideology and Women in North Korea." In *North Korea: Ideology, Politics, Economy*, edited by Han S. Park. Englewood Cliffs, NJ: Prentice Hall, 1996.

———. "The Pattern of North Korea's Track-Two Foreign Contact." North Pacific Policy Papers no. 5. Vancouver: Program on Canada-Asia Policy Studies, 2000.

Park, Pilho. "A Review of Major Legal Issues along the Foreign Investment Road to North Korea." Paper presented at the Symposium on North Korea's Engagement with the Global Economy: Prospects and Challenges, University of Wisconsin–Madison, April 12–13, 2002.

Pearce, Jane. "Looking at Long-Term Assistance." UNDP Pyongyang, *Interagency Quarterly* 1 (Autumn 1999).

Pecchio, Marie Rose. "Identification of an At Risk Group: Socially Deprived Children." Medécins Sans Frontières (MSF), Pyongyang, September 11, 1998.

Platkovskiy, Alexander. "Nuclear Blackmail and North Korea's Search for a Place in the Sun." In *The North Korean Nuclear Program: Security, Strategy, and New Perspectives from Russia,* edited by James Clay Moltz and Alexandre Y. Mansourov. New York: Routledge, 2000.

Powell, John. "Testimony to the Sub-Committee on East Asia and the Pacific of the US House of Representatives, 2 May 2002." Reproduced as "Special Report, North East Asia Peace and Security Network," May 20, 2002.

Private Voluntary Organization Consortium. "Field Trip: Nampo City Baby Home." Mimeo, Pyongyang, April 8, 1998.

———. "Field Trip: U.S. Monitors First Visit." Mimeo, Pyongyang, April 24, 1998.

Private Voluntary Organization Consortium in Democratic People's Republic of Korea. "Interim Report." Mimeo, Pyongyang, April 1998.

Pyongyang Chamber of Commerce. "Country Report." September 2001.

Quinones, Ken. Draft, chapter 2, "The American NGO Experience in North Korea." Mimeo sent to author, March 12, 2002.

Rawls, John. *A Theory of Justice.* Cambridge, MA: Belknap Press of Harvard University, 1971.

Reiss, Mitchell B. "KEDO and North Korea: Problems and Prospects on the Road Ahead." In *Solving the North Korean Nuclear Puzzle,* edited by David Albright and Kevin O'Neill. Washington, DC: Institute for Science and International Security Press, 2000.

"Resident NGOs in DPR Korea Involved in the CAP." Information leaflet, November 2001.

Ro, Jeong-Ho. "Making Sense of the DPRK Legal System." In *The North Korean System in the Post–Cold War Era,* edited by Samuel Kim. New York: Palgrave, 2001.

Robinson, W. Courtland, Myung Ken Lee, Kenneth Hill, and Gilbert M. Burnham. "Mortality in North Korean Migrant Households: A Retrospective Study." *Lancet* 354, no. 9175 (July 24, 1999).

Save the Children. "DPRK Assessment Report." Mimeo, August 18–31, 1997.

Scalapino, Robert A. "China and Korean Reunification: A Neighbor's Concerns." In *Korea's Future and the Great Powers,* edited by Nicholas Eberstadt and Richard J. Ellings. Seattle: University of Washington Press, 2001.

———. "Introduction." In *North Korea after Kim Il Sung,* edited by Dae-Sook Suh and Chae-Jin Lee. London: Lynne Rienner, 1998.

Shen, Shenying. "Politics and Strategies for Economic Development." In *North Korea: Ideology, Politics, Economy,* edited by Han S. Park. Englewood Cliffs, NJ: Prentice Hall, 1996.

Sigal, Leon V. *Disarming Strangers: Nuclear Diplomacy with North Korea.* Princeton, NJ: Princeton University Press, 1998.

———. "Mr. Perry's New Course on Korea." In *Solving the North Korean Nuclear Puzzle*, edited by David Albright and Kevin O'Neill. Washington, DC: Institute for Science and International Security, 2000.

Smith, Hazel. "Bad, Mad, Sad or Rational Actor? Why the 'Securitization' Paradigm Makes for Poor Policy Analysis of North Korea." *International Affairs* 76, no. 3 (July 2000).

———. "Brownback Bill Will Not Solve North Korea's Problems." *Jane's Intelligence Review*, February 2004.

———. *Caritas Five-Year Evaluation of Programmes and Projects in the DPRK.* Hong Kong: Caritas–Hong Kong, 2001.

———. "La Corée du Nord vers l'économie de marché: Faux et vrais dilemmas." *Critique Internationale*, Paris (April 2002).

———. "Defecting to Snatch Victory from Defeat." *World Today* 53, no. 3 (March 1997).

———. "Desperate Times in North Korea." *Far Eastern Economic Review*, February 14, 2002.

———. *European Union Foreign Policy: What It Is and What It Does.* London: Pluto, 2002.

———. "Korea: Gobbledygook." *World Today* 59, no. 2 (February 2003).

———. "The Koreas: Threat or Opportunity?" *World Today* 58, no. 1 (January 2002).

———. "Living with Absences: A Foreigner's Sojourn in Pyongyang." *Korea Society Quarterly*, Winter 2001/2002.

———. "Minimum Conditions for Humanitarian Action in the DPRK: A Survey of Humanitarian Agency Involvement and Perspectives." Paper presented at a workshop organized by the Centre for Humanitarian Dialogue, Geneva, December 2001.

———. "North Korean Foreign Policy in the 1990s: The Realist Approach." In *North Korea in the New World Order*, edited by Hazel Smith et al. New York: St. Martin's Press, 1996.

———. "North Koreans in China." In *Human Flows across National Borders in Northeast Asia*, edited by Tsuneo Akaha with the assistance of Anna Vassilieva and Shizu Naruse. Seminar proceedings, United Nations University, Tokyo, November 2002. Monterey: Center for East Asian Studies, Monterey Institute of International Studies, January 2003.

———. "'Opening Up' by Default: North Korea, the Humanitarian Community and the Crisis." *Pacific Review* 12, no. 3 (1999).

————. *Overcoming Humanitarian Dilemmas in the DPRK,* Special Report no. 90. Washington, DC: United States Institute of Peace, July 2002.

————. "Policy Reforms in the DPRK: Limits and Opportunities." Rome: World Food Program, 1999.

————. *WFP DPRK Programmes and Activities: A Gender Perspective.* Pyongyang: WFP, December 1999.

————. "Why Is There No International Democratic Theory?" In *Democracy and International Relations Theory: Critical Theories/Problematic Practices,* edited by Hazel Smith. London: Macmillan, 2000.

Smith, Hazel, et al., eds. *North Korea in the New World Order.* New York: St. Martin's Press, 1996.

Snyder, Scott, *Negotiating on the Edge: North Korean Negotiating Behavior.* Washington, DC: United States Institute of Peace Press, 1999.

Solarz, Stephen J. "Foreword." In Helen-Louise Hunter, *Kim Il-Song's North Korea.* Westport, CT: Praeger, 1999.

Staunton, Marie. Report of conversation with Mr./Ms (not clear from text) Kim, UNICEF officer, Huichon, August 5, 1997, recorded in "Trip Diary DPRK." Mimeo, August 6, 1997.

Steinberg, David I. "On Patterns of Political Legitimacy in North Korea." In *The North Korean System in the Post–Cold War Era,* edited by Samuel Kim. New York: Palgrave, 2001.

Takashi, Nada. *Korea in Kim Jong Il's Era.* Pyongyang: Foreign Languages Publishing House, 2000.

Thomas, Caroline. *Global Governance, Development and Human Security.* London: Pluto, 2000.

Trigubenko, Marina Ye. "Economic Characteristics and Prospect for Development: With Emphasis on Agriculture." In *North Korea: Ideology, Politics, Economy,* edited by Han S. Park. Englewood Cliffs, NJ: Prentice Hall, 1996.

United Kingdom Presidency Report. "European Union Technical Mission to the Democratic People's Republic of Korea, 9–16 May 1998." Mimeo, undated.

United Nations Children's Fund. *An Analysis of the Situation of Children and Women in the Democratic People's Republic of Korea 2000.* Pyongyang: UNICEF, DPRK, December 1999.

————. "An Analysis of the Situation of Children and Women in the Democratic People's Republic of Korea 2000, draft." Mimeo, Pyongyang, May 1998.

———. "DPRK Mission Report." Mimeo, Pyongyang, 1997.

———. "Draft Report on the Multiple Indicator Cluster Survey in the Democratic People's Republic of Korea, 1998." Mimeo, Pyongyang, 1998.

———. "Draft Situation Analysis DPR Korea 1997." Revised and edited. Mimeo, Pyongyang, June 13, 1997.

———. "Emergency Situation Analysis for DPRK." Pyongyang, undated but 1996 or 1997.

———. "Section 6, Interview Transcripts." In Emergency Fundraising Kit. Mimeo, Pyongyang and London, August 1997.

———. *Social Statistics: DPRK*. Pyongyang: UNICEF, undated but 2000.

———. "UNICEF Humanitarian Action, DPR Korea: Donor Update." New York, February 4, 2002.

———. "UNICEF Revised Funding Requirements: United Nations Consolidated Inter-Agency Appeal for the Democratic People's Republic of Korea: April 1997– March 1998." Mimeo, Pyongyang, undated but 1998.

United Nations Children's Fund and Institute of Child Nutrition. "Working Paper on Pilot Survey in Kangwon Province." Mimeo, Pyongyang, June 1988.

United Nations Conference on Trade and Development. *The Least Developed Countries Report 2002: Escaping the Poverty Trap*. New York: United Nations, 2002.

United Nations Department of Humanitarian Affairs. "United Nations Consolidated UN Inter-Agency Appeal for Flood-Related Emergency Humanitarian Assistance to the Democratic People's Republic of Korea (DPRK), 1 July 1996–31 March 1997," April 1996. Reproduced on http://www.reliefweb.int/ocha_ol/pub/appeals/96appeals/ dprk/prk_atx1.html#top.

United Nations Development Program. "1998 Annual Report of the United Nations Resident Co-ordinator in DPR Korea." Mimeo, Pyongyang, January 31, 1999.

———. "Report of the First Thematic Round Table Conference for the Democratic People's Republic of Korea." Geneva, May 1998.

———. *Second Country Cooperation Framework for the DPRK (2001–2003)*. New York: UNDP, June 2001.

United Nations Development Program and Agricultural Recovery and Environmental Protection. *Report of the Second Thematic Round Table Conference for the Democratic People's Republic of Korea*. Geneva: UNDP, June 2000.

———. "Status of Agricultural Activities." Mimeo, Pyongyang, 2001.

United Nations Development Program and the Democratic People's Republic of Korea Government. "Documents Prepared for the Second Thematic Roundtable Meeting on AREP for the DPRK." Mimeo, Pyongyang, 2000.

———. "Documents Prepared for the Thematic Roundtable Meeting on Agricultural Recovery and Environmental Protection." Mimeo, Pyongyang, May 1998.

United Nations Food and Agriculture Organization and World Food Program. "Crop and Food Supply Assessment Mission to the Democratic People's Republic of Korea." Special Alert no. 267. Mimeo, May 16, 1996.

———. "Crop and Food Supply Assessment Mission to the Democratic People's Republic of Korea." Special Alert no. 275. Mimeo, June 3, 1997.

———. "Crop and Food Supply Assessment Mission to the Democratic People's Republic of Korea." June 25, 1998.

———. "Crop and Food Supply Assessment Mission to the Democratic People's Republic of Korea." Rome, July 24, 2000.

———. "Crop and Food Supply Assessment Mission to the Democratic People's Republic of Korea." Rome, October 26, 2001.

———. "Food and Crop Assessment Mission to the DPRK." Rome, December 10, 1997.

———. "Special Report: Crop and Food Supply Assessment Mission to the Democratic People's Republic of Korea." Mimeo, December 22, 1995.

———. "Special Report: Crop and Food Supply Assessment Mission to the Democratic People's Republic of Korea." Mimeo, November 25, 1997.

———. "Special Report: Crop and Food Supply Assessment Mission to the Democratic People's Republic of Korea." June 29, 1999.

———. "Special Report: Crop and Food Supply Assessment Mission to the Democratic People's Republic of Korea." Rome, November 16, 2000.

United Nations Human Rights Committee. "Second Periodic Report of the Democratic People's Republic of Korea on Its Implementation of the International Covenant on Civil and Political Rights." GE.00-41814 (E), May 4, 2000.

United Nations Office for the Coordination of Humanitarian Assistance. "Consolidated Agency Appeal for the DPRK January–December 1998." Mimeo, 1998. Reproduced on http://www.reliefweb.int.

———. *Consolidated Agency Appeal for the DPRK January–December 1999.* New York: UNOCHA, December 1998.

———. *Consolidated Agency Appeal for the DPRK January–December 2000.* New York: UNOCHA, November 1999.

————. *Consolidated Agency Appeal for the DPRK 2001*. New York: UNOCHA, 2000.

————. "Consolidated Agency Appeal for the DPRK 2002." Mimeo, Pyongyang, 2002.

————. *Consolidated Agency Appeal for the DPRK 2003*. November 19, 2002, on Reliefweb, http://www.reliefweb.int/w/rwb.nsf/437a83f9fa966c40c12564f2004fde87/96b6c5fc02925530c1256c6f003815ce?OpenDocument.

————. *Consolidated Agency Appeal for the DPRK 2004*. Geneva: UNOCHA, 2003. Reproduced on http://ochadms.unog.ch/quickplace/cap/main.nsf/h_Index/CAP_2004_DPRK/$FILE/CAP_2004_DPRK_SCREEN.PDF?OpenElement.

United Nations Office for the Coordination of Humanitarian Assistance and the Democratic People's Republic of Korea. "Basic Facts." Mimeo, undated, probably 1998/1999.

————. "DPR Korea OCHA Situation Bulletin April 2002." Reproduced on http://www.reliefweb.int.

————. "DPR Korea: Situation Bulletin no. 06/02." June and July 2002.

————. *Humanitarian Situation Information Bulletin December 2000–January 2001*, January 31, 2001. Reproduced on http://www.reliefweb.int.

United States Institute of Peace. *A Coming Crisis on the Korean Peninsula? The Food Crisis, Economic Decline, and Political Considerations*. Special Report no. 19. Washington, DC: United States Institute of Peace, October 1996.

————. *Mistrust and the Korean Peninsula: Dangers of Miscalculations*. Special Report no. 38. Washington, DC: United States Institute of Peace, November 1998.

U.S. State Department. "Korea, Democratic People's Republic of, Country Report on Human Rights Practices, 2000." Released by the Bureau of Democracy, Human Rights and Labor. Mimeo, February 2001.

Von Hippel, David F., and Peter Hayes. "North Korean Energy Sector: Current Status and Scenarios for 2000 and 2005." In *Economic Integration of the Korean Peninsula*, edited by Marcus Noland. Washington, DC: Institute for International Economics, 1998.

Wada, Haruki. "Recovering a Lost Opportunity: Japan–North Korea Negotiations in the Wake of the Iraqi War." May 3, 2003. Reproduced on ZNet, http://www.zmag.org/content/showarticle.cfm?SectionID=44&ItemID=3569.

Wagner, Ellasue. *Korea: The Old and the New*. New York: Fleming H. Revell, 1931.

Waltz, Kenneth. *Theory of International Politics*. New York: Random House, 1979.

Williams, James H., David Von Hippel and Peter Hayes. *Fuel and Famine: Rural Energy Crisis in the DPRK*. Policy Paper no. 46. University of California, Institute on Global Conflict and Cooperation, 2001. Reproduced on http://www-igcc.ucsd.edu/publications/policy_papers/pp46.html#ftn2.

Winder, Joseph A. B. *Promoting Economic Cooperation between North and South Korea.* Washington, DC: Korea Economic Institute, October 19, 2001.

Wit, Joel. "Clinton and North Korea: Past, Present and Future." In *Solving the North Korean Nuclear Puzzle,* edited by David Albright and Kevin O'Neill. Washington, DC: Institute for Science and International Security, 2000.

Woodward, Bob. *Bush at War.* New York: Simon and Schuster, 2002.

World Food Program. "Access to Counties." Pyongyang, December 1999.

———. "Alternative Foods." Information sheet on "WFP in DPRK." Pyongyang, December 1999.

———. "Basic Agreement between the United Nations FAO World Food Program and the Government of the Democratic People's Republic of Korea Concerning Assistance from the World Food Program." Mimeo, June 9, 1986.

———. "DPR Korea: The Public Distribution System." Mimeo, Pyongyang, undated but obtained by author from WFP Pyongyang, February 2003.

———. "DPR Korea Update." Pyongyang, April 1999.

———. "DPR Korea Update no. 10." Pyongyang, October 1999.

———. "DPR Korea Update no. 40," Pyongyang, May 2002.

———. "DPR Korea Update no. 41," Pyongyang, June 2002.

———. "DPR Korea Update no. 52," Pyongyang, May 2003.

———. "Emergency Operation DPR Korea no. 5710.01: 'Emergency Food Assistance for Flood Victims and Children under Five.'" In WFP, *WFP Operations in DPR Korea as of 14 July 1999.* Rome: WFP, undated but 1999.

———. "Emergency Operation DPR Korea no. 5710.02: Emergency Food Assistance Following Floods." In WFP, *WFP Operations in DPR Korea as of 14 July 1999.* Rome: WFP, undated but 1999.

———. "Emergency Operation DPR Korea no. 5959: Emergency Food Assistance for Vulnerable Groups." In WFP, *WFP Operations in DPR Korea as of 14 July 1999.* Rome: WFP, undated but 1999.

———. "Outline for EMOP Submission: Emergency Operation DPR Korea No. 5710.00: 'Emergency Food Assistance for Flood Victims.'" In WFP, *WFP Operations in DPR Korea as of 14 July 1999.* Rome: WFP, undated but 1999.

———. "Recovery Assistance for Vulnerable Groups in DPR Korea." Draft, mimeo, Pyongyang, undated but 1999.

———. "Special Update: Newly Accessible Counties." Mimeo, Pyongyang, July 5, 1999.

———. "Stories from DPR Korea: Emergency Officers Talk to Beneficiaries." Pyongyang: WFP, 2000.

World Food Program in collaboration with United Nations Food and Agriculture Organization, United Nations Children's Fund, and Save the Children. *Nutritional Assessment to the Democratic People's Republic of Korea.* Pyongyang/Rome: WFP, November 1997.

World Health Organization Office of WHO Representative to DPR Korea. "Briefing on Health Situation in DPR Korea November 2002." Mimeo, February 12, 2003.

World Health Organization South-East Asia Region. "Emergency and Humanitarian Assistance Programme." Mimeo, January–February 1998.

Yamamoto, Toshimasa. "New Developments in Japan on Humanitarian Assistance to DPRK since the Summit of June 2000." Paper presented at the Third International NGO Conference on Humanitarian Assistance to North Korea. Mimeo, Seoul, June 2001.

Yang, Sung Chul. *The North and South Korean Political Systems: A Comparative Analysis.* Revised ed. Elizabeth, NJ: Hollym, 1999.

Yoshida, Kiyomi. "Supporting Activities of Japanese NGOs." In Executive Committee of the International NGO Conference on Humanitarian Assistance to DPRK, *International NGO Conference on Humanitarian Assistance to DPRK June 30–July 2, 2000, Conference Proceedings.* Tokyo: National Christian Council in Japan, 2000.

Yu, Xintian. "Expanding International Economic Cooperation on the Korean Peninsula." In *The Political Economy of Korean Reconciliation and Reform,* edited by James M. Lister. Washington, DC: Korea Economic Institute of America, 2001.

Yuan, Jing-Dong. "China and the North Korean Nuclear Crisis." CNS Monterey Institute of International Studies, January 2003. http://cns.miis.edu/research/korea/chidprk.htm.

Zabrovskaya, Lara V. "The Korean Peninsula and the Security of Russia's Primorskiy Kray (Maritime Province)." In *The North Korean Nuclear Program: Security, Strategy and New Perspectives from Russia,* edited by James Clay Moltz and Alexandre Y. Mansourov. New York: Routledge, 2000.

Zacek, Jane Shapiro. "Russia in North Korean Foreign Policy." In *North Korean Foreign Relations in the Post–Cold War Era,* edited by Samuel S. Kim. Oxford: Oxford University Press, 1998.

Zellweger, Kathi. "DPRK Trip Report, 6 August to 3 September 2002." Mimeo, Hong Kong, September 30, 2002.

Websites and web pages

asia.news.yahoo.com/020410/reuters/asia-99461.html

http://crm.kotra.or.kr/main/info/nk/eng/sntrade/cooperative.php3

http://english.joins.com/article.asp?aid=20010419112430&sid=E00

http://europa.eu.int/comm/external_relations/north_korea/intro/gac.htm#nk140403

http://nautilus.org/napsnet

http://news.bbc.co.uk/2/hi/asia-pacific/2604437.stm

http://nk.chosun.com/english/news/news.html?ACT=detail&key=1&res_id=4805

http://nk.chosun.com/english/news/news.html?ACT=detail&res_id=5530

http://quickstart.clari.net/qs_se/webnews/wed/bz/Qnkorea-un-food-china
    .R2HG_DNK.html

http://russia.shaps.hawaii.edu/fp/korea/berlin_declaration.html

http://ton-a-month.tripod.com/

http://www.abc.net.au/worldtoday/s424241.htm

http://www.acdi-cida.gc.ca/CIDAWEB/webcountry.nsf/
    0/7D484015AB33312E85256C04007DC8A9?OpenDocument

http://www.agnet.org/library/article/eb475.html

http://www.atimes.com/koreas/AK03Dg01.html

http://www.bekkoame.ne.jp/ro/renk/en/anessay.htm

http://www.careusaorg/newsroom/pressreleases/2000/apr/northkorea0404.asp

http://www.cdc.gov/mmwr/preview/mmwrhtml/00048030.htm#top

http://www.china.org.cn/english/2003/Jul/69917.htm

http://www.familycare.org/network/p01.htm

http://www.fas.org/irp/world/dprk/chosen_soren/

http://www.fides.org/English/1999/e19990423.html

http://www.hbaid.org/aa_north.html

http://www.ifrc.org/cgi/pdf_statistic.pl?allaps.pdf

http://www.kcna.co.jp/calendar/frame.htm

http://www.kcna.co.jp/index-e.htm

http://www.kcna.co.jp/item/1999/9908/news08/12.htm

http://www.kedo.org/news_detail.asp?NewsID=10

http://www.keepingapace.org/html/archives/war/nkorea.htm

http://www.korea-np.co.jp/pk/080th_issue/99020301.html

http://www.korea-np.co.jp/pk/122nd_issue/99120402.htm

http://www.korea-np.co.jp/pk/153th_issue/2000122122.htm

http://www.korea-np.co.jp/pk/174th_issue/2002013103.htm

http://www.kotra.or.kr.main/info/nk/eng/main.php3

http://www.ku.edu/~ibetext/korean-war-1/2001/12/msg00072.html

http://www.megastories.com/nkorea/glossary/unrest.html

http://www.nationalreview.com/comment/comment-hayward093002.asp

http://www.nautilus.org/napsnet/dr/0207/JUL23.html#item9

http://www.nautilus.org/napsnet/dr/9911/NOV02.html#item7

http://www.newsmax.com/showliners.shtml?a=2003/1/23/31026

http://www.nknet.org/enknet/ekeys/ekeys-frame.htm

http://www.nobel.se/peace/laureates/2000/

http://www.pbs.org/newshour/extra/features/jan-june03/nkorea.html

http://www.pcaps.iar.ubc.ca/pubs.htm

http://www.pyongyangsquare.com/aid/

http://www.reliefweb.int

http://www.reliefweb.int/w/rwb.nsf/0/
    ca57b6a0cfc9757bc1256cd1003f4df7?Open Document

http://www.reliefweb.int/w/rwb.nsf/a94094ac73e84191c125671c002fcbbc/
    52e0c11ac4ef989bc1256b9800444f3f?OpenDocument

http://www.reliefweb.int/w/rwb.nsf/vCD/Democratic+People's+Republic+of+Korea?
    OpenDocument&StartKey=Democratic+People's+Republic+of+Korea&ExpandView

http://www.theage.com.au/articles/2003/02/05/1044318668734.html

http://www.usa.or.th/news/press/2002/nrot102.htm

http://www.usspueblo.org/v2f/incident/incidentframe.html

http://www.vuw.ac.nz/~caplabtb/dprk/

http://www.wfp.org/country_brief/index.asp?country=34

http://www.who.int/archives/inf-pr-1997/en/pr97-71.html

http://www2.gol.com/users/coynerhm/chinese_influence_on_pyongyang.htm

http://wwwa.house.gov-international_relations-107-79392.pdf

http://www-igcc.ucsd.edu/publications/policy_papers/pp46.html#ftn2

Newspapers and magazines

The Age

Asahi Shimbun, English edition

Chosun Ilbo

Christian Friends of Korea, Activity Report

Economist

Financial Times

Foreign Trade of the Democratic People's Republic of Korea

Human Rights Watch Monthly Update

Japan Times Online

Japan Today

JoongAng Ilbo

Korea

Korea Economic Report

Korea Herald

Korea Now

Korea Times

Korea Today

Korean News

Los Angeles Times

National Review

New York Times

Oxford Analytica

Pyongyang Times

UNDP, *Interagency Quarterly*

Vantage Point

Index

About the Author

Hazel Smith is Professor of International Relations at the University of Warwick in the United Kingdom. She received her PhD from the London School of Economics in 1992 and was a Fulbright scholar and visiting fellow at Stanford University in 1994–95. In 2001–2 she was based in Washington, DC, as a Jennings Randolph senior fellow at the United States Institute of Peace. From April 2002 to August 2004 she was on secondment to the UN University in Tokyo. Her previous books include *European Foreign Policy and Central America* (1995) and *European Union Foreign Policy: What It Is and What It Does* (2002).

During her scholarly career, she has been regularly seconded to work with international humanitarian organizations. She is on the rosters of global humanitarian assistance experts maintained by the United Nations World Food Program (WFP), the United Nations Development Program (UNDP), and the European Union.

Professor Smith has worked, published, and broadcast extensively on the DPRK for nearly two decades. She has been a regular visitor to the DPRK since 1990, and has worked in-country with UNICEF, the World Food Program, UNDP, and NGOs for periods of up to a year. She continues to be consulted by governments, business, media, international organizations, and NGOs on the DPRK and Asian security and humanitarian affairs.

United States Institute of Peace

The United States Institute of Peace is an independent, nonpartisan federal institution created by Congress to promote the prevention, management, and peaceful resolution of international conflicts. Established in 1984, the Institute meets its congressional mandate through an array of programs, including research grants, fellowships, professional training, education programs from high school through graduate school, conferences and workshops, library services, and publications. The Institute's Board of Directors is appointed by the President of the United States and confirmed by the Senate.

Chairman of the Board: J. Robinson West
Vice Chairman: María Otero
President: Richard H. Solomon
Executive Vice President: Patricia Powers Thomson
Vice President: Charles E. Nelson

Board of Directors

J. Robinson West (Chairman), Chairman, PFC Energy, Washington, D.C.

María Otero (Vice Chairman), President, ACCION International, Boston, Mass.

Betty F. Bumpers, Founder and former President, Peace Links, Washington, D.C.

Holly J. Burkhalter, Advocacy Director, Physicians for Human Rights, Washington, D.C.

Chester A. Crocker, James R. Schlesinger Professor of Strategic Studies, School of Foreign Service, Georgetown University

Laurie S. Fulton, Williams and Connolly, Washington, D.C.

Charles Horner, Senior Fellow, Hudson Institute, Washington, D.C.

Seymour Martin Lipset, Hazel Professor of Public Policy, George Mason University

Mora L. McLean, Esq., President, Africa-America Institute, New York, N.Y.

Barbara W. Snelling, former State Senator and former Lieutenant Governor, Shelburne, Vt.

Members ex officio

Michael M. Dunn, Lieutenant General, U.S. Air Force; President, National Defense University

Condoleezza Rice, Secretary of State, U.S. Department of State

Peter W. Rodman, Assistant Secretary of Defense for International Security Affairs

Richard H. Solomon, President, United States Institute of Peace (nonvoting)

Hungry for Peace

This book is set in Adobe Garamond; the display type is Eurostile. Hasten Design Studio designed the book's cover; Mike Chase designed the interior. Helene Y. Redmond made up the pages. The text was copyedited by Chris Springer and proofread by Karen Stough. The index was prepared by Sonsie Conroy.